TRANSNATIONAL WRITING
PROGRAM ADMINISTRATION

TRANSNATIONAL WRITING PROGRAM ADMINISTRATION

Edited by
DAVID S. MARTINS

UTAH STATE UNIVERSITY PRESS
Logan

© 2015 by the University Press of Colorado

Published by Utah State University Press
An imprint of University Press of Colorado
5589 Arapahoe Avenue, Suite 206C
Boulder, Colorado 80303

  The University Press of Colorado is a proud member of
The Association of American University Presses.

The University Press of Colorado is a cooperative publishing enterprise supported,
in part, by Adams State University, Colorado State University, Fort Lewis College,
Metropolitan State University of Denver, Regis University, University of Colorado,
University of Northern Colorado, Utah State University, and Western State Colorado
University.

ISBN: 978-0-87421-961-6 (cloth)
ISBN: 978-0-87421-962-3 (ebook)

Library of Congress Cataloging-in-Publication Data
Transnational writing program administration / edited by David S. Martins.
     pages cm
   ISBN 978-0-87421-961-6 (paperback) — ISBN 978-0-87421-962-3 (ebook)
1. Writing centers—Administration. 2. Rhetoric—Study and teaching (Higher)
3. Report writing—Study and teaching (Higher) 4. Interdisciplinary approach in education. I. Martins, David S., editor.
   PE1404.T765 2014
   808.0071'1—dc23
                           2014010150

Cover photograph: Barriers of separation and distance/Flag#29/2008/79x47inch/mixed
media by Sara Rahbar / www.sararahbar.com.

CONTENTS

ACKNOWLEDGMENTS

There are many people who made this collection possible and sustained me throughout the process. The project began when my colleague at RIT Croatia, Rebecca Roja Charry, first posed her honest questions, which alerted me to the transnational dimension of my Writing Program Administration (WPA) work at Rochester Institute of Technology (RIT). Over the next four years, my conversations with Rebecca developed into a close collaboration that included curriculum development, team-teaching, program assessment, and co-authorship. My sincere thanks to Rebecca for engaging with me on this long-term inquiry.

There have also been many at RIT who encouraged and supported my work on this collection. In particular, Stan Van Horn, director of RIT's English Language Center, has been a regular companion in exploring the issues of internationalization, working with L2 writers, and program administration. We were supported by a Provost's Learning Innovation Grant, for which we proposed "Internationalizing Writing Instruction" by developing a first-year writing course that encouraged students to see cultural and language difference as an opportunity to make meaning rather than as a barrier to meaning-making. The first iteration of that course was taught by Paulette Swartzfager and Erin Karl. Through the process of designing that course, we have been able to engage in ongoing dialogue between the first-year writing program and the English Language Center, resulting in increased interaction between faculty in both areas and the uncovering of numerous issues of importance related to pedagogy, learning outcomes, and policy. Stan and I also facilitated a faculty learning community entitled "Global Context, Content, and Citizenship in the University Curriculum." During the ten-week reading and dialogue group made up of twelve faculty, staff, and administrators we explored arguments about internationalization, its impact on curriculum and teaching, and intercultural communication. Every conversation with Stan and my colleagues in the university writing program has deepened my understanding and appreciation of the issues surrounding language instruction in higher education.

A College of Liberal Arts faculty research grant provided financial support to build a small library of books focused on internationalization and higher education. Those materials—and the support the dean of the College of Liberal Arts, Jamie Winebrake, and RIT provost, Jeremy Haefner—led to my fellowship in the State University of New York's (SUNY) Collaborative Online International Learning (COIL) Institute. There Rebecca, my colleague in Croatia, and Michael Starenko, an instructional designer at RIT, were able to come together with international faculty partners to design a globally networked learning environment used in first-year composition (FYC). At the COIL Institute, we had the privilege of working with a great number of people, including Jon Rubin, Sarah Guth, and John Fowler.

The initial call for submissions conveniently coincided with the 2010 Thomas R. Watson Conference, where the theme was "Working English: Global Contexts, Commitments, Consequences." Many of the contributors to this collection were presenters and participants in that gathering. This "kick-off" for the project infused an energy and focus that sustained it to the end. Without the contributors, this collection would not exist. It has been their generosity, thoughtfulness, and perseverance that has made this collection as strong as it is.

Working on the collection enabled me to learn how to do my job better. Christine Licata, senior associate provost in academic affairs, encouraged me to take what I was learning and actively engage with the other faculty and staff immersed in transnational programming at RIT. With her support, I worked with Anne Wahl, Leah Bradley, and Bonnie Maddox in the office of Student Learning Outcomes Assessment, Dianna Winslow, director of FYC, and Angela Brodie in the university writing program, to design a direct assessment of student writing that included student work from four of RIT's global locations in Croatia, Kosovo, and the United Arab Emirates. Along with a sizable cohort of faculty teaching in Henrietta, faculty from each of the global locations participated in an online discussion of student work, as well as in the assessment of over 200 student essays. The experience for all involved was enlightening and gave each of us important perspectives on the range of student work produced in the program and how we all read and assess that work.

Jim Bowman, Rick Hunter, and Jeremy Sarachan read drafts of my introduction, and their feedback and tough questions helped me improve my thinking and writing. Michael Spooner and his colleagues at Utah State University Press have been wonderful to work with; all the stories of his cogent and able guidance are true. Additionally, the two anonymous reviewers provided generative feedback on the collection. And it was Sara Rahbar's (www.sararahbar.com) provocative and moving artwork that helped me visualize some of what I aspire to for this collection, and I am thankful for her generous permission to use a piece of her work on the cover.

Finally, my most heartfelt thanks goes to my partner in life, Jill Swiencicki. She is the one who helped me think though the material significance and political implications of transnational writing program administration, listened to me work through how to respond to chapter manuscripts, took our children to the park or let me steal time to write in a café, and generously read every draft of my introduction, challenging me to think more clearly, write more concisely, and argue more thoughtfully.

TRANSNATIONAL WRITING PROGRAM ADMINISTRATION

TRANSNATIONAL WRITING PROGRAM ADMINISTRATION
An Introduction

David S. Martins

- A professor in the United States "outsources" the grading of student writing to Bangalore, India
- Globally networked learning environments (GNLEs) connect students located in multiple countries, speaking different languages, to collaborate on writing
- Multicultural and multilingual students increasingly enroll at US-based community colleges and universities
- Student learning outcomes focused on cultural and language difference aim to "internationalize" first-year composition (FYC) curricula
- US-based colleges and universities establish international branch campuses
- Writing Program Administrations (WPAs) from the United States travel to countries around the globe to consult with faculty and administrators on developing writing programs
- Institutional and writing program websites target global and local audiences

The scenarios above provide just a few examples of how the "global" shapes and impacts the "local" contexts for writing programs. While local conditions remain at the forefront of WPA, transnational activities are thoroughly shifting the questions we ask about writing curricula, the space and place in which writing happens, and the cultural and linguistic issues at the heart of the relationships forged in literacy work. In the global expansion of higher education, the tension between economic and pedagogical interests strongly influences decisions made about what kinds of programs to offer and how to offer them. Writing teachers and administrators involved in the creation or development of international programs must negotiate these tensions based upon what they know and value about learning, teaching, and writing. This collection of essays demonstrates how "transnational writing program administration" challenges taken-for-granted assumptions regarding

DOI: 10.7330/9780874219623.c000

program identity, curriculum and pedagogical effectiveness, logistics and quality assurance, faculty and student demographics, innovative partnerships and research, and the infrastructure needed to support writing instruction in higher education. In the process, *Transnational Writing Program Administration* extends the theoretical underpinnings of WPA to consider programs, activities, and institutions that involve students and faculty from two or more countries working together and highlights the situated practices of such efforts. The collection brings multilingual graduate students at the forefront of writing studies together with established administrators, teachers, and researchers and examines the practices and theories that impact our conceptions of WPA as transnational.

My own introduction to transnational WPA came in 2009, when I started work at Rochester Institute of Technology (RIT) as the FYC program director. Although I knew the institute had multiple international branch locations, I was not thinking about them in relation to the first-year writing program until I received an email from a faculty member at RIT Croatia, in Dubrovnik, Croatia, asking permission to alter the RIT first-year writing curriculum to be more appropriate for the Croatian students in her class. Until that question was asked, I had not realized the specific ways my administrative work was, and would need to be, shaped by international contexts. Exemplifying the speeds at which globalization produces changes in higher education, my colleagues and supervisors at the time were initially unable to clarify my responsibilities with respect to curriculum development, assessment, or faculty development for RIT's branch locations. As the WPA, I was clearly working in conditions not of my own making, conditions which seemed increasingly influenced more by economic interests (e.g., potential revenue and risk management) than educational ones (e.g., student learning and faculty engagement).

By posing a simple question about her freedom to restructure the assignments in the course she teaches, my Dubrovnik colleague revealed two distinct, yet ultimately productive tensions: (1) the efficacy of current curricular structures for writing instruction at the two campuses, and (2) the degree of autonomy and control experienced by faculty teaching in the writing program. As the new FYC program director, I didn't understand the curricular connections between the two schools and was not at all clear about my role at any of the three branch campuses with respect to program assessment, curriculum design, and faculty professional development. Receiving these questions as I did challenged what had been a comfortable sense of the nature and scope of my work. But even more provocative was my uncertainty about the relevance of the learning outcomes and activities of FYC for the students enrolled at RIT and its branch campuses.[1]

Much has changed for me since my introduction to transnational WPA work. Since 2009, the administrators, faculty, students, and staff at RIT have been learning together about the rapidly changing transnational contexts of our teaching, learning, and literacy practice. Now, as the director of the university writing program, which includes FYC, writing across the curriculum (WAC), and a writing commons, I continually reframe and challenge the habits of thinking that inform my decisions about structuring writing programs. This collection represents my attempt to draw together some of the generative work being done in an emerging area of inquiry in writing program administration.

***

It is now taken for granted that, in the twenty-first century, US higher education is changing dramatically. According to the Institute of International Education (2010), there were 723,277 international students studying in the United States, a 32% increase since 2000/2001. The number of US students studying abroad has more than doubled in the last decade, with 270,604 in 2009/2010 compared to 129,770 in 1998/1999. The number of international branch campuses (IBCs) has also increased dramatically: according to a survey conducted by the Observatory on Borderless Higher Education, there were 200 degree-granting IBCs in 2011, compared to 162 branches identified in 2009, and less than 82 in 2006 (Lawton and Katsomitros 2012). Although there appears to be a slowdown in the number of IBCs being established, the kinds of partnerships being developed in countries like China and India are expanding, where national regulations restrict the type of relationships foreign institutions can have in those countries (Lewin 2012). For example, according to the Council of Graduate Schools, in 2008, 38% of US grad schools had international joint or dual-degree programs, up from 29% in 2007. An additional 31% of programs were instituted in 2009 (Skorton 2012). As the numbers of students traveling abroad—both to and from the United States—increases, as the number of cross-border programs also increases, and as online education becomes a more integrated facet of higher education, it is even more critical for WPAs to understand the specific opportunities and challenges of doing their work in transnational contexts.

"Transnational" can mean many different things. In their book *Transnational Education: Issues and Trends in Offshore Higher Education*, Grant McBurnie and Christopher Ziguras define transnational education as "any education delivered by an institution based in one country to students located in another" (McBurnie and Ziguras 2007, 1). While this notion of "transnational" clearly signals a changing relationship between institutions and students, its presumption of a one-way flow maintains a hierarchical relationship that privileges the position of the *delivering* institution, its pedagogical and curricular ideologies, its administrative structures, and often its labor and workplace practices. Unlike "global" or "international," the term "transnational" typically invokes a more critical, analytical orientation like that described by Wendy S. Hesford and Eileen E. Schell in the introduction to their *College English* special issue on transnational feminist rhetorics. Hesford and Schell (2008) argue that in rhetoric and composition, the term "transnational" has too often not been used in ways that recognize how "transnationality challenges traditional understandings of context" or "how all national formations are constructed within and often solidified by transnational connectivities" (464). The chapters in this collection do challenge our understanding of context, and draw specific attention to the connections forged in transnational work, by providing rich, critical descriptions of emerging activities of writing programs and deliberately paying attention to the relationships—personal and institutional, educational and economic—that produce those activities. Each chapter draws from and extends rhetoric and composition scholarship, and each aims to present a variety of methods and approaches for contributing to a more nuanced conversation about learning, teaching, and administration in transnational contexts.

Since the mid-1990s, there have been a growing number of publications in fields related to WPA discussing internationalization and the impact of globalization on writing instruction. In-press discussions have focused on a broad range of issues. Ever present in these discussions is a keen awareness of and attention to changes in the "local" contexts of writing programs, and of the ideological and political positioning that enables WPAs to serve as agents in bringing about meaningful change for students, faculty, and institutions. What these conversations reveal is that a prevalent activity for researchers and scholars in writing program-related fields has been a form of reckoning with disciplinary and institutional histories. Authors have historicized, come to terms with, critiqued, and attempted to rearticulate the various assumptions—about writing, learning, work, education, capitalism, politics, identity—that have shaped the narratives and practices of disciplinary research, pedagogy, and administration, as well as institutional structures and positions. This collection participates in this disciplinary ethos. Specifically, three interrelated themes shape the organization of this book: transnational positioning, transnational language, and transnational engagement.

TRANSNATIONAL POSITIONING

One lesson learned over the past twenty years of scholarship in rhetoric and composition is that, by offering writing teachers and administrators opportunities to see the localness of their work, transnational writing programs counter assumptions of the universality of writing instruction. For example, in 1995, Muchiri, Mulamba, Myers, and Ndoloi (1995, 176) dramatically demonstrated what composition researchers, teachers, and administrators "take for granted what is local to their institutions and nation." The authors describe a range of experiences that students in Kenya, Tanzania, and Zaire often have as they journey from their homes to the major city centers where the universities they are attending are located. The authors also highlight the experiences of faculty, who may themselves have extremely limited access to academic resources for research; there simply isn't access to academic texts, and the texts that are available may be dated. Within such contexts, the ability of students to see themselves engaged in a "world of research and debate" cannot be taken for granted: "The 'research site' that takes up so much of many composition handbooks seems to assume the student links into a network of new knowledge, through the library and the teacher. Composition teachers may forget just how fragile these links are" (188). Effectively, Muchiri and her colleagues remind all writing instructors and program administrators of the limitations of approaching US composition activities and structures from a narrow, local, privileged, Western view.

Extending the work of Murchiri and her colleagues in "Beyond These Shores: An Argument for Internationalizing Composition," Mark Schaub draws from his seven-year experience as a US-trained WPA working in Egypt to show how composition is an "isolationist discipline" (Schaub 2003, 89–95), and offers suggestions for (1) "how the field of composition can expand its horizons beyond North America," and (2) how to "make our classrooms more global." After noticing a waning of energy and urgency to internationalize writing instruction following the terrorist attacks on September 11, 2001, Schaub aims to encourage writing teachers and administrators to avoid "returning to isolationist thinking in our classrooms." Significantly, such isolationist thinking remains prevalent, but energetic voices have reinvigorated efforts to combat such thinking by offering clear methods of analysis and strategies for changing practices.

Christiane Donahue (2009), for example, critiques what she terms the "discourses of internationalization" as they relate to scholarly work and the teaching of writing, speech, and academic or scientific writing activities. She argues, "The U.S. picture of writing around the globe—its teaching, its learning, and our theories about these—has been highly partial, portraying the issue in particular ways, largely export-based, that I believe might create obstacles for U.S. scholars' thinking and thus impede effective collaboration or 'hearing' of work across borders" (214). She presents a provocative and complex portrait of "some of the linguistic, cultural, and discursive challenges in the discourses of internationalizing composition studies and how they suggest we might be misimagining our global roles and positions" (215). In this way, Donahue foregrounds the location of US composition teaching and scholarly work and attempts to reinvigorate the broader conversation about writing instruction and research. Donahue concludes her article by answering the question, "What can we, as a field, no longer do without?":

> We need international work because we can no longer do without deep understanding as the world shifts and slips. We need the ability to negotiate that comes from deep intercultural awareness; the ability to shift in understanding of our global position; the research trends and strong methods other scholars have developed; the deep familiarity with other systems and contexts, developed in so much more than the occasional encounter, fulfilling but exotic; the suspicion about market forces at work in the more glib general discussions about the value in internationalizing higher education. Without these, our "internationalizing" efforts will remain stuck in a-historical, a-contextual, and highly partial modes of intellectual tourism. (236)

In calling for deep intercultural awareness, familiarity with other relevant research trends and methods, other systems and contexts for education and research, and continued vigilance of economic factors, Donahue asserts her commitment to an ideal of self-awareness that relates to broader, cross-cultural, cross-linguistic understanding and experience. While the day-to-day pressures of teaching in and administering a writing program keep attention focused on "local" issues, concerns and problems, Donahue encourages an expanded sense of location.[2]

The recent publication of *Writing Programs Worldwide: Profiles of Academic Writing in Many Places* (Thaiss et al. 2012) presents an amazing portrait of writing instruction worldwide. As Chris Thaiss explains in his introduction, the editors' intent for the collection, in both its print and online versions, was "to inform decision-making by teachers, program managers, and college/university administrators in regard to how writing is conceived of, managed, funded and taught in higher education" (5). Through their efforts to build community, identify trends, and present rich diversity, the editors have provided an explicit presence to the expanding locations of writing instruction. Similarly, the chapters that comprise part 1 of this book further demonstrate the problems of the "export model" of international higher education, revealing an emerging internationalist perspective on the design and delivery of writing programs. In the process, these chapters effectively call into being new geographies and actualize new visions of teaching and learning.

Starting with a challenge to the basic definitions, Chris Anson and Christiane Donahue argue in chapter 1 that the common association of the term "writing program" with the teaching of college composition in the United States blinds us to the complex ways in which writing is programmatically woven into the teaching and research missions of higher education institutions around the world. Their chapter first complicates the standard historical narrative of WPA positions and works to construct a framework for analyzing the three sample "programs" they profile. Then, drawing on their experiences visiting and consulting at two institutions in Europe and one in Saudi Arabia, Anson and Donahue demonstrate the ways in which methods of instruction and research on writing are created from and adapt to the context-specific educational, curricular, and cultural needs and interests of their institutions. Chapter 1 demonstrates the value added from a different kind of conversation, one that does not focus on identifying where the "writing programs" are or who the "WPAs" are, but rather explores from a global perspective—and across institutional contexts—the activities, disciplines, and institutional structures and missions that utilize, study, and support writing in higher education.

The role of technology in the expansion of transnational locations of writing classrooms is significant. In chapter 2, "Tech Travels: Connecting Writing Classes across Continents," Alyssa O'Brien and Christine Alfano report on research funded through a grant from the Wallenberg Global Learning Network (WGLN). Their chapter describes the technological and pedagogical accommodations required when students work in globally-distributed teams on writing. Building on five years of work connecting university students across Asia, Europe, and the Middle East, O'Brien and Alfano share their research on writing in multimodal formats through virtual connections—not only blogging and video conferences, but also gaming and Second Life sessions engaging students in Sweden, Egypt, and the United States; Skype-facilitated peer review exchanges between Stanford and Singapore; and Polycom, class-to-class collaborative activities between Russia and the United States. In addition to its focus on strategies for adapting practices of traditional institutional settings and modifying technological apparatuses for collaborative learning in multimodal classrooms, chapter 2 explores the learning that can make such collaborations so much more than "simply" an exciting experience.

Cultural expectations for education are highlighted in the export of US-style education practices to the Middle East, as shown in two related chapters. For example, Alan S. Weber, Krystyna Golkowska, Ian Miller, Mary Ann Rishel, Rodney Sharkey, and Autumn Watts present a reflective case study in chapter 3, "The First-Year Writing Seminar Program at Weill Cornell Medical College—Qatar: Balancing Tradition, Culture, and Innovation in Transnational Writing Instruction." Based explicitly on the curricula of the main campus of Cornell University in Ithaca, New York, the faculty of the newly formed program has struggled to adapt the American-style writing instruction developed at the Knight Writing Institute in Ithaca for their unique group of learners. The authors conclude their chapter by describing efforts to promote the development of a literacy culture in which faculty and students negotiate strikingly different attitudes toward literature, identity, and textuality. In the second chapter focusing on writing programs in Qatar, Danielle Zawodny Wetzel and Dudley W. Reynolds trace four years of course materials from the FYC program at Carnegie Mellon University's Pittsburgh and Qatar campuses. Paying particular attention to the changes made over four years, their analysis of the linguistic and pedagogical assumptions behind those materials reveals an evolution in perspectives on curriculum, placement policy, program structure, and staffing. While the earlier course materials show a strong, unidirectional influence from the Pittsburgh campus to the Qatar campus, the later materials show a bidirectional influence between the two campuses, supporting the definition of a transnational program as one that is emergent, dynamic, and a site for collaboration. Zawodny Wetzel and Reynolds argue that perhaps one of the greatest challenges for transnational programs is determining the relationship between campuses and to what extent a global program is or needs to be homogeneous across campuses. Chapter 4 concludes that aspects of such relationships are determined contractually, but most of the relationship is negotiated between faculty at each location based on their perceptions of local and contextualized needs. "Adaptation Across Space and Time: Revealing Pedagogical Assumptions" argues that writing program administrators must approach a transnational writing program as dynamic and emergent rather than static or homogeneous.

Leadership is another compelling factor influencing the development of transnational writing programs. In chapter 5, "So Close, Yet So Far: Administering a Writing Program with a Bahamian Campus," Shanti Bruce encourages transnational WPAs to take what leadership scholars call an "unnatural leadership" approach and teach in an international classroom themselves in order to understand how the program works locally. Chapter 5 focuses on Nova Southeastern University's Bahamian campus, and includes discussions of various factors that significantly influence the design, experience, and impact of transnational writing programs: the international commute, "island time," classroom culture and language differences, and even weather conditions. Bruce urges WPAs to acknowledge the material consequences of seemingly trivial factors on pedagogy and program effectiveness.

The last chapter of part 1 highlights the importance of developing writing program infrastructure based on complex understanding of language difference among international and domestic students. In "Exploring the Contexts of US-Mexican Border Writing Programs," Beth Brunk-Chavez, Kate Mangelsdorf, Patricia Wojahn, Alfredo Urzua-Beltran, Omar Montoya, Barry Thatcher, and Kathryn Valentine highlight productive, programmatic responses to the ideological blinders that too often lead institutions to create more robust structures (though also often still inadequate) for supporting international students, leaving domestic students for whom English is not a first language with insufficient support. For these authors, the US-Mexico border region is a dynamic rhetorical space, presenting WPAs with a variety of challenges and opportunities to create effective placement mechanisms, develop dynamic curricula and writing pedagogies, identify productive institutional and programmatic collaborations, and design additional structures for supporting linguistic and culturally diverse students. Still, with all the efforts these authors document from their work in two border institutions, they acknowledge that much more work in this area is needed.

TRANSNATIONAL LANGUAGE

One immediate implication of transnational education, and one that has received critical attention within rhetoric and composition, is language difference. Part II: Transnational Language addresses language difference by expanding upon disciplinary discussions that have focused on "monolinguistic ideologies" in the teaching of college composition (see Canagarajah 2002; Horner and Lu 2008; Horner, Lu, and Matsuda 2010;

Horner, Lu, Royster, and Trimbur 2011; Horner and Trimbur 2002; Shuck 2006) and second language writers (Matsuda 1997; Matsuda, Fruit, Lee, and Lamm 2006; Silva 1990). These chapters provide provocative new methods for analyzing and understanding language differences in specific, transnational contexts.

Transnational writing programs offer particularly compelling opportunities to develop a more comprehensive understanding of the heterogeneity and fluctuating nature of the writing experienced in writing classes, and ultimately the efficacy of individual courses and program curricula. Still, the challenge for transnational writing teachers and administrators will be to take advantage of these opportunities. In the companion piece to the earlier chapter on border institutions, Barry Thatcher, Omar Montoya, and Kelly Medina-López offer a method and practice for taking advantage of those opportunities by developing a more nuanced understanding of language difference in writing classes. Drawing on analytical methods from linguistics and contrastive rhetoric, chapter 7 presents an "etic-then-emic" approach that enables the authors to engage meaningfully with "the predominant features of US writing curriculum as exemplified on the US-Mexico border." After characterizing varied border rhetorics and their related groups of students, the authors examine how these six groups might bring dynamic, contested, and complex rhetorical combinations of border rhetoric to the US writing classroom. The chapter concludes by briefly evaluating current curricula at New Mexico State University and The University of Texas at El Paso.

In their opinion essay appearing in *College English*, "Language Difference in Writing: Toward a Translingual Approach," Horner, Lu, Royster, and Trimbur (2011) called for a new disciplinary and pedagogical schema. The authors counter what they term as "traditional" and "accommodationist" approaches to language difference with a "translingual approach" that "sees difference in language not as a barrier to overcome or as a problem to manage, but as a resource for producing meaning in writing, speaking, reading, and listening" (303). Transnational writing programs expand meaning-making activities by offering writing teachers and administrators opportunities to develop new approaches to language difference in the writing classroom.

Hem Sharma Paudel develops just such a new approach to language difference in chapter 8, "Globalization and Language Difference: A Mesodiscursive Approach." Through a critique of four major approaches to language difference—world Englishes, English as a lingua franca, defense of national language, and the numerical model of multilingualism—Paudel endeavors to "develop a theory of translingual agency that, first, seeks to go beyond the paradigms of the dominant language theories that regard languages as discrete and stable entities and, second, also critiques the romanticized version of multilingual agency, where multilinguals are represented as naturally capable of shuttling across languages." He proposes a "mesodiscursive" approach to language difference that acknowledges the intermediary space between the polls of language fixity and radical contingency, and focuses on how language users create subtle differences in meaning while also imitating dominant discourse patterns. Such an approach enables writing teachers and administrators to see the difficulty of transforming language practice, due to the stabilizing forces that largely limit transformative potentials of language users.

Since the publication of "English Only and College Composition" (Horner and Trimbur 2002), WPAs have continued to extend and elaborate on the role of linguistic ideologies in the development of writing programs, their policies, and their related infrastructure. In the process, these conversations have set the stage for more systematic change in US writing instruction. On the level of institutional practice, for example, Gail Shuck (2006) takes seriously the challenge offered by Horner and Trimbur, and works to implement the ideas they articulate. By doing so, she demonstrates the immense task faced by transnational WPAs. As coordinator of the English language support programs at Boise State University, Shuck describes her efforts (1) to counter a monolingual ideology, while at the same time (2) acknowledging her complicity in that ideology because of its pervasive structuration of institutional positions, curricular structures, and placement and assessment practices. Throughout her essay, Shuck speaks to the infrastructures of composition that can be rethought in direct response to the classroom and institutional activities imagined as a counter to *monolingual ideologies.*

The last two chapters in part 2 focus on the relationship between language and writing program infrastructure. In chapter 9, "(Re-)Situating Translingual Work for Writing Program Administration in Cross-National and Cross-Language Perspectives from Lebanon and Singapore," Nancy Bou Ayash situates issues of (1) the multiplicity of language use "on the ground," (2) language policies, and (3) writing pedagogy within broader sociocultural, geopolitical, and economic changes. Paying special attention to how each issue informs and is informed by the other, she presents cross-national and cross-linguistic perspectives from the multilingual sites of the US, Singapore, and Lebanon. Exploring the differential treatment of language difference in policies and practices in these different locations, this comparative analysis offers US WPAs a more nuanced understanding of the possibilities for developing and institutionalizing translingualism in US-based writing programs.

In chapter 10, "Discourses of Internationalization and Diversity in US Universities and Writing Programs," Christine M. Tardy explores the dominant discourses surrounding internationalization and diversity, which are created and reinforced in US higher education through the public texts of university and writing program websites. While such genres have a primarily promotional aim, and their expressions of identity and ideology may or may not reflect actual institutional practices, these public texts are important for their role in establishing privileged norms and ideologies. Tardy presents a multimodal critical discourse analysis of the public websites of twenty-eight US universities and their writing programs, aiming to identify (1) the dominant discourses of internationalization and diversity as presented through these texts, and (2) the place and role of language within these discourses. Her findings illustrate a general neglect of language and relatively little emphasis on internationalization within the websites of writing programs. The chapter concludes by considering the ways in which writing programs are influenced by dominant university discourses, as well as how they might appropriate or disrupt these discourses to reflect program values that are desirable for meeting the challenges of writing in a globalized world.

TRANSNATIONAL ENGAGEMENT

Disciplinary conversations in composition, rhetoric, and literacy studies reveal a strong commitment to understanding the politics and pedagogy, the theory and practice, and the technologies and languages of literacy education conceived in globalized terms. Along with the recent discussions concerning "English only" or "monolinguistic ideologies" mentioned above, rhetoric and composition scholars have engaged directly with critiques of what Wendy Hesford (2006) calls the "global turn" in disciplinary activities. Margaret Himley (2003), for example, writes in "Writing Programs and Pedagogies in a Globalized Landscape" about her critical review of the required FYC sequence at Syracuse University. She describes what a writing program can teach about authorship in a world organized by fast capitalism and saturated with texts and networked connections. Himley poses many questions for WPAs to consider, encouraging writing instructors and administrators to engage each other and the students in their classes in an "archaeological analysis," which she describes as "an intellectual process that works to excavate the many meanings of events, artifacts, and texts, [which] is a nonlinear process of framing and reframing the object of analysis in order to understand it from many perspectives and through many interconnections" (63). It is a critical way of thinking, Himley explains,

> that recognizes what Eileen Schell calls "transnational linkages." It is a way of thinking and writing that locates us within emerging, [d]ynamic and global economic, cultural, political, and social systems of meaning. It is a way of thinking that values the dynamic nexus of the personal and the global as interconnected and complex networks of discursive and material meaning-making and that locates us all as global citizens. (64)

Hesford and Schell (2008, 464) elaborate on such an approach in their *College English* special issue on "transnational feminist rhetoric," which aims "to understand the 'cultural logics that inform and structure border crossings as well as state strategies' (Ong 1999, 5)."

The call for such transnational engagement has become even stronger: Darin Payne and Daphne Desser's *Teaching Writing in Globalization* offers chapters that "exemplify a critical remapping of disciplinary work as both a response to and an intervention into processes and products of globalization, at least insofar as they relate to writing and writing instruction in higher education today" (Payne and Desser 2012, 6). Bruce Horner's (2012) "The WPA as Broker: Globalization and the Composition Program" argues that WPAs must "take into account the global context in which their brokering is conducted in order to resist those effects of globalization that threaten the value of the work of writing and its learning and teaching" (58). In "Anxieties of Globalization: Networked Subjects in Rhetoric and Composition Studies," Rebecca Dingo and Donna Strickland strive "not to identify the bad (or good) effects of globalization, but to demonstrate the affectively driven rhetorical moves that link and sustain three subject positions shaped by globalization and central to the continued emergence and sustenance of rhetoric and composition studies: student, contingent worker, and administrator" (Dingo and Strickland 2012, 80). Responding to such calls, transnational writing programs can be seen as a way to counter masked complicity by offering writing teachers and administrators the opportunity to be deliberate about the ideology embodied by curricula and institutional practices.

Enacting a critical, transnational engagement, the chapters presented in Part III: Transnational Engagement extend the discussion of the cultural logics, contexts, and rhetorical moves shaping cross-border writing instruction and administration by drawing attention to labor practices, community colleges, and globally-networked learning environments. In chapter 11, Rebecca Dingo, Rachel Riedner, and Jennifer Wingard ground their discussion of WAC/WID (writing across the curriculum/writing in the disciplines) practices in a concrete example from the University of Houston, where a business professor outsourced grading from a WID class to Bangalore, India. In "Disposable Drudgery: Outsourcing Goes to College," the authors use the UH example to demonstrate why WAC/WID practitioners should map how local decisions are linked and have repercussions nationally and globally. To demonstrate these connections, Dingo, Riedner, and Wingard develop a transnational feminist framework that reveals linkages between specific labor sites of WAC/WID programs and ideologies of neoliberalism. Examination of the material, institutional, and ideological conditions in which WAC/WID practices occur enables them to show how UH's outsourcing proves local monetary decisions create unequal economic exchange, unequal power, and supranational effects. These practices sustain unequal and different iterations of material power that reinforce inequality across disciplines, departments, and, in this instance, global work sites. Through their analysis, the authors illustrate the significance of WAC/WID practitioners engaging in transnational feminist analysis.

In "Economies of Composition: Mapping Transnational Writing Programs in US Community Colleges," Wendy Olson demonstrates the importance of understanding how English language instruction functions in two-year colleges. Olson conducts her study of English language programs at two-year colleges in Washington State—specifically the pre-college writing classes "wherein students are introduced to academic writing expectations and conventions"—by focusing on what program descriptions and brochures, curricula, goals and objectives, and college missions reveal about course design, alignment with best practices in composition theory, and the pedagogical implications of curricular and programmatic formations. Accordingly, Olson examines the discrete ways in which economic globalization has shaped English as a literacy commodity for international students, within these particular open admissions institutions in the United States. As such, chapter 12 unpacks the complicated, and often contradictory, rise of language-intensive programs within the distinct, yet often overlooked, site of US community colleges.

Finally, Doreen Starke-Meyerring observes in chapter 13 that, as dwindling public funding for higher education pushes institutions to position themselves in global markets, WPAs are increasingly called upon to facilitate dominant neoliberal approaches to globalizing higher education through expansionist programs, which are designed to generate revenues from international tuition dollars. She argues that these approaches largely reproduce and repackage traditional, local, institutionally-bounded courses and programs—predominantly from the Anglophone West—for one-way sales in online or offshore global markets. In light of these pressures, "From 'Educating the Other' to Cross-Boundary Knowledge-Making: Globally Networked Learning Environments as Critical Sites of Writing Program Administration" offers an exploration of emerging globally networked learning environments (GNLEs) for their potential as critical sites for rethinking and repositioning writing programs and WPA work in higher education. By examining five dimensions of these emerging, partnered learning environments, Starke-Meyerring illustrates how GNLEs enable a critical engagement and allow writing teachers and administrators to carve out alternative learning spaces that can help question, redirect, and reshape dominant transmission models of "educating the Other."

***

As revealed in the controversy over Yale University's announcement that it had partnered with the National University of Singapore to form Yale-NUS College, the emerging activities of higher education in the twenty-first century are challenging taken-for-granted notions of academic administration (see Redden 2012; Smith 2012). Transnational higher education is raising high-stakes questions about faculty governance and decision making, academic standards and values, curriculum and pedagogy, and faculty and staff labor. WPAs adept at working in conditions not of their own making can bring clarity to these issues. The chapters in this collection raise provocative questions, provide insightful analyses, and present compelling models for teaching, research, and administration in transnational contexts. I know that each chapter productively challenged my own understanding of how to do my job.

In order to influence the conversations about international education on our campuses, WPAs have more work to do in rectifying our own historical and disciplinary limitations with prevalent linguistic ideologies, as well as disciplinary knowledge gaps. Challenging conventional practices, the essays in this collection demonstrate that transnational approaches to teaching and administering writing in global contexts require renewed, critical attention to shifting realities of higher education. Transnational approaches, as shown by each contributor, mean much more than simply focusing on "any education delivered by an institution based in one country to students located in another" (McBurnie and Ziguras 2007, 1); each author learns from the interaction of students and faculty across normally conceived borders—for example, between languages, cultures, economies, and institutions. Because the specific details of any transnational writing program present unique opportunities and challenges, the contributions to this collection do not offer sourcebook-like arguments for how to deliver cross-border programs. Instead, each chapter demonstrates the authors' critical perspectives on the infrastructures of WPA for global contexts, their theories of language and literacy produced in cross-cultural and cross-linguistic exchange, and their approaches to research suited for transnational pedagogy and writing studies.

While there are strong forces at work in maintaining the ideological commitments to specific configurations of curricular and administrative infrastructure—and which will make it even more difficult to enact changes to current models of teaching, learning, and writing—the globalization of higher education does offer opportunities to rethink and, therefore, restructure the delivery of higher education. Without such a rethinking, a business model of economic efficiency will dominate the discussion, while concerns of educational models will either be muted or remain secondary.

Notes

1. See Martins and Reed (forthcoming) for an extended argument about new models for teaching, learning, and writing in transnational contexts.
2. See also Horner, NeCamp, and Donahue (2011) for a discussion of "Multilingual Composition Scholarship," yet another way shifting locations impacts writing instruction and administration.

References

Canagarajah, Suresh. 2002. *The Geopolitics of Academic Writing*. Pittsburgh: University of Pittsburgh Press.

Dingo, Rebecca, and Donna Strickland. 2012. "Anxieties of Globalization: Networked Subjects in Rhetoric and Composition Studies." In *Teaching Writing in Globalization: Remapping Disciplinary Work*, ed. Darin Payne and Daphne Desser, 79–93. Lanham, MD: Lexington Books.

Donahue, Christiane. 2009. "'Internationalization' and Composition Studies: Reorienting the Discourse." *College Composition and Communication* 61 (2): 212–43.

Hesford, Wendy S. 2006. "Global Turns and Cautions in Rhetoric and Composition Studies." *PMLA* 121 (3): 787–801. http://www.jstor.org/stable/25486354.

Hesford, Wendy S., and Eileen E. Schell. 2008. "Configurations of Transnationality: Locating Feminist Rhetorics." *College English* 70 (5): 461–70.

Himley, Margaret. 2003. "Writing Programs and Pedagogies in a Globalized Landscape." *WPA: Writing Program Administration* 26 (3): 49–66.

Horner, Bruce. 2012. "The WPA as Broker: Globalization and the Composition Program." In *Teaching Writing in Globalization: Remapping Disciplinary Work*, ed. Darin Payne and Daphne Desser, 57–78. Lanham, MD: Lexington Books.

Horner, Bruce, and John Trimbur. 2002. "English Only and College Composition." *College Composition and Communication* 53 (4): 594–630. http://dx.doi.org/10.2307/1512118.

Horner, Bruce, and Min-Zhan Lu. 2008. "Resisting Monolingualism in 'English': Reading and Writing the Politics of Language. In *Rethinking English in Schools: Towards a New and Constructive Stage*, ed. Viv Ellis, Carol Fox, and Brian Street, 140–57. New York: Continuum International Pub. Group.

Horner, Bruce, Min-Zhan Lu, and Paul Kei Matsuda, eds. 2010. *Cross-Language Relations in Composition*. Carbondale: Southern Illinois University Press.

Horner, Bruce, Min-Zhan Lu, Jacqueline Jones Royster, and John Trimbur. 2011. "Opinion: Language Difference in Writing—Toward a Translingual Approach." *College English* 73 (3): 303–21. https://login.ezproxy.rit.edu/login?url=http://search .proquest.com/docview/851229387?accountid=108 and http://www.ncte.org/journals /ce/issues/v73-3, accessed March 30, 2011.

Horner, Bruce, Samantha NeCamp, and Christiane Donahue. 2011. "Toward a Multilingual Composition Scholarship: From English Only to a Translingual Norm." *College Composition and Communication* 63 (3): 269–300.

Institute of International Education. 2010. "Open Doors 2010 Fast Facts." *Open Doors Report on International Educational Exchange*. http://www.iie.org/Research-and -Publications/Open-Doors, accessed July 23, 2012.

Lawton, William, and Alex Katsomitros. 2012. *International Branch Campuses: Data and Developments*. Redhill: The Observatory on Borderless Higher Education.

Lewin, Tamar. 2012. "Colleges Slower to Branch Out Abroad." *New York Times*, January 12. http://www.nytimes.com/2012/01/12/education/colleges-slower-to-branch-out -abroad.html?_r=1&ref=tamarlewin.

Matsuda, Paul Kei, Maria Fruit, Tamara Lee, and Burton Lamm, eds. 2006. "Second Language Writers and Writing Program Administrators." *WPA* 30 (1–2).

Matsuda, Paul Kei. 1997. "Contrastive Rhetoric in Context: A Dynamic Model of L2 Writing." *Journal of Second Language Writing* 6 (1): 45–60. http://dx.doi.org/10.1016 /S1060-3743(97)90005-9.

McBurnie, Grant, and Christopher Ziguras. 2007. *Transnational Education: Issues and Trends in Offshore Higher Education*. New York: Routledge.

Muchiri, Mary N., Nshindi G. Mulamba, Greg Myers, and Deoscorous B. Ndoloi. 1995. "Importing Composition: Teaching and Researching Academic Writing Beyond North America." *CCC* 46 (2): 175–198. http://www.jstor.org/stable/i215234, accessed March 4, 2011.

Ong, Aihwa. 1999. *Flexible Citizenship: The Cultural Logics of Transnationality*. Durham, NC: Duke University Press.

Payne, Darin, and Daphne Desser, eds. 2012. *Teaching Writing in Globalization: Remapping Disciplinary Work*. Lanham, MD: Lexington Books.

Schaub, Mark. 2003. "Beyond these Shores: An Argument for Internationalizing Composition." *Pedagogy* 3 (1): 85–98. http://dx.doi.org/10.1215/15314200-3-1-85.

Shuck, Gail. 2006. "Combating Monolingualism." *WPA* 30 (1–2): 59–82.

Silva, Tony. 1990. "Second Language Composition Instruction: Developments, Issues, and Directions in ESL." In *Second Language Writing: Research Insights for the Classroom*, ed. Barbara Kroll, 11–23. Cambridge: Cambridge University Press. http://dx.doi.org /10.1017/CBO9781139524551.005.

Redden, Elizabeth. 2012. "Whose Yale College?" *Inside Higher Ed*, published March 28. https://www.insidehighered.com/news/2012/03/28/yale-faculty-raise-governance -questions-about-decision-open-branch-singapore.

Skorton, David. 2012. "Bringing Cornell to the World and the World to Cornell: A Presidential White Paper." Cornell University, Office of the President. http://president.cornell.edu/speeches/, accessed July 23, 2012.

Smith, Mitch. 2012. "A Call to Respect Rights" *Inside Higher Ed*, published April 6. https://www.insidehighered.com/news/2012/04/06/yale-faculty-resoultion-expresses-concern-about-singapore-campus.

Thaiss, Chris, Gerd Bräuer, Paula Carlino, Lisa Ganobscik-Williams, and Aparna Sinha, eds. 2012. *Writing Programs Worldwide: Profiles of Academic Writing in Many Places.* Anderson, SC: Parlor Press.

PART I

Transnational Positioning

1

DECONSTRUCTING "WRITING PROGRAM ADMINISTRATION" IN AN INTERNATIONAL CONTEXT

Chris M. Anson[1] and Christiane Donahue

The scene is familiar: you're moving across a rural landscape in a train, car, bus, or even on a bicycle. If this landscape is arable, eventually you'll pass by something you immediately recognize as *farmland*. The crops will be specific to the region, of course: corn, cotton, soybeans, pineapple, tobacco, poppies. But if someone were to ask you what goes on in those fields, what activity the fields represent, without hesitation you'd say *farming*. Even when we travel to the most remote and culturally distinctive regions of the world, "farming" activates familiar schemas for us.

In some ways, the concept of the "writing program," with its roots in the history of US higher education and the development of the almost ubiquitous first-year composition (FYC) requirement, is generic enough in most educators' minds to make a rough but workable analogy to the concept of farmland. The activities that take place in most writing programs—curricular oversight, teacher development, the placement of students into courses, and the attempt to make several or many different classes cohesive across a range of teachers—exist at the same level of generality as tilling soil, putting down seed, and harvesting what grows.

When we think about writing programs and their administration, it's tempting to construct them by activating familiar schemas that we map onto other educational contexts. Acknowledging that students may be fulfilling a variety of educational requirements structured in different ways, in various kinds of degree programs with different missions, and in other languages, we nevertheless imagine some kind of organizational center whose goals and activities share an affinity with the ones we know. At the helm is a *director*, someone with specialized knowledge and, usually, an advanced degree in rhetoric and composition. The principle activity is *teaching*, which is provided by a group of academic

DOI: 10.7330/9780874219623.c001

staff, sometimes tenure-line faculty, sometimes graduate students, but usually—especially at larger institutions—part-time or full-time instructors on contingent appointments. However, these assumptions often ignore major differences in what constitutes a "program," and how that program functions within its broader activity system—with various complex political, ideological, and social (f)actors at work. Consider, for example, the difference between a family-run soybean farm and a corporate-style wheat farm. These farms' economies of scale will be strikingly different. The larger farm will be in a more productive, competitive bargaining position than the smaller and may be able to withstand the ebbs and flows of the economy more effectively. Although there will be a hierarchy that governs both farms, the larger one will adhere to a carefully designed structure with specified roles and reporting processes, while the family farm will operate on the basis of tradition and unwritten rules of activity and productivity. The "farmers" in the corporate operation may include managers who have MBAs or advanced degrees in agricultural economics, while the titular head of the family farm may only be a high school graduate. When we compare the large, business-run US farm with one, say, in China, significant differences emerge from these countries' governance systems and overarching political and economic ideologies. Every operation within the farm itself—its roles, interpersonal relations, activities, finances, and measures of accountability— must be understood in light of these systems.

Over the past twenty years, the common refrain in US composition literature that references writing instruction and writing programs beyond US borders has been one of lack or even absence: "There is no . . ." Even as recently as 2007, Susan McLeod stated that "there was until very recently no comparable [FYC] course in universities based on the European model" (McLeod 2007, 23), with the exception of some in the Netherlands—a claim that simply does not bear out (see, for example, Donahue 2008). That misperception, we propose, has grown out of our tendency to look for what we know and, not seeing it, proclaim that it doesn't exist, such as arriving in a country where farming takes place out of sight in huge underground greenhouses when we expect it to be above ground. Sometimes the farm doesn't look like a farm. The "there is no . . ." belief persists for three additional reasons. It has grown out of our tendency, first, to equate any "writing program" with "first-year US-style composition curriculum," and, second, to restrict our knowledge to what we can read in English. Third, and perhaps more insidiously, the narrative serves *us* better by falsely reassuring us of our unique status in the world of writing instruction. And our overseas colleagues tend to oblige—because the programs can appear so different, the narrative is easier to enter. Only when pressed about classroom activities or curricular goals do alternate narratives emerge, usually ones that more closely resemble writing across the curriculum (WAC) or writing in the disciplines (WID).

And yet, both currently and historically, even within our US scholarship, there is evidence of a broader and less limiting understanding. It is not difficult to find references in book chapters to the roots of writing program administration (WPA) work in nineteenth-century developments fostered by Jardine or Bain in Scotland (Gaillet 2004). Current and forthcoming books (e.g., Thaiss et al. 2012) offer strong descriptions of full and partial programs. In the space of twenty minutes of Internet searching of websites and homepages, we can create tables of comparative writing program features in multi-country university networks (see appendix 1.1).

In this chapter, we will first briefly trace the place, role, history, and importance of WPA work in the United States, focusing on the contested nature of WPA and what constitutes a "writing program," because this underscores the heterogeneity of meanings and usually unconscious assumptions about what is meant by "program" and "administration" across the years and across types of US institutions. We will then explore how writing programs beyond the United States are shaped by and into unique institutional, disciplinary, and pedagogical contexts, demonstrating the importance of understanding the teaching of writing as situated within complex histories and cultures. To illustrate these principles, we will briefly describe some contextually evolving features of writing programs in three countries: a preparatory writing program at Dar Al-Hekma College in Saudi Arabia; a Center for University Methodology (Le Centre de Méthodologie Universitaire) at the Université Libre de Bruxelles; and a writing research center at The Université de Poitiers, one of France's oldest universities. These cases highlight the degree to which twenty-first century WPAs need a stronger sense of other approaches to higher education plans and infrastructures around the world. These examples will lead into a final section suggesting that, as dialogue with international writing studies and pedagogies continues to expand and invite greater cross-national collaboration, it is increasingly important that we map our frames, our language, and our assumptions onto writing work outside the US with caution, and with an almost anthropological sensitivity to context and the cultural and national sources of praxis. We will argue that seeing what has been persistently missed encourages us to revisit our entrenched beliefs about the "automatic" value of our courses, our field, and our research. This can help to widen possibilities not only for US-style WPA roles, but also for writing courses and pedagogies, enriching our development of new approaches and sharpening our sense of the local nature of existing WPA work.

THE "WPA" AS A US CONSTRUCTION: HISTORY AND CURRENT CONTOURS

Most generalized histories of composition instruction in US colleges and universities portray its development along a trajectory of increasing specialization. As the story goes, the ubiquitous US composition program has its roots in the slow democratization of higher education that took place in the mid- to late-nineteenth century. Most historians of rhetoric and composition point directly to Harvard as having created the progenitor "program," particularly after the establishment of the Boylston Professorship in Rhetoric and Oratory and the widening of Harvard's admission door to students who appeared to lack the communicative refinements of their predecessors (Reynolds, Bizzell, and Herzberg 2004). The precedent Harvard set—programs that sought to purge linguistic infelicities from the writing of young men—spread rapidly, both to newly established institutions and to older ones that, like Harvard, were starting to admit less prepared students and creating new areas of study that did more than train the next generation of lawyers, politicians, and clergymen (McDonald 1999). The eventual entrenchment of writing instruction in departments of literature, and the advent of New Criticism, solidified a focus on students' written products that has come to be known across the United States as the "current-traditional paradigm" (Adams and Adams 1987). As most historical accounts suggest, however, it was not until the development of the process movement in the 1960s and 1970s that the concept of the "writing program"—led by a growing cohort of specialists in writing process research—was fully developed.[2] As Crowley puts it, process pedagogy caused several "remarkable changes" to composition in the university, including the professionalization of the teaching of first year writing and a "reconceptualization of composition teachers as disciplined professionals" (Crowley 1998, 191).

Recently, US histories of both composition and WPA work have been complicating the story. L'Eplattenier and Mastrangelo's (2004) *Historical Studies of Writing Program Administration* highlights the earlier history—primarily, but not only, in the United States—through its analysis of stories of individual pioneers and whole communities. Notably, the influence of George Jardine (University of Glasgow) and Alexander Bain (University of Aberdeen) is carefully detailed by Lynée Gaillet (2004), who suggests that these scholars' early emphasis on writing, writing instruction, and writing in all disciplines is rarely noted in US scholarship. Similarly, David Gold's (2008) *Rhetoric at the Margins: Revising the History of Writing Instruction in American Colleges, 1873–1947* offers a neglected history of writing programs at three southern institutions (a black liberal arts college, a teacher-training school, and a public university for women). Gold's historical analysis of these institutions reveals the internal sources of their programmatic innovations, breaking the stereotype that progressive educational practice always trickles down from elite institutions and that what appears to represent instructional conservatism always has its source in conservative ideology. And Charles Paine's (1999) *The Resistant Writer: Rhetoric as Immunity, 1850 to the Present* documents the history of composition through the influence of competing institutions and practices. Such histories, described as alternate by Gaillet (2004, 185), suggest that there may well be alternate accounts of the current international WPA story.

From a contemporary perspective, scholars continue to struggle with the definition of a writing program, especially as institutionally systematic efforts to focus on writing still exhibit structural, curricular, and pedagogical diversity. For Janangelo (2011), writing programs in the United States are designed to help students to "write effectively for audiences both within and beyond the academy, develop their abilities as rhetors, and do their best work by composing and revising texts" in all kinds of venues, including first-year courses, disciplinary courses, or tutoring experiences. These venues have already clearly moved writing programs beyond FYC and, thus, WPA beyond its FYC profile. L'Eplattenier's suggestion that "the work of WPAs has existed as long as there have been institutions offering writing courses" would seem to support this broader interpretation as well, both in history and in current configurations (quoted in McLeod 2007, 45).

Just as "there is no agreed-upon concept of 'writing program'" (Schwalm 2002, 11), writing program *administration* in the United States as recently configured has been defined in various overlapping ways. Everyone who tries to pin it down encounters substantial diversity, leading Susan McLeod to say "context is all" (McLeod 2007, 8). Gaillet (2004) cites Olson and Moxley's outline of WPA activities—based on surveys of 250 English departments—to include "establishing liaisons with the community, promoting curricular reform, determining program policy in written documents, maintaining scholarship," and serving as leader and instigator of reform (174). This version of WPA work is set in opposition to the "feminist" administrative structure proposed by Dickson, which emphasizes collaboration, diversified authority, faculty-driven conversations about pedagogy, research, and administration, an atmosphere more in line with workshops and forums, strong support and mentoring, and effective rewards (175). In these "characteristic"-based descriptions of WPAs we also find the skills delineated by Cambridge and McClelland (1995), based on Gardner, including agreement-building, networking, diffusion of power, institution building, and flexibility. Perhaps an equally comprehensive, though differently detailed, way to understand the scope of WPA work is to consider the table of contents in Susan McLeod's (2007) *Writing Program Administration*. This volume places WPAs in roles as different as the unappreciated wife, the politician, and the manager, with domains of responsibility that may include curricula, ranges of courses, placement, accountability, staffing, multiple languages, and so on. These diverse descriptions suggest a different starting point for framing WPA in the world—not by associating it with a course (like a crop), but with a set of activities.

The WPA story at community colleges is an illuminating alternate account: community college faculty who are performing de facto WPA work without identifiable "programs." Community college voices underscore the fact that the four-year college account of a divide between English and writing, composition, or rhetoric is not *their* story (Andelora, cited in Calhoon-Dillahunt 2011), since composition is the mainstay of English departments (Holmstein, cited in Calhoon-Dillahunt 2011, 124). "Writing program," Raines (1990, 124) suggests, "does not evoke a precise image of what we [community colleges] do." The unique institutional histories of two- and four-year colleges provide contexts that are quite different; community colleges do not generally budget for WPAs, do not have coherent bodies of faculty employed at one institution, and do not provide for release time or professional development (123–24). And yet, clearly the activities of the WPA as defined above are in play. McLeod (2007) suggests that at least two aspects influence how WPAs develop: the size of what they must manage, and the point at which their work shifts from a task to a position. However, for colleagues in the 1,200 US community colleges, the first may be easy to discern, but the second is more likely to be unrecognized.

An alternative to FYC at a growing number of colleges and universities also provides a new account of WPA work and purpose.

This account moves us in the direction of European programmatic interests through its attention to WID, even in the first year, as well as its undergraduate research model that is often the base for writing instruction in other contexts. A recent study about writing programs in small colleges illustrates the move toward first-year seminars as the sole entry-level writing requirement, a move with interesting implications for writing and disciplinarity (Gladstein and Regaignon 2012). Interestingly, several of the individuals in L'Eplattenier and Mastrangelo's (2004) history of WPA work were at institutions—such as Vassar or Bryn Mawr—that fall into this category, suggesting stronger roots than are generally acknowledged in this kind of setting and pointing us back to university structures, governance, and missions as powerful contextual shapers of WPAs.

Finally, the disciplinary background of WPAs is also relevant to our analysis of the three sample programs. In the United States, early program directors characterize themselves as "converts" from literary studies, mainly because the field had no specialized doctoral programs when it began its trajectory toward professionalization and empirical research. Over time, increasing numbers of specialists in rhetoric and composition began taking the helm of writing programs, just as those programs began to diversify into FYC, upper-level composition (including courses designed for majors in various fields), technical and professional writing, and WAC. We will see that, in other contexts, writing program leaders or developers have their disciplinary formations neither in literary studies nor composition and rhetoric, but rather in applied linguistics, sociolinguistics, didactics, cognitive psychology, education sciences, or English as a Second Language.

CLIMATES FOR GROWTH: THREE PROGRAMMATIC INSTANTIATIONS

Three international examples offer alternative understandings of writing, programs, and administration, each grounded in deeply different cultural contexts. Writing has a unique place and role in the higher-education context of each country; research about writing offers insights into that writing, how it is understood, and how it—and students—institutionally develop. "Program" may seem uniquely North American, but, as we have suggested, the broader definition of program allows us to consider each of our three examples' programmatic contours. Finally, "administration" in each example must be understood in its institutional, theoretical, and scholarly dimension.[3]

Dar Al-Hekma College, Saudi Arabia

Our first example of transnational writing programs takes us to Jeddah, the second largest city in Saudi Arabia and the arrival point for hundreds of thousands of Muslims making the *Hajj* to Mecca, fifty miles to the east. We begin with this example because it demonstrates what happens when we try to import a curriculum with meaning in one national context into an entirely different context, as if "learning to write" is independent of complex cultural practices, ideologies, and activity systems. This example expands our idea of a writing program and its administration by asking us to consider how a US-oriented program is influenced by and adapts to its cultural and educational context.

Opening its doors in September 1999, Dar Al-Hekma College (hereafter DAH) was a project of the Al-Iim Foundation, which was established the same year in order to "provide state of the art higher educational facilities and services through academic institutions such as colleges and universities in the Kingdom of Saudi Arabia" ("About Dar Al-Hekma"). A "premier nonprofit institution," DAH was designed to serve the educational needs and aspirations of women and become a national and international model for excellence in teaching and learning—goals that attracted a visit by Hillary Clinton in 2010.

Boasting both Saudi accreditation from the Ministry of Higher Education and US accreditation from the Middle States Association and recently granted university status, DAH provides instruction almost entirely in English. Its roughly eighty faculty come from various countries in the region and around the world, and about half of them have advanced degrees from universities in the United States, Canada, and the United Kingdom, regardless of their country of origin. Oriented in the context of Saudi Arabia's Islamic principles, DAH's mission is to educate young women to take productive roles in Saudi society; its graduates "will be capable of bringing about positive change for the betterment of self, family, society and humanity with the aim of serving and pleasing the Creator" ("About Dar Al-Hekma"). With a current population of nearly 1,000 students pursuing BA and BS degrees, DAH was planned with an eventual enrollment goal of approximately 1,500. The college has a curriculum that offers a number of professionally-oriented degrees, and includes a well-regarded design school. Its facilities are first-rate: beautiful, well-maintained buildings; an excellent infrastructure; plentiful new technology; and spaces for students to work, study, socialize, and recreate. Full-time tuition, which varies slightly by college, averages about $8,000 per year, and several scholarships are available to reduce the costs for qualified students. The College Preparatory

Program (described below) costs about $250 per credit hour prior to full-time enrollment, and courses range from two to six hours per week.

One aspect of DAH's history makes it an especially interesting institution for studying international writing programs. To design its curriculum, the Al-lim Foundation commissioned the Texas International Education Consortium (TIEC) in Austin, Texas to create a "blueprint" for the college. Starting in 1998, TIEC was "responsible for the complete design of all programmatic, organizational, and operational aspects" of DAH, and used "the American model for academic programs and administrative organization" (TIEC 2012). TIEC appointed teams of US and Saudi experts to create the curriculum, design specific courses, choose textbooks, and consult more generally on the structure (and infrastructure) of the institution. As a relatively new institution saturated with Saudi values, but designed by a US educational consulting firm, DAH offers us an opportunity to consider a writing program in a state of international, cultural, and curricular development.[4]

Writing instruction takes place in the College Preparatory Program (CPP), a bridge program between high school and college that provides the necessary academic skills for students to be successful at DAH. The CPP is currently directed by Mariam Ghalayini, a Lebanese faculty member educated at the American University of Beirut. Although Ghalayini oversees the entire program, which includes math instruction, she has a strong background in writing studies, attends international conferences on writing center administration, and promotes writing across the DAH curriculum. In 2011, she established an international advisory board for the CPP, which includes several composition faculty at DAH, one from Lebanon, and one from the United States (Anson 2008). The board meets via teleconference twice a year, as well as during occasional onsite visits of the external members.

Students admitted to the CPP score between 380 and 499 on the TOEFL test. Those who fulfill the program's requirements are then qualified to be admitted to DAH (students with TOEFL scores of 500 and above can be admitted directly to the college). The program "fosters creative thinking, active learning and academic readiness for college level work" (Ghalayini, pers. comm., 2011). Three areas of instruction make up the CPP: English language, computer-assisted language learning, and mathematics. Writing instruction is part of an overall "standard curriculum in English as a second language" (Ghalayini, pers. comm., 2011) Several levels of courses are taught, and students' placement and progress are measured using standardized tests. At levels two and three, courses include six credits of writing, four credits of reading, five credits of listening and speaking, six credits of grammar, and two credits of study skills. At level four, courses include six credits of writing, three credits of reading, and three credits of study skills. An alternative level four curriculum, 1300C, requires twelve hours of English and two general-education courses at DAH. This option was added because students with more developed skills were eager to transition to full matriculation and felt that the CPP requirements took too long. Students enrolled in level two and three courses must also attend weekly sessions in a computer lab, where they "have the opportunity to be exposed to authentic language and reinforce their language skills acquired in their daily language" (Ghalayini, pers. comm., 2011). Using special software acquired by the CPP, the lab provides instruction primarily in grammar, listening, and speaking.

Because students are learning to write in a second language, writing instruction is part of an overall language preparation program in which the modalities (speaking, writing, reading, and listening) are separated. Taught in "bottom-up" fashion, writing instruction focuses on the fundamentals, especially grammar, and is "designed to address any academic deficiencies and to bridge gaps in basic English skills" between students' high school preparation and the demands of college ("Academic Programs" 2014). The program also has a thriving writing center and a strong interest in writing across the curriculum—initiatives led by Ghalayini, who is acquainted with the role of writing in US colleges and universities. Thus, unlike most US writing programs, DAH's program is administered as part of a broader program that includes four language modalities and math, and was initially created primarily as preparation for college admission and as a prerequisite for engaging in content courses that require proficiency in English. Among the many challenges this program faces is students' general lack of experience as writers in their native language (Arabic) and the lack of emphasis on written literacy in the home (in any language) because of the strongly oral nature of Saudi culture.

Like many universities in the Middle East, DAH has imported an American-style curriculum for second language learners but is uniquely adapting it to its own cultural and educational values. To some extent, this importation has led to various structural and ideological replications of well-documented concerns. For example, faculty responsible for teaching writing struggle with a higher course load (eighteen credit hours per week) than faculty in content courses, who teach fifteen hours. Furthermore, although DAH is a women's college, which would seem to provide gender parity among the faculty, all instructors of writing courses are women, whereas there are male faculty members in other areas of the curriculum.[5] Writing instructors' heavy teaching responsibilities undermine their engagement in the kinds of research we see at larger US institutions; instructors are evaluated primarily on the basis of their teaching. Unlike many US writing programs—which are associated with scholarship produced by rhetoric and composition specialists, the director, the associate director, and other administrators—the CPP is therefore primarily an educational service unit to DAH, a factor that suggests another adaptation of the US model to local conditions.

DAH shares with many US institutions assumptions about who should teach writing and how teaching requirements translate into instructors' working conditions. In the US, administrators and other faculty acknowledge the difficulty of teaching college-level discourse to novice writers, but, since most regions have a ready cohort of qualified instructors who are willing to be hired as contingent faculty, the disparities in working conditions in both countries look like they have the same source. While there is no dearth of English instructors available for hire at DAH (an American administrator at DAH was heard saying they are "a dime a dozen"), the differential load comes not just from market forces but from assumptions about course coverage and methodology, both of which were established with the help of the TIEC. The skills-based classes, which involve many workbook-like exercises on matters of language correctness, are assumed to be more mechanically (and therefore more easily) taught than the "sophisticated" and less "objective" curricula in interior design, nursing, and special education. Thus, the CPP's labor profile has its source in complex cultural and institutional values, which are shaped, in part, by the American curriculum it imported.

Curricular elements that were the artifacts of educational histories in the United States also needed to be changed or adapted to fit the Saudi context. For example, the TIEC had originally recommended that the CPP adopt Longman Publishers' NorthStar series of ESL books on reading, writing, speaking, and listening. The books are structured around topical readings that prefigure various writing tasks. However, it wasn't long before the CPP administrators and teachers realized that the series wouldn't work at DAH. Some chapters were about, or contained, material considered culturally insensitive or even offensive to Saudis. Other chapters were inappropriate for Saudi women, such as discussions of dating, cars (women are not allowed to drive in Saudi Arabia), or machines. Still others involved assignments and exercises that would be problematic for Saudi women to complete, such as talking to strangers in public places or making small talk with men and women while waiting for a bus or at the supermarket. Some of the pictures showed culturally objectionable scenes, such as people drinking cocktails, a couple publicly demonstrating signs of amorous affection, or a woman wearing sexy clothes on a date. The advanced book in the series had an entire section on homosexuality. Like the provision of a threshing machine to grape growers, the text was largely unusable. Eventually, Longman created a Middle-East version of the Northstar series after an American Muslim teacher "blew the whistle," but the CPP simply ordered a different set of books (Ghalayini, pers. comm., 2011).

The textbook problem illustrates another complex dimension of how the CPP is forming its identity as a program. On the one hand, DAH is clearly attracted to the instructional values, processes, and curricular features of US higher education. On the other, they appear to want these as ideologically neutral structures, into which they can fill culturally relevant (or entirely neutral) content. Some areas of the curriculum (e.g., science courses with universally acknowledged theories, research, or approaches) therefore may require less adaptation than others. If the goal of the English-language curriculum is mainly to build skills in written and oral communication, then any content will do, and the more culturally relevant the content, the better. If the courses were viewed (as many US foreign-language courses are) as a way both to learn the language and to understand the culture that speaks it—most naturally the US, given DAH's interests in an American-style curriculum—then it would not seem so problematic for students to read about women driving cars, operating machines, talking to strangers, going on dates, wearing elegant but somewhat revealing dresses, or having cocktails. Although all WPAs and instructors choose appropriate content for their courses, here we see an interesting conflict between the eager importation of instructional processes and the need to choose ideologically appropriate material through which those processes can be implemented. This aspect of writing program administration—choosing appropriate content for composition courses—makes DAH's program look similar to most programs in the United States. However, "appropriate content" in the United States is usually a question of matching the curriculum to desired outcomes, which sometimes *deliberately* challenge students to interrogate their cultural beliefs or expose the sources of sexism, racism, homophobia, and so forth (see George and Trimbur 2001). For DAH, on the other hand, choosing "appropriate content" is about matching the practice of second language skills to material that is culturally familiar, ideologically safe, and sometimes intellectually bland. The result—recently the subject of discussion by the advisory board—often leads students to complain of being disengaged from their writing and feeling a lack of purpose when coached to expand their ideas beyond the few sentences and paragraphs they manage, reluctantly, to produce.

Certain aspects of North American instruction now commonly employed in writing programs also proved to be difficult or impossible to implement effectively in the context of Saudi values and ways of working. Peer response and editing is one of the "most hated" practices for CPP students, mostly because of an ideology of privacy about one's thoughts and ideas (Ghalayini, pers. comm., 2011). Students don't like to share what they write, which they believe is personal, private, and acceptable only for turning in to the teacher. Although some students in the US may *also* have these feelings out of insecurity, they originate at DAH from a stronger cultural code of modesty and privacy. However, based on her involvement in the field of writing studies, Ghalayini believes that this practice should be reinforced until students become "more and more used to peer editing" and can "see the benefits they reap from such an exercise." What might be seen as a "global best practice" in writing classrooms must still be implemented in ways that respond to unique cultural contexts, power dynamics, and the perpetuation of values (see, for example, Kail and Trimbur 1987). These kinds of discoveries also remind us that the positive results of pedagogical research conducted in specific cultural and/or national contexts must be questioned and replicated in places where no one has previously imagined their relevance.

Though we see familiar elements in DAH's writing program—at least from a relatively bottom-up ESL perspective—they are still in need of unique adaptation to the cultural context of an institution influenced by Islamic values concerning gender roles, language use, the goals of education for women, teaching and learning practices, and a host of other factors. Some of these values are highly entrenched, while others continue to experience renegotiation and change (such as the kinds of jobs women can pursue and the relaxing of restrictions on Internet use and media viewership). Like the belief that all farming operates successfully on the basis of universal processes of work, distribution, reward, and utilization of the labor force, the DAH case exposes flaws in our assumptions about the universality of writing programs that might be imported or exported across cultures and national contexts. These assumptions are not just about the administrative or structural elements of writing programs, but also about appropriate, research-supported pedagogies and instructional practices that trickle down to the level of small classroom behaviors and activities.

***

Université Libre de Bruxelles (ULB), Belgium

Our second example foregrounds the work of Le Centre de Méthodologie Universitaire (CMU), which celebrated its thirtieth year in 2010. The center is our example that most resembles US-style writing program work, but it illustrates a unique evolution toward its current status. It has inspired initiatives in other European contexts, most notably in France, Switzerland, and Spain. The center's director, Marie-Christine Pollet, a linguist and didactician, points out that, while the current climate in Belgium (really, in Europe) is to strongly support college retention and first-year students' success, the center and ULB had long ago invested in that success across the disciplines (Pollet 2012). The CMU is interdisciplinary and "interfaculty"; its main purpose is to work with all first-year students on their writing, reading, and research abilities in French (the university's language). The team members at the center are linguists and faculty from different disciplines, working together to identify and address students' needs and create courses that support students' development. A subset of the faculty forms the core of a research group that studies reading and writing in secondary and postsecondary contexts, analyzes different modes of creation and transmission of knowledge in order to offer students ways to access that knowledge, and explores the secondary/postsecondary transition.

This program includes courses that develop students' understanding of texts, their note-taking, their ability to analyze and produce key outlines, their ability to comment on a text, their research and bibliographic approaches, and their fundamental revision approaches. Pollet reported in 2010 that the CMU's philosophy has evolved from an initial focus on prescriptive grammar and correctness to its current emphasis on acculturating students into university discourse communities, thus focusing on writing in the disciplines and the relationship between writing and knowledge construction. The center went through a middle stage that treated writing not as remedial and normative but as a technical skill, before coming to the current focus (Pollet 2010). This focus on "helping students to overcome the obstacles that the university and its new discursive environment provide" (Pollet 2012) is informed by parallel work, both in Brussels and in other francophone institutions, studying writing in general and university writing specifically. That work focuses particularly on the intersection between university writing and the construction of disciplinary knowledge, and it rejects the notion that we can teach decontextualized, generic, and transversal "techniques" rather than embedded, specific abilities (Pollet 2012). For US writing programs, this development is particularly interesting in the context of our own current, deep questioning of the first-year curriculum and its various approaches. While for decades we focused on *how* to teach first-year writing, now at least some WPAs are considering *whether* to teach first-year writing, particularly as a generic introductory course (Crowley 1998; Donahue 2008; Downs and Wardle 2007; Smit 2004).

The CMU maintains three principles in its work:

- every intervention it supports is grounded in a specific needs analysis, interdisciplinary collaboration, and team teaching;
- the basis for postsecondary teaching is a recognition that learning reading and writing is an ongoing process; and
- theory and practice must be brought to bear together. (Pollet 2012)

Several key areas of European writing research have directly shaped and, in some ways, been shaped by the work of the center: research focused on the writing process (Plane 2002); the effectiveness of peer review; many of the cognitive aspects of writing, such as the role of short- and long-term memory (Galbraith 1996; Kellogg 1996; Rijlaarsdam et al. 2004); and various aspects of genre and disciplinary knowledge construction (Boch and Grossmann 2002; Daunay 2011; Delcambre 2001; Jaubert, Rebière, and Bernié 2003; Reuter 1998). These areas have often been studied in elementary and secondary writing, and less frequently in higher education. More recently, new European fields have evolved, crystallizing attention that has developed for decades into a new strand, "university literacies," "in reference to specific writing and reading practices at the university . . . crossing two major and ancient fields of research, linguistics and the didactics of writing" (Delcambre and Donahue 2012). In the words of multiple researchers, this strand is built from long-term attention to postsecondary research strands:

- The "intertexuality/polyphony/citation" research strand has studied a range of specific university student writer practices related to source use (Boch and Grossmann 2001; Boch and Grossmann 2002; Guibert 2002, 2004; Laborde-Milaa 2002; Pollet and Piette 2002; Reuter 2001).
- The "entering new discourse communities" research strand had initially focused on writing in elementary and secondary school, but this set the groundwork for considering college writers, both undergraduate and graduate, in this context (Jaubert, Rebière, et Bernié 2003).
- The "particular types of higher education texts" research strand has extensively analyzed different types of writing and how each type functions in students' knowledge construction or construction of self (Boch 1999; Delcambre 2001; Derive and Fintz 1998; Guibert 2002;

Guigue 1998; Laborde-Milaa 2004; Lahanier-Reuter 2003; Masseron 2004; Penloup 2002; Pollet 2004; Reuter 1998; Souchon 2002).

The thirtieth anniversary conference at the CMU featured research embedded in the context described above. Several scholars described writing courses at other universities across postsecondary levels, as well as their disciplinary, theoretical, and research-based grounding. Others presented initiatives that link analyses of published scientific or academic writing to student writing, and that draw out pedagogical interventions and explorations of complex student positioning in advanced academic writing and of students' work with intertext and sources. This center has inspired other francophone institutions to develop courses, centers, research studies, graduate student positions, and other modes of higher education writing work. Examples include the fairly new program at l'Université de Grenoble III, which focuses on teaching students enrolled in linguistics how to research and write, as well as the courses now being offered to students at l'Université de Liège in mathematics, engineering, medicine, and the sciences.

Perhaps most interesting in this Belgian case are the questions the center is posing for its future—questions any US WPA might recognize:

- Should first-year courses be required for all or elective for some?
- How can we make first-year courses true projects of the institution overall and the departments specifically?
- How do we best balance theory and practice as we address our collaborators' needs?
- How can we continue to defend the high cost of these courses—in time and in faculty—to the administration?
- What year(s) are best for a focus on student writing? The first year is key, of course, but much research is now pointing to the equally important need for continued attention to writing throughout a student's higher education path.

L'Université de Poitiers, France

Our third example is from the Université de Poitiers, one of France's oldest universities, and asks us to recognize "writing," "program," and "administration" in shapes that less readily fill our expectations. Poitiers has a strong, well-developed cognitive research tradition that has focused on writing for decades. One of its research groups is the Centre de Recherches sur la Cognition et l'Apprentissage (CeRCA), or the Research Center for Cognition and Learning (RCCL; once called the Language, Memory, and Cognitive Development group), hereafter

CeRCA, for whom writing is both a cognitive and a social process. The lab focuses on research about lifelong development, memory, social regulation of cognition, language, and communication. Research laboratories structure higher education research as much as departments do in French higher education: faculty are hired into departments, but most of their research funding comes from the lab to which they belong—in the sciences, the social sciences, and the humanities. Teaching is in the department; service is to both the department and the research group.

CeRCA has played a key role in a multidisciplinary European networking project, "Learning to Write Effectively" (sponsored by COST, the European Cooperation in Science and Technology), whose purpose includes understanding how writing is developing in universities across Europe. The genres of writing across universities have been mapped and discussed, partly in an effort to better understand students' experiences, and partly to better share available research about university student writing. This effort, as with many current efforts in Europe, is heavily influenced by the top-down impositions of the Bologna Agreement and its effort to homogenize the state-funded educational system across Europe.

One of the more recent projects at the CeRCA laboratory, the "Eye and Pen" research project, provides a fine-grained description of the visual information fixated during a writer's pauses as well as during the act of writing. This device can be used to investigate the role of the text produced so far by a writer and of the documentary sources displayed in the task environment. The study of the engagement of reading during writing provides important information about the dynamics of writing processes based on this visual information (Alamargot et al. 2011; see Anson and Schwegler 2012 for a discussion of the potential of eye-tracking research).

By all US accounts, we would be likely to look suspiciously at this kind of work, given our uneasy relationship with cognitive and experimental research, our debates about cognitive and empirical research, our "social turn," and our recent acknowledgments as a field that we don't have the research capacity we think we should (Anson 2008; Durst 2006; Haswell 2005; Voss 1983). While cognitive research laid the groundwork for some serious advances in composition and rhetoric in the 1970s, especially in developmental studies, the past few decades of US higher education research in composition have rarely evoked working memory, developmental theory, or brain science insights. However, Denis Alamargot, the lead researcher in France and a cognitive and developmental psychologist, has positioned his work as a way to support undergraduate writers that he can then also study.

In the context of France's "plan licence," Poitiers is developing a writing center and has piloted a first-year writing course for French-speaking students. The "plan licence" is a government-funded initiative, instituted in 2007, to begin improving students' rate of success in undergraduate studies. It specifically targets undergraduate students, the least prestigious cycle of higher education in France with a notoriously high failure rate (Donahue 2008). We see that local context, institutional pressures, and political landscapes directly shape a broader transformation of university processes, as we saw in the United States with the introduction of open access universities or the rapid shift in the diversity of our student populations.

At Poitiers, Alamargot and his team developed a pilot course, and then surveyed the first-year student population in order to develop a broader outreach. We note that it is fairly rare today for a US writing program to be founded based on a specific needs assessment. The survey (see appendix 1.1) offered these key insights:

- Two-thirds of students spend from four to more than ten hours per week on writing projects.
- One of the most frequent types of writing, reported by 73% of respondents, is note-taking (French faculty routinely consider note-taking an important form of writing).
- Far less frequent forms include writing reports or exams; "dossiers" (small portfolios) are fairly frequent.
- About 90% report beginning a writing assignment between two and four days before it is due; the rest, one day before it is due.
- Two-thirds of respondents report that content, organizing material, coherence, and clarity are issues equal to or of greater importance than issues of grammar or correctness.
- Similarly, far more students expressed interest in obtaining support for their work with organization, writing drafts, and, to a slightly lower degree, managing writing as a process.

One particularly notable reply was to the question "If we opened a writing center, where should it be located?" By far the most preferred location was in the students' department, indicating a strong link to disciplinary work. Among other forms of support, the most favorable suggestion was to create a website, followed by a site offering real-time help from a teacher.

For 2012–2013, Poitiers planned to launch a course designed to teach twenty to forty members of the first-year class, as well as a writing center—the first in France.[6] However, Alamargot changed institutions, from the Université de Poitiers to the Université de Paris–Est Créteil

(UPEC), a newer university to the east of Paris, serving a considerably less privileged university population than Poitiers. At Poitiers, this meant that the plans were put indefinitely on hold. Recently, however, as the French higher education teacher training institutions have undergone a powerful reform that reintegrated them into the university system, Poitier's new teacher-training program has begun to reexplore the plans and reimagine a writing center. Meanwhile, at UPEC, Alamargot has initiated the process for establishing a writing center. He has obtained significant funding from organizations supporting innovation in higher education to analyze the institutional, cognitive, and pedagogical conditions and implement a center called CeRFRAP (Centre de Ressources et de Formation à l'Ecriture Académique et Professionnelle, or Resource Center for the Development of Academic and Professional Writing [RCDAPW]). Its purpose will be to improve undergraduate and MA students' ability to produce the different kinds of writing in their curriculum, including summaries, syntheses, note-taking, reading notes, argumentative texts, paraphrases, and citation. The programs offered by the RCDAPW will focus on helping students at all levels to develop their writing processes and approaches, to acquire strong strategies, and to renew their knowledge of grammar and mechanics.

These processes indicate intriguing parallels and differences to US WPA roles. Just as in the United States, where WAC programs are often noted to be dependent on one visionary or charismatic instigator, in France, initiatives are often in some way local. At Poitiers the initiative was driven by one research unit's desire to apply its research to the classroom and to create a kind of laboratory for further study of student writing. The role of the research laboratory and its director in shepherding this new attention to writing, both administratively and pedagogically, into student and faculty culture thus offers a significant variation, fully research-grounded, to the role of the typical US WPA. However, this local initiative was also nationally framed and informed by current reforms (such as the "plan licence" and the new teacher-training institutions) and historical trends. There is both a history of intervention courses focused on writing for first-year students—offered as early as the 1960s—and a range of local initiatives such as the one at the Université de Paris III described by Donahue (2008), in which faculty from different disciplines work with students in their first college term on reading, research, and writing abilities. The end result of the initial research at Poitiers is the possibility for writing centers and first-year writing courses—writing programs—at two different institutions, an old and tradition-infused university and a new university serving underprivileged populations. Local conditions and national frames have influenced both possibilities.

MANY PROGRAMS, MANY FARMS

These examples suggest that the more we try to map our frames, our language, and our assumptions onto writing work outside the United States, the more we miss in terms of that work and its potential to teach us. Starting with assumptions of national difference can lead to missing what is deeply shared; starting with assumptions of what a writing program *is* might lead to missing shapes and forms we simply haven't yet imagined. Instead, searching innovative practices, strong research, and writing courses or writing program administration in any form might open up new understanding. If, in fact, "context is all," then studying and understanding context, as we have tried to do with these three examples, is essential to any work we might do in trying to internationalize or understand the WPA scene.

We argue that the following common features are woven through the three examples presented here:

- They are programs because of their courses, the support they offer students or faculty, their missions, the faculty they bring together, the curricular design that fits particular models and practices, and the placement they oversee.
- They are also programs because of their research profiles—both the research of faculty and the research sponsored by or sponsoring the program's work. But, as we see at DAH, they may be programs that rely on the research of others to inform their practices.
- They have administrators—dedicated positions carrying out the work of the program; these positions have a particular profile, and include responsibility for being up to date on current scholarship and offering faculty development.
- They carry uncertain authority in the broader institution. Their agendas, and the perennial challenges and fragilities they face around issues such as budgets, assessment, and institutional respect are all too familiar, once we notice them.
- They share the battles for legitimacy, identity, and job description that we know all too well.

If we consider McLeod's (2007) table of contents summarized earlier in this chapter, we can see international WPAs as carrying out *activities* we share, rather than *courses* we share or stable *roles* that we play—being responsible for curricula, ranges of courses, positioning of students, accountability, staffing, working with multiple languages, and so on.

On the other hand, our examples point to essential and intriguing differences. If, as Rose and Weiser (1999), among others, have suggested, WPA work is scholarship, then the existing models we see—at least in these European case studies—would suggest not only shared work, but also the reverse: in these contexts, scholarship leads to writing programs as much as writing programs lead to scholarship.

The three cases here do not show this, but many initiatives outside of the United States begin with writing in disciplinary contexts and reject generic writing instruction. In France, for example, a ubiquitous first-year writing course called *techniques d'expression* was tried and rejected within a few years in the 1960s (Hassan, Daunay, and Fialip 2006). Current initiatives and longstanding attention to writing instruction in the upper level of undergraduate studies have been grounded in the disciplines. Another productive area of questioning might be in the history and current status of different disciplines that attend to writing instruction, research, and programmatic form. The role of "rhetoric" in the US evolution, for example, stands in contrast to "rhetoric" in European education, which heavily influenced attention to writing in both secondary and postsecondary studies until the early twentieth century. Rhetoricians might be part of one discipline, while others in the cases we have presented are applied linguists, sociolinguists, and "didacticians" (a uniquely European field that involves the theory and teaching of various subjects, including writing). This is a particularly interesting connection, given the longstanding alienation in both practice and research between US programs of rhetoric/composition and departments of education. In the Saudi case, there is much respect for the field of writing studies, and both teachers and administrators are eager to know the current thinking on—and implementation of— "best practices" for teaching writing within general education programs and across the curriculum. The burden placed on those interested in importing curricula from anglophone countries is to effectively translate approaches that work in those countries and apply them to an entirely different cultural context, where deeply-held codes of behavior and psychologically powerful assumptions about discourse affect how readily students will adapt to those approaches.

WPAs could internationalize by starting anew in our conversations. Some recent recommendations for the US field as a whole are quite relevant for WPA work specifically: reorienting our discourse (Donahue 2008); changing our assumptions and trying out a translingual attitude (Horner, Lu, Royster, and Trimbur 2011); and learning about other contexts by studying languages, reading as many abstracts in English of articles in other languages as we can, trying different terms in our literature searches, and contacting authors cited from contexts outside the United States. In addition, working with colleagues in modern languages (Horner, Necamp, and Donahue 2011), or with colleagues who work overseas, opens horizons that can be further broadened by initiating "equal exchange" projects with our international colleagues and building on each other's strengths. The European, African, Asian, South American, Canadian, and other journals that cover developments in the areas of college writing instruction, research, and curriculum are worth reading, and might well be the journals of the other disciplines mentioned above: didactics, linguistics, English for Academic Purposes/ English for Specific Purposes (EAP/ESP), or education.

Finally, our examples suggest that WPA work is most often grounded in systemic institutional plans, not just the charisma of a single dedicated individual—precisely what McLeod (2007) suggests is vital for success. University structures and governance, as noted in our earlier section on WPA work, shape the specifics of WPA work, whether nationally or internationally. The program at DAH clearly has a leader at the helm, but she must mediate between a highly structured curriculum set up with the help of a US-based consulting firm, her own understanding of composition from an international perspective, and the culturally-specific practices and beliefs that students, faculty, and other administrators bring to college—a task that involves the participation and response of many stakeholders. At the Université de Lille III, where much recent work on university literacies has been focused, a student support center has been developed. It is not run by one person, but by a team, including a member of the research lab in education. In other contexts, the roles of departments and research labs might differ from the ones we have described, adding further complexity to the question of how one defines "program" and "administration."

Thus, when we take apart the notion of "program" and its contested aspects, we see both shared work and different insights. This leads us to ask why identifying a "program" in the US sense actually matters. Earlier efforts to identify WAC work across Europe met with resistance, befuddlement, or irritation, because the starting point for surveys and queries was always in a US frame and included US terminology. The results of such efforts could have been changed by something as simple as querying faculty about research methods courses rather than writing courses at their institutions—where, it turns out, much in-depth writing instruction takes place, including attention to revision, peer review, drafting, and conferencing. Calling a French university individual carrying out writing work and instruction a "French WPA," for example, fails to capture the right understanding or structure, yet there is deep exchange to be had.

The future of US understandings of international WPA work lies, we argue, in asking questions such as: How are local values related to the availability and use of resources? Where do others, in other structures, develop these resources? And how might we globally reconsider our modes, methods, and models for studying transnational writing work? Perhaps more importantly, when discussions of such questions take place among and between institutions in different parts of the world, the shared understandings of commonalities and differences in the structures, curriculums, teaching practices, roles of research, and ideologies of education enrich, complicate, and extend our work in fruitful ways that, in turn, encourage the growth of new ideas and new ways to harvest them.

Notes

1. The order of authorship is purely alphabetical.
2. A Google Ngram search for "writing program" shows a dramatic increase in the appearance of the term in published books and documents beginning in the late 1970s; "writing program administration" rises almost vertically starting in 1980.
3. The first of the examples is at an institution that delivers instruction in English to students for whom English is not their primary language; the other two are writing programs in Europe that work with students in the dominant language of those countries. This distinction is often elided in literature on teaching writing beyond US borders, and yet it is at the heart of some fundamentally different missions and institutional structures.
4. Because of significant personnel turnover at the TIEC since DAH was established, it was not possible to obtain a full history of its efforts to create the DAH curriculum. The person in charge of the writing curriculum was an expert in ESL rather than general composition studies, but was not willing to share information about her involvement.
5. Of course, it is difficult to say with any certainty whether the gender disequilibrium that characterizes many American university writing programs, as well as the asymmetrical relations of power therein, are the result of systemic forces or the fact that DAH is a women's college.
6. France does have student learning and career support centers, such as the one at l'Université de Lille 3, and there is a writing center at the American University in Paris. However, we do not consider the AUP writing center—an excellent, forward-thinking center with years of experience—a French writing center, any more than AUP would be considered a French university.

References

"Academic Programs." 2014. Dar Al-Hekma University. https://sisweb.daralhekma.edu
    .sa:8251/portal/page?_pageid=333,138592&_dad=portal&_schema=PORTAL.
    Accessed September 10, 2014.

Adams, Katherine H., and John L. Adams. 1987. "The Paradox Within: Origins of the Current-Traditional Paradigm." *Rhetoric Society Quarterly* 17 (4): 421–31. http://dx.d oi.org/10.1080/02773948709390797.

Alamargot, Denis, Gilles Caporossi, David Chesnet, and Christine Ros. 2011. "What Makes a Skilled Writer? Working Memory and Audience Awareness During Text Composition." *Learning and Individual Differences* 21 (5): 505–16. http://dx.d oi.org/10.1016/j.lindif.2011.06.001.

Anson, Chris M. 2008. "The Intelligent Design of Writing Programs: Reliance on Belief or a Future of Evidence." *WPA: Writing Program Administration* 32 (1): 11–36.

Anson, Chris M., and Robert A. Schwegler. 2012. "Tracking the Mind's Eye: A New Technology for Researching 21st Century Writing and Reading Processes." *College Composition and Communication* 64 (1): 151–71.

Boch, Françoise. 1999. *Pratiques D'écriture et de Réécriture à L'université. La Prise de Notes, entre Texte Source et Texte Cible.* Villeneuve d'Ascq: Presses universitaires du Septentrion.

Boch, Françoise, and Francis Grossmann. 2001. "De L'usage des Citations dans le Discours Théorique. Des Constats aux Propositions Didactiques." *Lidil* 24:91–112.

Boch, Françoise, and Francis Grossmann. 2002. "Se Référer au Discours D'autrui: Comparaison entre Experts et Neophytes." *Enjeux* 54:41–51.

Calhoon-Dillahunt, Carolyn. 2011. "Writing Programs without Administrators: Frameworks for Successful Writing Programs in the Two-Year College." *WPA* 35 (1): 118–35.

Cambridge, Barbara, and Ben McClelland. 1995. "From Icon to Partner: Repositioning the Writing Program Administrator." In *Resituating Writing: Constructing and Administering Writing Programs,* ed. Joseph Janangelo and Kristine Hansen, 151–59. Portsmouth, NH: Boynton/Cook Heinemann.

"CeRCA." 2014. Université de Poitiers. http://cerca.labo.univ-poitiers.fr. Accessed October 1.

Crowley, Sharon. 1998. *Composition in the University: Historical and Polemical Essays.* Pittsburgh: University of Pittsburgh Press.

"About Dar Al-Hekma." Dar Al-Hekma College. Accessed 15 September 2013. https://sisweb.daralhekma.edu.sa:8251/portal/page?_pageid=253,138545&_dad=portal&_schema=PORTAL

Daunay, Bertrand. 2011. *Les Écrits Professionnels des Enseignants. Approche Didactique.* Rennes: Presses Universitaires de Rennes.

Delcambre, Isabelle. 2001. "Formes Diverses D'articulation entre Discours D'autrui et Discours Propre. Analyses de Commentaires de Textes Théoriques." *Lidil* 24:135–66.

Delcambre, Isabelle, and Christiane Donahue. 2012. "Academic Writing Activity: Student Writing in Transition." In *University Writing: Selves and Texts in Academic Societies,* ed. Montserrat Castello and Christiane Donahue. Amsterdam: Emerald Publishing.

Derive, M.-J., and C. Fintz. 1998. "Quelles Pratiques Implicites de L'écrit à L'université? Quelques Réflexions à Partir de L'analyse d'un Corpus de Sujets de Partiels et D'examens en DEUG de Psychologie." *Lidil* 17:43–56.

Donahue, Christiane. 2008. *Ecrire à L'Université: Analyse Comparée, France-Etats Unis.* Villeneuve d'Ascq: Presses Universitaires du Septentrion.

Downs, Douglas, and Elizabeth Wardle. 2007. "Teaching about Writing, Righting Misconceptions: (Re)Envisioning "First-Year Composition" as "Introduction to Writing Studies." *CCC* 58 (4): 552–85.

Durst, Russell. 2006. "Writing at the Postsecondary Level." In *Research on Composition,* ed. Peter Smagorinsky, 78–107. New York: Teachers College Press.

Galbraith, David. 1996. "Self-Monitoring, Discovery through Writing, and Individual Differences in Drafting Strategy." In *Theories, Models and Methodology in Writing Research,* ed. Gert Rijlaarsdam, Hugh van den Bergh, and Michel Couzijn, 121–41. Amsterdam: University Press.

Gaillet, Lynée Lewis. 2004. "A Genesis of Writing Program Administration: George Jardine at the University of Glasgow." In *Historical Studies of Writing Program Administration: Individuals, Communities, and the Formation of a Discipline*, ed. Barbara L'Eplattenier and Lisa Mastrangelo, 169–90. West Lafayette: Parlor Press.

George, Diana, and John Trimbur. 2001. "Cultural Studies and Composition." In *A Guide to Composition Studies*, ed. Gary Tate, Amy Rupiper, and Kurt Schick, 71–91. New York: Oxford UP.

Gladstein, Jill, and Dara Regaignon. 2012. *Writing Program Administration at Small Liberal Arts Colleges*. Anderson, SC: Parlor Press.

Gold, David. 2008. *Rhetoric at the Margins: Revising the History of Writing Instruction in American Colleges, 1873–1947*. Carbondale, IL: Southern Illinois University Press.

Guibert, Rozenn. 2002. "L'entraînement à la Synthèse comme Apprentissage du Dialogisme." *Spirale* 29:145–64.

Guibert, Rozenn. 2004. "Formation aux Dialogismes." *Pratiques* 121–122:28–44.

Guigue, Michel. 1998. "Lectures et Données de Terrain: Deux Modes D'accès au Savoir Difficiles à Tisser dans la Rédaction D'écrits Longs." *Lidil* 17:81–98.

Hassan, Rouba, Bertrand Daunay, and Martine Fialip. 2006. A French Perspective on Higher Education Writing Research. WDHE conference, Milton Keynes, UK, 11–12 May.

Haswell, Rich. 2005. "NCTE/CCCC's Recent War on Scholarship." *Written Communication* 22 (2): 198–223. http://dx.doi.org/10.1177/0741088305275367.

Horner, Bruce, Min-Zhan Lu, Jacqueline Royster, and John Trimbur. 2011. "Language Difference in Writing." *College English* 73 (3): 303–21.

Horner, Bruce, Samantha Necamp, and Christiane Donahue. 2011. "Toward a Multilingual Composition Scholarship: From English Only to a Translingual Norm." *College English* 63 (2): 269–300.

Janangelo, Joseph. 2011. "Issue Brief: Writing Programs." *National Council of Teachers of English*. NCTE, 1998–2011. http://www.ncte.org/college/briefs/wp. Accessed 17 September 2013.

Jaubert, Martine, Maryse Rebière, & Jean-Paul Bernié. 2003. "L'hypothèse "Communauté Discursive": D'où Vient-elle, où Va-t-elle?" *Les cahiers THEODILE* 4, 51–80.

Kail, Harvey, and John Trimbur. 1987. "The Politics of Peer Tutoring." *WPA: Writing Program Administration* 1 (1–2): 5–12.

Kellogg, Ronald. 1996. A Model of Working Memory in Writing. In *The Science of Writing: Theories, Methods, Individual Differences, and Application*, ed. C. Michael Levy and Sarah Ransdell, 57–71. Hillsdale, NJ, England: Lawrence Erlbaum Associates.

Laborde-Milaa, Isabelle. 2002. "Polyphonie Enonciative: Représentation D'étudiants en Position D'évaluateurs de Leurs Pairs." *Spirale* 29:181–200.

Laborde-Milaa, Isabelle. 2004. "'Auto-Reformulation et Investissement du Scripteur: Abstracts et Quatrièmes de Couverture de Mémoires de Maîtrise.' Pratiques: Théorie, Pratique." *Pédagogie* 121–22:183–98.

Lahanier-Reuter, Dominique. 2003. "Lecture-Ecriture et Gestions de Tableaux." *Les Cahiers THEODILE* 3:83–97.

L'Eplattenier, Barbara, and Lisa Mastrangelo, eds. 2004. *Historical Studies of Writing Program Administration: Individuals, Communities, and the Formation of a Discipline*. West Lafayette, Indiana: Parlor Press.

Masseron, Caroline. 2004. "Note sur L'apprentissage du Compte-rendu." *Pratiques* 121–22:217–44.

McDonald, Louise Gaylord. 1999. *Powerful English for the Active and Productive Man: How College English Became Difficult Enough to Build Character at Harvard College, 1890–1900*. PhD. Diss., University of Minnesota.

McLeod, Susan. 2007. *Writing Program Administration*. West Lafayette, IN: Parlor Press.

Paine, Charles. 1999. *The Resistant Writer: Rhetoric as Immunity, 1850 to the Present.* Albany: SUNY Press.

Penloup, Marie-Claude. 2002. "Construire le Concept D'écriture de Recherche pour le Mémoire de Maîtrise." *Enjeux* 54:151–65.

Plane, Sylvie. 2002. "Apprendre L'écriture: Apports de la Didactique, Questions pour la Didactique." *Pratiques* 115–116:7–13.

Pollet, Marie-Christine. 2004. "Appropriation et Ecriture de Savoirs chez des Etudiants de Première Année. Une Voie Difficile entre Stockage et Elaboration." *Pratiques* 121–122:81–92.

Pollet, Marie-Christine. 2010. "Journées d'Etude du Centre de Méthodologie Universitaire." Bruxelles: Université Libre de Bruxelles, 7 Décembre.

Pollet, Marie-Christine. 2012. "From Remediation to the Development of Writing Competencies in Disciplinary Contexts: Thirty Years of Practice and Questions." In *Writing Programs Worldwide: Profiles of Academic Writing in Many Places (Perspectives on Writing)*, ed. Chris Thaiss, Gerd Brauer, Paula Carlino, Lisa Ganobscik-Williams, and Aparna Sinha, 93–103. Anderson, SC: Parlor Press.

Pollet, Marie-Christine, and Violaine Piette. 2002. "Citations, Reformulation du Discours D'autrui: Une Clé pour Enseigner L'écriture de Recherché?" *Spirale* 29:165–80.

Raines, Helon. 1990. "Is There a Writing Program in This College? Two Hundred and Thirty-Six Two-Year Schools Respond." *College Composition and Communication* 41 (2): 151–65. http://dx.doi.org/10.2307/358154.

Rose, Shirley, and Irwin Weiser. 1999. *The Writing Program Administrator as Researcher.* Boston: Heinemann.

TIEC, and the Texas International Educational Consortium. Accessed December 12, 2012. http://www.tiec.org/exp_mideast_dahc-desc.html.

Reuter, Yves. 1998. "De Quelques Obstacles à L'écriture de Recherche." *Lidil* 17:11–23.

Reuter, Yves. 2001. "Je Suis Comme un Autrui Qui Doute. Le Discours des Autres dans L'écrit de Recherche en Formation." *Lidil* 24:1–27.

Reynolds, Nedra, Patricia Bizzell, and Bruce Herzberg. 2004. "A Brief History of Rhetoric and Composition." In *The Bedford Bibliography for Teachers of Writing*, 6th ed., ed. Nedra Reynolds, Patricia Bizzell, and Bruce Herzberg, 1–18. New York: Bedford/St. Martins.

Rijlaarsdam, Gert, Hugh van den Bergh, and Michel Couzijn, eds. 2004. *Effective Learning and Teaching of Writing. A Handbook of Writing in Education.* 2nd ed. vol. 14. Studies in Writing. Boston: Kluwer Academic Publishers.

Schwalm, David. 2002. "The Writing Program (Administrator) in Context: Where Am I, and Can I Still Behave Like a Faculty Member?" In *The Allyn & Bacon Sourcebook for Writing Program Administrators*, ed. Irene Ward and William J. Carpenter, 9–22. New York: Allyn & Bacon.

Souchon, Marc. 2002. "L'analyse de Productions Ecrites D'étudiants de Première Année à L'université." *Enjeux* 54:101–14.

Smit, David. 2004. *The End of Composition Studies.* Carbondale: Southern Illinois University Press.

Thaiss, Chris, Gerd Bräuer, Paula Carlino, Lisa Ganobscik-Williams, and Aparna Sinha, eds. 2012. *Writing Programs Worldwide: Profiles of Academic Writing in Many Places.* Anderson, SC: Parlor Press.

Voss, Ralph. 1983. "Composition and the Empirical Imperative." *JAC* 4 (1): 5–12.

Appendix 1.1. The Writing Program Activities in the Matariki Network of Universities

Dartmouth College	• Institute for Writing and Rhetoric • Student Center for Research, Writing, and Information Technology • Professional development offerings
Durham University	• "Writing across Boundaries" and "Writing on Writing" programs • English Language Centre • College tutors
Queen's University	• Writing center • Handbook, tutoring, and workshops • Undergraduate and graduate networks • Courses: effective writing 1–2, modular, and analytical
University of Otago	• Minor in writing • Writing courses: academic, professional, and creative • Writing clinic and ESL support
University of Tübingen	• Writing center (one of the first in Germany)
University of Western Australia	• Online tutorials in writing • Student services • Consultations available with StudySmarter team (similar to a writing center, but not specific to writing) • Facilitated writing groups, writing retreats, and writing communications
Uppsala University	• Evolving interest in writing, undergraduate–graduate (PhD)

2
TECH TRAVELS
Connecting Writing Classes across Continents

Alyssa O'Brien and Christine Alfano

At Stanford University in California, three students sit around a large plasma screen, composing a storyboard on a digital whiteboard with students at the University of Örebro in Sweden. In Egypt, a student works late at night on a blog post, responding to a question from an American student about standards of living in Cairo and the recent revolution. In Khabarovsk, Russia, students prepare their speaking notes for a joint presentation on the oratory skills of world leaders, to be projected through Polycom video-conference technology. In each case, all of these students are participating in the Cross-Cultural Rhetoric (CCR) project, a transnational collaborative endeavor aimed at fostering intercultural competencies in writing and speaking for students who need to know how to communicate and collaborate with others across the globe. Administered out of Stanford University's Program in Writing and Rhetoric, and with the collaboration of technological specialists from Stanford's Wallenberg Hall, CCR works across multiple platforms and time zones to connect students in writing classes across five continents. Since its first pilot "connections, " our umbrella term for bringing students together through various technological means, CCR has sought to foster student development in the areas of rhetorical knowledge, critical thinking and writing, processes, understanding of conventions, and composing in electronic environments—the very categories espoused by the Council of Writing Program Administrators in their outcomes statement (Council 2000).

In this chapter, we provide an account of how we have investigated and tested best technology practices for global connections. We argue that discrepancies among universities with regard to infrastructure, access, and equipment can be resolved through creative accommodation and by conceptualizing the relationship between technology and pedagogy as a symbiotic one. We contend that accommodations need to be made according to a sliding scale of technological sophistication

DOI: 10.7330/9780874219623.c002

and access on behalf of partner institutions, with the aim of using the optimal technology available to meet a learning outcome. At the same time, we argue that additional accommodations must be recognized and negotiated, such as scheduling cross-cultural exchanges across diverse time zones; meeting in the middle in terms of pedagogical goals and learning objectives for each institution; and establishing parity of workload, accountability, and contribution on the part of both students and teachers.

Three research questions guide this chapter's argument about the need for technological and pedagogical accommodation. First, how can we adapt our practices to implement a sliding scale of technology in order to connect students across universities with different levels of Internet access, technological equipment, institutional support, and instructor involvement? Second, how can we modify our technological apparatus in order to meet the goals of our pedagogy, so our pedagogy drives our media setup and not the other way around? Relatedly, when is it necessary to make pedagogical accommodations in order to work with available technologies, and what can be learned from these adjustments? Third, how can this relatively new and innovative use of class time be more than an exciting mediated experience, and simultaneously help writing courses meet the WPA outcomes for FYC? These outcomes, delineated by the Council of Writing Program Administrators in April 2000 and amended July 2008, identify the knowledge, skills, and attitudes that FYC courses should instill in students (Council 2000).[1]

In the following pages, we provide a brief overview of the origins and administration of CCR. We then turn to lessons from our work, establishing three different kinds of technologically-mediated connections across diverse countries. In the process, we seek to address this chapter's three core questions of technological adaptation, pedagogical accommodation, and outcome-based learning. We conclude with an assessment of this work from a WPA perspective, and we offer further questions about the implementation, management, and future development of such globally-interactive and digitally-facilitated writing pedagogy.

ORIGINS AND ADMINISTRATION OF CCR

The CCR project began in 2005 as a research collaboration between two universities: Stanford University in California and the University of Örebro in Sweden.[2] The project was originally funded by the Wallenberg Global Learning Network (WGLN), an organization which aimed to connect Swedish universities with Stanford in order to improve Swedish educational practices and outcomes. The WGLN funded our project focused on "Developing Intercultural Competencies through Collaborative Rhetoric" for two years. During its pilot and grant-funded years, CCR was led by principal investigators (PIs) Andrea A. Lunsford of Stanford University and Brigitte Mral of Örebro University. This collaboration brought together faculty and staff from both institutions (Christine Alfano, Dan Gilbert, Alyssa O'Brien, and Robert E. Smith from Stanford, and Anders Eriksson and Eva Magnusson from Örebro). The goal was to design new activities, technologies, and best practices for globally connecting students in order to facilitate their development as writers, speakers, and culturally-sensitive collaborators using digital media.

Within the first three years, the research team developed a curriculum for fostering intercultural competencies, built and tested video-conference collaboration stations, established a CCR blog, and generated a wide range of best practices for global learning through technology. In 2008, although Stanford continued to collaborate with Örebro, we expanded our range of connections to include additional universities, and the administration of CCR methodologies became more collaborative on a global scale, with input and knowledge-sharing across five countries: Australia, Egypt, Russia, Singapore, and Sweden. At that point in time, we began to refer to our Stanford-based efforts under the title of "The Stanford Cross-Cultural Rhetoric Project," and we established an independent website (http://ccr.stanford.edu) as our public presence. Today, Stanford's CCR project resides under the umbrella of Stanford Introductory Studies in the Program of Writing and Rhetoric (PWR), with funding from the vice provost for undergraduate education; a small budget covers technology, student workers, and materials costs.

From its inception, the Stanford CCR project aimed to extend the benefits of transnational writing exchanges to many members of the university community. Since its launch in 2005, nearly twenty of PWR's full-time lecturers have participated in the project as instructors for classes that connect with other classes across the world. This participation gives individual lecturers opportunities to develop international networks and collaborate with faculty at other institutions on lesson plans, course material generation, and assessment of student work. Participating classes have included writing courses with a range of themes, from those focused on intercultural issues (such as Visual Rhetoric across the Globe; The Rhetoric of Tourism; and Global

Controversies and the Rhetoric of Leadership) to those with a broader focus (such as What's So Funny? Humor, Race, Class and Gender; The Rhetoric of Food Science and Politics; Environmental Rhetoric; New Technologies of Identity; and The Rhetoric of Gaming). Over the years, as many as ten PWR sections per quarter have incorporated a CCR component, whether that be a video-conference connection, a blog exchange, a guest speaker video-conferenced into class, or an international peer review exchange via Skype.

In administering these transnational interactions among students, we have sought to align CCR's goals with the goals of the writing program. CCR's emphasis on strategic and successful intercultural communication complements Stanford's emphasis on first- and second-year writing courses producing effective arguments—in multiple genres and media—with a keen understanding of differences in audience and rhetorical situation. We designed a lesson plan template that scaffolded the development of skills in intercultural communication through activities centered on textual analysis and production. Our pedagogy evolved to focus on small group activities, and, accordingly, in addressing our technology infrastructure, we continually sought to use video-conference software that would support this type of small group work. While that technology has changed over the years, as we detail below, our priority continues to be on fostering student development as writers, speakers, and culturally-sensitive collaborators using digital media. With that goal driving our CCR work, we learned valuable lessons in technological and pedagogical accommodation across different platforms, institutions, and educational contexts.

MAKING ACCOMMODATIONS: ATTENDING TO SPACE

From an administrative perspective, one of our first concerns in launching our project was identifying viable spaces—both virtual and physical—to use for this new kind of transnational writing program work. This section details our experiences and recommendations regarding space based upon our collaboration with universities in Australia, Egypt, Russia, Singapore, and Sweden. We argue that space options can be negotiated across universities if participants keep in mind the end goal of connecting students for active learning.

In terms of virtual spaces, we researched the setup of different learning formations. In 2005, when we first piloted our cross-cultural connections, the then-emerging video-conference model employed in university settings was the broadcast video lecture: students assembled together in a physical auditorium space to listen to a speaker through a video stream. This broadcast model proved unsuitable for a project devoted to helping students develop their skills in cross-cultural *communication*; our premise of dialogic exchange necessarily led us to move toward a format where students could be more actively engaged in discussion. Accordingly, in the early months of the project, we piloted connections between Stanford and Örebro students that brought classes together for a shared group discussion in small, globally-distributed teams of three students on each end. Early feedback and assessment using exit surveys confirmed that optimal student learning took place in small groups, resonating with much of the scholarship in the rhetoric and composition community about the benefits small group learning environments (Bruffee 1973; Elbow 1973).

To meet this need for small group interactions, we had to set up in a *physical space* that would best leverage our technical, institutional, and curricular resources in order to help construct a productive, small group learning experience for our students. Consequently, we decided at Stanford to run the video conferences from one of our tech-enhanced classrooms in Wallenberg Hall.[3] Our rationale for this very pragmatic decision was that we aimed to utilize resources already available to a class in its own room, rather move the students to a separate space. This solution did, however, initially restrict participation in the project to those classes already scheduled in one of our "smart" tech-enhanced classrooms. Limited involvement is thus one drawback of relying on pre-established spaces.

But here is where the need to be creative in administering this kind of work emerges. In our case, the fixed space necessitated the development a plan for reconfiguring the room to accommodate several simultaneous small group video conferences. The room was, fortunately, already equipped with five computer stations intended for student collaboration and distributed around the perimeter of the room. Thus, it seemed well designed to be repurposed to allow for five small group video-conference stations. Our first solution entailed bringing in portable sound dividers and echo-cancelling microphones to separate the different groups and reduce ambient noise. The drawback of this solution was that these panels did not sufficiently reduce the ambient noise; the video-conference connections required greater acoustic isolation for each group than we could achieve by holding multiple connections in one classroom or, similarly, in one large computer lab.

We learned that the ideal space solution for small group video conferences was an individual small room for each group, with acoustic isolation. Accordingly, we experimented with different configurations—using space in our writing center, private offices, and empty classrooms, and even moving laptops or rolling collaboration stations into hallways. For one video conference, we reserved space for thirteen different simultaneous groups, spread over three floors of a single building.

At the same time, our partners in Sweden, Egypt, and Australia faced a similar challenge. The writing programs at these institutions did not have dedicated small room spaces outfitted with the appropriate technology for making digital collaboration possible. In Örebro, Sweden, for instance, the first small group video conferences were held in faculty offices and empty classrooms, allowing for acoustic isolation for each connection. Subsequently, the Swedish team in Örebro used grant money from the WGLN, along with matching funds from the university president, to design and create a space that would make small group learning available. Largely the vision of Eva Magnusson, the space was named "The Rhetoric Room." This innovative technology classroom was equipped with a series of collaboration stations separated by dividers, a setup similar to our Wallenberg Hall classroom. However, although The Rhetoric Room promised stronger CCR connections between Stanford and Örebro, it became apparent that, even with its advanced design, it suffered from some of the same limitations that we had experienced in our Stanford spaces. Yet the process of making accommodations for these unforeseen issues helped us become more flexible in our overall approach to technologies and solutions that would optimize connections.

Specifically, our solution combated ambient noise by having Örebro students use headsets to try to minimize the interference. Over time, a new practice evolved: while some students remained in The Rhetoric Room but used headphones (with as many as four audio connections per collaboration station), others would take laptops into the surrounding hallways to carry on video conversations with their Stanford partners. Subsequently, when we initiated small group video-conference connections with the University of Sydney, Australia, and Uppsala University in Sweden, we negotiated not only how to locate the best possible space for the working groups, but also discussed providing the ancillary hardware (headsets and dividers) that would improve connections and optimize learning. When University of Sydney students connected from a computer lab and, later, from their new writing center space, the student teams used headsets and dividers to reduce noise.[4] Similarly, in Egypt, student groups met in dedicated spaces such as faculty offices or, when assembled in one room, they used headsets and dividers to approximate group isolation.

At Stanford, we were able to pioneer an even more advanced use of space when we were granted permission to reserve a series of private conference rooms on the fourth floor of Wallenberg Hall for our video conferences. While we did not "own" the space, the ability to use it and make long-term reservations for our connections allowed us to move to a more stable platform for our tech setup. With this change in location, we were able to stress stability (using desktops instead of laptops, fixed screens instead of rolling ones), which in turn fostered the necessary conditions for stronger, more reliable video connections. Thus, we argue that space problems can be negotiated through creative accommodation and by partnering pedagogical aims with institutional possibilities.

CONNECTING PEDAGOGY AND TECHNOLOGY: HARDWARE AND SOFTWARE SOLUTIONS

Securing available institutional space enabled us to take an important step for CCR: we could develop, test, and implement the most optimal hardware setup for these connections. The result was the construction of five computer "collaboration stations," specifically designed for digital dialogic work in writing classes. Composed of a large plasma screen for video and for sharing a collaborative whiteboard writing space, a desktop or laptop connection, an echo-cancelling microphone or headsets to reduce noise, and a webcam for visual representation of participants, these stations provided a stable platform to support our pedagogical emphasis on small group work.

In reflecting on the benefits of these stations, we have come to identify four key points essential to successful implementation. First, providing these collaboration stations in a small, dedicated conference room (or faculty office or empty classroom) ensures that the groups will have acoustic isolation. Second, the computer plasma screen and whiteboard facilitates and improves collaborative writing activities. Third, echo-cancelling microphones (or multiple headsets) allow for three to five people to hear and speak without producing a troublesome echo on the other side. If this point is not observed, the consequences include reduced participation and lack of communication, which Paloff and Pratt (2005) have noted as two challenges to successful online student collaboration. Fourth, the projection of webcam images on a large plasma screen offers a maximized viewing area for students and replicates face-to-face contact.

Furthermore, even the type of webcam matters in terms of configuring power dynamics across countries. Early on in our work, we used moveable webcams and positioned them on top of plasma screens. Our partners in Örebro acquired laptops with embedded webcams, resulting in images that were closer to the face and more in line with eye contact. As Anders Eriksson (2008) noted in a post on our instructor's blog, because Stanford students were seated at a desktop collaboration station and removed from the webcam, Örebro students perceived them as if from what he called "a God's Eye view," with the US students in "a subordinate position," looking up at them. Conversely, since the Örebro students often gathered around a single laptop, their faces appeared large, filling the screen on the Stanford side, an effect of the hardware that resulted in invisibility for some members of the team. That is, not all the Örebro students could be seen because of the narrow webcam field on the laptops, reducing some group members to disembodied voices during their conversations. From an administrative standpoint, the difference in perspective caused by hardware has strong implications in the distribution of responsibility, accountability, and authority across student teams, and even in the establishment of relationships across institutions.

Along with negotiating the best use of physical spaces and constructing the working hardware solution for small group learning, we also researched and tested a crucial component of video-conference infrastructure: the *software* platform. Indeed, we found the hardware and software to be interdependent variables in the support of pedagogical and curricular objectives.

More specifically, based on our research into globally-distributed teams working together in small groups, we sought a video-conference platform capable of hosting multiple simultaneous small group connections, which led us to Marratech (O'Brien and Alfano 2009).[5] Designed by a Swedish-based company, Marratech found early favor in academia (Correia and Sorensen 2007; Heeler and Hardy 2005; Molka-Danielsen et al. 2007) and was already in active use in Swedish universities at the time of our project's pilot. After beta testing, we concluded that this software would be particularly beneficial for global connections among groups in geographically dispersed writing classes, both for the way its infrastructure supported multiple computer platforms and levels of access as well as for its other technological capabilities, most notably its ability to simultaneously show a video stream, provide a collaborative whiteboard and text box, and run a record function. In working with Marratech, we learned communication practices that could be transferred across mediums. That became even more important when we had to switch software platforms due to industry availability or institutional mandate.[6] The important point here is that administering CCR with Marratech taught us best practices that we would then apply to connections using other software platforms, including Skype, Polycom, and Adobe Connect.

Specifically, we recommend that WPAs considering software options for such transnational connections select a solution based on the following four criteria:

1. The versatility of the software to meet diverse pedagogical needs or possible lesson plans;

2. The technical existence of a two-way whiteboard to serve as a shared writing space;

3. The option for unobtrusive observation on the part of instructors; and

4. The adaptability of the software across a range of institutional situations or contexts.

In terms of the first criterion, our work with Marratech during our earliest connections with Örebro (and Adobe Connect in later years) revealed that one of its strongest assets was its ability not only to host multiple connections, but also its versatility in terms of switching between those connections during a single video-conference session. In other words, the software in its most basic configuration allowed us to pair globally-distributed groups in one-to-one video chat sessions. But it also supported multiple simultaneous connections, meaning that we could simulate a virtual auditorium space where up to thirty-five individual computers could link in at any one time—a capability we leveraged both for opening remarks in a lecture format, as well as closing presentations, reflections, and student discussions at the end of our video-conference sessions. In this way, software made possible a great number of pedagogical arrangements, activities, and learning outcomes.

While we valued small group interactions, we also recognized an educational need to assemble all participants in a single virtual space. This configuration is a crucial tool in collapsing distinctions between schools and cultures; in these moments, students perceive themselves not as one of two institutionally-located groups, but as participants in a broader conversation across cultures. Thus, the software's versatility opened pedagogical possibilities, meaning we could easily reconfigure our virtual space to meet the needs of our lesson plans. Our virtual chairs were not bolted to the floor, so to speak; we could rearrange the "furniture" to best suit particular learning objectives, prioritizing pedagogical goals over technological constraints.

Second, we have identified that the ideal software needs to offer a collaborative whiteboard space. As our research indicates, student learning is maximized by pairing discussion and analysis of texts with the active production of a collaborative deliverable (O'Brien and Alfano 2009). The shared whiteboard provided the globally-distributed student groups with a real-time canvas for creating a variety of shared texts, from discussion notes to information graphics, advertisements, storyboards, and even presentations. When there is a shared whiteboard space, both "sides" can write, draw, exchange PowerPoints, and compose collaborative texts. In both Marratech and Adobe Connect, that shared whiteboard space is possible. We have also turned to Google Docs and Google Draw (paired with Skype or Gmail chat) to serve as similar whiteboard writing spaces in our connections with Egypt, Australia, and Singapore. Stanford students connected through Skype with students at the National University of Singapore. Using either the Skype "share document" feature or a shared Google Doc to exchange their writing, the students then conducted an international peer review. As administrators of CCR, we projected the laptop connection onto a large plasma screen to allow for increased video size and improved readability of the written document under discussion. In all cases, establishing a strong video-audio connection was most important, along with a shared whiteboard space for a group of students to work together as one team. In other words, the principal take-away is that the software solution, while it might consist of a series of creative adaptations, should include the means for collaborative digital writing.

Third, the optimal software solution allows for instructors or researchers to unobtrusively visit the small groups and observe their learning. In the first years of CCR, Marratech's room-switching function and record feature (allowing future playback of recorded sessions) made it an ideal platform for our research and for assessing the progress of each group. Today, we use Adobe Connect to achieve the same goal: the instructor can visit the virtual rooms of the students working together, without disturbing them in the way that opening a physical door would do. These software solutions allow us as course instructors to easily and discretely move between virtual rooms without leaving our own computers. Currently, Skype does not yet offer this option, and we are forced to confront various concerns about the shift of the role of the instructor in student learning, which has been under discussion since the rise of e-learning in the early 2000s (Bonk, Wisher, and Lee 2004).

Finally, we recommend selecting a software solution that is flexible in terms of digital access for international partners with unequal resources. One concern from the beginning of our project was that the digital divide might inhibit participation by other international institutions, particularly those with different technology budgets, support, or hardware capabilities. Since Marratech worked across both Mac and PC platforms, we anticipated it would minimize hardware conflicts and help us negotiate hardware differences between institutions. In addition, Marratech's hosting structure seemed ideally suited to the elimination of any obstacles arising from financial inequities between institutions: one university could pay an annual fee to "host" rooms on Marratech, and then others could acquire the software as a free download in order to access those hosted rooms. Our WGLN grant, and later our funding from Stanford University, allowed us to serve as the Marratech host for our CCR sessions, and we created six to eight virtual rooms for the globally-distributed teams involved in our project. In our current use of Adobe Connect, we use the software for free at Stanford and the license is maintained and supported by Örebro University. For the Skype-based connections we hold with Australia, Egypt, and Singapore, there is no additional institutional overhead cost or technology support barrier; moreover, both Skype and Google Docs are very familiar to students and increasingly used in the educational arena.

NEGOTIATING PARITY, SCHEDULES, CLASS SIZES, AND PEDAGOGICAL OBJECTIVES: WORKING ACROSS INTERNATIONAL TIME ZONES

Beyond negotiating the technological components of transnational connections, we also recommend attending to the challenges of managing both time zones and competing objectives in curricular and pedagogical outcomes. Early on in our project, we recognized that certain scheduling accommodations would need to be made to account for time zone differences. For example, because of the nine-hour difference between California and Sweden, the best match seemed to be to pair morning Stanford classes with evening Örebro classes. On the Stanford side, this immediately limited the number of classes that could participate in the project to those that met at 9 a.m., putting particular constraints on our room reservations and decreasing the number of students who could engage in the exchanges. On the Örebro side, since the university did not offer many evening classes, the sessions were initially run as extra meetings on top of regular class obligations and held from 6 to 8 p.m. This discrepancy caused both an inequity in student engagement and an uneven rhetorical situation. For many of the Stanford students, 9 a.m. classes impinged on their sleep; for the Örebro students, many of whom were older, the evening hours meant time away from dinner and families. The student experience, consequently, was initially mixed: participants began the connections with different perspectives on the stakes involved in their own participation, which at times was perceived as a difference in engagement and commitment to the activity. From an administrative perspective, we soon recognized that in order to facilitate equal and productive encounters between students, we needed to establish parity of requirements and accountability for all participants in the project. As time progressed, Örebro was able to work with its registrar to introduce into its rhetoric curriculum an official Cross-Cultural Rhetoric course that required evening class sessions. At Stanford, we moved most of our CCR-themed courses to early morning time slots and worked more closely with our partners to agree on how students' work in the class factored into their overall grades for individual courses. The take-home message here is that successful transnational collaboration needs to address the logistics of scheduling at optimal times, instill parity of both workload and accountability, and contend with diverse rhetorical situations.

We leveraged these lessons when we brought on board students from the American University in Cairo (AUC), Egypt, and needed to negotiate across different curricular structures, cultural norms involving family time, and the logistics of travel in Cairo. Initially, during our first two years of collaboration, the AUC campus was located near Tahrir Square in downtown Cairo.[7] However, in February 2009, the university moved its campus to the suburb of New Cairo. Located in a more remote desert area, the new campus necessitated a much longer commute, with the majority of students, faculty, and staff bused to campus in the morning and back to downtown Cairo in the afternoon, away from technology classrooms and equipment necessary for global connections. Consequently, the original connection time of 6 p.m. Egypt to 9 a.m. Stanford became problematic, since 6 p.m. was the commute hour and AUC effectively shut down in the evening. To remedy this unexpected logistical obstacle, we once again made accommodations and tried to work creatively as a global team of teachers. One solution we implemented was to ask AUC students to connect from home using their personal computers (or to meet at each other's houses and connect on a shared computer), without institutional infrastructure or hands-on help from the instructor or technologist.

What we discovered was that residential bandwidth in Cairo tended to be less robust than institutional levels for supporting the feature-heavy demands of Marratech; the connections were unstable and even unpredictable, and were disrupted many times by video lag or distorted audio. Frequently, the connections dropped altogether. To compensate, we moved several of the groups to Skype (communicating with students via text message). Since Skype is more minimalist in its features than Marratech, it therefore requires less bandwidth to maintain a sustained video connection. For the most part, students welcomed the transition; many had used Skype in their personal lives and were familiar with the platform. At the same time, we learned the importance of decentralizing the administration of the project to enable students to connect during times and from locations that worked best for them. Thus, from a WPA perspective, we predict that cross-cultural connections among students in the future might be pedagogically prepared and coordinated by administrators, but, more importantly, students can and should increasingly take ownership for their connection spaces and equipment, as well as for the rigor of their collaborative work as globally-distributed teams.

For our connections that exceeded a nine-hour time difference, we again had to think creatively and accommodate the needs of both institutions. This was the case when we connected with students in Australia, Russia, and Singapore; we would negotiate a mutually beneficial time during which students would be required to attend the video conference in order to ensure parity of participation and accountability.[8]

A further challenge emerged when we found ourselves trying to match up uneven class sizes. The University of Sydney's WRIT1001 course enrolled as many as 400 students. To accommodate these large numbers, we extended the schedule of the Stanford-Sydney sessions over the course of three days, with four or five video conferences per day of approximately one hour each, and we invited multiple Stanford classes to participate, distributed across these many sessions. In negotiating connection options, we prioritized meeting times that aligned with Sydney's established class times in order to stabilize the schedule on one side. On the Stanford side, although we required Stanford students to attend video-conference connections outside of their regular class hours, we took care to offer a variety of session possibilities to address their diverse scheduling constraints. Multiple Stanford PWR classes—employing a variety of course themes and drawing from both our freshman-level and sophomore-level classes—participated in these exchanges. The lesson learned here is that administering uneven class-size connections involves a heightened level of collaboration, but it is indeed possible to resolve schedule logistics and co-create a lesson plan that meets the curricular demands and enrollment parameters of different courses in order to help students develop skills in intercultural communication.[9]

In all cases, we have discovered that it is crucial to establish video-conference connections during either officially scheduled class times or mandated special sessions in order to ensure attendance and participation. This has proved for us and for our international partners to be a good administrative decision. In piloting non-required, optional video-conference connections, we had very low turnout from the students; therefore, we recommend nesting transnational video conferences within established courses and institutionally-sanctioned meeting times.

On the matter of negotiating pedagogical objectives, we have gained important insights concerning transnational collaboration. From a WPA perspective, the lesson is that partner institutions should collaborate on all details whenever possible, from technology purchases up through the design and implementation of lesson plans and grade assignments. There must be a shared vision about the goal or purpose of connections, learning outcomes desired, and workload distribution among students. We realized the need for such conversations early on, when we—as teachers and new project administrators in 2005—encountered our first challenges during the initial months of the pilot. As we started to plan the pedagogical and technological implementation of our project with our partners Anders Eriksson and Eva Magnusson at Örebro, we immediately recognized that the requirements for a successful international collaboration were nearly identical to those for a more local partnership, as we had experienced with our colleagues at Stanford. Specifically, we needed frequent, preferably face-to-face, contact; an ability to share and collaborate on materials; the opportunity for productive discussions about pedagogical goals; time for both individual and joint reflection; and shared values on learning outcomes and assessment.

To meet these expectations, we began using the very same video-conference protocol that we intended to ask our students to use, and we established regular weekly video-conference meetings with our Örebro partners. Called "Teacher Tuesdays," these meetings began at 6 a.m. in California and 3 p.m. in Sweden; we matched our early morning coffee in the United States with our Swedish colleagues' mid-afternoon coffee break between classes. In the process, we became familiar with the technology and developed best practices for team-building and international collaboration. During these sixty to ninety minute sessions, we not only drafted lesson plans, reflected on our collaboration, and established pedagogical guidelines and assignment sequences for our cross-cultural curriculum, but we also practically explored the problems and potential of audio/video-enabled communication. In addition, we made good use of asynchronous collaborative tools—using a project wiki and later Google Docs—to coauthor activity sheets and post class schedules. In this way, we experimented with and piloted the same tools and techniques of collaborative writing that we planned to ask our students to use in their intercultural communication practices. Through this process, we attempted to confront some of the institutional, cultural, and logistical challenges identified by Belz and Muller-Hartmann (2003) as common when conducting a transnational teaching partnership.

In our subsequent partnership with Uppsala University in Sweden, we found ourselves connecting courses that had fundamentally different goals: Uppsala focused on modern rhetoric, while Stanford focused on writing and speaking across a range of time periods and disciplines. Consequently, we collaborated to construct lesson plans that met the curricular goals of both institutions.[10] Our solution developed collaborative activities that could be completed real-time and focused on a rhetorical approach to humor, leadership, and advertising. We then asked students to harness their new, deeper understanding of rhetoric as it crosses cultures and produce collaboratively-authored texts. These texts resulted in new media composing, such as generating a website, developing content for a storyboard, drafting a speech on the whiteboard, and imitating the platforms of Facebook and Twitter through humorous "top ten" lists.

Just as with our University of Sydney partnership, we had to negotiate an uneven number of students across institutions. In Uppsala, the modern rhetoric class enrolled forty students, while our Stanford classes had a maximum of fifteen students. Our solution included dividing the Uppsala class in half, with twenty students connecting to fifteen Stanford students from one section, and then repeating the lesson plan for the second set of Uppsala students connecting with a different Stanford section. This structure allowed for all Swedish students to have the same educational experience, a Swedish requirement, and it gave twice as many Stanford students the chance to develop intercultural communication and composing abilities first-hand. We delineate these solutions because it was only through our collaboration and negotiation as administrators in different countries that we found best practices for bridging differences, strategies which we hope will be useful to other WPAs. In fact, we quickly applied these lessons when we initiated new partnerships with universities in Russia and Australia. The need to come to a shared vision of the purpose and possibilities for the connection was most evident when we connected undergraduates from a range of disciplines at Stanford with graduate students studying economics and law in Russia (O'Brien and Kovbasyuk 2013).

ADAPTING TO AVAILABLE TECHNOLOGY: FOSTERING SMALL GROUPS WITH BROADCAST VIDEO

We have argued for creativity, flexibility, and accommodation with regard to space, hardware, software, parity, scheduling, and meeting pedagogical goals when administering transnational connections between writing classes. What happens, however, when the only video-conference technology infrastructure available is not suited for small group collaboration? What happens to best practices and the lesson we learned that students reach writing outcomes most when they can collaboratively author work at the site of the intercultural exchange?

We faced these questions from the beginning of our connections with Khabarovsk State Academy of Economics and Law in Far East Russia. It became clear during our pedagogical planning sessions that that different levels of computer access, concerns over uneven bandwidth, and a pedagogical desire for full class-to-class connections would make using globally-distributed team technologies (such as Marratech, Adobe Connect, or Skype) impossible to implement. We turned instead to the one technology supported by both universities: Polycom video-conference technology. Polycom provides high-definition video and strong audio, with a capability for switching over to a PowerPoint presentation in place of the video stream. It is often already supported and funded by most universities, avoiding additional expenses, although there are considerable space and technological arrangements to be made.

As a first step in making accommodations for our Russian partners, we experimented with where to place the video camera, since our initial attempt at using Polycom in our 2005 pilot had met with disastrous results. During that early effort to connect entire classes, we relied on Polycom and positioned students in front of a large screen to communicate their research projects and ideas with each other. In exit surveys, students remarked that the tech setup for Polycom had been disorienting, inhibiting their ability to engage in a close conversation with their international partners. With the webcam situated on a low table, but the students looking at their counterparts on a more elevated screen, it was extremely difficult to create eye contact. This setup in turn disrupted the possibility for a mutual or shared gaze that research suggests is a key component in productive conversation and online video collaboration

(Bailenson, Beall, and Blascovich 2002; Grayson and Monk 2003). Our early use of Polycom placed the webcam to one side, and students had difficulty achieving a sense of connection with their international partners since they could not make eye contact. The encounter more closely approximated performance than conversation or collaboration. In our research, we recognized this as a failure of transparency (O'Brien, Alfano, and Magnusson 2007); that is, the participants' constant awareness of the technological interface stalled their ability to make a deep connection.

Returning to Polycom for our Khabarovsk connections with several years of research behind us, we made certain adjustments that streamlined the experience for both sides. First, we approximated face-to-face conversation by aligning the camera within the line of sight for the viewing audience, creating a greater sense of a shared gaze. Second, we capitalized on Polycom's more advanced options, using the camera's zoom feature to spotlight specific students when they were speaking, thereby simulating a proximity of field that we have argued is a key component of productive, digitally-mediated collaboration (O'Brien, Alfano, Magnusson 2007). We also learned through experimentation that we could use the zoom feature to approximate small group configurations based on our strategic placement of students in the room, and, consequently, in the video frame. This realization provided a breakthrough moment, for it enabled us to simulate small group discussion and interaction. Third, we rearranged the physical space to best support this sense of proximity, creating what we called a "contact zone" at the front table for students to work more closely with their Russian colleagues, with the rest of the class observing as an audience behind them. By strategically positioning the Polycom camera directly below the screen, we were able to more closely approximate the sense of a mutual gaze between groups, crucial to creating a foundation for interpersonal bonding, productive dialogue, and optimal learning.

By making accommodations with hardware placement, software features, and spatial arrangement, we incorporated the benefits of small group pedagogy into the connection, despite using a technology principally designed to support large group or class-to-class conversations. We made adjustments in our administration of the project and reconceptualized the technology-pedagogy impasse as more of a symbiotic relationship than an adversarial one. Our successful reintroduction of Polycom into the CCR project represented not only how we had learned to turn limitations into opportunities for innovation, and to manage transnational connections across technological disparities and institutional differences, but also how WPAs seeking to engage in this work can generate creative solutions that prioritize student learning above technical, spatial, and institutional challenges.

FACILITATING ASYNCHRONOUS TRANSNATIONAL CONNECTIONS

While we have mainly focused thus far on video-conference connections, it is important to include a reflection on the use of asynchronous communication technologies for fostering cross-cultural student learning. Scholars, such as Robert Godwin-Jones (2003), have heralded the potential for blogs and wikis to support robust online collaboration and projects, such as Lina Lee's (2009) at the University of New Hampshire, who successfully turned to blogging for intercultural learning. In CCR, we have relied on blogging technology since our initial connections (O'Brien and Alfano 2009). As the administrative hosts of the CCR blog using a Stanford server, we have worked to streamline the logistics of authorship permission and develop a model of tech support that could make the blogging platform (first, Movable Type and, later, Wordpress) accessible both to tech-savvy users as well as tech-novice instructors and students.

As we continued to administer the project, bringing in more countries across more time zones, the blog became a rich repository for writing and reflection by student participants, processing the lessons about intercultural communication they learned during a video conference. It also served as a showcase for student work generated by the globally-distributed teams—a place to publish the tangible outcomes of their collaboration. For example, online photo essays posted on the blog—featuring photographs taken by students of their schools and local cultures—facilitated rich discussions online and in the classroom about stereotypes and cultural authenticity. And posts detailing student research projects and textual analysis provided the foundation for serious academic discussions of research methodology, topic selection, and cultural assumptions. In one CCR blog post, AUC student Manar Nesseem reflected on Egyptian gender stereotypes, using a photo he took of a billboard as visual evidence for his analysis of cultural norms. Through establishing and facilitating such virtual connections in the asynchronous medium, we recognized the truth of Jill Walker's (2005) assertion about the benefits of raising the stakes for students by publishing their writing in a "public space" to a real audience; our CCR blog writers became active participants in public, transnational discourse, and derived a more complex view of writing in a networked environment (Benson and Reyman 2009).

We recommend that WPAs seeking to launch international partnerships look to blogging as a stable, reliable platform, where students can
compose at their own pace and with whatever language aids or writing
resources they might need for their assignment. Furthermore, the blog
mandates particular attention to writing itself, making it an ideal complement to video conferencing in writing courses, as well as a pedagogical practice that enables students to develop in significant ways as writers, in accordance with WPA outcomes.

ASSESSING TRANSNATIONAL WRITING
PEDAGOGY THROUGH WPA OUTCOMES

In our ongoing assessment of the CCR project, we have collected six
years of exit survey data that consistently shows high scores on student
learning outcomes (O'Brien and Alfano 2009). In surveying, debriefing,
and working with our students since 2005, we have come to realize how
valuable the cross-cultural collaboration opportunities are for them as
developing writers and communicators. Taken together, the qualitative
comments made by students in exit surveys might offer an appropriate
closing argument for this kind of transnational writing pedagogy.

Specifically, students articulated learning how writing and ·rheto-
ric travels across cultures: "I was struck by how similarly my classmates
and the Swedish and Australian students analyzed and reacted to visual
and written rhetoric. It was especially interesting to hear the Australian
group critique an Australian-produced travel ad about vacationing in
Australia." Students identified the importance of learning communication strategies for cross-cultural situations: "I received some first-hand
experience in communicating with international students—people with
absolutely different backgrounds. I think that is the most valuable thing
I've learned yet." Others showed metacognitive awareness as a habit of
mind: "My favorite part was hearing the opinions on interesting topics of
students my age in another country, and not through polls or documen-
taries, but through people I was able to speak to in a video conference."

These comments reflect the WPA Outcomes Statement for First-Year
Composition. Accordingly, we might evaluate the work of such transnational writing program initiatives by "the common knowledge, skills,
and attitudes sought by first-year composition programs in American
postsecondary education" (Council 2000). The first category of the
WPA outcomes statement is "rhetorical knowledge." We contend that
such outcomes can and should be met in new media platforms, such as
video-conference or blogging technologies. Our aim should be to teach

students how to focus on a purpose, respond to the needs of different audiences, respond appropriately to different kinds of rhetorical situations, and write in several genres. When connecting internationally with other students in mediated writing spaces—including on a shared whiteboard, blog interface, or computer screen—students engage with different audiences and learn real-world response strategies. In terms of the second WPA category, "critical thinking, reading, and writing," we argue it is through transnational writing collaborations that students learn how best to collaborate on writing-based assignments. In this way, students view the steps of the writing process as a series of tasks to be negotiated with others from diverse cultural contexts and across institutional settings, with varying expectations concerning what it means to read and write well. Through such collaboration, students learn to integrate their own ideas with those of others, and thereby begin to understand the relationships that stretch across language, knowledge, and power.

The WPA outcomes then stress "processes." By exchanging drafts for peer review or writing collaboratively on a shared whiteboard, we claim, students develop flexible strategies for generating, revising, editing, and proofreading; they learn that it takes multiple drafts to reach a final product. In this way, they come to understand the collaborative and social aspects of writing processes first-hand, and learn to balance the advantages of relying on others with the responsibility of doing their own part to improve a text. With regard to "knowledge of conventions," we propose that connecting and writing through video-conference technologies and blogs gives students first-hand experience with using a variety of technologies to address a range of audiences and, thus, learn common formats for different kinds of texts. Finally, the WPA outcomes statement places strong emphasis on the need for students to "compose in electronic environments." Writing in a digitally-mediated virtual space is a productive way to meet this mandate, since students can communicate through webcam, microphone, shared whiteboard, chat box, and blog interfaces. With greater recognition of the learning opportunities afforded by such technologies, more interactive and real-world engagements among students can take place, preparing them both for their futures in a digitally-mediated global world, as well as for their careers working with people from diverse cultural backgrounds and institutionally-determined perspectives on knowledge production.

However, we argue the value of connecting students across continents exceeds learning skills for communication. In terms of attitudes, such transnational exchanges help students develop the WPA-identified "habits of mind," supporting student success with regard to curiosity (the desire to know more about the world), openness (the willingness to consider new ways of being and thinking in the world), and engagement (a sense of investment and involvement in learning). By placing students in direct communication with others from around the world and requiring them to complete a writing-based task as a team, we encourage the development and growth of such habits. Transnational writing practices also instill creativity (using novel approaches for generating, investigating, and representing ideas), persistence (sustaining interest in and attention to short- and long-term projects), responsibility (taking ownership of one's actions and understanding the consequences of those actions for oneself and others), and flexibility (adapting to situations, expectations, or demands), since the writing product is one that needs to be invented with creativity, negotiated with intercultural communication skills, adapted based on the abilities and preferences of the participants, and completed with students learning how to balance individual ownership against group authorship. Finally, we have seen that when video-conference or blogging connections are followed by reflection, such writing tasks help foster the WPA-required habit of metacognition (the ability to reflect on one's own thinking as well as on the individual and cultural processes used to structure knowledge).

Yet, what is perhaps most remarkable about transnational collaborations across writing classes, universities, and countries is that, since students are located in diverse cultures and academic environments, they develop these habits of mind through *first-hand, active* learning, where lessons are immediate and students gain these skills through engaged participation. To ensure such learning, however, administrators of transnational writing projects need to take great care to place available technologies and pedagogical goals or expectations in a symbiotic relationship, which requires making creative adjustments as necessary to ensure optimal learning.

Nationally and internationally, there is great interest in fostering more transnational connections. Steven Fraiberg (2010, 119) calls for "further partnerships with international classrooms and speakers of world languages" through technologies such as online video-conferencing. He argues that writing studies today ought to "offer students opportunities to imagine global audiences and to receive responses from cross-cultural perspectives." Transnational WPA efforts can fulfill this need by looking to digital writing pedagogies that bring students together for active learning of collaborative composition and intercultural communication learning practices, which impart real-world lessons about audience and text and develop individual writing abilities.

However, certain questions arise from our research. We have seen how we must adapt our practices to a sliding scale of available technology, and also modify our technological apparatus to come to creative solutions for meeting learning outcomes for writing students. We have made the case for negotiation among administrators and instructors concerning time zones, parity of student workload, pedagogical aims and activities, and composition in electronic environments. The next questions to confront us emerge as technology continues to improve and students begin to initiate such collaborations on their own using Facebook, Google Video Chat, Google+, Facetime, or other newly-minted means of communication. Will such increasingly common global interactions better prepare students for classroom-based technological exchanges? Alternatively, will familiarity with digitally-mediated communication render students more skeptical or even cynical about the potential educational value of transnational activities in the writing classroom? What is the role of WPAs in establishing and managing cross-institutional connections when many of the hardware and software requirements delineated in this chapter are becoming increasingly available without additional cost or official sanction? Finally, as video-conference technology in particular continues to evolve, becoming more capable of multi-user simultaneous connections and communication through an unimaginable range of innovative tools, what are the possibilities for connecting student writers across even greater discrepancies or differences at the institutional and cultural level?

These questions await answers. What we do know for certain is that the expanding internationalization of our universities affords us greater opportunities for connecting students in dynamic and highly productive ways. The field has already begun the transition to implementing a writing pedagogy that fosters the collaborative composition of transnational writing texts through various technological means. We argue that such connections should become an increasingly common practice of writing program administration for our twenty-first century, interconnected world.

Notes

1. See the complete set of WPA outcomes for FYC at http://wpacouncil.org/files /wpa-outcomes-statement.pdf.
2. For a history of the research endeavor funded by the WGLN, see http://ccr.stan ford.edu/wgln.html.
3. Once the home of Stanford's Center for Innovation in Learning (SCIL), Wallenberg Hall began renovations in 1999 to house advanced resource classrooms. The

redevelopment was made possible through a $15 million grant from the Knut and Alice Wallenberg and Marcus and Marianne Wallenberg Foundations in Sweden, with the purpose of advancing education and encouraging faculty innovation in teaching at Stanford. Today, the building offers several tech-equipped smart classrooms intended to create flexible, creative learning environments, as well as workshop spaces, breakout areas, research facilities, and traditional classroom spaces.

4. When the University of Sydney launched its new Writing Hub in 2010–2011, it opened a space that had been designed at least in part to foster transnational collaboration. This innovative writing center featured a combination of video-conference-equipped computers and headphones with audio splitters (so that multiple students could connect to the same computer), thus establishing a stable infrastructure for our connections.

5. Our success with Marratech in class-to-class video conferences led us to use it as our e-meeting software for our 2007 and 2008 International Symposia, two virtual conferences in which we connected WPAs and research-scholars across eleven countries.

6. Subsequent to our adoption of Marratech, the platform was acquired by Google and partnered with Elluminate in 2007. This transfer of ownership changed some of the software's suitability for our needs, yet the lessons we learned from it remain relevant for administrators seeking to connect students across continents.

7. We established a partnership with the Rhetoric and Writing Department at AUC and thank our colleagues for their collaboration, particularly writing instructors Ghada El Shimi, Sanaa Makhlouf, Mark Mikhael, and Wafaa Wali, as well as Department Chair Emily Golson. Moreover, because Egypt is on the same time zone as Sweden, we were able to host three-way video conferences with Cairo, Örebro, and Stanford, all connecting at the same time for students to produce collaborative writing projects.

8. When working with our colleague Johan Geertsema of the University Scholars Programme at the National University of Singapore, we set up connections for 4 p.m. at Stanford and 8 a.m. in Singapore the following day. Similarly, in connecting our students with those of our colleague Olga Kovbasyuk at Khabarovsk State Academy of Economics and Law in Russia, we set up 4 p.m. Stanford classes that met with Russian classes convening at 10 a.m. the next day.

9. We thank Susan Thomas, William Foley, Ben Miller, and Ariel Spigelman at the University of Sydney for their ongoing collaboration with the Stanford CCR project.

10. We are grateful to Uppsala University colleagues Patrik Mehrens, Sofi Qvarnstrom, and Janne Lindquist Grade for their creativity, flexibility, and commitment to the CCR project.

References

Bailenson, Jeremy N., Andrew C. Beall, and Jim Blascovich. 2002. "Gaze and Task Performance in Shared Virtual Environments." *Journal of Visualization and Computer Animation* 13 (5): 313–20. http://dx.doi.org/10.1002/vis.297.

Belz, Julie A., and Andreas Muller-Hartmann. 2003. "Teachers as Intercultural Learners: Negotiating German-American Telecollaboration along the Institutional Fault Line." *Modern Language Journal* 87 (1): 71–89. http://dx.doi.org/10.1111/1540-4781.00179.

Benson, John, and Jessica Reyman. 2009. *Learning to Write Publicly: Promises and Pitfalls of Using Weblogs in the Composition Classroom.* Computers and Composition Online; Accessed 8 September 2011.

Bonk, Curtis J., Robert A. Wisher, and Ji-Yeon Lee. 2004. "Moderating Learner-Centered E-Learning: Problems and Solutions, Benefits and Implications." In *Online*

Colllaborative Learning: Theory and Practice, ed. Tim S. Roberts, 54–85. London: Information Science Publishing.

Bruffee, Kenneth. 1973. "Collaborative Learning: Some Practical Models." *College English* 34 (5): 634–43. http://dx.doi.org/10.2307/375331.

Correia, Ana-Paula, and Elsebeth Sorensen. 2007. "The Urge for Collaboration: The Evaluation of a Virtual Learning Collaboration across the Atlantic." In *Proceedings of World Conference on Educational Multimedia, Hypermedia and Telecommunications*, ed. Craig Montgomerie and Jane Seale, 1779–1785. Chesapeake, VA: AACE.

Council of Writing Program Administrators. 2000. *WPA Outcomes Statement for First-Year Composition*. http://wpacouncil.org/files/wpa-outcomes-statement.pdf.

Elbow, Peter. 1973. *Writing Without Teachers*. New York: Oxford University Press.

Eriksson, Anders. 2008. "Camera and Authority." *CCR Instructor's Blog*. April 27.

Fraiberg, Steven. 2010. "Composition 2.0: Toward a Multilingual and Multimodal Framework." *College Composition and Communication* 62 (1): 100–26.

Godwin-Jones, Robert. 2003. "Emerging Technologies: Blogs and Wikis: Environments for On-line Collaboration." *Language Learning & Technology* 7 (2): 12–6.

Grayson, David M., and Andrew F. Monk. 2003. "Are You Looking at Me? Eye contact and Desktop Video Conferencing." *ACM Transactions on Computer-Human Interaction* 10 (3): 221–43. http://dx.doi.org/10.1145/937549.937552.

Heeler, Phillip, and Carolyn Hardy. 2005. "A Preliminary Report on the Use of Video Technology in Online Courses." *Journal of Computing Sciences in Colleges* 20 (4): 127–33.

Lee, Lina. 2009. "Promoting Intercultural Exchanges with Blogs and Podcasting: A Study of Spanish-American Telecollaboration." *Computer Assisted Language Learning* 22 (5): 425–43. http://dx.doi.org/10.1080/09588220903345184.

Molka-Danielsen, Judith, David Richardson, Mats Deutschmann, and Bryan Carter. 2007. "Teaching Languages in a Virtual World." Nokobit Proceedings., 97–109. Trondheim: Tapir Akademisk Forlag.

O'Brien, Alyssa J., and Christine L. Alfano. 2009. "Connecting Students Globally Through Video-Conference Pedagogy." *Journal of Online Learning and Teaching* 5 (4): 675–84.

O'Brien, Alyssa J., Christine Alfano, and Eva Magnusson. 2007. "Improving Cross-Cultural Communication through Collaborative Technologies." In *Persuasive Technology*, ed. Yvonne de Kort, Wijnand IJesselsteijn, Cees Midden, Berry Eggen, and BJ Fogg, 125–131. Springer (4744). http://dx.doi.org/10.1007/978-3-540-77006-0_17.

O'Brien, Alyssa J., and Olga Kovbasyuk. 2013. "Fostering Intercultural Dialogue via Communication Technologies." In *Meaning-Centered Education: International Perspectives and Explorations in Higher Education*, ed. Olga Kovbasyuk and Patrick Blessinger, 65–81. New York: Routledge.

Paloff, Rena M., and Keith Pratt. 2005. *Collaborating Online: Learning Together in Community*. Jossey-Bass.

Walker, Jill. 2005. "Weblogs: Learning in Public." *On the Horizon* 13 (2): 112–8. http://dx.doi.org/10.1108/10748120510608142.

3

THE FIRST-YEAR WRITING SEMINAR PROGRAM AT WEILL CORNELL MEDICAL COLLEGE – QATAR
Balancing Tradition, Culture, and Innovation in Transnational Writing Instruction

Alan S. Weber, Krystyna Golkowska, Ian Miller,
Rodney Sharkey, Mary Ann Rishel, and Autumn Watts

INTRODUCTION AND BACKGROUND
American Style Writing Instruction in the Arabian Gulf

Krystyna Golkowska, Writing Program Coordinator
Mary Ann Rishel, Professor (ret.), Writing Faculty

The Gulf state of Qatar pioneered a major change in its educational system when the former Emir, His Highness Sheikh Hamad Bin Khalifa Al-Thani, and his wife, Her Highness Sheikha Moza bint Nasser, founded the Qatar Foundation in 1995, which asked six American universities to develop branch campuses in Qatar, a complex known as Education City in Doha. Inviting US schools to set up branch campuses within the country forms part of a larger strategy to shift Qatar's reliance away from oil and gas revenue, which dominates the economy, toward a knowledge-based economy emphasizing education, research, and biotechnology. To achieve this goal, however, more Qataris must be trained in STEM fields (science, technology, engineering, and mathematics) instead of seeking high-paying jobs in the military and government, which employ the majority of nationals.

In 2000–2002, through a partnership with Weill Cornell Medical College in New York City and philanthropist Sanford Weill, Weill Cornell Medical College in Qatar (WCMC–Q) opened its doors as the first American medical school in the region. In the following year, English and academic writing were instituted to fulfill the requirements of the medical college in New York City and the main campus in Ithaca, New York. The faculty was charged with adopting the curriculum of the

DOI: 10.7330/9780874219623.c003

John S. Knight Writing Institute for Writing in the Disciplines, a program housed in the College of Arts and Sciences and serving the entire Cornell community. Since the First-Year Writing Seminars (FYWS) at WCMC–Q were to have the same goals and outcomes as those on the main campus, course objectives included using the liberal arts approach to thinking, critical inquiry through scholarly essays, and consideration of the role literature holds in medicine. The challenge for WCMC–Q administrators and faculty arose from the need to deploy an American model of writing instruction in a conservative Muslim country that privileges oral communication. Moreover, English language preparation among students was inadequate, and, as the later sections of this chapter will explain, there were also issues including the absence of writing centers in the region, misperceptions of local cultural taboos, and the students' culturally specific engagement with literature, identity, and textuality. Thus, instructors were immediately faced with the need to not only teach humanistic content, but also to translate and implement educational paradigms that originated from a different system of learning and teaching beliefs.

Teaching FYWS in Qatar is further complicated by the structure of the Pre-medical Education Program. Pre-med students at WCMC–Q are expected to satisfy all the requirements for application to the Medical Program in two years instead of four (as is the case in the United States), which places heavy demands on students and faculty. Consequently, the curriculum consists primarily of science courses and offers only two mandatory courses in the humanities besides the FYWS: Psychology and Medical Ethics. There is no possibility of electives, and the demands of the science-heavy curriculum exact their toll, including a larger number of laboratory practicum hours than on the main campus. To increase student motivation, FYWS courses are designed to engage future doctors. For example, the first semester courses have usually been taught under the Cornell rubric "Reading and Writing about Literature" or "Writing across Cultures," but in the second semester instructors offer courses in drama, Islamic medicine, or stories by and about doctors. Students' linguistic proficiency, cultural competence, and religious sensitivity are taken into consideration in the process of selecting course themes and materials.

The overview below of the history of WCMC–Q's FYWS will suffice here to exemplify some successful initiatives and serious dilemmas that both faculty and administrators have had to face in developing the Writing Program in Doha. Writing classes began in the fall of 2004, with three sections of sixteen students each, in a seminar entitled "Beyond the Bones: Writing about Literature and Society." To assist students in developing an interpretative frame for reading narrative, the fall course offered literature that explored moral codes and social values arising from an international arena. From anthologies of international fiction and nonfiction, students examined how culture shapes the way we think and how epistemologies—such as socially constructed thought—can determine the values and choices of both the individual and the community. The syllabus and guidelines for these three sections were identical, although each instructor experimented with different readings for units within the course. The spring 2005 sections addressed oral presentations in the sciences and humanities, which complemented rhetorical elements in their essays.

As the WCMC–Q Pre-medical Education Program and writing programs continue to grow, the primary goals and objectives of the FYWS have remained unchanged. The seminars continue to emphasize critical thinking, close reading of texts, and writing with clarity and coherence. At least six essays developed through revised drafts (approximately thirty pages of polished prose) are required; readings are determined by the theme of each seminar and are limited to seventy-five pages per week in order to allow time for writing and revision. WCMC–Q shares many of the challenges facing other schools in Qatar that use English as the language of instruction and adopt an American-style curriculum. More often than not, Education City instructors have to accommodate students who lack linguistic proficiency (in both their native Arabic and English) and cultural competence. The new emphasis on science in national schools has resulted in the reduction in weekly hours of language instruction, both Arabic and English. Students come to WCMC–Q from many countries in the region and the world. Even those coming from Qatar graduate from secondary schools implementing different educational systems, some of which originate in Pakistan, India, Egypt, Lebanon, western Europe, and the United States. The Writing Program has no placement exam, and the level of readiness for a college-level writing course is uneven. To address this concern, the writing faculty use a diagnostic essay, which factors into decisions regarding student placement. An effort is made to evenly balance each section not only in terms of gender or ethnicity but also proficiency.

In reality, this imbalance results in writing instructors having to teach a bi-modal class, with some native and near-native English proficient students learning beside students with challenges such as limited vocabulary, low reading speed, little exposure to literature, and limited cultural literacy. The above-mentioned factors have necessitated modifications regarding the number of students per section, the amount of individual attention they receive, and the type of texts they use. The FYWS in Ithaca, New York were not initially designed to accommodate ESL (English as a Second Language) learners. While classes on the main campus are capped at seventeen students, WCMC–Q classes are often no larger than twelve in order to facilitate more one-on-one tutorial work with weaker students and to provide faculty the time to develop new and innovative assignments, course modifications, and teaching strategies to serve this unique student population. Moreover, pre-medical writing faculty offer an additional weekly fifty-minute workshop as part of the course, as well as meet with students individually or in small groups more often than their counterparts in Ithaca.

In view of the low number of Qatari students who are academically ready to face the challenge of pre-medical courses, WCMC–Q created a one-year Foundation Program in fall 2006. At first the program only offered courses in chemistry, biology and physics, but soon it became apparent that one of the main challenges was students' English proficiency, which in some cases did not allow them to understand their English language textbooks. As an immediate solution, a general ESL course was taught in spring 2007, and in August 2007 a new faculty was hired to build the Foundation ESL Program. The ESL program began in the fall of 2007, offering two EAP (English for Academic Purposes) courses, ENGLF 102 and ENGLF 103. The curriculum emphasized students' linguistic and cultural competency, and the two core courses were accompanied by tutorials such as TOEFL: skills and strategies, SAT preparation, academic discussions, and oral presentations. Another addition to the curriculum was the Foundation Summer College Program, a six-week session on the main campus in Ithaca, during which Qatari students took two three-credit courses, an English writing course and a course in bio-scientific terminology, later substituted by a course in philosophy. This experience proved invaluable for the students not only for honing their academic skills, but also for introducing them to the Cornell community and American culture.

Despite these efforts, some Qatari students continued to struggle in the Pre-medical Program and had to be decelerated, possibly due to low English proficiency, since standardized test scores indicated high levels of competence in mathematics and science. In an attempt to modify the pre-medical curriculum, WCMC–Q tried to introduce a three-year track. Consequently, a bridge writing course modeled on Ithaca's bridge Writing Workshop 137/138 was introduced in fall 2009 to prepare students for FYWS. Unfortunately, the idea of a three-year track was subsequently abandoned and the course is no longer offered. The writing faculty feels that all students would benefit from at least one more course in sociology, anthropology, or literature, as well as continued ESL support. For some students, this could be the key to success in the medical education program.

One of the factors that has proved helpful in ensuring the success of the FYWS in Qatar is close cooperation with the main campus. To guarantee that the quality and amount of writing meet the standards of the main campus, the director of the Cornell University FYWS at the Knight Institute acts as course director for WCMC–Q and works closely with the FYWS coordinator in Doha. The course director from Ithaca visits Doha every other semester to review writing faculty performance, observe classroom teaching, and help develop assessments. To further ensure consistency, WCMC–Q writing instructors are evaluated using end-of-semester forms generated by the Knight Institute. Implemented more recently, reciprocal visits of WCMC–Q writing faculty to Ithaca have also proved invaluable. Since WCMC–Q faculty come from different universities—and even different countries—links to Cornell's main campus contribute to fostering unity and cohesiveness in the FYWS program in Qatar.

At the same time, although the identity of FYWS at WCMC–Q remains closely tied to that of the writing program in Ithaca, a number of modifications were introduced to maintain focus on the curriculum's core values in a very different sociocultural context and under specific institutional constraints. The goals and objectives of the program continue to raise questions about the relationship of the seminars to the main campus, where students have over 125 choices for seminars each term within their four-year bachelor's degree program. Given WCMC–Q's restriction of a two-year pre-medical program, the limited option of five seminars at most becomes consequential. While Ithaca has encouraged a structure that is parallel to Qatar's, this mirroring of the main campus can be simplistic, and therefore more difficult to administer and assess. Among future questions, WCMC–Q faculty will need to ask how large a role the humanities, arts, and social sciences will play in a medical degree program.

THOUGHT ESSAY AND CASE STUDY

The following thought piece by Alan Weber and case study by Ian Miller exemplify two of the key challenges that all writing faculty at WCMC–Q face: engaging the Gulf writing student who has been educated in a different pedagogical paradigm, and understanding the relationships that Qatari and Arab expatriate students forge between literature and their own identity. Through a historical, philosophical, and sociological analysis, Weber attempts to delineate the worldviews of the Gulf Arab student and explain how their perceptions might impact their approaches to knowledge, literacy, and the kind of writing expected in FYWS. Miller, in an intimate portrait of the Gulf writing teacher in action, analyzes how the differing approaches that Western and Eastern cultures take to the construction of meaning—as well as the relationship of the self to literature—produce one of the most profoundly challenging issues in teaching literature and writing in the Gulf as a means of self-discovery and self-expression.

Engaging the Gulf Writing Student

Alan S. Weber, Writing Faculty

Western educational paradigms based on Greek philosophical academies and the medieval Quadrivium and Trivium have prospered on the notion of the dialogic mind: the belief that dialogue, *disputatio*, and *dialexis*—the cross-readings and refashionings of authorities—foster the critically inquisitive mind and create new knowledge. Its modern methods—the argumentative persuasive essay, class discussion, writing as discovery, and peer review, for example—have become so ingrained in European and American pedagogy that they often manifest themselves as unproblematic, universal axioms about how we all learn. However, Islamic education, particularly in the Arabian Gulf—which, unlike North Africa and other Muslim nations, has been relatively free of Western cultural influence until the late twentieth century—has developed along its own lines. One of the most salient features of traditional Islamic education is that it is difficult, and certainly not encouraged, to question authorities within a religiously-based curriculum. The discussion below examines the various epistemological and historical factors that have impacted education and intellectual life in the Gulf, and which have resulted in a complex higher education writing classroom where predominantly European and American instructors are teaching a mixture of local Gulf and Asian expatriate students who were previously educated using an extremely diverse high school curricula.

The first and most fundamental sin in Islam is providing companions to Allah, or *shirk*. The abhorrence of polytheism is common in Islamic writings about the *jahaliyya*, or age of ignorance before the revelation of Islam, in which the worship of many gods was closely linked to barbarities such as infanticide. In conservative interpretations of Islam, this creates a curious association of monotheism and monologism with modernity, and diversity and multiplicity with perversion or error, while Western educational paradigms have embraced the modern age as poly-vocal, multicultural, and global. Salafist Islam, the dominant form in Qatar, situates itself as the most radically monotheistic of the Muslim worldviews, in which the principal of *tawhid* or oneness stands at the heart of theological inquiry. *Al Kitab al-Tawhid* is also the name of a com-monly read text by Mohammed Ibn 'Abd al-Wahhab, the eighteenth-century founder of the conservative and puritanical interpretation of Islam called Salafism by its proponents and Wahhabism by its detrac-tors. A version of this book was used as a textbook in the early public schools of Qatar in the 1950s and 1960s, before the introduction of the Egyptian curriculum.

Al-Wahhab has recently lent his name to the new national mosque in Doha, Qatar. His father was a Hanbali scholar, the school of Islamic jurisprudence whose philosophy of law has several important implica-tions for literacy and its followers' relationship with texts and authority. Ahmad ibn Hanbal grounded all knowledge in the Qur'an and pro-phetic tradition (*ahadith*). A related and frequently voiced statement by Qatari WCMC–Q students is that all knowledge can be found in the Qur'an, and there is no reason to doubt the sincerity of this belief, whether it is grounded in a literal or metaphorical understanding of rev-elation. Ibn Hanbal rejected consensus of the faithful (*ijma'*) as a valid method for determining legal questions and knowledge not explicitly spelled out in sacred texts. In addition, he disagreed with the use of *qiyas* or analogies, a common Greek epistemological tool in both ancient and modern inquiry, as a means of achieving certainty.

Thus ibn Hanbal's brand of theology, epistemology, and jurispru-dence emphasized that religious scholars were the only ones truly equipped to interpret scripture, primarily by using the most literal inter-pretations of primary texts. The fact that the first Gulf educational insti-tutions, the *kuttab* schools, followed a similar approach—by employing a banking model of instruction focused on the teacher, as well as empha-sizing memorization and de-emphasizing interpretation—is probably partially related to Hanbali influence in the region.[1] Of course, this reli-gious model of education downplays the role of dialogue and debate in the educational process, since Qur'anic meanings are not negotiated among learners. Obviously this method does not fit in with the scien-tific method of hypothesis-building and justification through evidence, although early scholars such as Al Bukhari—in order to determine the strength and validity of sayings (ahadith) of the Prophet—followed a literary interpretative process of weighing evidence, assessing sources, and examining the context in which the sayings were uttered. These ahadith collections—written by Al Bukhari, Abu Dawood, Sahih Muslim, etc., in the Sunni tradition and Al-Kulayni, Al-Tusi, etc., in the Shia tradition)—have become reified and unquestionable sources of Islamic authority, only rarely subject to further interpretation. Why the powerful religious educational traditions of *kalam* (theology) and Al Bukhari have become so inflexible in the Arabian Gulf has not been adequately answered by educational historians, but a veneration for tradition and the past probably plays an important role.

In addition, political-theological alignments in the modern Gulf, in which conservative monarchies do not allow political debate that challenges the status quo of the ruling families, precludes the kind of participatory and questioning society that is encouraged in Western democracies. Specifically, the rise of the Saud dynasty, which conquered and unified the Arabian peninsula, is generally attributed to an eighteenth century pact between Muhammad bin Saud and Wahhabist sheikhs that continues to this day. In return for fealty and religious justification for bin Saud's violence against other Muslims (by declaring them *kaffirs*, or unbelievers, for not adopting the unitary Wahhabist interpretation of Islam), the Al as-Sheikh family has been granted almost total control over educational institutions in Saudi Arabia and over interpretations of Shari'ah law. Part of the exercise of this political power is the co-opting of the concept of *bid'ah*, or innovation, which originally meant that any new element in Islamic practice that contravened scripture had to be rejected as heresy.

However, the term *innovation* has been subtly extended in conservative Gulf societies to include cultural and political change as well, implying that attacks on any facet of the status quo are equivalent to attacks on Islam itself, since they are "innovations." Thus, "innovations"— Qatar's Education City, for example—are sometimes criticized in national newspapers such as *Al Wataniya* as "unIslamic." Education City students often dress in western clothes, and unmarried males and females intermingle in class (WCMC–Q was the first co-ed university in Qatar). In contrast, Qatar University (the national university) maintains a separate male/female campus and a new student group lobbied for and won an Islamic dress code in 2012. These events, of course, are symbols of a wider feeling of cultural erosion in the face of a majority expatriate population.

Qatar and the United Arab Emirates are internationally unique in that 86% and 91% of the population respectively consists of expatriate workers, who provide the labor that is fueling the recent explosion of infrastructural development in the Gulf.[2] Qataris make up only 6% of the entire labor force in Qatar, and only about 25% of teachers are Qatari nationals. Every government planning document since the late 1990s has warned against the potential erosion of Islamic and Qatari values from this large influx of foreigners, particularly teachers who are in culturally sensitive positions. Furthermore, the Secretary General of the Gulf Cooperation Council has explicitly called non-citizen immigrants, who make up approximately 40–50% of the entire Gulf population, "a security threat."

Thus, the constant and threatening presence of the "other" in their midst has caused a noticeable retreat into an "imagined" unitary Gulf identity (to borrow Benedict Anderson's phrase[3]) of Bedouin heritage. Although, historically, the Gulf has hosted a diverse spectrum of non-Bedouin cultures and peoples—settled pearl traders; manumitted slaves; pirates; oasis-based date farmers and ranchers; and Persian, Balochi, and Indian trading families—Bedouin symbology has now been widely adopted throughout the Gulf as a way to solidify "native" Gulf identity. Some of these familiar symbols include hawking, camels, the *khanjar* (dagger) or sword, the *ardha* war dance, and the *thobe* and *abaya* or its variations. Unlike their cosmopolitan and multilingual neighbors living on the Arabian peninsula littoral—who have traded and interacted with Mesopotamia, Persia, and India for millennia—the interior Bedouins take pride in the simplicity of their customs and material culture, their directness and honesty of way of life, and their unbroken bloodlines, which confer honor and status. They do not mingle with other cultures and rarely marry outside their own tribe (first and second cousin marriage is estimated at 54% in Qatar). Neo-Bedouin identity suits ruling families well, since according to its own mythology it has remained completely free of Western influence, and the lower economic tiers of the Gulf are made up of Bedouin tribes who were sedentarized in the 1950s–1970s; thus, it carries populist appeal.

This imagined native "Bedouinized" identity glosses over the reality of the Gulf's historical transience and its intermixture of peoples. Strict adherence to Sunni Salafist doctrines also provides a common unifying trope for the ruling and high-status tribes of the Arabian Gulf, although, again, this ostensible homogeneity in reality disregards the large Shia and crypto-Shia populations in Bahrain and eastern Saudi Arabia, as well as the fact that most Omanis are Ibadis, a breakaway Kharajite sect that is neither completely Sunni nor Shia in practice. Public discussions about this religious diversity are uncomfortable, and are often sidestepped under a nascent Gulf patriotism that is transform-ing the previously strictly-tribal relations. In addition, the well-attested historical presence of Jewish families in the Gulf—along with Nestorian Christians, Hellenistic Greeks, Hindu Indians, and Zoroastrian Persians (under the pre-Islamic Sassanian dominance of the Gulf)—is minimized in school curricula in the same way that modern descendants of these communities (still living in the Gulf) have become mostly invisible in the media.

Bahrain, Dubai, and now Qatar have recently been opening up their societies toward Western tourists, Western university branch campuses, and expatriate professionals from around the world. However, secular-ism cannot be entertained in the current political climate in the Gulf as a response to multi-ethnic and multi-religious societies, and, in fact, the concepts of diversity and multiculturalism do not exist in national laws, constitutions, or social structures. Furthermore, the *kafala* system of labor law creates a two-tiered system of rights, with immigrants accorded diminished protections from the state. In many ways, clearly Gulf soci-eties represent communities that are yearning for the identity of a uni-fied existence, through de-emphasizing the differences present in their previously-variegated history, and dispensing with the problems of diver-sity and multiculturalism (expatriate workers) by simply not recognizing non-tribal, indigenous elements of their social groupings as belonging to their communities.

What are the practical implications for the writing classroom of this survey of the educational, social, and cultural conditions of the Arabian Gulf? The kuttab tradition of early education, which has continued into Qatar's high school curriculum, makes it difficult for students to interro-gate authorities and establish their own voices in writing. Autumn Watts details below how WCMC–Q students were initially uncomfortable work-ing with peer tutors, having preconceived notions that knowledge could only come from expert authorities. There was also a specific concern for Muslim women in Qatar, since they are socialized to speak in a soft voice and avoid contradicting males, especially male members of their fami-lies. Thus, writing provided an alternate space for them to speak within their culture; and, in the author's experience, women more than Qatari men generally entered the classroom with higher technical writing skills and a distinct voice, since many of them kept private writing diaries.

Challenging an elder person or authority figure in Qatar is discour-aged; however, writing instructors want their students to critique and unpack authority as part of the discovery process. Due to the previously discussed social structure of the Gulf, students can be diffident about engaging "otherness." They may be wary of criticizing others for fear of offending, or they may be unable to grasp the reality that they are living in a multicultural society, since there is so little public discourse about what that actually means. The notion that most Gulf educational systems use a banking model is commonplace among Gulf educators, including both professionals trained in Western as well as Arabic-speaking countries. Thus, when expatriate educators arrive in the Gulf (I must emphasize again that 75% of teachers in Qatar are expatriates) with new educational practices and paradigms such as flipped classrooms, there is bound to be confusion among students about their roles and responsibilities as writers.

The WCMC–Q program is particularly fortunate in that the course director who oversees the FYWS at the Ithaca, New York campus— Katherine Gottschalk—taught at WCMC–Q for one semester. She therefore thoroughly understands the adjustments that must be made to the FYWS within the complex cultural context of Qatar, while still maintaining Cornell standards and expectations. The FYWS are, after all, full credit-bearing Cornell courses.

Although British and American education has touched the Gulf for almost fifty years, due to the students who were sent abroad to complete undergraduate through post-graduate degrees, the impact of Western educational methodologies has only recently been felt, strongly, in the last decade with the opening of Western branch campuses in Qatar, Dubai, Abu Dhabi, and Kuwait, as well as the increasing number of partnerships with American universities. The Gulf is clearly still at the encounter phase with Western educational paradigms. The next decade will determine if the historical and intellectual legacies of Qatar will meld with or accommodate the methodologies of modern American writing instruction—and Western education in general—in the educational experiment known as Education City; or, in a best-case scenario, if they will modify American thinking about writing instruction and programs toward a more inclusive, international set of writing practices.

Cloud of Unknowing: Navigating Cultural Difference

Ian Miller, Writing Faculty

The first essay I assigned the Foundation Writing class at Weill Cornell Medical College in Qatar[4] asked the students to define how our sense of place shapes us as people. The outcomes of the assignment and rubric were clear, but students found the task frustratingly open-ended, although we'd spent two weeks reading a series of essays and stories by modern American writers—Stuart Dybek, Lorrie Moore, and Richard Rodriguez—that examine the subject.

> *"Professor,* you ask us to write about place, but we must choose that place ourselves?"

> "Yes," I said. "Bearing in mind the other writers we read and discussed as examples, I'm asking you to define an important place and analyze the meaning it has for you in accordance with the requirements of the assignment."

> "But what is this meaning?"

> "Yeah," said another. "What do you want us to say?"

> "Well, that's sort of the point. You have to define that meaning for yourself. You need to integrate the ideas we discovered in the texts with your own thoughts, your own sense of history and belonging, the experiences that have made you who you are."

> "But what are the right thoughts?"

> ". . ."

> "Professor, if you tell me what you want me to do then I will do it. I will be successful because I have completed what you have asked. But if not, how do I know I'm finished? How do I know I have done what you have set for me to do? If the path is open, how do I know its end?"

Here's what I believe about the stuff I teach:

1. Writing is a recursive engagement with the scope and force of what it means to be alive.

2. Literature allows us to access the human experience in all its guises of culture, language, tradition, and conflict.

3. Through written engagement with textual content (social, historical, political, and literary), we become more aware of our own experiences and disguises.

4. As a result of this heightened awareness, we're led to an enriched understanding of our own voices and the words we craft into written form.

Reflecting on the flurry of questions received at the outset of that first assignment, I realized that much of the confusion derived not only from my teaching philosophy in practice, but from my own interpretation of self as well. Moreover, I was dealing with a milieu that seemingly approached texts as fixtures not to be critically interrogated. In both the Foundation and the Pre-medical Programs, students—local and international alike, though overwhelmingly Muslim—expressed discomfort at the idea that *readers* define the meaning of a story through close textual analysis. "But what about the writer?" they ask. "Only the writer can know for sure what the story means. Not us."

I don't pretend to grasp the complexity of this disconnect[5], but I believe it has something to do with the fact that the Qur'an, particularly in the Gulf region, is not up for open interpretation—i.e., the text is fixed—*especially* in a public and secular setting, a notion that might color one's approach to the act of explication in general. However, through immersion in reading and written response (personal as well as critical), the propagation of a culture of literacy, and the reformulation of the classroom as a "private space," students can come to accept and enjoy that knowledge in the humanities is emboldened by the collaborative spirit that resides between the artist and the scholar-reader.

In Donald Barthelme's riotous short story, "A Manual for Sons," the author of the manual (the instructor, in fact) states, "Fathers are teachers of the true and not-true, and no father ever knowingly teaches what is not true. In a cloud of unknowing, then, the father proceeds with his instruction."[6] Without suggesting that I enact or fulfill some latent patriarchal role as writing instructor, I do—however blindly—try to reach a modicum of truth within myself about what I do and do not want to share with my students. In my mind, an essential element of critical thinking, as problematized as that term has become in education, is what I call sense-making: when students take an object (a text) and interpret it in such a way (e.g., discussing what others have said about similar objects in dissimilar contexts—say, a psychoanalytical reading of a postcolonial text) that new meaning is created, a dialectical exercise that questions strictly binary thinking about authorship, ownership of meaning, and the production of narrative.[7]

Yet, like Barthelme's fathers, I must weigh this truth (or *view* of a truth) in my own cloud of unknowing, which in Qatar is compounded by the gulf between my own cultural understanding of self—a jambalaya of George Berkeley, Emmanuel Lévinas, Bert Hellinger, psychoanalysis, and twentieth century American literature—and the familial and religious processes with which many of my students self-identify.[8] Additionally, since I teach writing as an examination between self and story, wherein students synthesize narrative material into analytical thought and written argument/analysis, how the self perceives the story—textual and/ or ideational—is fundamental to the writing process. The challenge of a cross-cultural classroom lies in the myriad of perspectives, histories, epistemological matrices, and social competencies—in a word, the *stories* I cannot readily access due to cultural distance.

Of all the distances between my students—as a general collective— and myself, the most pronounced involved the way they tended to self-identify along lines of family and religion versus any particular school of political thought or secular philosophy. My self-perception is inextricably tangled with my liberal arts education, whereas a number of my students, particularly the boys—who often arrived at WCMC–Q from high school science curriculums that emphasized rote memorization of facts and information disembodied from concepts—may have only read a handful of books in their lives (usually less, sometimes none) before taking my writing seminar. In these cases, the idea of, say, explicating a film beyond the image momentarily flashed upon the screen is utterly foreign.[9]

To initially navigate the cultural and educational divide, I immersed students in a culture of literacy, a heavy regimen of reading and writing. I wish I had a less colonial and more sophisticated answer to offer. Simply, I demanded *a lot* of intake and production. On the first day of class I provided every student with a Moleskine journal, explaining that they could expect up to eighty pages of reading a week, with two to three specified journal assignments that were collected and graded bimonthly,[10] as well as six critical essays over the course of the semester. "The idea," I said, tautologically, "is to read as you write and write as you read." In a reflective letter, one student, who'd struggled at the outset but was ultimately successful, described how in the beginning "it was so hard . . . I lost hope . . . [but] just a few weeks later I found myself deeply integrated into the course. I started understanding and going deeply into field I never even knew it existed [*sic*]. I started to learn how to analyze a book. Previously I would only read for entertainment, but now it means more to me."

After four years at WCMC–Q, the "Moleskine" is as infamous as it is revered, a rite of passage students routinely praise as much as they bemoan. And it works. Many of these kids have never written much of anything by hand, which is a different type of writing than doing so on a computer. By nature, hand writing is more personal, tactile and spontaneous, less rehearsed, and more responsive. Students take a bit of time to get used to it, but once they do they assume real ownership of the process. The Moleskine becomes a running diary of what they're learning in the seminar, as well as a place to reflect on their first year in college.[11] Obviously, the Moleskine also provided me with an opportunity to better understand the stories of these students, their feelings about family, religion, and education, as well as how they were finding their way within the body of the course.

As if by osmosis, the more students read as they wrote and wrote as they read, the more they began to understand and appreciate the reciprocal relationship between a reader and a writer, and that sense-making exists in the gap between the binary of audience and author. The immersion into a culture of literacy works much in this way: exposure breeds familiarity breeds critical distance breeds introspection. My seminars go on to postulate the following:[12]

1. We understand our lives and the condition of our living through story.

2. By interacting with the narratives of others—via reading, writing, listening, and watching—we enhance our empathic ability to recognize and respond to the common humanity shared by all.

3. We create narratives to provide meaning to events and experiences, which thus lends basis to the promotion or criticism of any given action.

Story runs the world. Story is an argument that enables students to explore how human values and actions are subject to a slew of situational, historical, and political influences. As a result, students appreciate the world in larger, more flexible and tolerant terms, a perspective that allows them to better contextualize their own values and actions with regard to others.

In addition, I gave my students a series of assignments and readings that spoke to questions of family and religion, topics deeply relevant to their lives. What do these terms signify? How do they work? What does it mean to be an individual and yet still belong to a family as much as a religion? How do these tensions shape our decisions, our judgments? What are the consequences of our belief systems? By what template do we initiate or justify action? Finally, how do these questions manifest, complicate, and resolve (or not) themselves in literature? Now, cultural and religious sensitivities dictate that certain queries must be broached cautiously. For instance, the concept of God in society (even the concept of God as a concept) or gender roles in the family, issues at once engaging and resonant for students, are also taboo. To accomplish this task, I billed our classroom as a private community, a safe space where students could openly converse and where ideas were kept within the confines of that space. I adhered to a strict policy of confidentiality, which gave the necessary symbolic illusion that students could freely discuss what was already on their minds. In a society where face and reputation are the strongest units of currency, students needed to be assured that, as far as the outside world is concerned, "What happens in Miller's seminar stays in Miller's seminar."

By integrating a culture of literacy with issues of authorship, self-identity, and the prescribed outcomes of the FYWS—coupled with a "private" classroom—students had the opportunity to publicly investigate their lives in an academic setting, a wholly new and refreshing experience for many educated in rote systems of learning. While the students found the course intellectually stimulating and personally relevant, they also helped me adjust for my own cultural disconnects and points of unknowing. And though it's difficult to schematize and assess what I've learned from my students in objective terms (it's a lot), the process of our discourse certainly works both ways. The semester will usually begin with most, if not all, the material and discussion points presented by me. However, after a few weeks, several hundred pages of reading, and a dozen Moleskine assignments, students begin to take ownership of both the material and the discussion. They begin to produce the dialogue, projecting their thoughts, feelings, and critical assessments onto the texts as a way to formulate a new understanding of a short story, novel, film, or poem. Approaching the demands of their assignments with rigor, armed with textual evidence, and emboldened by a burgeoning ability to critically investigate constructions of identity, self, and otherness, students abandon notions of right answers and successful completions and instead strive to create meaning for themselves.

Constructing a Culturally Intelligible Writing Center

Autumn Watts, Former Writing Center Coordinator

Any university typically requires student assimilation into academic culture. The student must learn how to write, think, argue, and behave according to certain norms. As a foreign institution within a hosting culture, however, WCMC–Q's student and faculty acculturation must be more reciprocal. The university model is also a transnationally familiar one. The layout of the room, the role of the instructor and the student—all of these share certain embedded norms that make a "classroom" intelligible to all participants. The performance of the roles of "student" and "professor" arise from historical understandings that comprise the common paradigm of education.

Conversely, while writing centers have existed for some time in US higher education, in the Middle East and North Africa (MENA) region they remain a very recent innovation, although the Middle East-North Africa Writing Centers Alliance (MENAWCA) was formed in 2007 with a newsletter and bi-annual conference to facilitate writing center professional development. However, writing centers are less well-narrated than classrooms in the MENA region, and therefore less intelligible. There are fewer base norms to draw upon; function, purpose, and practice must be invented and reiterated until absorbed within the university culture. For example, collaborative learning and peer tutoring—the heart of writing center practice—are culturally-specific models. They must be adapted, not transplanted, from the origin to the hosting environment. If "student" and "professor" are familiar, normalized roles, "consultant" and "client" remain shifting and negotiable. The writing center of WCMC–Q therefore exists within multiple overlapping contexts: a writing center within a US medical school within Qatar, and within a greater education movement throughout the Middle East.

I began my position as the writing center coordinator in 2007, and found myself confronted with a writing center that saw very few visitors. An early survey of the students revealed they associated the writing center with "bad" writers who needed help from someone else: a double stigma. Moreover, few students or faculty outside the writing program understood what a writing center could offer, and how it could help them.

While such challenges are universally common to writing center work, especially in the MENA context, overcoming them meant articulating the writing center in a way that would cross-culturally define and communicate its purpose. This entailed answering the following questions: Who uses, or doesn't use, the writing center, and why? What does "getting help" mean? How is the center understood within diverse perspectives? How is it understood within mine? What are the gaps between these understandings? I considered, for example, how even my gender might impact the writing center. Should my door remain open (for respectability in a Muslim culture) or closed (for face-saving privacy) during a session? Rather than expecting students to adapt to and embrace writing center services, I realized I needed to learn how the writing center could adapt to and embrace the clients I hoped to serve. I had to learn how to make the writing center visible and productive, assimilated and intelligible.

This adaptation entailed revamping the positive image of the writing center and de-stigmatizing its services. However, the students—many of whom arrived from a vastly different education model—remained reluctant to visit. Unfamiliar with writing center philosophy, they believed they should only ask for help from their professor, the perceived authority. Instead of working collaboratively with a writing tutor to define their work and ideas, students were trained to seek the "right" answer from their teachers, as is common in hierarchical, top-down educational models, which emphasize memorization of facts and form the most common education model in Qatar's government-funded Arabic schools. Opening up the writing center to support staff and faculty as well as students helped redefine that association. Gradually, students began to perceive the writing center as a space for feedback, discussion, and continuing growth, rather than a "fix it shop" for weak writing.

The biggest challenge, however, was initiating a peer tutoring program. This challenge arose from several factors. Students were less comfortable seeking help from peers and distrusted their credibility— indeed, one of my writing center colleagues in Qatar reported disbanding a peer tutoring program due to a lack of interest.[13] In addition, the accelerated premedical program meant that our students at WCMC–Q often had less free time and a more intensive class schedule than a typical American university student. Consequently, peer tutoring was perceived as an extracurricular activity without capital for their future goals in medicine. In short, attracting tutors also meant illuminating the merit of the work itself and its alignment with doctorly values—ethics, patience, empathy, and serving the community.

I finally arrived at a decentralized "peer consultant" program, offering fixed walk-in hours as well as flexible by-arrangement appointments: held anytime, including weekends and evenings, and anywhere, including the dorms, the library, or on Skype. Like their North American counterparts, the peer consultants received extensive training to cultivate their tutoring skills as well as the philosophy and ethics of writing center practice, with a strong emphasis on cultural competence and ESL learning. Involving the peer consultants as collaborators encouraged agency and investment in their work, leading to increased commitment, professional growth, and fresh innovations. They have pioneered initiatives such as the "Adopt a Class" program, and they conduct personalized outreach for a particular course or upcoming assignment. Peer consultants also maintain a Facebook page and design and lead their own writing workshops. Perhaps most importantly, they energetically promote the writing center among their classmates and often lead by example, visibly embracing the services themselves. As peer consultants are renowned for high academic achievement, such modeling has greatly contributed to renovating the writing center image within the student body, and has seeded a culture of peer learning that continues to flourish.

Ironically, my attempts to change student attitudes toward the writing center merely replicated the very same top-down model I sought to challenge. Only when I invited and trusted the peer tutors to engage their classmates and produce their own culture of peer learning did our program finally thrive. Like a third cousin, what we have arrived at bears little resemblance to our origin campus in Ithaca, New York, and even less to its hosting models. Instead, I think it offers a synthesis of qualities from both contexts, one that embodies what I believe are the foremost core values of writing center work: collaborating, eliciting, listening, and empowering.

Toward Creating a Literacy Culture in Qatar

Rodney Sharkey and Alan S. Weber, Writing Faculty

As part of our wider aim at WCMC–Q, writing faculty are engaged in a number of activities that promote the notion of a literacy culture, both absorbing and producing language and literature in a reflective and creative way. Reading literacy is a recent phenomenon in Qatar, due to the late introduction of public education in the 1950s, and even today it is rare to see a Qatari reading a book, magazine, or newspaper outside of a university setting. Instead, Qatar has developed an elaborate oral culture, now facilitated by the cell phone and exemplified by the social custom of the *majlis*, where men gather in a salon and orally exchange news, poetry, and stories while simultaneously instructing younger boys in culture and religion. The majlis of an important sheikh also has a political dimension concerning tribal decisions. Women engage in similar informal, gender-segregated gatherings. Also, in the pre-oil era, local cultures were focused primarily on survival in the harsh desert environment, and—outside of orally transmitted folktales and Bedouin poetry—there is only a negligible and very recent Qatari literary/visual arts tradition. Orally recited poetry, however, is highly esteemed and cultivated. Some of the initiatives to create a literacy culture are relatively straight forward, such as establishing a robust and popular debate club through which students meet twice weekly and debate a wide variety of current affairs and/or philosophical topics. Debate is a particularly effective way of providing a voice for young women in the Gulf region, and also helps students understand the principles of dialectics.

Publication initiatives involve printing selections of WCMC–Q student essays in hard- and soft-bound copy. Students are invited to submit a favored essay to a bi-annual competition where the winning essay is selected by a panel of FYWS faculty at the main campus in Ithaca, New York. Subsequently, a collection of the best essays is published in a handsome volume. To date, three volumes of *Qira'at: Essays from the Students of Weill Cornell Medical College – Qatar* have been published. The process teaches students the importance of revision, reflection, and rewriting, as well as the arduous process of preparing writing for professional publication. WCMC–Q medical and pre-medical students have the strongest record of any other Qatar university in winning national essay contests, and students are increasingly serving as co-authors with faculty on peer-reviewed professional articles.

The writing center also produces an annual collection of creative writing entitled *Between Seminar Rooms*, in which students present their poetry, short stories, and more general literary musings for the delectation of their peers. Further initiatives include an annual literary lecture series, in which faculty present a lecture on an area of interest and/or expertise to the college and the general public alike. There are also very generous research grants available from the Qatar Foundation to assist student research in all areas of intellectual enquiry, and often students undertake language-related research with these grants. For example, books have been produced on concepts such as narrative medicine in Qatar and the positive role the humanities plays in consolidating the character of professional doctors.

Finally, at the commencement of learning each fall term, and in an annual campus-to-campus gesture, WCMC–Q and Cornell University participate in the New Student Reading Project, where freshmen read a nominated book and attend campus-wide readings and accompanying lectures. In such diverse ways, writing faculty at Weill Cornell Medical College in Qatar continually attempt to foster and promote a vibrant and rewarding literacy culture for our students.

Notes

1. See Ian Miller's section below for direct evidence in Qatar of modern first-year college students' difficulties—due to their previous government school education—in adapting to American-style education, which emphasizes independent learning and personal ownership of knowledge.

2. For more information on the relationship between Arabian Gulf economic development, the labor market, and education, see Alan S. Weber, "Education, Development and Sustainability in Qatar: A Case Study of Economic and Knowledge Transformation in the Arabian Gulf," in *Education for a Knowledge Society in Arabian Gulf Countries*, ed. Alexander W. Wiseman, Naif H. Alromi, and Saleh Alshumrani, International Perspectives on Education and Society 24 (Bradford, UK: Emerald Group Publishing Limited, 2014), 59–82.

3. Benedict Anderson first advanced the concept of "imagined communities" in his 1983 book *Imagined Communities: Reflections on the Origin and Spread of Nationalism*, and his theories have been critiqued fruitfully in sociology and literary studies.

4. Although I now teach the FYWS—wherein the practice of writing is often approached through the study of literature, and classes are populated by local and international premedical students with varying analytical and linguistic skills—I spent my first two semesters at WCMC–Q teaching in the Foundation Program, the equivalent of pre-college courses in basic science and English. Foundation students are predominantly Qatari, and are graduates of government and "independent" high schools, where the medium of instruction has been assessed (most notably by the RAND Corporation)

as quite poor by international standards. Moreover, there exists little to no uniformity in secondary education.

5.   See Dr. Alan Weber's section, "Engaging the Gulf Writing Student," for a situational and historical compendium on the matter.

6.   Donald Barthelme, *Sixty Stories* (New York: Penguin Books, 2003), 245.

7.   While I recognize my pedagogical approach as ethnocentric to my training in the United States, one of WCMC–Q's objectives is to deliver an American higher education in Qatar, ideally no different than what students would receive at the home campuses in New York.

8.   Again, see Dr. Alan Weber.

9.   Due to the excessive heat and prevalence of shopping malls with multiplexes, movies are the most widely disseminated form of secular narrative in the Gulf, thus providing a ready foray into ways of talking about story.

10.   A crosscut of actual Moleskine prompts: (1) "How does CG Jung 'prove' the existence of the collective unconscious, and how does he differentiate his theory from Freud's? (one page)" (2) "As you watch *The Dark Knight* this weekend, I want you to meditate on the following: How might a mask at once *mask* a person's identity while concurrently revealing one's essence? Can masks be physically false but psychologically true? If masks subvert and thereby expose the illusion of appearances, can masks then work to unmask reality—and, if so, what in the world does that mean? (four pages)." Naturally, the Moleskine serves as an excellent opportunity for prewriting. Thesis statements, claims, instances of textual evidence, and points of analysis routinely spring from Moleskine responses.

11.   I routinely find pictures and more personal entries—notes to friends or letters to the self—which I encourage them to produce, but with the understanding that I respect those parts of the journal as private.

12.   Remember, this is a medical college, and empathy—as a concept, experience, and response—should be integral to a physician's training.

13.   We were fortunate in a small country like Qatar to have considerable dialogue among writing center directors (facilitated also by MENAWCA), and we were able to learn from each other's programs, initiatives, and mistakes.

4

ADAPTATION ACROSS SPACE AND TIME
Revealing Pedagogical Assumptions

Danielle Zawodny Wetzel and
Dudley W. Reynolds

A TRANSNATIONAL PARTNERSHIP

In 2004, the Carnegie Mellon University (CMU) administration in Pittsburgh signed an agreement with the Qatar Foundation, promising they would build together a branch campus in Doha, Qatar for two specific undergraduate programs: business and computer science.[1] The Qatar Foundation's goal was to build in one area, called "Education City," a variety of programs from top universities in the United States. Education City was to be a hub of "American-style" education, comprised of programs from Virginia Commonwealth University, Texas A&M University, Weill Cornell Medical College, Georgetown University's School of Foreign Service, and Northwestern University. Students who graduated from programs at Carnegie Mellon in Qatar would receive the same diploma as those students graduating from Carnegie Mellon in Pittsburgh. The instruction, faculty were told, was to be "the same" between campuses, and the 2011–2012 CMU "Factbook" states that both campuses hold "the same standards and curriculum" (Carnegie Mellon University 2011, 11).

Without question, this agreement with the Qatar Foundation presented new and profound challenges for CMU faculty. The university had planted graduate programs in a variety of places around the world, so the notion of internationalizing the university's brand was not a new one. However, this time the university was taking on the enterprise (and responsibility) of building an authentic, Carnegie Mellon *undergraduate* experience. In addition to the academic major programs, this experience was to include metacurricular programming, academic advising, professionalization, career counseling, and—of course—the first-year

DOI: 10.7330/9780874219623.c004

writing, general education course. Overnight, CMU's one required writing course in Pittsburgh went global.

The purpose of our work here is to provide a record of curricular adaptation and change within a transnational writing program in order to more broadly consider decision making across campuses and in a global university context. Methodologically, we also use our course materials as a lens by which to reflect on our work as pedagogues and teachers. By examining how these materials change over just a few years, we can ask (1) what kinds of changes have occurred and (2) what, if anything, those changes teach us. As writing program administrators, pursuing these questions enables valuable reflection on what we choose to change or keep constant, and, perhaps most importantly, why we change. For us, alterations in our course materials demonstrated how influence and change can be motivated from a variety of rhetorical forces that shape a transnational writing program.

For those interested in the globalization of higher education and accountability within a university system, we provide an account of how a program's shifting boundaries can influence writing program structures, faculty, and students. For example, the global context influenced CMU–Pittsburgh to dedicate more resources to teaching English to multilingual students by funding courses and building an infrastructure for supplemental instructors. In exploring the global university context, we draw upon institutionalist organizational theory to explain how some writing program changes suggest that movement toward conformity can be motivated by a need to meet academic norms, and, perhaps, by a need for credibility and legitimacy. We also discuss how variation within the curriculum highlights perceptions of students' needs within each campus context. But variation can be a tricky concept in any writing program, as discourses of accountability and standardization trigger a move toward conformity rather than variation. From our perspective, accountability need not lead to homogeneity, but rather to a rational account or justification of commonalities and differences.

In this chapter, we first provide some contextual background about the two campuses and explain how the Doha campus shaped opportunities for multilingual students on the Pittsburgh campus. Second, we describe some of the changes we have observed in teaching materials from both campuses, changes toward both convergence and difference. We use these changes as evidence for theorizing transnational WPA as a rhetorically dynamic, organizational process that is shaped by a variety of influences, including university policy, context-specific factors, and disciplinary knowledge.

We assume that, within a transnational program, writing program administrators should expect—and welcome—influence and change from all sites where writing instruction occurs. By expecting a dialogic exchange of practices and ideas, perhaps we can begin to move away from what Donahue (2009, 212) has called the "import/export" model of internationalizing writing pedagogy. We have learned—by reflecting on the CMU–Doha/CMU–Pittsburgh events and the First-Year Writing course materials—that influence in transnational education is not deterministic, moving in one direction only. Rather, influence is a negotiated, dynamic process that can originate from both campuses.

INTERNATIONALIZATION, MULTILINGUALISM, AND COMPOSITION

In the era of the global university, we struggle to locate ourselves within a contentious discourse that highlights the greed of the corporate university and the colonial reach of Westernized literacy practices. Some higher education and composition researchers have critiqued "internationalization" and "transnational education" as simply a vocabulary trick that masks the corporate university's attempt to globalize an institutional brand and ultimately create revenue (Donahue 2009; Wilkins and Huisman 2012). Some higher education administrators—including the CMU provost, who signed the original contract with the Qatar Foundation—claim that the motivation for globalizing university programs is not only to expand an institutional presence, but also to bring new collaborations and opportunities for research and learning to the source campus (Kamlet 2010, 83).

Other concerns relate to the colonial reach of the West. For example, internationalizing the teaching of English may encourage linguistic hegemony and imperialism, as well as weaken local languages (Pennycook 1994). The move to globally extend the teaching of English writing might diminish "other" literacy practices in cultures outside of the United States (Donahue 2009, 214). These arguments appear not only in academic publications, but also in more popular ones (Phillipson 2012). Some literature documents the notion of English as an important commodity—and the pedagogical complications associated with that kind of ideology—as students and teachers become driven by English language testing (Reichelt 2005). Suresh Canagarajah warns us that we might fail to think of English as "a plural language that embodies multiple norms and standards. English should be treated as a multinational language, one that belongs to diverse communities and not owned only by the metropolitan communities" (Canagarajah 2006, 589). Of course, even in his own argument for the pluralization of English within the teaching of composition, Canagarajah reminds us that such practice is difficult to negotiate as we balance the need to accommodate readers with students' goals and perceptions of their own languages and identities.

Given these perspectives on institutional agendas, the globalization of American education, and the privileging of a Western view of language and literacy, we acknowledge that there are several competing concerns that shape the first-year writing program in Doha and Pittsburgh. Some of these concerns relate to maintaining CMU's educational brand within a global context, and some relate to maintaining disciplinary norms and practices. Globally, these concerns should enable reflective practice for our pedagogies, but we are also aware of the fact that these concerns can paralyze instruction, confining decisions to circles of endless critique on the language and literacy practices we choose to teach. In order to help us move away from an unproductive use of these concerns, writing program administrators should view English and any "language practice" as a resource (Brandt 2001; Horner, Lu, Royster, and Trimbur 2011, 397; You 2006, 200). Additionally, as Deb Brandt (2001) explains, we must challenge ourselves to consider the contexts that shape how and why individuals acquire various literacies:

> To treat literacy as a resource is to emphasize that it takes its shape from what can be traded on it. This perspective attends to the competitions that surround literacy, the struggles to harness it for profit or ideological advantage, the struggles for the prerogative to manage or measure it, and the ways that these incessant struggles set the terms for individual encounters with literacy. Above all, this perspective emphasizes the instability of literacy, its links to political and economic changes and to the shifting standards of value and conditions of access that accompany those changes. (7)

If English language and literacy can be seen as tools or resources, then it is our obligation as writing program directors to facilitate conditions that will not simply impose structures, but rather shape our students' abilities to use language and literacy practices to achieve their own goals. These goals will enable our students to consider what their literacy education will help them achieve. This perspective requires an adaptive and flexible view of curriculum, so students' needs and local contexts in Qatar can shape any First-Year Writing "brand" agenda from Pittsburgh. This adaptive understanding of curriculum is important for our progression beyond viewing the composition course as a gatekeeper and toward what Yancey (2004, 306) has called the "gateway," a necessary change since composition has been historically rooted as a "rite of linguistic passage" for students who wish to continue in the university (Kaufer and Zawodny Wetzel 2014). For the first-year writing course to be a gateway toward expert knowledge making and authoring practices that are meaningful to students, the instruction must be structured in a way that allows teachers to meet unfolding needs within their unique, situated, rhetorical contexts.

DIFFERENT LANGUAGE AND LEARNING CONTEXTS FOR CARNEGIE MELLON

We design our courses as responses to our students' needs and institutional contexts; therefore, we explain a few particularities between CMU in Doha and in Pittsburgh. The most obvious differences between CMU–Pittsburgh and CMU–Doha are language and campus size. In Pittsburgh, most undergraduates claim that English is their stronger, sometimes only, language. Therefore, multilingual students in Pittsburgh face what we have called an "English as Second Language" (ESL) context. In Doha, multilingualism is the norm among students. All students use at least two languages, sometimes more. Doha students live in what is traditionally called an "English as Foreign Language" (EFL) or World Englishes context, and, for most of these students, English is not their stronger language. While multilingual students in Pittsburgh can expect to attend class with many students who speak only English, in Doha, multilingual students attend class with only other multilingual students.

In addition to language disparities, campus size and context differs significantly. In Pittsburgh, the university enrolls as many graduate students as it enrolls undergraduates. Currently the CMU–Pittsburgh campus enrolls roughly 1,410–1,450 freshmen students. Roughly 17% of the undergraduate population is international, and an increasing number of students declare themselves as "nonnative" English speakers on their applications for university admission. The majority of multilingual students who attend CMU–Pittsburgh hail from Asian countries such as China, India, and South Korea. Many Pittsburgh undergraduates bring multilingual resources to the campus, but their academic reading and writing education has occurred within the United States or within a US-centric school outside of the United States.

Conversely, CMU–Doha now enrolls roughly 100 freshmen each year, and currently there are no graduate education programs. Not unsurprisingly, many of the students who enroll at CMU–Doha are Qatari. Slightly more students come from expatriate families living in Doha, and a small number are international students (meaning that they typically completed high school outside of Qatar and live in dormitories). These students bring another kind of diversity, as many come from countries like Egypt, Pakistan, and India, where English is just one of many languages. Thus, in Doha, all of the students bring rich multilingual resources to the campus. While Pittsburgh undergraduates represent a variety of educational experiences, the Qatar students demonstrate a more diverse range of academic reading and writing backgrounds.

These linguistic and contextual differences are important to note because they shape the material and political conditions of faculty work, as well as the teaching materials we create. The agreement between the Qatar Foundation and CMU mandated an equivalent educational experience for students in Doha and Pittsburgh. However, the very different student groups and their linguistic and educational backgrounds suggest that equivalency is a problematic concept. Just as Matsuda, Ortmeier-Hooper, and You (2006, viii) have argued for the importance of noting the political contexts that shape the teaching of second language writers in our programs, we assume these features are worth noting not just as points for comparison, but also for recognizing various agendas and concerns that shape university policy and curricula. We have provided this very brief account of the different campus contexts in order to prime some of the later discussion about curriculum, especially concerning difference.

IDENTIFYING CHANGE AND INFLUENCE
IN DOHA AND PITTSBURGH

Using Doha to Argue for Curricular Change in Pittsburgh

Here we discuss one of the clearest examples of influence that Doha had upon Pittsburgh, and how Doha became an argument for change in Pittsburgh. Because of Doha's influence, multilingual students—and their writing—became more visible in Pittsburgh, not just within the first-year writing program but also within the university's structure. Until 2006, when CMU opened its doors in Doha, Qatar, there was no regularly-funded first-year writing course for undergraduate multilingual students in Pittsburgh, nor was there any systematic course placement process for students. Doha triggered a shift in Pittsburgh: the university recognized its second language writers in Pittsburgh by funding a dedicated composition course as well as a placement process.

This change in course offerings between the two campuses did not just "happen" in an ad hoc manner. Instead, stakeholders on the Pittsburgh campus used the emergent Qatar campus as an opportunity to argue for change. When the academic departments were approached to make a schedule of classes for the Qatar campus, the former heads of the Departments of English and of Modern Languages rallied to explain how multilingual students in Qatar would need some version of an ESL academic writing course. They used this event as an opportunity to show how far behind the university's policies were in addressing the curriculum needs for multilingual students in Pittsburgh. Since the charge was that the educational experience between CMU–Pittsburgh and CMU–Doha should be "the same," they argued that multilingual students in Pittsburgh should get the same attention that multilingual students in Doha receive (Tucker 2012).

What has resulted since the Doha campus opened is that the First-Year Writing Program in the Department of English now offers a regularly funded course for multilingual students in Pittsburgh. Moreover, there is now an online placement process that incoming students must complete before arriving on campus, which is connected to the advising structure of the university. All instructors within the First-Year Writing Program have also been exposed to additional training about multilingual students' potential needs within the writing classroom. This change in the Pittsburgh course offerings has led to a number of new connections among campus units, which are invested in the educational trajectories of these multilingual students. Overall, the addition of this one course and its placement process has raised the visibility of multilingual students in Pittsburgh, based on the assumption that good practices in Doha would be good practices in Pittsburgh. Influence from the Doha campus enabled Pittsburgh to "catch up."

Using Doha to Argue for Enhanced Course Structure

Just as the Doha campus helped Pittsburgh's multilingual students become more visible, it also supported arguments for enhancing the second language writing pedagogy within the first-year program. As we stated earlier, the rapid growth on the Doha campus led to a situation in which Dudley Reynolds needed to respond quickly to emerging needs. For example, Dudley changed the course's structure to boost the amount of feedback that students received on their reading and writing, as well as to make more time in the course for that feedback to occur. Between 2007 and 2009, the following changes occurred:

- The number of course units or hours per week changed from nine to twelve.
- The number of days per week the course met changed from three to four.
- The number of people providing instruction per section changed from one to four.

In 2008, the 76100 course became a twelve-unit course and met four times per week. There was a lead instructor, a supplemental instructor handling discussion sections, and two course assistants who were undergraduate students on campus. Thus, the total number of individuals involved in providing feedback was four. Two days per week were taught by a lead instructor and were dedicated to teaching about reading texts and the academic discourse features that should appear in students' writing. Two days per week were taught by a supplemental instructor and were dedicated to a small group discussion (eight to ten students) of the course readings. By fall 2009, the number of students and the workload for faculty had grown enough to require that nine individuals deliver the twelve-unit course. Two were lead instructors (regular teaching faculty), three were supplemental (experienced teachers with master's degrees), and four were undergraduate course assistants. Dudley reshaped the structure of the 76100 course to make more room for reading discussion and to accommodate shifting enrollments and staffing possibilities.

Similar to the argument discussed in the last section, this enhanced structure in Doha's courses opened up rhetorical space for a familiar argument in Pittsburgh: how could CMU–Pittsburgh's multilingual students have fewer opportunities and less support than multilingual students in Doha? Once again, Doha enabled Pittsburgh to argue for teaching assistants who could provide additional, individualized feedback and conferencing within the course. Change in Doha, paired with the university's collaboration with the Qatar Foundation, prompted a request for change in Pittsburgh. In two very concrete ways, the argument for equivalency between the educational experiences in Doha and Pittsburgh served as a mechanism for triggering change for Pittsburgh's multilingual students. Based on these changes in Pittsburgh, we can say that influence within a transnational program need not flow from the "main" campus only, but rather should be constructed through dynamic, negotiated interactions.

ARTICULATING SIMILAR BUT DIFFERENT INSTRUCTIONAL
PRIORITIES IN DOHA AND PITTSBURGH

In the previous section we discussed how, for larger curriculum and resource decisions, the "sameness" argument was a tool for raising the visibility and meeting the needs of multilingual students in Pittsburgh. In this section, we suspend this discussion to examine aspects of 76100 course materials from 2007 to 2010 in order to identify points of similarity and difference between the campuses. In other words, while the previous section outlined the ways in which the programs in Doha and Pittsburgh became similar, this section describes some ways that the programs—particularly within the 76100 course—needed to be different. Because of the public nature of syllabus documents, how we express our course objectives can raise tensions if administrators interpret the educational process as appearing different rather than "the same" between our campuses. Our unofficial guide however, was a statement made by former English Department Head David Kaufer at a campus Communication Symposium in June 2008, and repeated by our Vice-Provost for Education Amy Burkert at the 2012 Communication Symposium: "We need to be the same, except when we need to be different." We have interpreted this statement for FYW to mean that our goals are stable but the means to achieve those goals will most likely vary with the needs in our local contexts.[2] Our approach is consistent with what WPA research has shown us—creating standards across multiple sections and teachers of writing is a complex task (Carter-Tod 2007), especially in a global university context.

Because we did author (independently) these course materials, we acknowledge that our ability to distance our own personal stakes from these materials is somewhat constrained. However, our experiences with these materials—in both designing and teaching them—do not disqualify us from using them as evidence for an argument about change and adaptation in a writing program. Since these materials are now part of our history, we can distance ourselves (although not entirely) from them for the purpose of analysis and reflection.

We examined syllabi, major writing assignments, and rubrics from our course 76100 Reading and Writing in an Academic Context. We wanted to use these documents mainly because they communicate, both to students and to the larger university context, the instructional design of the course, its major activities and assessments. We read the materials closely and looked for changes in several key areas, including course objectives, writing assignments and rubrics, and assigned readings. We also looked for changes in how we represented language in these documents, in order to explore whether we emphasized any particular language ideology throughout the four years. From this, we noted that the admissions profile for multilingual students in Pittsburgh has been quite stable, whereas a lot of change has occurred in Doha since the inaugural class.

Prioritizing Students' Needs in Course Objectives

While the overall goals of the First-Year Writing Program provide a structure for some conformity between the Doha and Pittsburgh campuses, there are obviously differences between the programs, especially regarding how the teachers frame and deliver their courses. The overall goal at CMU–Pittsburgh is to provide students with the authoring practices that enable them to build new consensual knowledge in a community of experts. This goal is one that holds the courses together, regardless of variation in context-specific objectives or assignments. Because all students in 76100 will eventually enroll in 76101, the curricular relationship between the two courses must be a tight one. While we acknowledge the influence of 76101 in the two-course sequence for multilingual students, in this section we outline the range of specific course objectives in only the 76100 courses on both campuses.

The course objectives—written between 2007 and 2010—demonstrate that the Doha course shifted toward reading instruction and analysis more than teaching writing processes (see table 4.1). However, the Pittsburgh course remained consistently focused on teaching reading and writing as an integrated priority within 76100, as the objectives suggest. By 2010, the objectives of the Doha 76100 course prioritized reading and analysis over writing. In particular, the course emphasized externalizing reading and analysis practices to build a metacognitive awareness of reading. In fact, the third objective (communication) could refer to multiple modes of expression, including oral and written communication. These objectives from 2010 in Doha are reproduced below:

In *Reading and Writing for Academic Contexts* we will work on three broad areas:

1. Developing expertise on issues through reading

2. Analyzing the construction and usage of written texts

3. Communicating what we are learning about objectives 1 and 2

This shift toward framing the course more in terms of academic reading with some writing was the most defining adaptation within the

Doha course. The shift occurred because of Dudley's concern about students' lack of exposure to academic texts in their high school backgrounds, as well as a concern that they needed a larger discussion component in the course that would help them unpack the significance of their reading. Dudley also hoped to build upon what appears to be, for most of the Doha students, a strength—their discussion skills. He wanted them to understand how discussion relates to learning. The decision to change from meeting three days per week to four days per week enabled more discussion.

Table 4.1 shows the 76100 course objectives as they evolved in the course syllabi between 2007 and 2010. While the overall goal for the first-year program states that students should learn how to become a contributing author within an academic community, the students in Doha and Pittsburgh brought various resources and educational experiences with them. While the students in Doha excelled at discussing and expressing their views together, they needed more work on their ability to read, comprehend, and analyze academic texts.

Not surprisingly, the major assignment sequences from 2007 to 2010 reflect these different priorities that the course objectives demonstrate (see table 4.2). While Pittsburgh remained committed to a portfolio-based course with writing process reflection assignments, Doha moved toward a final project that highlighted students' research and reading practices for locating and mapping an academic conversation of sources. For Pittsburgh, demonstrating metacognitive strategies for controlling writing processes was a higher priority than establishing strategies for navigating a text-based, academic conversation.

These differences are based upon different contexts and the needs we perceived within them. Overall, the evolutionary differences between the 76100 objectives stem from the emergent nature of the Doha campus prior to 2010. The most distinct difference between the campuses is the extent to which reading and writing are integrated priorities within the course. Both of these differences indicate how we perceived students' needs within each campus structure. In other words, our curricular priorities show clear instances where we determined that "we need to be the same—except when we need to be different." The syllabus documents also point toward more internal changes within the Doha course materials. We did not find this rate of change to be surprising, given the emergent nature of admissions on the Qatar campus and the relatively stable admissions process in Pittsburgh.

Table 4.1 76100 Objectives in Doha and Pittsburgh Syllabus Documents, 2007–2010

	Doha	Pittsburgh
2007	-Develop proficiency in reading and writing academic texts in English. -Develop awareness of characteristics of language use in an academic context. -Interrogate the implications of global- ization for academic and professional literacy in the twenty-first century.	-To increase reading proficiency in Eng- lish, particularly within an academic context. -To introduce students to the fundamen- tal writing practices of summarizing, comparing, and analyzing written texts in English. -To increase students' rhetorical aware- ness of audience when writing in English. -To introduce students to functional norms for communicating in academic English.
2008	This class will help you develop the advanced academic literacy practices expected of university students. These literacy practices include: -identifying problems and needs that can best be met through reading or writing, -employing effective strategies for getting the information you need from a text, -formulating goals when you write regarding the effects you want to have on your readers, -evaluating and appreciating the message and goals of the author(s) of a text, and -relating something you are reading or writing to other texts as a way of under- standing patterns of human interaction and knowledge creation.	This course is for students who want to build increasingly expert literacy prac- tices in academic English. In the course, we will:[3] -draw on both discourse analytical and metacognitive strategies for reading in academic English; -summarize, compare, and analyze texts; and -draw on genre conventions for writ- ing academic essays in English, espe- cially from a functional and rhetorical perspective.
2009	In academic contexts, reading and writ- ing are the tools that we use to interact with other scholars, to work through issues that are important for our societ- ies, and to create products that entertain, inform, and persuade. In this course we will emphasize learning how these academic conversations work by reading a lot, analyzing and discussing what the readings mean, and writing papers that create arguments based on our interpre- tations of the readings. Next semester, in 76101, you will build on this awareness of the structure and tools of academic conversation to focus more on crafting your own contribution.[4]	This course is for students who want to build increasingly expert literacy prac- tices in academic English. In the course, we will: -draw on both discourse analytical and metacognitive strategies for reading in academic English; -summarize, compare, and analyze texts; and -draw on genre conventions for writ- ing academic essays in English, espe- cially from a functional and rhetorical perspective.

continued on next page

Sharing a Philosophy of Language within Different Frameworks

Another point of convergence between Doha and Pittsburgh revolved around the different representations of English in the course docu- ments. Regardless of the different priorities in 76100, the function and

Table 4.1—*continued*

	Doha	Pittsburgh
2010	In Reading and Writing for Academic Contexts we will work on three broad areas: (1) Developing expertise on issues through reading, (2) Analyzing the construction and usage of written texts, and (3) Communicating what we are learning about (1) and (2).	This course is for students who want to build increasingly expert literacy practices in academic English. In the course, we will: -draw on both discourse analytical and metacognitive strategies for reading and writing in academic English; -read for major claims and evidence; -write with quotations and paraphrase of source texts; -summarize and compare texts in writing; -argue for a position that other authors might find controversial or different from other positions; -build strategies for demonstrating control of conventions for writing in English; -draw on genre conventions for writing academic essays in English, especially from a functional and rhetorical perspective; -analyze models of effective writing in English for the rhetorical strengths and weaknesses of those models; and -engage in collaborative peer review processes for our writing.

practice of academic English appear to be represented similarly on both campuses. Unlike the influence exerted upon our courses through the argument for equivalency, we suppose the underlying motivation for common representations of language results from the normative pressures within our academic disciplines. We isolated statements about language and categorized them by type. Overall, we found three major categories or themes for these references to language. Sometimes multiple categories could be present in the same statement, but these instances were rare. We categorized these statements in terms of how they provided:

- a rationale for instruction,
- linguistic resources to encourage particular effects through writing, and
- a reference to standards or norms to encourage control of language.

If a language statement provided a rationale for instruction, that rationale typically addressed course objectives or outcomes in a reflective, rhetorical way so that students could understand the "why" behind the course structure. Statements about linguistic resources aimed at supplying students with the options and linguistic materials needed to persuade a reader or produce a particular kind of effect. This

Table 4.2 Assignment Sequences in Doha and Pittsburgh, 2007–2010

	Doha	Pittsburgh
2007	Readings on Globalization Restaurant Review Museum Catalog Entry Summary Synthesis Final Project: Position Essay	Readings on Language and Education Comprehensive Summary Selective Summary Comparison Position Essay Final Project: Portfolio & Reflection Memo
2008	Readings on Environmental Sustainability Analysis (Summary) Reaction Comparison Focused on Similarities Comparison Focused on Differences Final Project: Bibliography Resource Guide	Readings on Why College Matters Comprehensive Summary Selective Summary Comparison Position Essay Final Project: Portfolio & Reflection Memo
2009	Readings on Environmental Sustainability Analysis (Summary) Reaction Comparison Focused on Similarities Comparison Focused on Differences Final Project: Website Resource and Presentation at Local High School	Readings on Why College Matters Comprehensive Summary Comparison Focused on Similarities or Dissimilarities Mini-Synthesis Position Final Project: Portfolio & Reflection Memo
2010	Readings on Environmental Sustainability Explication (Summary) Reaction Connection Final Project: Academic Conversation Analysis (a map of ten sources)	Readings on Identity in a Digital Culture Comprehensive Summary Comparison of Similar Arguments or of Very Different Arguments Mini-Synthesis Position Final Project: Portfolio & Reflection Memo

"resource" approach to language also provided a "why" for students—the "why" behind various linguistic options. The third category, referencing standards to encourage language control, included statements about nonstandard language forms. In the table below, we give examples from both campuses for each of the categories (see table 4.3).

These examples illustrate how we signal through our course materials various ways of understanding language. We observed each of these three categories in four years of course materials across both campuses, which we argue signals a common philosophical orientation toward language that is consistent with the norms of the discipline at large. While we did not see change in the course materials for these types of language statements, we do think this homogeneity speaks to the shaping power of academic disciplines and professions across transnational boundaries.

Table 4.3 Statements about Language in Doha and Pittsburgh 76100 Course Materials

Type of Statement	Doha	Pittsburgh
Rationale	A lot of meaning can be packed into written language because readers can take longer to process a sentence than listeners to a conversation (2008, assignment description).	When we make choices for the language in our overall claim, we make choices about the language and concepts that follow (2007, assignment description).
Resource	Does the language consistently mark the summary as an interpretation of someone else's ideas? (2007, rubric).	Will your reader know when text or ideas are from you or the source text because of your use of reporting verbs? (2010, rubric).
Standard	Your paper will be assessed on your control of the grammar and vocabulary that are normally used in academic English writing (2010, syllabus).	Carefully edit and proofread all texts, paying special attention to those error patterns you will be tracking over the semester (2009, syllabus).

THE SIGNIFICANCE OF CONVERGENCE AND DIFFERENCE IN A TRANSNATIONAL PROGRAM

We have shown how the program structures, the 76100 course objectives, and the syllabi show points of change toward similarity and difference within a transnational program. The situations that shaped these points are important for understanding the complex decisions that WPAs make so that writing education can thrive in a global context. Understanding WPA in a global context is complicated precisely because we must mediate the dynamic processes of our programs as they interact with institutional agendas, program structures, and unfolding teaching contexts. Our decision making is shaped by institutional concerns, such as accountability toward long-term structures like the agreement between the Qatar Foundation and Carnegie Mellon, or the professional standards of a particular discipline or field. It is also shaped by local concerns, such as student profiles or staffing resources. We suggest institutionalist organizational theory as a means of interpreting the influences that shape pedagogical difference and convergence within our programs. We discuss convergence first, and then we close with some thoughts about difference.

Institutionalism as a Dialogic Interpretive Lens

As we stated earlier, one of the goals for this chapter is to give a sense of what an emerging transnational writing program might look like through a lens that assumes a writing program is a dynamic process and not a static entity. This approach enables us to investigate points of change over time, as well as to analyze variation in the courses rather than rigid structures. We believe this approach makes sense not only from organizational and linguistic theories of emergence (Hopper 1988), but also from a perspective that values the voices of local teachers, as reflective practitioners (Schon 1984), and their students (Lunsford and Ouzgane 2004). (Unfortunately, this chapter does not include students' voices from Pittsburgh and Doha, so this chapter is a preliminary stage for understanding the dynamics of teaching reading and writing in a transnational program.[5])

As writing program administrators, the curricula we design are rhetorical and pedagogical responses to particular exigencies that we perceive within our university or college contexts. In responding to emergent needs, we draw upon prior practices to shape our teaching. In this way, writing programs are both intertextual and rhetorical processes. Bakhtin (1986) says this "occupies a particular *definite* position in a given sphere of communication. It is impossible to determine its position without correlating it with other positions" (91, emphasis in original). We argue that the same can be said of a program's design and practices. All pedagogical practices exist within dialogic and, hence, rhetorical relationships. Moreover, organizational theory, particularly the strand previously called *neoinstitutionalism* and now *institutionalism* (Meyer 2008), allows us to theorize about these relationships between organizations, or, for this chapter, between campus programs.

Organizational theory is basically a discipline devoted to understanding how organizations become structured in particular ways. If we see campuses and writing programs as types of organizations, then organizational theory may help us to explain the dynamic structures of a transnational writing program. Institutionalism asks questions regarding the forces that shape particular kinds of variation and change within an organization's structure. As they are described by research literature, these forces are basically rhetorical, because they are motivated by a rhetorical need for legitimacy (Meyer and Rowan 1977).

Since the first-year courses in Pittsburgh and Doha are geographically separate entities, with their own unique organizational and pedagogical concerns that still must be accountable to the overall university, we can describe our programs as "organizational peers" that are accountable to the university's mission. As transnational peers, WPAs in charge of the first-year programs have a unique relationship in that we are accountable to each other for the work we do as we establish our joint legitimacy within our institutional frameworks and professions.

Institutionalism provides a framework for explaining what research calls *isomorphism*, or the similar structures and practices that exist across the boundaries of different organizations. Despite its different analytical focus, institutionalism offers a useful vocabulary for considering rhetorical motives that shape writing program structures and texts to resemble each other. DiMaggio and Powell (1991, 67) list three kinds of isomorphic change:

- coercive isomorphism, linked to problems with political legitimacy
- mimetic isomorphism, linked to problems of uncertainty
- normative isomorphism, linked to needs related to professionalization

This concept of isomorphism might explain the points of convergence between our campuses. We used documents from 2007–2010 to locate points of commonality and difference and to understand our own efforts toward homogeneity and variation in our approaches to teaching at our respective campuses. Within a university structure that demands accountability between the two campuses, it is imperative that WPAs can explain the reasons why some curricular aspects are "the same" and some are not.

In general, isomorphism explains the "moves" decision makers take toward establishing legitimacy among their peer organizations. For us, our first-year writing program is accountable to other programs within global universities. These explanations of organizational change are helpful for describing transnational writing programs in that they are theoretical perspectives with dialogic and rhetorical underpinnings.[6] They are rhetorical in part because (1) they emphasize the role of interaction between peer organizations; (2) they describe change in terms of exigencies, such as a need for legitimacy, credibility, or efficiency; (3) they account for homogeneity in terms of the relationships between organizations in a particular field or context; and (4) they assume a dynamic, social context within which an organization functions. We believe that institutionalism enables us to consider the organizational and sociohistorical contexts of WPA practices, leading to a richer understanding of prior contextual norms as both "constraining and enabling" (Giddens 1984, 25) in new and unfolding rhetorical situations within a global context.

Institutionalism provides an explanatory framework for the arguments we make to establish our legitimacy within a field of practice—or, for our purposes, within a transnational writing program. One of the arguments we recorded earlier was that multilingual students in

Pittsburgh deserved the same kind of educational affordances as multi-lingual students in Doha. Additionally, another argument has become part of our decision making processes: "We need to be the same, except when we need to be different." This kind of discourse reflects what insti-tutional theorists Meyer and Rowan (1977) observed about isomorphic organizational language: "Vocabularies of structure which are isomor-phic with institutional rules provide prudent, rational, and legitimate accounts" (349).

Because institutional theory offers a framework for understanding isomorphic change, or change for the sake of establishing legitimacy, we draw upon it here to analyze some of the changes we observed in our course materials. We suggest that when writing programs "go global," those programs become accountable across new boundaries in new ways. For our particular case, the language of accountability was that the campuses needed to be the same as much as possible. For Carnegie Mellon, that language created a sense of professional norming that enabled the program to both add a course for our multilingual students and to include supplemental instructors to enhance writing feedback in the 76100 course. Moreover, other changes toward homogeneity within the course assignments could be linked to this sense of institutional norming. We find this institutional framework to be helpful because it indicates that convergence can result from dialogic relationships rather than one-way directed influence, which is consistent with our experi-ences between Doha and Pittsburgh.

We also demonstrated how, not unsurprisingly, there are many points of difference across materials in a transnational program, and that those differences can be linked to the various needs we perceive within our local contexts. According to organizational scholar Jens Beckert (2010), the same influences that shape convergence or isomorphism across insti-tutional structures can also shape difference. This corresponds with our account of differences between the two campuses. For example, Dudley adapted the 76100 course objectives to prioritize reading and discussion because he found his students did not have sufficient experience with reading. However, in Pittsburgh, Danielle emphasized writing processes and editing for a portfolio because she perceived students' needs as grounded in a US-centric communication context with US-centric audi-ences. These differences—and the fixity with which we hold to these differences—appear to be our responses to the unique cultural contexts and constraints we negotiate on each campus. Our moves to differen-tiate our courses in these specific ways point to a professional norm within composition studies that values the unique rhetorical contexts of our students, as well as to the unofficial idea that difference could exist between the two Carnegie Mellon campuses because we considered it necessary to be different.

Based upon our own understanding of CMU's writing program context, we suspect that the most likely institutional explanation for homogeneity across the boundaries of our courses lies within the need for professionalization, as that thread is the one most connected with academic professions and the need to establish professional credibility within a field. The adjustments toward convergence and difference that we have discussed in this chapter are moves we justified according to our training and expertise in reading and writing pedagogy, rhetoric, composition, and second language acquisition. Because WPAs are academics accountable to a field of continuing scholarship, this normative force appears to be the strongest as we establish our legitimacy within our field. Normative isomorphism also allows for individuals to act according to shared values, such as the values that WPAs share, or the values that Carnegie Mellon faculty share.

However, we do not assume that the other two types of isomorphism are necessarily absent in the CMU relationship, especially since WPAs are also accountable to the political structures of their universities. Since DiMaggio and Powell (1991, 67) claimed these analytical categories are not "always empirically distinct," and since research has pointed to cases that show more than one type of isomorphic force at once (Walpole 2000), we would be naïve to assume that other forces (e.g., politics and uncertainty) are not present. For our 2007–2010 work, we hesitate to say that political pressure or coercion dictated the structures of the writing program, even though the argument for equivalency was invoked to help Pittsburgh "catch up" to Doha. In this instance, since it was the faculty who argued for pedagogical improvements for multilingual writers in Pittsburgh, any coercion for change originated from the faculty's use of the agreement between Carnegie Mellon and the Qatar Foundation.

CONCLUSION

This chapter points to the dynamic nature of a writing program "gone global," in which WPAs negotiate accountability and standards in a transnational context. We have shown that, within a transnational program, there can be points of convergence and variation in course structures, and that these points can be understood in terms of the professional and academic norms or values we share. Moreover, these similarities and differences must coexist in order for a transnational program to succeed in different parts of the world and with different students. Additionally we have shown how influence within a transnational program can move in different directions and shape the allocation of resources on both campuses.

We have also demonstrated a practical method for reflecting upon our practices, our course designs, and what influences them. By examining our materials and locating points of change toward convergence and variation, we learned things about ourselves and our work that we had not noticed in the regular routine of instruction.

Finally, we offer a picture of convergence and difference that raises a potential problem for writing program administrators. Our local interactions prompt us to make local responses for change toward difference, but our university structures at times prompt us to respond toward conformity. How we negotiate these influences requires careful reflection on our practices to ensure that we are ultimately striving to serve our students. Within the field of composition, the "norm" is to value the differences of our local contexts and our students in those contexts. Yet this move to value the local teaching context can, perhaps, potentially work against the mission of a global university that has been charged to protect its brand. We think others should pursue more work in transnational program accountability, especially taking into consideration that accommodating local contexts need not upset university policies. Apparent contradictions—even productive ones—can coexist in a transnational program if we view universities as dynamic, complex processes.

Notes

1. The campus now offers majors in information systems and biological sciences as well.
2. We continue to describe the 76100 course on both campuses as an experience in which students will (1) learn to write for readers rather than write for correctness; (2) locate points of connection among texts and learn strategies for representing those in writing; and (3) learn strategies for controlling language in academic discourse expectations.
3. The Pittsburgh 2008–2010 materials listed extensive outcomes, which we have not included due to space constraints.
4. The Qatar 2009 and 2010 syllabus documents also included extensive learning outcomes.
5. Our colleague Silvia Pessoa is conducting a longitudinal study of multilingual students' writing and development across four years at CMU-Doha. Her data includes both students' texts and interviews.
6. Our intentions here are to highlight what institutionalism offers our theories about transnational WPA. For a good starting point in organizational theory, see W. Richard Scott's (2008) text, *Institutions and Organizations*.

References

Bakhtin, Mikhail Mikha lovich. 1986. "The Problem of Speech Genres." In *Speech Genres and Other Late Essays*, ed. Caryl Emerson and Michael Holquist, and translated by Vern W. McGee, 60–102. Austin: University of Texas Press.

Beckert, Jens. 2010. "Institutional Isomorphism Revisited: Convergence and Divergence in Institutional Change." *Sociological Theory* 28 (2): 150–66. http://dx.doi.org/10.1111/j.1467-9558.2010.01369.x.

Brandt, Deborah. 2001. *Literacy in American Lives*. Cambridge: Cambridge University Press. Kindle Edition. http://dx.doi.org/10.1017/CBO9780511810237.

Canagarajah, A. Suresh. 2006. "The Place of World Englishes in Composition: Pluralization Continued." *College Composition and Communication* 57(4): 586–619. http://www.jstor.org/stable/20456910.

Carnegie Mellon University. 2011. *Factbook 2011–2012, Vol. 26.* Office of Institutional Research. Pittsburgh, PA. http://www.cmu.edu/ira/factbook/facts2012.html.

Carter-Tod, Sheila. 2007. "Standardizing a First-year Writing Program: Contested Sites of Influence." *WPA: Writing Program Administration* 30 (3): 75–92.

DiMaggio, Paul J., and Walter W. Powell. 1991. "The Iron Cage Revisited: Institutional Isomorphism and Collective Rationality in Organizational Fields." In *The New Institutionalism in Organizational Analysis*, ed. Paul J. DiMaggio and Walter W. Powell, 63–82. Chicago: University of Chicago Press.

Donahue, Christiane. 2009. "'Internationalization' and Composition Studies: Reorienting the Discourse." *College Composition and Communication* 61 (2): 212–43. http://dx.doi.org/10.2307/40593441.

Giddens, Anthony. 1984. *The Constitution of Society: Outline of the Theory of Structuration.* Berkeley: University of California Press.

Hopper, Paul. 1988. "Emergent grammar and the *a priori* grammar postulate." In *Linguistics in Context: Connecting Observation and Understanding*, ed. Deborah Tannen, 117–34. New York: Ablex.

Horner, Bruce, Min-Zhan Lu, Jacqueline Jones Royster, and John Trimbur. 2011. "Opinion: Language Difference in Writing: Toward a Translingual Approach." *College English* 73 (3): 303–21.

Kamlet, Mark. 2010. "Offering Domestic Degrees Outside the United States: One University's Experiences over the Past Decade." In *Higher Education in a Global Society*, ed. Madeleine B. d'Ambrosio, Paul J. Yakoboski, and D. Bruce Johnstone, 83–107. Northampton, MA: Edward Elgar. http://dx.doi.org/10.4337/9781849805315.00012.

Kaufer, David, and Danielle Zawodny Wetzel. 2014. "Rhetoric, Composition, and Design." In *Oxford Handbook of Rhetorical Studies*, ed. Michael MacDonald. Oxford: Oxford University Press.

Lunsford, Andrea, and Lahoucine Ouzgane. 2004. "Composition and Postcolonial Studies: An Introduction." In *Crossing Borderlands: Composition and Postcolonial Studies*, ed. Andrea Lunsford and Lahoucine Ouzgane. Pittsburgh: University of Pittsburgh Press. Kindle Edition.

Matsuda, Paul, Christina Ortmeier-Hooper, and Xiaoye You. 2006. "Preface." In *The Politics of Second Language Writing: In Search of the Promised Land*, ed. Paul Matsuda, Christina Ortmeier-Hooper, and Xiaoye You, vii–xiii. West Lafayette, IN: Parlor Press.

Meyer, John W., and Brian Rowan. 1977. "Institutionalized Organizations: Formal Structure as Myth and Ceremony." *American Journal of Sociology* 83 (2): 340–63. http://dx.doi.org/10.1086/226550 http://www.jstor.org.

Meyer, John W. 2008. "Reflections on Institutional Theories of Organizations." In *The Sage Handbook of Organizational Institutionalism*, ed. Royston Greenwood, Christine Oliver, Roy Suddaby, and Kerstin Sahlin-Andersson, 790–809. Thousand Oaks, CA: Sage. http://dx.doi.org/10.4135/9781849200387.n35.

Pennycook, Alastair. 1994. *The Cultural Politics of English as in International Language.* London, New York: Longman.

Phillipson, Robert. 2012. "Linguistic Imperialism Alive and Kicking." *Guardian Weekly.* 13 March. http://www.theguardian.com/education/2012/mar/13/linguistic -imperialism-english-language-teaching

Reichelt, Melinda. 2005. "English-Language Writing Instruction in Poland." *Journal of Second Language Writing* 14 (4): 215–32. http://dx.doi.org/10.1016/j.jslw.2005.10.005.

Schon, Donald. 1984. *The Reflective Practitioner: How Professionals Think in Action.* New York: Basic Books.

Scott, W. Richard. 2008. *Institutions and Organizations: Ideas and Interests.* 3rd ed. Thousand Oaks, CA: Sage.

Tucker, G. Richard. 2012. "Closing Remarks." Presentation at the Carnegie Mellon University Communication Symposium. June 27.

Walpole, MaryBeth. 2000. "Under Construction: Identity and Isomorphism in the Merger of a Library and Information Science School and an Education School." *Library Quarterly* 70 (4): 423–45. http://dx.doi.org/10.2307/4309461.

Wilkins, Stephen, and Jeroen Huisman. 2012. "The International Branch Campus as Transnational Strategy in Higher Education." *International Journal of Higher Education* 64 (5): 627–45. http://dx.doi.org/10.1007/s10734-012-9516-5.

Yancey, Kathleen Blake. 2004. "Made Not Only in Words: Composition in a New Key." *College Composition and Communication* 56 (2): 297–328. http://dx.doi.org/10.2307 /4140651 http://www.jstor.org/stable/4140651.

You, Xiaoye. 2006. "Globalization and the Politics of Teaching Second Language Writing." In *The Politics of Second Language Writing: In Search of the Promised Land,* ed. Paul Matsuda, Christine Ortmeier-Hooper, and Xiaoye You, 188–201. West Lafayette, IN: Parlor Press.

APPENDIX 4.1. ELABORATED OUTCOMES FOR 76100 IN DOHA (DISTRIBUTED TO TEACHERS BUT NOT NECESSARILY TO STUDENTS)

By the end of this course you should be more proficient at:

1. Employing analytical reading strategies, including:

1.1. Articulating the argument of a text as a purposeful activity involving rhetorical moves and desired effects on specific audiences and being able to identify each component;

1.2. Recognizing and interpreting evaluative language, register markers, and visual scaffolding;

1.3. Employing techniques appropriate for lengthy and/or complex readings including previewing, skimming, outlining, and content summaries;

1.4. Compensating for unknown vocabulary through confirmation checks, inferencing, and dictionary usage for high-frequency or high-profile terms; and

1.5. Constructing visual representations of move and concept structures.

2. Formulating summary reactions to a reading, including:

    2.1. Articulating personal responses through margin notes, journaling, and public discussion;

    2.2. Identifying similarities and differences between readings with respect to topic covered, purpose for writing, intended audience, central argument, means for developing argument, examples used, proposals for action;

    2.3. Imagining how others might react to a reading and identifying alternative interpretations and positions on issues that arise in public discussion; and

    2.4. Leading an academic discussion of a text, identifying key issues and potential polemics.

3. Producing a summary evaluation of a reading appropriate for a given purpose, including:

    3.1. Demonstrating familiarity with range of purposes for summary evaluations including distillation of argument, introduction to content, and commentary on technical aspects such as writing style or method for appealing to an audience and being able to categorize appropriately the summary evaluation produced;

    3.2. Differentiating between summarizing and repeating (i.e., paraphrase, quotation) text content and being able to strike an appropriate balance between the two;

    3.3. Commanding language conventions for summarizing texts including identification of text, subject-verb selection, and tense usage; and

    3.4. Commanding mechanical conventions for source attribution, referring to authors and text titles, and incorporating quotations.

4. Creating a rhetorical product (written text, oral presentation, multimedia) that characterizes relations between texts as the basis for a complex argument, including:

    4.1. Locating, with support, texts relevant to a topic;

    4.2. Categorizing other texts as counterpoints to argue against, historical preliminaries, sites of confirmation, components of a larger issue, or suggestions for further exploration;

    4.3. Understanding the role that reference to other texts plays in establishing academic credibility (and avoiding perceptions of plagiarism);

    4.4. Developing a move structure for achieving an argument that locates other texts within the rhetorical product;

4.5. Choosing the appropriate medium and genre for achieving the purpose and being able to identify associated conventions for presentation; and

4.6. Demonstrating a production process that includes the procurement of feedback and revision across multiple drafts.

APPENDIX 4.2. OUTCOMES FOR 76100 IN PITTSBURGH (DISTRIBUTED TO STUDENTS FOR SELF-ASSESSMENT)

By the end of the course, students should have

- Learned specific vocabulary to support reading comprehension (keywords, claim & evidence, central & peripheral, etc.)
- Learned strategies or methods to support reading comprehension (annotation, visual analysis, etc.)
- Understood that different genres require different type of reading strategies
- Learned to make different kinds of claims about texts (summary claims, comparison claims)
- Increased their ability to write precise claims that organize a reader's understanding
- Learned to support claims with quotations and paraphrase from sources
- Learned to develop their own claims to make an argument in their writing
- Learned to enhance clarity by writing clear characters and action
- Learned how to use language of attribution, such as reporting verbs
- Learned specific strategies for producing coherently written texts
- Learned to use the language of cohesion, such as metacommentary
- Learned specific language to improve the clarity of sentence-level writing (articles, connectors, etc.)
- Learned to move beyond simply proofreading when revising an academic paper in English
- Understood how writing is a process in this course (planning, drafting, revising, and getting feedback)
- Learned to evaluate and incorporate feedback from others to revise their own writing
- Understood their goal for writing in English is communication with readers rather than correctness
- Increased their ability to identify their strengths and weaknesses for writing in English

5

SO CLOSE, YET SO FAR
Administering a Writing Program with a Bahamian Campus

Shanti Bruce

As a part of my position as WPA at Nova Southeastern University (NSU), I send faculty to teach on the Caribbean island of New Providence, which is considered the crown jewel of The Bahamas. Five times during each ten-week term, these professors must make their way there, teach, and return within thirty to forty-eight hours. In order to truly understand this process, I took what leadership scholars Dotlich and Cairo (2002) call an "unnatural leadership" approach and put myself in their position. I assigned myself these courses in order to learn about the process firsthand. In this chapter, I share my experiences and reflections on what I learned about transnational WPA (TWPA) work.

INTRODUCTION
When I assumed the role of WPA at NSU in Fort Lauderdale, FL, I became responsible for staffing writing and literature courses on the main campus and at several branch campuses. After the full-time faculty's courses were scheduled, the remaining courses fell to me. My first semester, I had 100 courses to manage. Three of those were at NSU's Bahamas Student Educational Center in Nassau, on New Providence Island. Majors on this campus were primarily offered by the school of business. The College of Arts and Sciences supported these majors by teaching the required business writing course, as well as an occasional literature or history elective. Classes there met during five weekends over a ten-week term: two hours on Friday evenings and four hours on Saturdays. This schedule was intended to serve the needs of the working Bahamian adults who enrolled in the programs offered.

With so much to learn as a first-time WPA, I continued to staff the Nassau courses with two adjunct faculty members who had taught there

DOI: 10.7330/9780874219623.c005

in the past. These instructors knew how to manage the travel and the courses, so I asked them to continue filling the positions. Even though I had never met them, I rehired them both via email, passed along any weather updates that came to me, and at the end of the term, I made sure their grades had been entered.

That first fall went smoothly on the main campus. I got to know my colleagues and worked to balance teaching, scholarship, and WPA work. I observed many of the main campus writing instructors I was supervising, and I met with each of them to talk about their classes. I held workshops on teaching in computer classrooms, a first step toward my goal of eventually moving the composition courses into labs. I also became chair of NSU's Master's in Writing program and began a curriculum review process with the faculty. The connections I made on the main campus were strong, but I felt detached from the courses being held in The Bahamas. While the Nassau courses accounted for a small percentage of my scheduling responsibilities, I needed to learn more about them for a number of reasons. First, unlike the other courses I staffed, these courses required faculty to be approved by an immigration department and flown to and from a location multiple times. Second, these courses supported a collaboration with another school on campus, the H. Wayne Huizenga School of Business and Entrepreneurship, which was the state of Florida's largest business school, so it was important that our support was consistent and of quality. Finally, I knew a time would come when the instructors who currently traveled to the Caribbean were no longer available, and I knew I would need to be able to prepare new people to step into those roles. I needed to learn more about the travel, the campus, and the students, and while the current instructors were willing to talk with me about the work, I felt I would better understand it if I went there myself.

In her article "Coming of Age as a WPA: From Personal to Personnel," Jeanne Marie Rose (2005) looked to management theory to help her reflect on WPA work. She cited Peters and Waterman's recommendation that leaders use "Hewlett Packard's philosophy of 'management by walking around' or MBWA" (75). Their approach encouraged leaders to walk around and talk with those in the trenches. I did just that during my first semester on the main campus, and I was able to learn a great deal. I imagined going to the island for a day to visit the campus and meet a few of the students would have given me similar insight, and while that would have been helpful, I wasn't convinced it would give me a complete picture of what it was like to work there for an entire term. From my own study of leadership in writing programs, I had learned that the best way for me to understand the work would be to do it myself. My study revealed that many professionals from programs across the country value leaders who are willing to do the difficult jobs themselves. Respondents to my national survey said "good leaders are 'not afraid of the heavy lifting or dirty work,'" and "they 'step up to the plate'" (Bruce 2005, 190–91). They also believe "effective leaders are 'in the trenches'" (191). As a part of my study, I talked with Jeanne Gunner, who has held numerous academic leadership positions. She said, "The best leaders in our field are people who are teachers themselves. There's a connection that sustains them, so they don't get *elevated* out of the trenches. They stay there" (Bruce 2005, 195). I agreed with Gunner as I realized teaching my own courses on NSU's main campus had provided additional insight I wouldn't have gained if I had only observed others teaching.

That summer offered me an opportunity to follow Gunner's advice and get into the trenches in The Bahamas. Business writing and world literature courses were on the schedule, so I assigned them both to myself. This was considered a "double," since I would have to teach the courses back-to-back: 6–8 p.m. and 8–10 p.m. on Friday evenings, and 8 a.m.–12 p.m. and 1–5 p.m. on Saturdays. Combining this with my twelve-month position on the main campus ensured that this would in no way resemble a summer vacation, but as I suspected, going there myself as a participant-observer helped me to truly understand the process. From getting permission to work there from immigration and experiencing the travel and teaching conditions, to learning directly about the student body from the students themselves, I got the information I needed to evaluate the curriculum and prepare future faculty.

UNDERSTANDING COMPLICATIONS OF THE INTERNATIONAL COMMUTE

Preparing to teach a course typically begins with creating a syllabus, but for these courses, I began by renewing my passport so that I could provide a copy to NSU's Assistant Director of Operations. She is in charge of sending it, along with other official documents about assigned courses, to The Bahamas Immigration Department, which has to approve all NSU professors before they work on the island. Once approved, the Immigration Department sends an official letter stating that Immigration is aware of the teaching assignments and dates. This documentation must accompany each person on every trip, and must be presented to the Immigration Officers upon arrival at the island airport, if requested.

After completing the approval process, I worked with NSU's Travel Office to arrange my flights and hotels for the five weekends I would be traveling. There is a week off between the first and second, as well as the third and fourth, weekends. Students and faculty have two weeks off between the fourth and fifth weekends. This meant that I was scheduling many weeks in advance. The travel agents adhered strictly to the airline guidelines that stated passengers must be at the airport two hours before international travel, and it was decided that there was no way I could finish my late Saturday course, which ended at 5 p.m., and catch the last flight off the island at 6 p.m. This meant returning home on Saturday was not an option. Thus, I would be spending Friday and Saturday nights on the island each time.

While I was going through the steps to arrange my travel to the island as a teacher, my main concern was how this firsthand experience—the preparation and the teaching—would help me, as the new TWPA, understand this particular student center, the curriculum we were offering, and the student body we were serving. I wanted to learn how the collaboration between the schools worked and gain an understanding that would allow me to evaluate what we were doing there and how well we were doing it. I needed to know the details of the preparation and travel so that I could prepare future instructors. If the preparation and travel went smoothly for the instructors, they could spend more time focusing on their students and their work in the classroom. For this job, I realized, adjuncts had to be willing to prepare much more than a syllabus, and all for the same pay. This was something to take into account when hiring instructors.

Because of my "double," I had to plan twelve hours of class meetings per weekend, while also planning assignments for students to complete during the interim two or three weeks. This proved to be challenging. I needed to use class time effectively, and I had to make sure all assignments were clear because of the amount of time that would pass between class meetings. I was beginning to understand how much pressure the instructors teaching these courses would feel. Leadership scholars Dotlich and Cairo (2002) discuss the benefits of putting oneself in uncomfortable positions such as this. They insist that the "best leaders commit unnatural leadership acts" (3) and believe the impulse to act in an "unnatural" and even uncomfortable manner is what distinguishes today's effective leaders. When I decided I wanted to teach these courses, it came as a surprise to my colleagues. In my position, I am neither required nor expected to fulfill this role myself. My twelve-month job keeps me busy on the main campus throughout each week, making this move particularly unnatural in my context.

Planning for twelve (almost straight) hours in the classroom also felt unnatural and uncomfortable. I had to find a way to design the classes so that the students would remain engaged with the material for the duration of each meeting. I also had to find a way to make sure I had the stamina for it. While I was preparing as a teacher, I continued to evaluate each step of this process from my perspective as the TWPA. I am responsible for designing all standard syllabus templates, and all adjuncts are required to use these templates, so teaching the courses in this format helped me to identify what would and would not work in this unique learning situation. I had previously looked at the syllabus and come up with assignments that I thought could be completed during thirty-minute or hour-long segments. After meeting the students and teaching with the books and the syllabus for the duration of the term, I learned how to improve the class plan. For example, I learned that if I wanted to assign a group project in the business writing course, class time would have to be given for group preparation. Not everyone could meet outside of class because, as I discovered, not everyone lived on the same island and not every island had consistent Internet access. Meeting for group work can be a problem for students in any class, but when students are separated by a plane ride, getting together is impractical and costly. I didn't eliminate the group project from the course, but I did reduce the amount of work it required and, therefore, the amount of class time that would have to be dedicated to it.

My trips were scheduled to begin in July and end in September, which happened to be right in the middle of hurricane season (June 1 to November 30). This meant that my trips, though carefully planned, were subject to change at any time due to threatening storms, flights being canceled, and airport closings.

When my first travel day came, I arrived at the airport weighted down with books, syllabi, a laptop, and business attire for two days. I happened to meet several business professors on the plane who were all going to Nassau to teach as well. They were adjunct faculty who had made many trips to The Bahamas, and they enjoyed telling me about their experiences on the island, recounting stories of lost luggage, missed planes, and power outages. When we arrived, we exited through the back of the plane onto the tarmac and walked toward the airport. Once inside, we were ushered into lines where we were required to present our documents to immigration officers. The officers recognized a few of the business professors. As they chatted, the professors introduced me to the officers. I told them this was my first weekend, and they welcomed me to the island. Next, we walked through baggage claim and came to the stations where luggage was being searched. The lines were long, and once again, a few of the officials recognized the business professors I was with and waived all of us around the lines. The area outside was a bit confusing, but the seasoned professors knew right where to stand to get a taxi quickly.

In this situation, I did what Dotlich and Cairo (2002) recommend; I gave up some control and trusted the people I was with to help me get to where I needed to be. Dotlich and Cairo say this is a "pragmatic" approach, and while they "do not advocate blindly trusting everyone," they explain that "when appropriate, leaders today need to trust first and ask questions later" (22). My willingness to be a follower in this situation helped me build new relationships, which Dotlich and Cairo say is another important task for today's leaders, and it made my term more manageable and enjoyable.

During the ride to the hotel, I thought about the long luggage lines and the confusing taxi area and wondered how long the whole process would have taken if I had not been with those professors. I had done my share of international traveling, so I knew I would have figured it all out eventually, but I wasn't convinced it would have been in enough time to make it to the hotel and catch the designated NSU bus to the campus before my first course began. As it turned out, I had just enough time to check into the hotel, change clothes, and gather my materials before the early bus was ready to take those of us with early courses (beginning at 6 p.m.) to the campus. I realized then that many of the professors I had flown in with were not scheduled to teach until 8 p.m., and others who were scheduled to teach at the same time as me had arrived on earlier flights.

My first class had not yet begun, but I had already learned valuable information I would use as the TWPA. First, future instructors needed to book earlier flights when they were working with the travel office, especially on the first weekend. They needed time to learn the process and to make mistakes. Second, when I considered instructors for this position, in addition to looking for quality education and experience, I would need to look for seasoned travelers who could be flexible, who wouldn't be thrown when the unexpected happened, and who could handle the somewhat rugged experience of commuting to and teaching on the island. Third, I would need to encourage future instructors to look out for the business professors who would be traveling with them on their flights. They came from all over, so I couldn't help them meet ahead of time, but I knew they would be easy to spot since the gate at the Fort Lauderdale airport is small, and the Friday morning flights to Nassau were usually half full.

During this first trip, I also noticed that the other professors, the *business* professors, were in loose fitting, short-sleeved Tommy Bahama button downs and Polo pullovers, and they didn't change before we left to teach. Some wore shorts, and most wore sandals. That would be the last time I packed bulky business attire and heels. The "bus" turned out to be a cramped van, and we all piled in for the half hour ride to the campus. The former British colony retained the English preference for driving on the left side, and the twists and turns of the road showed the beauty of the island, as well as the poverty.

When we arrived at the campus, I saw that the classroom building resembled a two-story motel with each door opening to the outside. I found the campus office, and one of the staff members greeted me and walked me to my classroom. The sign on the door read, "Business Writing: Dr. Bruce Shanti." I mentioned to her that my names were reversed and that "Bruce" was actually my last name. She apologized for the error and said they had been surprised to see that I wasn't a man when I walked into the office. All of the instructors I flew in with were men, so perhaps their surprise was understandable. Throughout the weekend, the staff offered several apologies for the error, but I was not offended. Perhaps this was an innocent mistake, or perhaps there was an expectation that professors were males.

I tried to settle into the room as it was getting close to 6 p.m., and I wanted to be prepared when the students arrived. The window box air conditioner had a hard time combating the tropical heat, and I was feeling drenched with sweat in no time. The concrete floors under my heels made my legs ache. No wonder the other professors donned loose clothing and comfortable shoes. This would certainly be an important note I would share with future instructors.

As the clock ticked toward 6 p.m., my room remained empty. Typical first day, I thought. I figured the students were finding their way, and we'd start a bit late. By 6:10 p.m., only one student had taken her seat, so I stepped outside to see if others were on their way. Indeed, cars were still arriving. A few of the students gathered in small groups, and a couple of professors were outside having casual conversations. To me, the atmosphere felt unusually calm for a first day.

Around 6:30 p.m., my classroom was finally full. As I reviewed my roster and got to know each student, it became clear that there would be no men in the course. The students were all working women. Many of them were eager to share that they were single moms who saw this university degree as the way to move up both in their jobs and in their status in their country. My second course, which began more promptly at 8 p.m., included one man, which I learned was an anomaly.

Three quarters of the way through my second class, I noticed the students getting antsy. I also began hearing noise coming from outside and could see through the windows that several students and a few instructors were walking around. We still had about thirty minutes of class left, so I assumed the others must have gotten out early because it was the first day. With only five weekends of class meetings, I had definitely planned to stay the entire time. At 9:40 p.m., I finally stopped. My students seemed agitated and kept looking out the windows. I finally asked what was wrong, and they explained, politely but anxiously, that it was time to go. I looked at my watch and the clock on the wall, and confused, I pointed out that we still had class time left. They looked around at each other and back at me. They explained that it was *really* time to go. They never stayed to the very end, and if I was planning to stay, several of them had to leave anyway because their rides were outside waiting for them. Some had been waiting for a while, and they had to go.

A bit unsure about how to proceed, I wondered if they were trying to take advantage of my being a new professor at the campus or if the other instructors had made a habit of cutting out early, causing students to expect classes to run short. The issue of time had not come up during my conversations with the previous writing instructors, but what had come up was the students' dedication to their studies. Dotlich and Cairo (2002, 19) acknowledge that "natural leaders want correct answers. They are comfortable viewing situations as having a right course of action and a wrong one." However, Dotlich and Cairo (2002, 20) explain that "sometimes . . . leaders grapple with whether it is better to make demands on people that may increase performance but negatively affect the work environment or to ease up on these demands in order to make people feel valued." They say that today's leaders "may opt for one approach now but remain open to switching to another approach as circumstances change." In that moment, I decided to listen to the students and respect their concerns. I knew I wanted more information about this time issue, but I conceded and told them I looked forward to seeing them on Saturday for our next meeting. And with that, they were off.

I gathered my materials and walked outside the classroom. I found our bus, driver, and all of the other instructors waiting for me. They laughed and asked if I had run late. I dismissed their jibes and climbed in for the ride back to the hotel. When we arrived, the other professors said we had to hurry if we were going to eat dinner. Our hotel was all-inclusive, which was helpful for the university because they didn't have to reimburse for each meal because meals were included. We went inside, and no one took the time to go to their rooms first. Instead, they rushed down the spiral staircase to the lower level where the buffet was in the process of being closed down for the night. The dining room was deserted, and we all grabbed plates and filled them with fried plantains and anything else we could get our hands on before it was removed. Finally at the table, the professors explained that we got in just after the dinner hour, and we would have to be up early to catch breakfast as well.

This situation was especially troubling and unexpected. I was shocked that class times conflicted with mealtimes. I talked with the other professors about it, and one of them said he brought snacks with him in his luggage because of this issue. Another said he tried to take extra food at breakfast, so he would be sure to have something for dinner. I never thought I would have to worry about the instructors I hired getting enough food to eat. When I returned to work on the main campus after that first weekend, I explained the situation to upper administrators. They said they were unaware of this issue and would approve reimbursement for instructors who needed to buy food at other restaurants and stores during their stay. Perhaps the administrators had not heard about it because adjuncts did not want to risk sounding like they were complaining. As a full-time faculty member and TWPA, I felt I could talk openly about problems such as this.

UNDERSTANDING "ISLAND TIME"

The morning came quickly, and once again, I found myself alone in the classroom waiting for my students to arrive. 8:00 a.m. came and went, and none of the students were present. Similar to the night before, it wasn't until almost thirty minutes after the official starting time that the class was full and ready to begin. Once they were all there, I set my books and roster aside, and I asked them to please explain to me what was going on with the time. A stickler for punctuality on the main campus, I was concerned about their respect for the course, and as the TWPA, I was especially sensitive to contact hours. The women in the room, many my age and older, explained to me that they were on "island time." I listened carefully and learned about the way the concept of time is interpreted in the islands. I had heard of island time and was well aware that punctuality is not valued in the same ways around the world, but I hadn't expected these academic courses, being offered by a US university, to be affected by this concept. I thought the US academic culture would have been transplanted along with the campus and the professors, especially since quick flights and day cruises regularly transport Floridians and Bahamians between the two countries. The students said people in The Bahamas think in terms of "island time," which means that nothing starts or ends at the officially posted time. The students were in sync with the way things work on the island, and what I initially saw as being "late" or "early" was not seen that way by the students or the other faculty and staff on campus. A student in Fort Lauderdale might try to *get away with* being tardy or skipping out early, but these students meant no disrespect and were, in fact, surprised that I expected them to adhere to traditional US expectations. In The Bahamas, "island time" is a longstanding concept that needs to be respected. Insisting on starting exactly at the posted time risked disrespecting their culture.

My colleague, Dr. Andrea Shaw, is from Jamaica and has studied the way island time is represented in literature. After this experience, I met with her and asked if she could define it for me. She said there isn't really one set definition. It is more of a feeling, a concept, something that is understood in the culture. According to Shaw, the island view of time "is an aspect of life which appears sacrosanct to most people in the 'first world.'" She explained that in her study of Gloria Naylor's *Mama Day*, time in the novel's magical, island setting "is not experienced as a mechanized occurrence marked by the chiming of bells or the buzzing of alarm clocks, but as the passage of seasons and events." Shaw also mentioned her study of the novel *Praisesong for the Widow* by Paule Marshalle, which is set in the Caribbean island of Carriacou. She said, in that story, the main character, Avey, from North America, "realizes that time functions on a different plane from what she is accustomed to, starting with the anxiety of a lengthy wait for a taxi. She is disconcerted by the change in the flow of time." When Avey forgets to wear her watch, Shaw explained, readers see "Avey's subconscious submission to island time." Shaw said that what I had seen as "tardy" could very well be the effect of island time, meaning that it was natural and appropriate and not deserving of the negativity associated with the word "tardy." Shaw also mentioned how many people speak of being on "Cuban time," a phrase that indicates another island where events begin much later than one might expect based on the set time.

***

The rest of my first class went well, as did my second. I kept my second class as close to 5 p.m. as possible, letting them go when I was confident that we had covered what we needed to cover and before they took to staring out the window. As I walked toward my colleagues who were already in the bus, I heard "Let's go!" and "Come on!" I realized they were in a hurry, and a few of them looked downright concerned. I got in the bus, and instead of going to the hotel, we went straight to the airport. Several of the instructors had tickets for planes that were scheduled to take off in less than an hour. I asked how this was possible since I was told by the travel office that I couldn't fly out until Sunday each time. The professors explained that they did not want to stay two nights, and with island time affecting the class schedule, they could make the last plane. They exited, and the few of us who were left spread out in the bus and relaxed as we made the trip back to the hotel. I was exhausted from twelve hours of teaching and five bus rides in less than twenty-four hours. I felt as if I had learned as much as my students in the past two days, and I went over just how different this situation was from anything I had experienced at any of the universities I had taught at in the States.

The concept of "island time" was perhaps the biggest difference I encountered during the term. For me, in the workplace and out, time is time. Variations don't exist. Barbara Adam (1994) explains that "most social science treatises on time establish time as a social fact. As ordering principle, social tool for co-ordination, orientation, and regulation. . . . To theorists with a functionalist bias time is always social time," she explains, "because it reflects, regulates, and orders social life" (42). I was used to living by the clock and the order it demands. My work is structured around class time, contact hours, office hours, syllabus schedules, due dates, terms, and semesters. When I'm lucky, I get lunch time, and I am forever after that elusive free time. The rule of time is evident in how we think and speak about it. "The importance of language in relation to the human awareness of time," Adam explains, "is pointed out by many" (92). She references Fraisse's argument that "Only humans . . . communicate information that not only refers to the present but to things that existed in the past and are planned, anticipated, and conceived for the future" (92).

As a writing teacher and WPA, language and time are at the center of my work, so this new concept of "island time" presented a challenge. At the Nassau campus, the staff, students, and my colleagues all respected island time. Even the bus driver mentioned that she might have to leave me if I kept my class too late. But what about contact hours? What about our responsibility to the students and the integrity of the degrees they were earning? I didn't sense that the students didn't care about their education. It was, in fact, quite the opposite. I found their dedication, as

a whole, quite strong. They showed great respect for education and perceived it as their gateway to a better future. The seriousness with which
they approached each course assignment made it impossible for me to
believe that their adherence to "island time" was in any way a measure
of their care for the class or respect for the discipline.

Adam's (1994) explanations of the many manifestations of time
throughout the ages led her to conclude that "time is still a fact of life
but it has emerged as a multi-layer, complex fact of life; multiple in its
forms and levels of expressions" (169). Elliott Jaques (1982, 3) went so
far as to claim that no people "living *at* the same time live *in* the same
time." I had walked into a new culture and been challenged to accept a
new expression of time. Two of Dotlich and Cairo's (2002) "unnatural
leadership" acts include (1) being open to new ways of doing things and
(2) being willing to "challenge the conventional wisdom" (25). In this
situation, I became open to the way a different culture interprets the
class times we set when making schedules. With this adjustment, I connected with my students and earned their trust. I don't believe Hewlett
Packard's "managing by walking around" strategy would have given me
the same understanding of how island time affects the classroom. Going
there and experiencing it firsthand prompted my discussions with the
students and Shaw, which both proved to be great learning experiences,
but actually watching the clock in the classroom while waiting for my students to arrive and securing my place on the bus before it left me made
it real. It would have helped to have learned about island time before
I began this journey, but I know that simply hearing about it from the
comfort of my office on the main campus, or hearing someone mention
it while I visited the Nassau campus for an afternoon, would have left
me with a superficial understanding. Those in the trenches truly understood island time, and now, so did I.

I find myself reflecting on this issue more than any other I encountered during my experience teaching in The Bahamas. While I did learn
a great lesson about the culture and the way these students understand
and express time, and while I can certainly step outside of my own comfort zone in order to respect another way of living, I cannot honestly
say that I have become fully comfortable with this felt sense approach
to time and the classroom. I recognize that I am very much a product
of my culture and have a strong attachment to the way I have always
interpreted punctuality. However, as a TWPA managing courses being
taught in vastly different places, I have had to accept that the time students spend in the Bahamian classroom is a bit shorter than the time
spent in Florida classrooms. Because of this, I adjusted the course plans

to include more assignments during the interim weeks in an effort to engage the students with the curriculum longer, thereby mitigating the effects of lost class time. I also consider this cultural difference when I hire instructors. Those who have what might be thought of as "type A" personalities can be great candidates for courses taught in the US, but they are not my first choice for these Bahamian courses. One of the instructors I have come to depend on to teach these courses is a great fit because she has a free spirit, which helps her to easily adapt to this and other challenges that arise, all the while making sure her students enjoy rich classroom experiences.

CULTURE AND LANGUAGE IN THE BAHAMIAN CLASSROOM

I learned a great deal during that first weekend, but I knew there was much more for me to learn. The next time I entered the classroom, I began by asking my students to tell me all about their country. I thanked them for explaining island time to me and told them I wanted to learn everything I could about The Bahamas from those who call it home. The students appreciated my interest and enthusiastically shared with me. I learned about Junkanoo, the street carnivals that are a celebration of live music and elaborate costumes, and the popular Fish Fry in Nassau where conch is cooked in myriad ways. They explained the country's commitment to its tourism industry. They said everyone on the islands understands that without tourism, their economy wouldn't survive. Therefore, there is an understanding among the people who live there, including those prone to criminality, that "no one messes with tourists." Interestingly, casinos operate on the islands for the tourists, but the locals are not allowed to gamble. These conversations dovetailed nicely with the discussions and assignments in business writing, and many students used the proposal assignment to come up with a way to improve industry on the island. Finally, they shared their country's devotion to Christianity and family. This made for interesting discussions during the World Literature I course when we studied Genesis, which they knew well and loved, and made for unique challenges when I brought in flood myths from around the world that bore strong resemblances to Noah's story and clashed with some of their long-held religious beliefs. These lively discussions engaged the students with each other and the curriculum.

During these discussions, I wasn't afraid to show what I didn't know. I was willing to listen and learn from my students. Dotlich and Cairo (2002) discuss leaders "who have made critical mistakes because they refused to admit that there was a gap in their knowledge" (17). They encourage today's leaders to "expose [their] vulnerabilities" (17) and insist that, "at times, the appropriate response is to be perplexed" and "to admit that you are uninformed about a subject or a situation" (18). They say "it is also important for leaders to be learners" (18). This approach worked for me. I learned about my students, and they, in turn, learned that I was truly interested in them, their home, and their stories. This all helped me immediately in my role as the teacher in the classroom, but it also offered me the insight I was looking for as the TWPA. I gained a better understanding of the student body the program serves. I learned what they felt they needed in order to get ahead in their workplaces: improved writing and document design skills and, most importantly, they needed a completed college degree. I learned how to create standard assignments that incorporated what mattered to the students into the curriculum, such as business proposals for improving island industry and job application materials since many believed they would be moving on and moving up once the degree was finished. I also found that asking them about their culture was a great way for future teachers to connect with these students. For me, it had prompted great discussions, and since then, other teachers have reported building the same wonderful connections using this approach.

Learning by listening was also a significant finding in my study of leadership in writing programs. In my study, interview participants often mentioned listening as an important quality of leaders of writing programs. Lizbeth Bryant, a director of composition, "spoke of a leader whose 'style came from an ideology that he had about teaching composition: expressivism, listening to people and working with them.'" Michele Eodice, writing center director and former president of the International Writing Centers Association said, "Good leadership involves listening, diplomacy, the ability to see the big picture, and the ability to empathize with people" (Bruce 2005, 197–98). It was interesting to see these assertions supported by my experiences.

The conversation I had with the students about their culture marked a turning point in the term. The students warmed up to me and were eager to continue talking with me and sharing their stories during class discussions and breaks. One student surprised me when she came up to me and urged me not to put my purse on the floor. I always keep an organized desk, so after I set up my materials, I put my purse on the floor underneath it. I picked it up at her request, but by the next day, out of habit, I had returned it to the floor. She came up to me again and explained that they believe this action will make me "go broke." I obliged and picked it up, and during that class, I noticed that none of the women had anything on the floor. They all respected that superstition. If my following suit made them feel better, that was fine with me. In fact, I appreciated them looking out for me. I realized I had probably placed my purse there on the first weekend as well, but none of them had tried to deter me from that practice.

The Nassau campus happened to be near a cemetery, so talk of their culture regarding funerals as elaborate social functions also took place. Evidently, the dress is formal, the services long, and the after parties even longer. I learned that "sweethearts" sometimes made appearances at these funerals. They were laughing when they told me this, but I didn't get it, so they explained it to me. In The Bahamas, "sweetheart," which I had always thought to be a term of endearment, is a derogatory term used for the other woman or man in an extramarital affair. There, you don't want to be called someone's "sweetheart." This reminded me that even seemingly common words, such as "sweetheart," can have very different meanings in other countries.

"Sweetheart" was only one of many language differences. When the first assignments came in, they included many British English spellings. It wasn't a surprise because I was aware of the political history of the island, but I had wondered if the students would have gotten used to using US spellings in their previous courses. I also thought there was a chance they would try to adopt US spellings because of their interest in the US. The most common differences included adding "u" to words such as behaviour, colour, endeavour, favourite, honour, humour, labour, and neighbour, and using an "s" where many US words would have a "z," such as analyse, apologise, authorise, customise, empathise, finalise, generalise, memorise, and organise. Spellings such as catalogue, centre, and learnt were also often used.

While these students were earning a degree from a US university, and while the textbooks and professors all used standard US English, the reality was that these students lived in a culture where variations of English were both accepted and expected. In addition to British and US influences, Bahamian language blends traces of African and Creole. Coming into this situation and insisting on standard edited US English would have been wrong. In this situation, I needed to take a different approach. Horner, Lu, Royster, and Trimbur (2011, 303) "call for a new paradigm: a translingual approach" that "sees difference in language not as a barrier to overcome or as a problem to manage, but as a resource for producing meaning in writing, speaking, reading, and listening." This approach makes sense in The Bahamas because the language these students were using functioned in acceptable and important ways in their culture. Horner et al. explained, "When faced with difference in language, this approach asks: What might this difference do? How might it function expressively, rhetorically, communicatively? For whom, under what conditions, and how?" (303–04). My Bahamian students planned to stay in their country either working in their current jobs or in those to which they planned to apply upon graduation. Rejecting their language in the classroom might have caused them harm in the workplace because they might have begun producing writing more appropriate for a US audience. Horner et al. said, "a translingual approach directly counters demands that writers must conform to fixed, uniform standards" (305) and that "the possibility of writer error is reserved as an interpretation of last resort" (304). In my class, I noticed the students placed "Re": in the center of their memos, which went against the standard textbook's instructions to place it flush left. I spoke with them about this difference and learned that, far from writer error, this choice made their memos accurate and professional according to Bahamian standards.

It can be easy to make assumptions about common customs and language use when entering an English speaking country, but even on an island so close to the US, differences can be stark. When I prepare future instructors to teach these courses, I talk with them about the importance of accepting these cultural and language differences. I meet with them individually since only one instructor is now going per term. Our individual meetings give us a chance to talk about the differences they are likely to encounter. I share my experiences and examples of student work I received. I also invite them to talk with me during the term when they begin to see these differences. We also talk about being careful not to assume every difference we see is an appropriate cultural difference. Sometimes, grammar, spelling, structure, and document design are wrong and need to be corrected. After all, students are in this course to learn these skills. I also remind instructors that these differences are not acceptable on our campuses in the US because those students will be writing for a different audience, one that is expecting to see standard US conventions.

MATERIAL CONDITIONS

The material conditions at the center proved to be a challenge. While the classrooms were clean and equipped with technology, the oppressive heat was difficult to contend with, even for a resident of South Florida. While the heat can be uncomfortable, the storms can truly cause life on the island to come to a standstill. One Saturday morning, we arrived at the campus and found that the power was out. It had been raining and continued to rain all day. My students and I spent close to four hours having class with no electricity, which meant no lights, no technology, and most importantly, no air conditioning. Towards the end of that morning class, the students began to ask if they could go home because they feared their homes might be flooding. The storm showed no signs of stopping, so campus staff decided to cancel the afternoon classes. The professors all went back to the hotel and sat in the open lobby watching the wind and the rain. The area was full of unhappy tourists who either wanted the sunny beaches they were promised in advertisements or wanted the airport to reopen so they could go home. We gathered together and waited it out. The power came and went, and I thought about ways to make up the lost class time.

With six hours of class per course each weekend, missing a weekend means missing one fifth of a term. When bad weather, illness, or other unexpected situations arise, faculty may not be able to get to the island for classes or leave when classes have ended, and instructors are not the only ones flying to campus. Some of the students fly in from surrounding islands. In my class, a few came from the island of Eluthera. Faculty and students alike have families, jobs, and other responsibilities that require their attention, and an additional day in Nassau does not figure into those plans. These issues pose administrative dilemmas. If storms or other unexpected problems cause an instructor not to be able to reach the island, six hours of class time must be made up. Some students have access to the Internet, so Blackboard and email could offer a solution, but not everyone has consistent access. If an instructor on the main campus has to miss class, another instructor could cover those classes, but even if someone was willing to fly to The Bahamas to cover a class, that person would not have been approved to work by the Immigration Department. Part-time faculty often work multiple jobs, so being stranded on an island can impede their ability to fulfill other commitments. I can't offer further compensation, so to avoid this unfair situation, I am careful to explain all of this when I interview new people for this work. I explain that while every effort is made to ensure schedules and even safety, the unexpected can and does happen, and many of these situations are out of my control. I provide instructors and curriculum, but in this middle management position, I have had to accept that there are many aspects of the program I can't change. I would prefer the students and faculty meet more often for shorter periods of time, but I would rather work within this current system than deny these students an opportunity to work with NSU to obtain a college degree. I would like these instructors to be paid more since they spend so much time in transit and on the island, but salaries are way out of my purview. I can—and do—make suggestions, but these are policies I do not set. As for making up class time, each situation is treated individually. Often, more time is given for assignments, new deadlines are set, the Internet is used as much as possible, and in rare situations, classes have been rescheduled.

On the day of the torrential storms that I experienced, I noticed one of the adjunct business instructors was especially concerned. I didn't know him well because he was quiet and kept to himself. One of the other instructors explained to me that this particular instructor worked for a number of schools and, in addition to his island courses, taught about ten online courses per semester. He absolutely could not afford to be without electricity. Whenever I saw him outside of classes, he was glued to his laptop. He was the only one of us who was ever on the Internet when we were away from the campus because Internet was not included in our stay at the hotel. I also opted not to pay the exorbitant international calling rates for my cell phone, so I had it turned off from Friday afternoon until Sunday when I returned to Florida. It was an interesting situation, and I knew it might be difficult for some instructors to be in a foreign country for two days without convenient phone and Internet connections. A variety of job and familial obligations could make this lack of communication uncomfortable at best.

CONCLUSION

I continue to reflect on my experiences teaching at NSU's Bahamas Student Educational Center in Nassau. As a new TWPA, my strategy was to go there as a teacher in order to learn how to support the program as an administrator. If I had not taken this approach, I may never have fully understood the challenges that can—and do—arise in this unique work. I wouldn't have felt the fatigue, watched the rain while waiting for the airport to reopen, or gotten to know the students, the facility, and the other instructors.

Transnational writing programs take many forms and operate in many contexts. That being said, I offer this advice to anyone entering into transnational writing program administration.

Go there.

Traveling to the country and the campus provides great insight into the local culture, everyday challenges, and campus conditions. Actually being there—on the ground, with the people, in the moment—is the best way to begin to develop a real understanding of the local context.

Teach there.

When possible, I encourage TWPAs to get into the trenches of the international classroom. For me, going beyond "managing by walking around" taught me what I needed to know about my program. Now that I have established that foundation, I feel as if I could employ the MBWA method with positive results. This is concurrent with what I learned through my study of leadership in writing programs. The people I interviewed consistently said that strong WPAs "maintain classroom connections" (Bruce 2005, 195). Being in the classroom—for the duration of a term—will reveal how the program is really working.

Speak with faculty.

Speaking with a variety of instructors working at a campus can help you discover what they feel is and is not working when it comes to curriculum, resources, and material conditions. This information can help you support them in their work. Speaking with them in the environment in which they teach is even better because faculty will likely bring up even more important issues, positive and negative.

Speak with the students.

Students are full of information about the local environment and their experiences in the classroom. They may offer a much different perspective, and this information can help you shape the program to fit their needs. Furthermore, it can be a wonderful experience to meet the student population your program is supporting.

Accept that the international campus will be different.

Inconsistency is often regarded as a negative, but it is unrealistic to expect a program administered in different countries to be exactly the same. Differences in course delivery, contact hours, and even curriculum focus can be okay. These differences do not, in and of themselves, mean the classes are less effective or the degree is of a lower quality.

Donald A. McAndrew, former director of a composition and TESOL Ph.D. program, said, "To sustain the process of leadership, literacy leaders must transform themselves constantly through reflection on their role as leaders, learn from their experiences, take risks, and change as curiosity and introspection direct" (McAndrew 2005, 128). In my role as a WPA supporting a transnational program, I have accepted that differences in contact hours are inevitable. I learned that cultural differences can be great, even when proximity and language make a place seem familiar, and most importantly, I have learned that taking an "unnatural leadership" approach works. I put myself in uncomfortable situations, and I learned from them. I admitted to gaps in my understanding and gave up some control of situations. I was a learner as well as a leader and a teacher, and this served me—and the program—well.

I currently have three faculty members who rotate in the Nassau writing faculty position because I learned firsthand, and those I have since sent have confirmed, that it is a taxing job, one that should not be repeated immediately. I assign these instructors to main campus and online courses in the interim and assign them to The Bahamas only when they feel ready to again embark on the demanding travel and teaching schedule. According to Dotlich and Cairo (2002, 25), being open to new ways of doing things is an important "unnatural leadership" act. When I began staffing the Nassau courses, I believed it would be easiest to assign one person to all of the courses. It seemed to make sense that if one person went to the island over and over again, that person would fully grasp the travel routine and any quirks the job might entail. After doing the job myself, I realized the demands could make the quality of instruction suffer should one person become too worn out from the weight of the work.

At the end of my term teaching at NSU's Bahamas Student Educational Center, to my surprise, my students presented me with several gifts. Among those gifts was a handmade purse, but it was another that I found most intriguing. This gift was a ceramic plate that included information about all of the islands and the culture of The Bahamas, from food and animals to cultural events and holidays. They handed me the plate and said, "This is your syllabus!" I took it and promised to study it. It still sits on a shelf in my office, and it reminds me that good things can happen when I dare to act as an unnatural leader by getting into the trenches, giving up some control, exposing vulnerabilities, and challenging conventional wisdom.

References

Adam, Barbara. 1994. *Time and Social Theory*. Cambridge, UK: Polity Press.
Bruce, Shanti. 2005. "An Analysis of Leadership Practices in Composition Studies." PhD diss., Indiana University of Pennsylvania.
Dotlich, David L., and Peter C. Cairo. 2002. *Unnatural Leadership: Going Against Intuition and Experience to Develop Ten New Leadership Instincts*. San Francisco: Jossey-Bass.
Jaques, Elliott. 1982. *The Form of Time*. New York: Crane Russak.

Horner, Bruce, Min-Zhan Lu, Jacqueline Jones Royster, and John Trimbur. 2011. "Language Difference in Writing: Toward a Translingual Approach. *College English* 73 (3): 303–21.

McAndrew, Donald A. 2005. *Literacy Leadership: Six Strategies for Peoplework.* Newark, DE: International Reading Association.

Rose, Jeanne Marie. 2005. "Coming of Age as a WPA: From Personal to Personnel." *WPA: Writing Program Administration* 28 (3): 73–87.

6
EXPLORING THE CONTEXTS OF US–MEXICAN BORDER WRITING PROGRAMS

Beth Brunk-Chavez, Kate Mangelsdorf, Patricia Wojahn, Alfredo Urzua-Beltran, Omar Montoya, Barry Thatcher, and Kathryn Valentine

INTRODUCTION

The US–Mexico border region is a dynamic rhetorical space with multiple language varieties and complexly related cultural and rhetorical traditions. Not surprisingly, this dynamic complexity presents a variety of challenges and opportunities to writing program administrators situated on the border. According to the Conference on College Composition and Communication (2009) Statement on Second Language Writing and Writers, writing teachers and WPAs should work to "recognize and take responsibility for the regular presence of second language writers in writing classes, to understand their characteristics, and to develop instructional and administrative practices that are sensitive to their linguistic and cultural needs."

The CCCC Statement on Second Language Writing and Writers was developed in response to the monolingual, monocultural orientation of most US writing programs, which are geared toward either homogenized English writers (Matsuda 2006) or English as second language (ESL) writers. Even though writing programs serving each of these populations share certain goals and interests, particularly at the post-secondary level, their historical development has resulted in separate fields with their own specific concerns, theoretical underpinnings, research traditions, and pedagogical approaches.

Following this dichotomous model, most US border universities allow only officially classified international students to enroll in ESL courses, while students who have progressed through the US school system must enroll in "mainstream" writing courses, regardless of their

DOI: 10.7330/9780874219623.c006

English language abilities or rhetorical and cultural backgrounds. Furthermore, the "regular" writing courses tend to approach rhetoric and writing from predominantly homogenized US curricular models. However, a large percentage of students in mainstream writing classes at US–Mexican border universities are bilingual or multilingual learners, variously referred to as English language learners (ELL), language minority, Generation 1.5, immigrant/domestic/resident ESL, and/or Spanish-dominant students. These students bring complex combinations of Mexican, Latino, and cross-border rhetorical traditions to the US writing classroom. We argue that border institutions can do more to attend to the strengths and needs of these bilingual/multilingual populations of students who—although familiar with some aspects of US culture and schooling—have unique linguistic, cultural, and educational backgrounds that clearly distinguish them from their monolingual counterparts. Such attention will prepare students for writing challenges both on and beyond the border.

In the context of the key characteristics of varied US and Mexican rhetorical traditions, this chapter first examines the writing programs at New Mexico State University (NMSU) and The University of Texas at El Paso (UTEP), two border universities with a growing population of bilingual/multilingual students.[1] We identify various aspects of institutional and curricular paths, particularly in relation to first-year composition and the specific situations facing domestic students for whom English is not a first language, situations in which they—and their richness and complexities—are, we argue, all too often ignored. We end by proposing several strategies that US writing programs at the border and beyond could employ to better serve the range of students who enter our classrooms.

WRITING PROGRAMS AT THE US–MEXICO BORDER

It is easy to make assumptions about students who enter writing classrooms. For instance, some people might assume that students are less than twenty years old, eager to learn, focused on their studies above all else, familiar with a range of school-based academic and literacy practices, and prepared to interact with ease in the English language. All too often, one or more of these assumptions is inaccurate. A growing number of US high school graduates enter higher education while still learning to read, write, and otherwise employ the English language (Roberge, Siegal, and Harklau 2009, 3). Such students, whether immigrants or the children of immigrants, represent a category of multilingual students that is less visible than the two more familiar categories of students: "native" English speakers and international students (Ferris 2009, 3). The complexity of this third group in the US–Mexico border context is perhaps even greater—and far more contested—than in non-border contexts. Our chapter focuses on these students by examining the institutional procedures, curricula, and pedagogies of our border writing programs, and then identifies areas with rich potential for productive change.

We share such details because many institutional processes, such as those facilitated by the admissions and placement offices, are beyond the responsibilities of WPAs. Knowing more about the complex context of our students, such as their language and cultural backgrounds as well as their academic success rates, can and should inform the decisions and work of the WPA. This topic is relevant for all WPAs, not just those working on the borderlands. As of 2011, 16.5 percent of U.S. college students aged 18–24 are Hispanic (Pew Research Center 2012, 7), making them the largest minority group going to college (8). The following information represents our attempt to better understand our students' experiences and reflect on our practices as they potentially affect the writers in our classrooms.

UNIVERSITY ADMISSIONS

Many students' first interactions with a university occur during the admissions process. Generally, students are divided into three groups: graduates from US high schools, transfer students from other US institutions (community colleges or other four-year colleges), and international students. Additionally, the admissions process varies significantly for domestic and international students. At NMSU and UTEP, domestic students have to meet the basic entry requirements mandated by New Mexico and Texas respectively. Applicants are required to have graduated from an accredited high school or academy (or have passed the General Education Development (GED) test) and have fulfilled the recommended high school curriculum, which includes at least two semesters of English at the high school level. If potential students don't have these courses (or any other courses included in the recommended curriculum) on their high school transcripts, they cannot be admitted into a four-year university and will need to attend a two-year college until prepared to transfer. Students at both institutions must also submit scores from standardized tests such as the ACT, SAT, and—for UTEP students—the Texas Student Success Initiative.

International students are defined as those applicants with a non-immigrant student visa. Most of the undergraduate international students at our institutions have graduated from Mexican high schools. These students, however, are often quite different from other international students. Some are actually US citizens (as it is not uncommon for Mexicans living in border cities to have American or dual nationality), although they may have attended school in Mexico and are Spanish monolingual. Therefore, they cannot be truly considered "international," if this term is based on citizenship status. To further complicate this group, some students may have attended all or part of their schooling in the United States, which is also quite common in the border region. In fact, some students go back and forth between US and Mexican schools, which has important financial advantages later on—for instance, attending a US high school for a period of thirty-six months qualifies UTEP students for in-state tuition when they attend college.

Given the number of transnational students from Mexico, UTEP has developed a "parallel" system of admission. These applicants take either the *Prueba de Aptitud Academica* (Academic Aptitude Test, or PAA) or the Test of English as a Foreign Language (TOEFL). If they take the PAA, this score is used in conjunction with their high school GPA for admittance to UTEP; they are thus identified as ESL learners and are required to take the ESL placement exam, unless they report a TOEFL score higher than 600 (paper-based) or 100 (internet-based). Depending on their placement score, these students may need to take various English for Speakers of Other Language (ESOL) courses before taking the ESOL equivalents of FYC courses. At NMSU, international students who graduated from a US high school do not automatically qualify for admittance; records of attendance from any international secondary school are also required. International students must demonstrate English proficiency by a TOEFL score of at least 500 (paper-based), 173 (computer-based), or 61 (internet-based). Those students who do not meet the qualifying levels of proficiency can, however, be admitted after successfully completing a program available through the Center for Intensive Training in English (CITE) at NMSU.

While the dual admissions processes for domestic and international students may be clear, it is still uncertain what languages students speak when entering our universities. The UTEP application for international students asks them to identify their first language, but the corresponding admission form for domestic students does not ask for their native or dominant language. There is, however, an optional question that asks students to report on "other languages" they may speak. In other words, the admissions process assumes that international students speak, read, and write in languages other than English, but that domestic students do not. Nonetheless, as we will explain, responses to this optional question for domestic students have allowed UTEP administrators to learn more about the student population's linguistic backgrounds and preferences.

We argue that more universities could do as UTEP is doing and add questions on the admission forms that allow, minimally, for identifying the numbers of US citizens for whom English is an additional language. If this information is communicated from admissions to faculty, WPAs could be informed and thus proactive in making decisions about hiring, training, and program development. NMSU administrators, for instance, are at a disadvantage without knowing how many students enter the university with a home language other than English. To remedy this, the WPA and others are developing a survey to identify home languages, language preferences, and the like. The plan is to distribute the survey to FYC students at the university and its four affiliated two-year colleges. For instance, decisions about how many, if any, instructors to hire with expertise in teaching both writing and ESL cannot be made without considering the population.

WRITING COURSE PLACEMENT

The process of placement is likely more important, and certainly more accessible, to WPAs than that of admissions. Often WPAs are focused on the writing proficiencies of their students, and the question of which writing courses are more beneficial (i.e., mainstream composition, ESL, basic writing, or some other alternative) does not have an easy answer at either of our institutions. Various writing faculty and administrators at both institutions maintain that all students who graduate from a high-school in which English is the language of instruction should be placed into mainstream basic writing or FYC courses, an argument that ignores border students' various backgrounds and the adaptations they will need to carry out in order to succeed. Other writing faculty and administrators argue that considerations should be made for students who are—or have been—identified "non-native" or "multilingual," and they recommend specialized writing courses. The boundaries between native and non-native English language users—and their corresponding rhetorical preferences—are not clear; thus, issues of placement are more complex than our processes allow (Ferris 2009). The reality is that the placement process is not often informed by WPAs or writing experts, and frequently this process is invisible. At our institutions, students tend to be placed through indirect measures (such as ACT or TOEFL scores), which Haswell (1998) argues are the most problematic type of placement mechanism.

Many ESL researchers have argued there "should be no one-size-fits-all" approach to placement, particularly given the "differences between domestic and international L2 writers" (Ruecker 2011, 95; see also Braine 1996; Matsuda 1999; and Matsuda and Silva 1999). Ideally, each student deserves individual attention, but for most institutions it would be virtually impossible to review and assess each student's profile to decide whether she or he would benefit from placement in a mainstream, ESL, or some other type of course. Instead, just as with the admissions process, there are parallel placement processes; students are automatically tracked into either mainstream or ESL writing courses based on the institution's policies regarding students' educational backgrounds, the diagnostic tools used or advising procedures available, the programmatic choices available, or a combination of these. At both NMSU and UTEP, there is no middle ground between the monolingual English/ESL dichotomy; in other words, two classifications are used for all types of border students. As a result, both native and ESL classrooms have a complex mix of students, and, thus, teachers and students alike may perceive that only some of the students' needs are being met (Matsuda 2008).

As we have suggested, these issues often become invisible as students are tracked into either the mainstream composition or the ESL composition course sequences. Domestic students at both of our institutions are tracked into mainstream courses, either basic writing or FYC, depending on the placement score they achieve on the ACCUPLACER writing exam (UTEP) or the ACT (NMSU). International and transnational students are tracked into ESOL courses automatically as a result of having taken the PAA or TOEFL tests. At both institutions, international students' TOEFL scores determine if an additional ESL placement test is necessary. Additionally, students are placed into a range of ESOL courses. At UTEP, ESOL students can start taking subject-matter courses while they are enrolled in ESOL courses, either core curriculum courses delivered in a bilingual format (usually taught in Spanish but with textbooks and materials in English) or mainstream courses taught completely in English. There is no procedure in place at either institution that enables students to transition from mainstream English courses to ESOL courses or vice versa, particularly because students arrive at each program through different admission and placement procedures.

From the students' perspective, the placement process is equally complicated. As research outside the US–Mexico border maintains, some multilingual/ESL students thrive in mainstream classes, finding them challenging but beneficial, while others prefer and benefit from participating in an ESL writing course (Costino and Hyon 2007). Aside from institutional placement procedures, some students might try very hard to avoid being placed in ESL courses, especially if they have experienced some level of discrimination as ESL learners or have come to see ESL as a label that carries a stigma (Bashir-Ali 2006; Ruecker 2011; Vandrick 1997). In universities where students are able to self-select, the timing of courses and the enrollment of their friends can influence their choices. In short, we simply do not know how individual border writers relate to these placement issues.

In order to achieve a better understanding of students' perspectives, Ruecker (2011) surveyed students in UTEP's first-semester writing classes (both general English [ENG] and ESOL). He found that 73 percent of the ESOL students were satisfied with their placement, while 96 percent of ENG students were satisfied. The most common response among those satisfied with their ESOL placement was that the course was "better for their needs" and could therefore support their learning more effectively (102). Among those not satisfied with their placement in the ENG sections were domestic ESL learners "concerned [that] their English was not good enough" or that they would be "more comfortable" with students like themselves—non-native English speakers (102). Each semester ESL instructors at NMSU report being approached by resident students who say they would be more comfortable taking an ESL course. Almost always, these students must be turned away due to the program only accommodating international students.

Along a slightly different vein, Ruecker (2011) also asked whether ESOL students would prefer to be in a writing course with only non-native English speakers or a class that included both native and non-native English speakers. The results were surprising: 79 percent said they wanted to be in a class that included both. In addition, about a quarter of the students in both tracks felt that labels such as "ESL" carry negative connotations and therefore would prefer to be placed in a course without such a label. Such results call for alternatives to the mainstream and ESL binary. Silva (1994) and Matsuda and Silva (1999) propose other models, such as cross-cultural composition courses with an equal mix of native and non-native English speakers or a model of self-directed placement (SDP) where students can view course syllabi and then choose for themselves.[2] Given these findings, NMSU now reserves two sections of

ENGL 111 for students from the College Assistance Migrant Program (CAMP). These students will comprise half of the population in each section, with the other half consisting of students who enroll through the regular enrollment process.

Clearly, our placement procedures do not ensure that students enrolled in mainstream composition courses are entirely comfortable communicating in English and, therefore, will be successful in the course. Recent data from the Center for Institutional Evaluation Research and Planning indicates that, of the students who graduated from a US high school and enrolled in UTEP's ENG 1311 for the 2010–2111 academic year, 38.7 percent reported being most comfortable speaking both English and Spanish and 8.6 percent reported being most comfortable speaking Spanish. Comparatively, 52.8 percent of the students reported being most comfortable speaking English. Nearly half of the students who were enrolled in mainstream courses indicated a more varied language background and experience, a great contrast to the normative monolingual English model. We suspect that even non-border institutions will find data with trends such as these, trends that warrant more attention if we are to teach to the populations present in our universities.

COURSE/CURRICULUM STRUCTURE AND TEACHING APPROACHES

Much like the admissions process, the current curricula at our institutions are not specifically designed to address the variety of rhetorical and cultural contexts our students bring with them. Thus, part of our call for this chapter includes examining the implications of this disconnect and perhaps addressing them (positive or negative) in our future work. This is not to say that individual instructors do not make some of these adjustments, but we feel that, *programmatically*, more can be done with respect to the issues we raise. This section briefly describes the writing curricula at our institutions and outlines areas that might present challenges for border students.

Drawing heavily on the Writing Program Administrator's Outcomes Statement (Council of Writing Program Administrators 2008), both of UTEP's first-year courses have recently been redesigned as rhetorically-based courses, with emphasis on audience, purpose, context, genre, and exigency in all assignments. This closely aligned two-course sequence seeks to help students think, read, and write critically; understand a theory of discourse communities; engage as a community of writers who dialogue across texts, argue, and build on each other's work; draw on existing knowledge bases to create "new" or "transformed" knowledge; develop a knowledge of genres as they are defined and stabilized within discourse communities; address the specific, immediate rhetorical situations of individual communicative acts; and develop procedural knowledge of the writing task in its various phases and using a variety of media. However, much remains to be explored as to how well the assumptions of this rhetorical base fit in with the complex rhetorical preferences of border writing students.

At NMSU, students generally begin their writing requirement by taking ENG 111: Rhetoric and Composition, the first of two required general education writing courses. After successfully completing ENG 111 (or its equivalent for international students), these students are then funneled into a second required writing course: a 200-level course connected to specific fields of study—business communication, technical or scientific writing, or writing in the humanities and social sciences. The FYC course is a four-credit semester-long class that focuses on rhetoric and argument as a means of introducing and reinforcing strategies of academic writing. The NMSU program, like the UTEP program, emphasizes critical thinking, rhetorical abilities, the ability to research effectively using a variety of sources, the capacity to arrive at one's own informed and considered opinion, strategies for persuasion, awareness of distinct strategies used in various disciplines, and the rhetorical means of establishing trust and credibility through the use of logic, factual support, and standard English conventions. The program also assumes that writing is a process, and that writing well almost always requires rethinking and rewriting.

Both UTEP and NMSU offer a series of professional development workshops for all instructors. Topics for these workshops have included teaching and tutoring ESL writers, teaching effective hybrid or online courses, and understanding the rhetorical basis for writing instruction. Although instructors at both institutions approach the course material in their own ways, there are certain principles that the UTEP program promotes:

- Writing should be taught and practiced as a process.
- Students should have multiple opportunities for feedback.
- Courses should help students develop their technological literacies and learn how to learn online.
- Students should be given the opportunity to reflect upon and improve their self-regulating strategies.
- Instructors should consider what skills and strategies students are expected to develop as they move beyond our courses.

At NMSU, the program emphasizes pedagogical principles that help students to:

- practice writing processes, from invention, drafting, and revising to editing and polishing;
- read actively and think critically;
- use writing to persuade, inform, and engage an audience through considered and supported thesis development;
- explore new methods of academic inquiry, rhetorical analysis, and argumentation; and
- develop academic research abilities.

Toward these ends, teachers are encouraged to build courses that are student-centered and workshop-oriented, with peer review and critique as regular practices. Also common are practices emphasizing writing as process, with expectations of notes, rough drafts, peer and instructor feedback, revised drafts, and final/polished drafts—the latter edited with an eye to a particular target audience, ideally academic.

Overall, both institutions attempt to build a writing program with a rich view of literacy and learning. However, much remains to be explored as to how well the assumptions of these programs fit the complex rhetorical experiences, knowledge, and preferences of border writing students. Moreover, a great deal of student participation is expected, including peer reviews, which could conflict with previous classroom experiences students have encountered in other cultural situations. It is also possible that some writing assignments rely on culturally-specific information outside the range of multilingual students' experiences. Additionally, multilingual students typically require extra response time from their instructors in more than one medium; for instance, teacher comments on student writing are more effective if supplemented with an individual student-teacher conference (CCCC 2009). However, such conference time must be built into the curriculum, which may make it difficult to cover the multiple assignments required in each course.

SUCCESSES AND INTERVENTIONS WITH US CURRICULUM IN A BORDER CONTEXT

Given the potential disconnect between the predominantly US curricula and the border students enrolled in the writing courses, readers of this chapter might assume a large number of various problems. Although we have not seen a wide range of concrete evidence for this, we suspect the domestic ESL students at our institutions are largely a silent minority, who may blame themselves for the obstacles they encounter. However, institutional data at UTEP suggests that the problems may not loom as large as we might envision. At UTEP, when the curriculum, delivery, and evaluation systems were implemented in 2009, some instructors resisted the change, believing that the program would be too challenging, particularly for ESL students. However, preliminary data indicated these concerns were unfounded. We were able to correlate our students' language preferences mentioned above with their placement and their pass rates for 2010–2011. For the first-semester course, the pass rates for these groups were almost identical. Students who selected Spanish as their language of choice—and graduated from a US high school—performed just as well as both the students who selected English and those who selected English and Spanish. The pass rate was between 77 percent and 79 percent for all three groups of students.

We attribute this rate of student success to, first of all, the flexibility, hard work, and determination of students. Programmatic structures have no doubt contributed as well. At UTEP, graduate student instructor preparation includes one year of tutoring in the university's writing center prior to serving as an FYC instructor. During that time, graduate students receive instruction and best practice tips for working with ESL students, in addition to the intensive experience of working with these students one-on-one. Periodic mandatory workshops stress the importance of giving students linguistic space within the confines of an English-dominant curriculum. For instance, students are given the option of mixing languages in their drafts, of using Spanish when conducting primary and secondary research, and of speaking Spanish or Spanglish when working collaboratively with their classmates. Several of the assignments in both courses provide instructors and students with the opportunity to explore the languages they speak within their discourse communities and understand when and why they switch between them. Finally, instructors are accustomed to living in a community where Spanish is commonly heard in multiple domains and many of the graduate student instructors are bilingual themselves.

At NMSU, data about success rates for various groups are not available, given that students are not asked about languages they know or use more comfortably as part of the admissions process. However, nearly 80 percent of students overall pass the ENGL 111 course in fall semesters, with approximately 70 percent passing the course in spring semesters. According to our data, students who retake the course the second time have a small chance of passing. This is an area we feel needs further exploration and one that calls for performance measures for ESL students, among other groups. Questions we wish to explore include the following: Who are the people who do not pass ENGL 111? What are their characteristics? Are there distinct characteristics of those who pass ENGL 111 the second time around as opposed to those who do not? How can we meet the needs of students who struggle with a basic requirement such as ENGL 111? What are their needs, and what types of support do we offer them? What support *could* be offered?

In the interim, NMSU programmatic structures may contribute to student success. Instructor preparation begins before the fall semester, during an intensive week of training in which an ESL director offers an informative workshop. Graduate students become instructors of record in their first semester, while also taking a semester-long practicum on writing theory and pedagogy, one unit of which addresses teaching writing to ESL students. Typically once a year, an additional workshop may be offered as professional development that focuses on the needs and resources of ESL students. Other structures in place at our institutions may also contribute to student success. Some of these are described in the sections that follow.

PROGRAM COLLABORATIONS

The division of labor between composition and ESL writing courses (Matsuda 1999) is manifested in various ways. At our institutions, the mainstream and ESL composition courses are offered by different departments; faculty who teach one group of students may not feel prepared or have the desire to teach the other group, further exacerbating the native/ESL dichotomy. We have found that the institutional division of ESL and mainstream courses can impede collaboration and cooperation. Both programs see great potential in the idea of sharing resources and identifying and addressing common problems, but this sharing proves challenging. Recently, members of the ESL and mainstream programs at NMSU and UTEP have taken specific actions to better coordinate their programs.

At NMSU, faculty have made regular meetings together a priority. Together, they tackle the long (and sometimes contentious) debates over whether or not mainstream and alternative courses for multilingual writers should be—for all intents and purposes—equivalent, or whether different agendas should drive curricula and implementation (Atkinson and Ramanathan 1995). After initial discussion, the two programs at NMSU identified large discrepancies in the aims of their respective FYC courses, as well as a complication in that those teaching ESL courses were not trained in composition and vice versa. The two departments are now in the early stages of working together to propose an additional ESL course that will prepare students for the mainstream course and, equally important, are considering how to go about preparing mainstream instructors to work more effectively with ESL students. Similarly, at UTEP, the ESL composition courses have been modified so that course objectives are better aligned with those in mainstream FYC courses, and syllabi, assignment sheets, and other materials developed in the latter have been shared and modified, as needed, by the ESL faculty. In addition, the directors and some faculty of both programs have occasionally met with academic advisors and admissions coordinators to discuss general processes and specific instances where students may have been inappropriately placed.

Despite these efforts, the mainstream and ESL programs remain independent and disconnected in important ways, not just within the institutional structure but also in terms of the way administrators, instructors, tutors, and the students themselves perceive these programs and their mission, pedagogical approaches, methodologies, and academic exigencies. However, conversations concerning advising, placement, and curriculum are beginning to bridge the two programs in ways that will ultimately benefit all students. Most certainly, the research related to this chapter and other projects has helped to illuminate the benefits and challenges of the writing programs at our border campuses.

WRITING CENTERS

One important approach to helping border ESL students succeed is for WPAs to realize that writing classes cannot be the sole source of instruction. University writing centers are a natural companion for this endeavor. Therefore, it is important for FYC programs and writing centers to complement each other's work. UTEP's writing center serves both undergraduate and graduate students from all disciplines in the university, though the majority of students come from the College of Liberal Arts. (The second largest group is from The School of Nursing and the College of Health Sciences.) Most of the tutors are undergraduates, but first-year graduate students also contribute significant tutoring hours. Approximately half of the students who come to the writing center have ESL-related concerns. Some of these issues are minor, such as a few surface errors—sometimes viewed as writing "accents"—that do not impede the communication of ideas. Other students have vocabulary and syntactical concerns that reflect a lack of experience writing and reading in English. The majority of ESL students at the writing center fall into these two groups. A third group of students usually consists of international students, most often from Mexico, whose writing is greatly influenced by the rhetorical traditions and expectations of their native cultures.

Writing center tutors, both graduate and undergraduate, receive substantial training with regard to ESL students. The founding director of the writing center (a second language writing specialist), as well as PhD students with second language specialties, have created training materials for tutor workshops that cover issues such as second language acquisition processes, contrastive rhetorics, and error analysis. In addition, ESL concerns are regularly brought up during weekly meetings, and any sample student writing that is discussed usually includes an ESL student's paper. The goal is to make every tutor an ESL specialist.

NMSU's writing center, operated through the Department of English at NMSU, also serves both undergraduate and graduate students at the university. Typically, the largest group of students who use the center are those enrolled in FYC, with the next largest group being international students—often graduate students—from a variety of disciplines. All of the tutors are graduate assistants who also teach general education writing courses through the English department; they are assigned to the writing center in their first year of teaching at NMSU. In a typical year, approximately half of the tutors are new to the center. A few of the consultants identify as non-native speakers of English and/or international students. Most of the students using the center identify English as their first language and come to the center with a range of writing concerns. A much smaller group of students identify as Spanish speakers; presumably, some of these students come to the center with ESL concerns. Students who speak a variety of other languages are also represented, but in much smaller numbers.

At NMSU, writing center tutors receive substantial training in the teaching of writing, both for the classroom and for the writing center. This training includes attention to working with ESL students in the writing center, as well as discussions on language diversity. In addition, tutors attend ongoing professional development meetings, where they discuss specific ESL tutoring sessions and learn about working with ESL students from presentations that draw on writing center and second language writing scholarship.

WRITING FELLOW PROGRAM

Another type of program made available to directly assist students at both UTEP and NMSU was the Writing Fellow Program (WFP). In the

WFP at UTEP, writing tutors were placed in FYC and workplace writing classes to help students as they focused on writing assignments in their courses, some on a whole-semester assignment and some on an as-needed basis, indicated by the instructor. Writing fellows also helped faculty design and implement writing assignments. Unfortunately, budget cuts have resulted in what is hoped to be a temporary cessation of the program.

The WFP at NMSU, a joint effort of the Student Success Center (an academic support center for students across campus) and the writing center, was created to offer students assistance with writing projects assigned in the classroom. Initially introduced on a trial basis in three sections of ENG 218: Technical and Scientific Writing, the WFP employed the use of an assigned writing fellow (a select graduate-level student from the NMSU writing center) who worked in the classroom to provide direct access to tutoring services and writing resources via scheduled writing workshops, individual meetings, and online and face-to-face support. Focused on engaging each student enrolled in the course, the writing fellow provided services on all writing assignments over the course of a semester. This collaborative process allowed students to interact freely with a dedicated writing fellow, explore potential issues or questions about writing, and co-develop an appropriate course of action to improve writing capability. In particular, ESL students sought the one-on-one assistance from the writing fellow in numbers that led him to inform the WPA that there seemed to be a greater need in this area than had previously been acknowledged.

The WFP aimed to provide general writing assistance to all students, although it specifically targeted first generation students. In the future, this program could be re-envisioned to more fully address the specific writing needs of bilingual or multilingual students who are seeking help with their English writing. Because the funding for this program was not continued, students needing assistance are now directed to other support systems, such as the university's writing center and the Student Success Center. We consider it unfortunate that this type of program was not continued, a program that supported our aims to strengthen the diversity we see in our FYC courses and beyond.

THE ASSURED PROGRAM

Another program at NMSU is specifically designed to support students from migrant families. The Agriculture Science Summer Undergraduate Research and Education (ASSURED) program at NMSU is designed to provide first- or second-generation students of migrant farm workers the opportunity to work on intensive research projects and gain a better understanding of science and writing. Funded by the National Science Foundation and held during the summer, ASSURED pairs ten undergraduate students with faculty mentors and staff to work on research initiatives related to their interest. While conducting research, the students are required to attend weekly writing workshops designed to assist them in writing a research paper. Because most—if not all—students in the program are ESL writers, these writing workshops are administered by trained ESL faculty or graduate assistants from the NMSU English department. During these writing workshops, students work one-on-one with faculty to better facilitate their understanding of the research writing process. Students are provided with the writing strategies and resources necessary to create a small research paper, as well as an academic poster and presentation. Each written paper is designed to be submitted for consideration in the *Journal of Young Investigators*.

THE CAMP PROGRAM

Another program at both NMSU and UTEP assists students from migrant families. College Assistance Migrant Program (CAMP) is a federally-funded program that specifically helps migrant or seasonal farm worker students, with an aim of seeing them to graduation. To that end, CAMP offers a variety of support mechanisms (such as monthly visits with an advisor) during the students' first year at NMSU. CAMP also tries to continue to interact with the students after that first year, checking up on their needs and their progress. Additionally, UTEP has a federally-funded CAMP program, which offers similar support systems designed to help students from migrant families succeed.

CONCLUSION

In her article on the responsibilities of WPAs with respect to English language learners, Miller-Cochran (2010) stressed that it is up to WPAs to take steps in "gaining an understanding of the linguistic and cultural influences that affect students and their written language" (217). Yet currently, like most US universities, the writing program placement processes at UTEP and NMSU are modeled after the monocultural–foreigner approach, geared toward either homogenized English writers (Matsuda 2006) or ESL writers. Likewise, the FYC program curricula at both universities have not been fully adapted to the border context. While the curricula at both institutions draw on best practices as established by the Council of Writing Program Administrators, they are not created to explicitly address the complex rhetorical context of the US–Mexico border. We have identified the potential needs of just some of the types of students on our campuses.

Despite this approach, the overall pass rates at both schools are fairly high (from 70% to 80% in first-semester classes[3]), and research conducted at UTEP has shown that students who self-identify as bilingual or who are predominately Spanish speakers had identical pass rates as those who self-identified as preferring to communicate in English only. Perhaps the pass rates at both universities can be partially attributed to teacher training and several successful interventions. Both the NMSU and UTEP writing programs include ESL writing concerns in their pedagogy courses. Both institutions have writing centers staffed by tutors whose training includes second language writing, and both writing centers are frequently used by ESL students. NMSU also offers a summer program (ASSURED) to assist students from first- or second-generation migrant farm labor families, many of whom are resident English language learners, and both institutions offer the CAMP program for this same population. The former WFP provided focused assistance to ESL students at both universities. Overall, the practices at both institutions follow guidelines established by the CCCC Statement on Second Language Writing and Writers (CCCC 2009). However, our programs are left with questions that we are only beginning to address:

- What are the implications of the disconnect between the border context and these universities' writing placement procedures and curricula? Preliminary data about pass rates suggest this disconnect hasn't negatively impacted students' success rates, but what about other indicators of success? At NMSU, one study is underway to identify characteristics of students who earned As in first-semester composition compared to those who did not pass the class with the required C or above. With this data, we hope to extract factors—such as language and cultural diversity—that can impact student performance. All writing programs can benefit from conducting research of this nature. Similar research can also identify patterns in overall retention and graduation rates.
- How can writing programs move away from what Matsuda (2006) has called "the myth of linguistic homogeneity?" How can we privilege students' multilingual backgrounds in the writing class? Some shifts we have made at UTEP may be subtle, but they are meaningful. For example, students begin the two-course sequence by considering the many discourse communities they belong to. They are encouraged

to think about the various language practices within those discourse communities, and to reflect on the times and ways they move between different languages. Many instructors are comfortable permitting small groups to complete their in-class projects in Spanish. Finally, when appropriate, students are encouraged to complete both primary and secondary research in their first language. This might include reading relevant articles published in Spanish for their literature review or rhetorical analysis projects. Or, for their documentary assignment, it can mean interviewing a research subject in Spanish and providing subtitles for their audience. During the program's monthly workshops, writing instructors exchange ideas for effective ways to incorporate students' languages into what has long been perceived as an "English-only" class.

- How can we make more people aware of the multilingual nature of our students and the implications for such diversity? One solution is to network with institutional entities across our campuses. WPAs can be instrumental in raising awareness of opportunities and challenges. At most institutions, there is a separation between academic areas and other areas, such as student services. We argue that all who come into contact with the diverse students at the border and beyond need to be brought together to work together. At NMSU, for instance, a grant from the provost's office allowed for this type of model to be implemented. The grant, running from fall 2012 through fall 2013, allowed for monthly meetings among representatives from the following offices on campus:

  ○ Academic Support Programs and Services Center (ASPSC)—the program committed to providing quality educational services that achieve academic, personal, and career success for all student-athletes.

  ○ College Assistance Migrant Program (CAMP)—helps migrant or seasonal farm worker students succeed in college.

  ○ Academic ESL/CITE Programs—designed to meet the needs of primarily international students.

  ○ Student Success Centers—two centers that provide centralized, university-wide academic support, including learning assistance and tutoring for students from all disciplines and at all levels of academic standing.

  ○ Teaching Academy—the entity that serves NMSU educators through training, mentoring, and networking.

  ○ TESOL Program—offers both undergraduate and graduate education designed to prepare preservice and inservice teachers to work with culturally and linguistically diverse (CLD) students in the context of classrooms, schools, and the community.

  ○ Writing Center—offers one-on-one tutoring for NMSU students regardless of level of experience; helps with anything from understanding assignment directions to revising final drafts.

○ Writing Program—the first- and second-year writing program
housed in the Department of English, reaching almost every
student through ENGL 111 and/or the required 200-level writing course.

Each of these entities work together to build and enhance more
inclusive understandings and approaches across campus with respect
to our students. These meetings have lead to action items for the various entities to accomplish. In addition to these monthly meetings, our
institution has used the grant money to have an outside expert lead a
series of introductory and follow-up workshops. As someone who has led
educational training workshops on ESL-related writing and composition
around the world, this workshop leader has helped faculty and others
who serve our diverse population gain more inclusive understandings
and approaches for tutoring and teaching. The grant money also supports a number of faculty in attending the summer New Mexico Higher
Education Assessment Workshop. There they work intensely for two
and a half days on their respective assessment projects and leave with
an action plan for implementation. The team of faculty has developed
an assessment plan for curricular and cross-unit interventions, which
were cultivated after a year spent focusing on the cross-campus needs of
English language learners.

In beginning conversations across campus about issues related to the
diversity of our student population, and in drawing such issues to the
attention of upper-administration, our WPAs and others have been able
to focus attention on our multilingual students and acquire support that
will (1) help identify our students' linguistic and cultural profiles; (2)
provide professional development opportunities for instructors, staff,
and program administrators across units that are consistent with the
diverse population we serve; (3) disseminate findings; and (4) develop
cross-unit and collaborative interventions that ensure the academic success of our diverse students, all while tapping into opportunities (made
possible by cross-cultural sharing) that acknowledge and embrace diversity. We believe this model looks encouraging, and we hope that others
will consider similar steps in expanding conversations about our linguistically and culturally diverse students across campus.

However, institutions need not necessarily seek an outside expert on
ESL or related issues. We suggest that institutions identify the many valuable resources that could easily be made available to address aspects of
multilingual writing classrooms. One of our co-authors (Barry Thatcher)
is a resident expert on intercultural communication and Spanish–English
L2 writing (specifically cross-border composition, US–Latin American

rhetorical theory and writing, and research methods). Thatcher is piloting an English composition course reserved just for Mexican nationals who are in an exchange program with NMSU. They are ESL writers who are caught between the formal ESL and English department programs. Preliminary results are very promising. There is also a Teaching English to Speakers of Other Languages program in the Department of Education that has faculty with relevant areas of expertise as well. And NMSU has a Center for Latin American and Border Studies, with faculty engaged in issues relevant to our diverse populations. Each of these entities could be tapped to play key roles in informing our institutions about the possibilities for optimizing diverse student work.

In the meantime, we advocate that WPAs become familiar with the literature on teaching writing to linguistically and culturally diverse students. We recommend beginning with recent books, such as Kirklighter, Cardenas, and Murphy's (2007) *Teaching Writing with Latino/a Students: Lessons Learned at Hispanic-Serving Institutions*; Ferris's (2009) *Teaching College Writing to Diverse Student Populations*; Horner, Lu, and Matsuda's (2010) *Cross-Language Relations in Composition*; and Matsuda, Cox, Jordan, and Ortmeier-Hooper's (2011) *Second-Language Writing in the Composition Classroom: A Critical Sourcebook*.

In this chapter, we have outlined a number of cases where our border institutions were either responsive or unresponsive to the strengths and needs of domestic ESL students. We can do more, at both institutions, to become more aware of their diverse presence in our classrooms. We can also do more to work with programs that are already providing support for ESL students at our institutions, getting to know their mission and identifying areas where joint efforts could benefit both our students and our programs. "Exploring the context of US–Mexican border writing programs" is merely the first step in laying the framework for much-needed research, evaluation, and development of a border writing curriculum.

Notes

1. New Mexico State is a mid-size university located in Las Cruces, New Mexico. In fall 2010, it had a student population of 23,000. Forty-four percent of the students were Hispanic, 79 percent attended full-time, and 75 percent were in-state students. The University of Texas at El Paso is located in El Paso, Texas. In fall 2010, it had a student population of over 22,000 students. Seventy-six percent of the students were Hispanic, 61 percent attended full-time, and 83 percent were from El Paso County.
2. SDP is the placement process recommended by the CCCC (2009) Statement on Second Language Writing and Writers.
3. This pass rate is consistent with pass rates in other first-year courses at the university.

References

Atkinson, Dwight, and Vai Ramanathan. 1995. "Cultures of Writing: An Ethnographic Comparison of L1 and L2 University Writing/Language Programs." *TESOL Quarterly* 29 (3): 539–66. http://dx.doi.org/10.2307/3588074.

Bashir-Ali, Khadar. 2006. "Language Learning and the Definition of One's Social, Cultural, and Racial Identity." *TESOL Quarterly* 40 (3): 628–39. http://dx.doi.org/10.2307/40264549.

Braine, George. 1996. "ESL Students in First-Year Writing Courses: ESL Versus Mainstream Classes." *Journal of Second Language Writing* 5 (2): 91–107. http://dx.doi.org/10.1016/S1060-3743(96)90020-X.

Conference on College Composition and Communication (CCCC). 2009. "CCCC Statement on Second Language Writing and Writers." http://www.ncte.org/cccc/resources/positions/secondlangwriting.

Costino, Kimberly, and Sunny Hyon. 2007. "'A Class for Students Like Me': Reconsidering Relationships Among Identity Labels, Residency Status, and Students' Preferences for Mainstream or Multilingual Composition." *Journal of Second Language Writing* 16 (2): 63–81. http://dx.doi.org/10.1016/j.jslw.2007.04.001.

Council of Writing Program Administrators (CWPA). 2008. "WPA Outcomes Statement for First-Year Composition." http://wpacouncil.org/positions/outcomes.html.

Ferris, Dana. 2009. *Teaching College Writing to Diverse Student Populations.* Ann Arbor: University of Michigan Press.

Fortuny, Karina, and Ajay Chaudry. 2009. *Children of Immigrants: Immigration Trends.* Washington, DC: Urban Institute. http://www.urban.org/publications/901292.html.

Haswell, Richard. 1998. "Searching for Kiyoko: Bettering Mandatory ESL Writing Placement." *Journal of Second Language Writing* 7 (2): 133–74. http://dx.doi.org/10.1016/S1060-3743(98)90011-X.

Horner, Bruce, Min-Zhan Lu, and Paul Kei Matsuda, eds. 2010. *Cross-Language Relations in Composition.* Carbondale: Southern Illinois University Press.

Kirklighter, Cristina, Diana Cardenas, and Susan Wolff Murphy. 2007. *Teaching Writing with Latino/a Students: Lessons Learned at Hispanic-Serving Institutions.* Albany: State University of New York Press.

Matsuda, Paul Kei. 1999. "Composition Studies and ESL Writing: A Disciplinary Division of Labor." *College Composition and Communication* 50 (4): 699–721. http://dx.doi.org/10.2307/358488.

Matsuda, Paul Kei. 2006. "The Myth of Linguistic Homogeneity in U.S. College Composition." *College English* 68 (6): 637–51. http://dx.doi.org/10.2307/25472180.

Matsuda, Paul Kei. 2008. "Myth: International and U.S. Resident ESL Writers Cannot be Taught in the Same Class." In *Writing Myths: Applying Second Language Research to Classroom Teaching*, ed. Joy M. Reid, 159–76. Ann Arbor: University of Michigan Press.

Matsuda, Paul Kei, and Tony Silva. 1999. "Cross-Cultural Composition: Mediated Integration of U.S. and International Students." *Composition Studies* 27 (1): 15–30.

Matsuda, Paul Kei, Michelle Cox, Jay Jordan, and Christina Ortmeier-Hooper, eds. 2011. *Second-Language Writing in the Composition Classroom: A Critical Sourcebook.* Boston: Bedford/St. Martin's.

Miller-Cochran, Susan. 2010. "Language Diversity and the Responsibility of the WPA." In *Cross-Language Relations in Composition*, ed. Bruce Horner, Min-Zhan Lu, and Paul Kei Matsuda, 2010–20. Carbondale: Southern Illinois University Press.

Pew Research Center. 2012. *Hispanic Student Enrollments Reach New Highs in 2011.* http://www.pewhispanic.org/files/2012/08/Hispanic-Student-Enrollments-Reach-New-Highs-in-2011_FINAL.pdf.

Roberge, Mark, Meryl Siegal, and Linda Harklau, eds. 2009. *Generation 1.5 in College Composition.* New York: Routledge.

Ruecker, Todd. 2011. "Improving the Placement of L2 Writers: The Students' Perspective." *Writing Program Administration: Journal of the Council of Writing Program Administrators* 35 (1): 91–117.

Silva, Tony. 1994. "An Examination of Writing Program Administrators' Options for the Placement of ESL Students in First-Year Writing Classes." *WPA: Writing Program Administration* 18 (1–2): 37–43.

Vandrick, Stephanie. 1997. "The Role of Hidden Identities in the Postsecondary ESL Classroom." *TESOL Quarterly* 31 (1): 153–7. http://dx.doi.org/10.2307/3587980.

PART II

Transnational Language

7

GLOBAL WRITING THEORY AND APPLICATION ON THE US–MEXICO BORDER

Barry Thatcher, Omar Montoya, and
Kelly Medina-López

INTRODUCTION
Global and Border Theory and Practice of Writing

Globalization and transnationalism generally mean the growing interdependence of people and cultures (Grewal 2008), with globalization focusing generally on economic independence and transnationalism focusing more broadly on interdependence.[1] Both examine the conditions, connections, and factors that facilitate and structure interdependence among people, due in large part to global finance, economy, energy, law, immigration, health, and so on. Because of the evident global connection related to oil prices, for example, most people acknowledge the de facto existence of globalization. In other words, what happens in the Middle East has a direct impact on what I pay for gasoline; we are now dependent on each other.

For researchers and program administrators of English writing courses, globalization does not have the same dramatic, public effect as oil prices, but it does have two key impacts. First, the number of ESL and ELL speakers/writers around the world is an issue of globalization. There are more ESL speakers in China than native speakers of English. More than a decade ago, John Swales (1997, 373) argued that English is a "Tyrannosaurus Rex" because it is the dominant language of science, business, academia, and information technologies and is trampling cultural and linguistic norms around the world. Pennycook (1995) similarly argues that English and its teaching/learning strategies are significantly influencing world cultural patterns, citing problems of development as connected to this influence. Not much has changed since 1999, except for an acceleration of this global influence of English, perhaps in part

DOI: 10.7330/9780874219623.c007

due to internet technologies. Thus, when ESL students attend our US writing classes, they bring their theories and practices of English as taught and experienced in their ESL class, directly influencing their pedagogical and curricular expectations.

Second, globalization has also meant that US writing classes have a much larger percentage of students whose primary language is not English, and who are not familiar with the cultural and rhetorical patterns expected by US institutions. This is especially true along the US–Mexico border and concerning Mexican–Latino immigrants, the subject of this article. The new 2010 US government census reports that "More than half of the growth in the total U.S. population between 2000 and 2010 was because of the increase in the Hispanic population. Between 2000 and 2010, the Hispanic population grew by 43 percent, rising from 35.3 million in 2000 to 50.5 million in 2010" (Census 2011). The Pew Center also reports that, in the same time frame, Hispanic enrollment in US universities surged by 24 percent (Hispanic 2012).

Thus, globalization has meant a significant influx of students in US universities, many of whom speak English as a second language and are not familiar with the cultural writing practices of the United States. The largest influx is from Latin America, most notably Mexico. WPAs have certainly noticed this influx of ESL students, which has generated an admirable amount of inquiry, research, and more reflexive practice. This realization and subsequent development is fully explored throughout this book and merits no further discussion here.

But how can WPAs address globalization—or even the similar term, transnationalism—in meaningful ways? First, because of globalization, researchers are beginning to interrogate US approaches to writing instruction, exploring how previously invisible curriculum, pedagogies, and materials are designed by, for, and according to predominant US cultural and rhetorical traditions. They are also hypothesizing about how to best engage these traditions. Foremost have been Canagarajah (2006), Horner and Trimbur (2002), and Matsuda and Atkinson (2008). Further, a number of researchers have complicated the term "ESL," primarily focusing on students that are caught between languages, such as Generation 1.5 (G1.5) students (Harklau et al. 1999).

However, as helpful as these studies are, few of them dare describe the actual features or patterns of the predominant US writing curriculum, including its rhetorical assumptions and strategies. This failure has two causes. First, many studies apply lots of heat, labeling the US curriculum as hegemonic, invisible, debilitating, colonizing, and so on, but none have identified features beyond general history (Horner and

Trimbur 2002), the fact of invisibility (Matsuda and Matsuda 2009), or multilingualism pedagogy (Canagarajah 2006). Second, and at the other end of the spectrum, many researchers take a *local approach*, demonstrating the highly unique patterns of literacy, but rarely connecting these patterns to the broadly-competing rhetorical approaches in the classroom (Scenters-Zapico 2010).

Giving in to the local approach or not daring to describe predominant rhetorical patterns leaves writing teachers, administrators, and researchers to wonder: what are ESL, G1.5, and multilingual students having to acculturate to when they enroll in US writing classrooms, and how can we ethically and sensitively help them achieve their goals? What is perhaps not apparent—but is addressed in this chapter—is the role of theory and methodology. Why have the theories and methodologies employed by these ESL and G1.5 researchers made them unable or unwilling to validly and reliably draw out these rhetorical attributes and describe, or at least hypothesize, how they function in the ESL and multilingual classroom?

These theoretical and methodological weaknesses have four sources. The first is US ethnocentrism: Much of the current research on G1.5/ESL writers examines writing in US contexts, drawing on US-based theories of rhetoric and writing, which naturalizes or makes invisible the cultural and rhetorical foundations of these "diverse" contexts. For example, the collection *Transnational Literate Lives in Digital Times* (Berry, Hawisher, and Selfe 2012) documents general world trends in digital literacies outside the United States and portrays the "global" digital literacies of foreign graduate students living in the United States. However, instead of grounding the experience of these graduate students in their home literacies and, then, their complex transitioning to US contexts, the core of this text shows how these graduate students un-reflexively assimilated US rhetoric and writing theory, which they used as the foundation for their voices. For example, one Mexican national was quite taken with Villanueva's (1993) *Bootstraps* and Mejia's (2004) article in *Crossing Borderlands*, using both as touchstones for grounding his digital literacies and forming his own voice and approach to digital literacy and storytelling. Villanueva's and Mejia's texts are entirely US-based, with little or no research/theory from Mexico or Latin America. Ironically, this approach assumes that a well-educated Mexican national can only speak about his digital literacy experiences using US-sourced theory and research. The ethnocentrism is obvious.

Second, the great majority of ESL, G1.5, and multilingual research in the United States assumes a US context that is safely ensconced where predominant US values still reign, in spite of evident multiculturalism. Consequently, perhaps the continued perpetuation of predominant US values is because a large variety of ESL students (from many backgrounds and languages) come together in the US classroom, and they generally have two things in common: the need/desire to learn English, and the default use of the US cultural and rhetorical paradigm as common ground from which they can learn English (Matsuda and Matsuda 2009). It would be impossible to interrogate and accommodate the great variety of cultural and rhetorical traditions, or to use another non-US tradition as the curricular base. Thus, ESL writers bring their highly varied and complex rhetorical and cultural traditions to the writing classroom, but—in order to make the classes work—this incredible diversity is homogenized into the US paradigm (Matsuda and Matsuda 2009), a kind of US ethnocentrism.

A third problem is that these methods generally focus on language and composition styles of students *in the classroom*, assuming that the rhetorical patterns these students draw from—and that the US curriculum is based on—are mostly academic and linguistic. There is research attending to key retention and performance factors—such as individual motivation, family support, and educational traditions (Ruecker 2012)—but, generally, this approach ignores the rhetorical traditions that originate outside the classroom and are not directly connected to language use[2]. This purely academic approach is narrow and ethnocentric in two ways. First, the formal writing programs, curricula, and classes that are common in US, Canadian, and Northern European countries are situated very differently in other parts of the world, where, in many places, they minimally exist in the same developmental and institutionalized way. Mexico, for example, has minimal writing courses, especially for science and engineering (Garza Almanza 2009). Thus, it's difficult to compare the rhetorical traditions of a well-developed writing program to one that does not formally address writing theory and rhetoric.

Instead, it's much more likely that the broadly combined cultural and rhetorical traditions from industry, politics, religion, and socioeconomic structures form the foundation of traditions that both US natives and ESL, multilingual, and G1.5 students bring to the writing classroom. Consequently—as Connor, Nagelhout, and Rozycki (2008) and Matsuda and Atkinson (2008) argue—researchers, teachers, and WPAs would be well served by paying attention to the developments of intercultural rhetoric and writing, which examine the interaction of different rhetorical traditions in a variety of academic and nonacademic writing contexts.

Fourth, related to the academic and linguistic focus, common methodologies used to denaturalize the US writing classroom have significant validity problems for global contexts. First, many theorists draw on literary and critical, textual hermeneutics when exploring global writing in US classrooms (Canagarajah 2006), but these theories are not designed to assess the planning, composing, reviewing, and evaluating of multilingual student writing, only the sociopolitical dynamics of mostly literary texts. Second, when some researchers use empirical methods, which are extensively validated in US composition contexts, they fail to globalize the methods themselves, again using US-sourced methods to assess global contexts. Most methods used to address global writing are not designed for global inquiry. Instead, they are a mix of broad frameworks (often derived from literary theory hermeneutics) that are localized at the individual level, leaving a significant gap between the predominant rhetorical traditions of a specific context and the rhetorical strategies of individual students. This is clearly evident in Berry, Hawisher, and Selfe (2012)'s argument, where they discuss broad digital history on the one hand—citing global growth of information technologies—but, on the other hand, they can only connect a half dozen graduate students to their own digital lives, both interpersonally and locally (using US theory). Consequently, this work cannot connect the features of the larger hegemonic status of predominant US patterns to how these patterns actually influence writing in the classroom.

These questions about theory and methodology are critical; as of yet, our field of ESL, multilingualism, and rhetoric and writing studies has yet to address them, so they are precisely the focus of this chapter. Drawing on our extensive experience, we propose both a methodology and practice for engaging with the predominant features of the US writing curriculum, as exemplified at the US–Mexico border.[3] This chapter first describes a global writing theory and practice by drawing on work in intercultural rhetoric and professional communication. Next, it grounds that theory by exploring features of the US–Mexico border, exemplified by health communications. Finally, it examines the features of writing curricula at UTEP and NMSU, hypothesizing about the types of rhetorical patterns that border students are drawing upon to engage with this curriculum.

GLOBAL THEORY OF WRITING AND RHETORIC

As explored earlier, our current state of research and theory demonstrates a wide gap between a general claim of US hegemony and a determined belief that this hegemony must be influencing concrete practices. How do we bridge that gap? Following what Barry Thatcher has fully developed elsewhere (Thatcher 2010; 2012b), we believe that the most ethical and effective approach to research on intercultural and border populations is the "etic-then-emic" approach that is grounded in the human capability framework. Despite a great variety of approaches to intercultural theories and methods (Gudykunst 2005), almost all intercultural researchers reference a kind of tension between *emic* (local–insider) and *etic* (outsider–universal) constructions (see Headland, Pike, and Harris 1990). Since this approach is so critical to global writing, we will define and operationalize them here.

Emic and *etic* are terms first developed by linguist Kenneth Pike (1967). Emic derives from the term *phonemic* and etic from *phonetic*. A phoneme is the smallest linguistic unit of meaningful sound, depending on language and culture. Phonetic is the smallest unit of language sound that can be made by humans across all languages. For example, English and Spanish speakers (not writers) have different phonemes for the same letters in the alphabet. For many Spanish speakers, the consonants S and C or B and V often sound the same and are used (more or less) the same in spoken, but not written, language. Thus, it is common, for example, to see Spanish signs in stores that have mixed these pairs up, using "serrado" (closed) for the correct "cerrado" (open), or "avierto" (open) for the correct "abierto" (closed). Since most Spanish speakers cannot tell the difference between these two consonant pairs, each pair is usually a single phoneme, or, in other words, indistinguishable in spoken language. However, English speakers distinguish between C and S and B and V, so each of the pairs is a separate phoneme, which forms four phonemes instead of two. This difference between Spanish and English phonemes is a culturally specific difference, or an *emic* difference, based not on universals but on cultural evolution and use of the two languages.

This emic approach has been operationalized in anthropology as "the intrinsic cultural distinctions that are meaningful to only the members of a given society in the same way that phonemic analysis focuses on the intrinsic phonological distinctions that are meaningful to speakers of a given language" (Lucy 1996). Thus, only members of a given culture can judge the emic descriptions of their culture or language because this knowledge is insider-based, or only available to those from that culture. In other words, a Spanish speaker would have to learn that the English pairs B and V and C and S are separate phonemes—they mean something different, unlike Spanish.

As previously mentioned, the etic approach derives from the term *phonetics*, which is an area of linguistics that studies the physical elements of speech sounds and their processes of production, reception, and perception. A phone is a speech sound made by a distinct working of the mouth, tongue, throat, and air. Unlike phonemes, phones are not language or culture specific; in fact, any normal speaker of a given language can physically articulate all of the phones available to the human species. Thus, phonetics is universal and often explores how different languages utilize phones to form phonemes, exemplifying the etic-then-emic approach.

These emic and etic distinctions developed into competing paradigms. The emic approach argues for the intrinsic incomparability of one culture to another, while the etic camp argues for the need to provide neutral frameworks or approaches for comparing cultures. This division focuses squarely on epistemology. Emics argue that knowledge is fundamentally local and is culture specific, while Etics argue that—just like possible speech sounds—there are similar universals of knowledge and behavior across cultures (see Morris et al. 1999 for a better discussion of this distinction). Despite these often stark differences, most anthropologists and linguists agree that researchers should use both emic and etic approaches (Bhawuk and Triandis 1996; Lucy 1996; Morris et al. 1999). Emic gets at the intuitive and empathic elements of culture and is critical for carrying out ethnographic fieldwork. In addition, emic often produces important variables for later etic hypotheses. Etic approaches, on the other hand, are essential for cross-cultural comparison, but they must be qualified with emic details.

For intercultural and global research, etic approaches are best operationalized as "common human thresholds of interaction" (Thatcher 2010; 2012b) that all humans share, regardless of their culture. From this perspective, they are not viewed as positivistic, modern narratives, but rather as dynamic frames constructed through constant cultural development and structuring, much like Darwinistic scenes of evolution (Bourdieu 1999; Mesoudi 2011; Pagel et al. 2013). For example, Thatcher draws upon a variety of intercultural researchers (Hall 1976; Hampden-Turner and Trompenaars 2000; Hofstede 2010; House et al. 2005) for etic frames, which usually include: relations between the group and one person; rules/norms; public versus private boundaries; status; sources of virtue or guidance; time; the role of context in communication; and the handling of inequality in communications. Each frame is universal to humanity; for example, all cultures create and apply rules, demonstrate how a person relates to others, and deal with time or the role of context in communication. However, the ways cultures conceptualize and operationalize these common human thresholds are unique and dynamic, and, thus, they are effective for comparing cultures and then enriching these comparisons with emic details.

For ESL and multilingual researchers, one tremendous benefit of the etic-then-emic approach is the ability to explore and conceptualize global rhetorical contexts, revealing the kinds of rhetorical and cultural adaptations and acculturations that many of our students must carry out in order to be successful in the writing classroom. The next section provides a model of this kind of global inquiry, first exploring the dynamics of the US–Mexico border and, second, using the etic-then-emic approach to examine the rhetorical patterns in health communications.

THE US–MEXICO BORDER AS A MEANS OF EXPLORING A GLOBAL WRITING THEORY

The US–Mexico border region is a dynamic rhetorical space, with multiple language varieties (Spanish, Spanglish, and English), and at least four complexly-related cultural and rhetorical traditions (Mexican, Anglo, cross-border, and Latino). Not surprisingly, this dynamic complexity brings challenges to US writing programs. Among the theoretical and methodological reasons already discussed, one reason why the border is so unexplored is that the border variable complicates the dynamic nature of multilingual and multicultural writing, perhaps demonstrating a uniqueness that may or may not exist outside border areas. Thus, a dynamic model emerges for understanding the relation of border composition, rhetorical traditions, and global writing curriculum and administration.

First, the border is not a context where numerous languages and rhetorical traditions are, by necessity, homogenized into a single US paradigm; instead, there are two strongly competing languages (Spanish and English) and rhetorical traditions (Mexican and US; see Baca 2000). Since the US side of the border region *was* Mexico 160 years ago, many of the social, cultural, and institutional foundations were originally based on Mexican models. Consequently, US institutions have had to map onto—or be created in the context of—Mexican models. The Mexican side of the border region is clearly based on Mexican models, both historically and currently, yet the US influence is clear and undeniable (Vila 2000). As a result, on the US–Mexico border, the Spanish language and Mexican rhetorical traditions are a legitimate and powerful alternative to English and US traditions (Baca 2000). A US–Mexico border sociologist, Pablo Vila (2000), explains how these cultural and social foundations took root, both in El Paso, Texas, and right across the border in Ciudad Juárez, Mexico. In many ways, these sides of the border are substantially similar, but—because of the strength of either US or Mexican legal, political, and educational institutions—each side is also distinct. Current border research is attempting to understand which cultural and rhetorical values can cross the border, which cannot, and which ones get reconstituted or revised on the other side (Thatcher 2012a; Vila 2000). For example, Thatcher (2012b) found that US border universities exhibited strong US rhetorical approaches on their websites, despite being situated within a few miles of Mexico. On the other hand, Mexican border universities showed a strong US cultural influence in their website design, exhibiting a more hybrid approach. This asymmetrical influence—US ignoring the Mexican influence, while Mexican assimilating a US influence—is typical of border situations (Vila 2000). This is the complexity of daily life on the border, and it is a rich context for exploring global writing programs.

Thus, WPAs at US border universities face many curricular and cultural challenges: How can they design writing programs that address the complex border situation, while preparing their students for writing situations outside the border region? How do border university students relate to the writing curriculum? And how might WPAs help border students understand and build strength from their multicultural and multi-rhetorical situation? To begin exploring these questions, this section first identifies key—but general—characteristics of US and Mexican rhetorical traditions. This comparison lays the groundwork for typifying border rhetorical and cultural combinations, or *rhetorical functionings*, showing how students might draw from—and relate to—these traditions in their US writing classrooms. Finally, the next section explores a basic rhetorical structure of writing in order to hypothesize how these six different functionings might relate to US-based writing curricula. This more abstract and theoretical chapter contextualizes the other chapter in this collection that explores the writing programs at New Mexico State University (NMSU) and The University of Texas at El Paso (UTEP).

US AND MEXICAN RHETORICAL TRADITIONS

For this section, drawing on ESL research, we present key differences in writing strategies between US English writers and Mexican Spanish/ESL writers. Using an example of health communications along the

US–Mexico border, we outline five differences between US and Mexican rhetorical traditions. We present these differences not as absolute, essential characteristics, but as predominant strategies that border writers draw upon in a variety of academic and nonacademic contexts. For those scholars predisposed to the local approach, this discussion will feel (and be) too broad, but—as articulated by almost all intercultural researchers—it's important to understand the broad, etic frame in order to situate the local.

Much research has compared the different writing styles of US and Mexican rhetorical traditions in academic contexts (see Abbott 1996; Crawford 2007a; Crawford 2007b; Montaño-Harmon 1991; Kail, Sanchez y Lopez 1997; LoCastro 2008; Simpson 2000; Valero-Garcés 1996). Most of this research concludes that, from an English writer's perspective, Mexican Spanish writers have more run-on, longer, and more complex sentences; constant lexical repetition for thematic cohesion (as compared to syntactic parallelism); more additive and causal conjunctions; and frequent, conscious deviations from topics. And, not surprisingly, most—if not all—these differences tend to show up in Mexican ESL compositions (Montaño-Harmon 1991; Simpson, 2000).

Further, most research comparing the writing instruction of L1 (first language) Spanish writing and L1 English writing concludes that Mexican writing instruction emphasizes: (1) vocabulary building by using synonyms, antonyms, paraphrasing, and derivations; (2) writing practice that focuses on tone, style, and vocabulary based on written models from literary figures; (3) practice in elaborating a given idea through writing in various ways, as the student attempts to develop the theme in greater depth; and (4) work on correct grammar and mechanics at the sentence level (Montaño-Harmon 1991, 418). Likewise, much research in professional communication (Thatcher 2006, 2011) has documented rhetorical differences between Mexican and US professional writers. These writing and pedagogical differences originate from different rhetorical traditions, especially concerning the styles and rhetorical purposes of writing, as opposed to orality (Leon-Portillo 1996; Thatcher 2006; Valadés 1996).

However, despite these apparently clear differences between predominant Mexican and US writing styles, it is often difficult to understand how these differences might influence writing instruction and program administration, especially at US universities. These contrastive rhetorical characteristics are so broad that they are devoid of meaning in specific contexts, a point Thatcher (2012b) demonstrates elsewhere. How do we analyze this well-developed body of research in contrastive rhetoric, which clearly shows different patterns in Mexican compositions? And how do border writers, who are often caught between these two rhetorical traditions, draw on both traditions in US writing classrooms? In order to understand the relevance of rhetorical difference, we need to move beyond some stylistic features and explore more fully the cultural and rhetorical reasons for these differences. This understanding will help US writing instructors and program administrators understand both *how* and *why* border writers draw upon both rhetorical traditions in complex, strategic ways. This how and why is precisely what many current ESL and multilingual approaches are missing.

To illustrate these differences, we turn to two examples of health communications that are commonly used along the US–Mexico border, a topic that is more thoroughly developed by Thatcher (2012a) elsewhere. We employ these two examples because they are used for the same context, are written by Mexican and American authors, and they describe the same content. In other words, they are as much an etic frame as possible (Thatcher 2010). These samples demonstrate the full array of rhetorical differences that often surface not only in writing styles, but also in rhetorical features such as purpose, audience–author relations, information needs, document organization, and stylistic preferences.

Both health pamphlets are produced by the National Institute of Health and address cholesterol and heart health (National Institute of Health 2013). The first example is a *fotonovela*, a pamphlet that was developed by Mexican health experts contracted by the NIH for the Mexican-American and Latino community in the United States. Figure 7.1 is a selection of four pages from the twenty-four-page English version. In English, *fotonovela* means a photo drama pamphlet, and, as a genre, the fotonovela has been a critical component of health instruction for Latino communities, not just in the United States, but in all of Latin America (see hablamosjuntos.org). This fotonovela has been very successful in the United States, as noted by its main author, Hector Balcazar (Balcazar et al. 2011), one of our colleagues in multiple border health and literacy research projects.

Figure 7.2 shows an NIH pamphlet with the same content, but delivered for a non-Latino or generic US audience.

We present these two pamphlets as a way to more fully understand the broad rhetorical differences between the United States and Mexico, especially since these differences are so relevant on the US side of the border, the site of this inquiry. Of course, no two documents can exemplify such a complex comparison, or thoroughly represent both populations, but we present them as examples in order to help readers

Figure 7.1

understand the complex, but broad, etic intersections at the US–Mexico border and how these intersections influence border writing classrooms.

The next section briefly summarizes five key rhetorical differences, following the intercultural, etic-then-emic comparative model previously discussed. This model assesses the rhetorical approaches of two documents using common human thresholds of analysis, or, in other words, comparison variables that both groups of people share (Bhawuk and Triandis

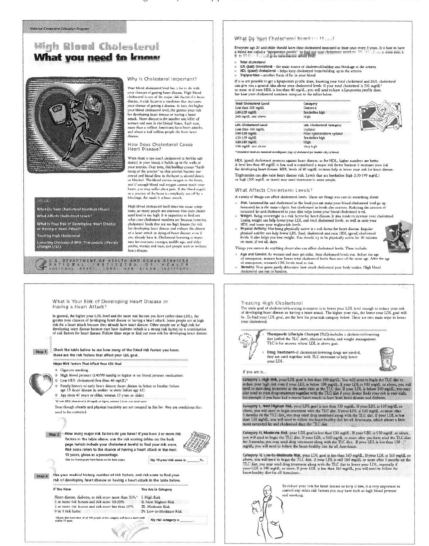

Figure 7.2

1996; Lucy 1996; Thatcher 2010; 2012b). These variables are: individual–collective, rules orientation, degree of involvement, context, and time.

Collective and Individual Orientations

This variable or value set assesses levels of independence or dependence among groups of people and demonstrates how these differences manifest themselves in various writing and communication patterns. People in more independent or individualistic cultures tend to be more self-reliant, competitive, and act in their own self-interest for personal growth (Hampden-Turner and Trompenaars 2000). In collective societies, individuals tend to be integrated into strong, interdependent groups, to which they are extremely loyal (Hofstede 2010). As much research has documented, collectivism is a dominant value in Mexico, while the United States consistently ranks very high on individualism (Albert 1996; Castañeda 1995; Condon 1997; Hampden-Turner and Trompenaars, 2000; Hofstede 2010; House et al. 2005; Kras 1991).

These differences show up in both NIH manuals. It is obvious from Figure 7.1, or the *fotonovela*, that there is a strong collective orientation. The entire health scenario is grounded in the Ramírez family, including the specific roles of grandmother, father, mother, and two children. The first page of this pamphlet does not define cardiovascular health; rather, it lays out the family as the context for discussion. Members of this family are not seen as independent equals, a characteristic of individualistic cultures; instead, each member of the family is seen in a specific, traditional role with their corresponding hierarchies, further reinforcing the collective orientation of the pamphlet. This approach emphasizes the interpersonal relationships among family members and the social hierarchy involving the grandmother, father, mother, and children. Interestingly, the tighter urban space in the Ciudad Juárez, Mexico view similarly demonstrates a collective value. In academic writing contexts, this value of collectivism often manifests itself in more formal and role-sensitive writing strategies, including great care for social hierarchies (Kras 1991), a modeling of appropriate rhetorical approaches, and more formal vocabulary, syntax, and grammar (Montaño-Harmon 1991; Simpson 2000).

On the other hand, Figure 7.2 indicates strong patterns of individualism. The first page of the pamphlet shows a lone person, isolated from social context. There is no grounding in a specific time, place, context, or social relation; rather, there is a strong emphasis on an objective analysis of cholesterol levels, divorcing these levels from anything other than the individual. In addition, the figure of the lone person running in the heart and the checklist emphasize personal achievement and self-creation. Further, from a US cultural standpoint, there is a friendlier document design pattern, which allows individuals to quickly locate desired information. Conversely, the document design of the fotonovela is not as friendly to US readers because it is designed around social interaction, not the important information about heart health.

Much ESL and second language (L2) research has documented the presence of individualism in US writing programs. This includes: seeing the individual as the unit of analysis (Ramanathan and Atkinson 1999); a strong division between personal and objective communication strategies, which resolve interpersonal conflicts by going back to the uniqueness of the individual rather than to one person's political or social context (Stewart and Bennett 1991); a dumbed-down readership level so as to uncomplicate the interpersonal dependence of communicators (Kras 1991); and an emphasis on personal achievement, self-creation, and reader-friendly document design patterns (Thatcher 2012b).

These collective–individual differences perhaps point to difficulties more collective writers may have in more individualistic US composition programs. For example, in most US writing classrooms, students are required to take a stance on a controversial topic and write an essay that attempts to persuade readers on that issue. The focus of this type of assignment is on what the writer—as an individual—thinks or believes, which avoids intimately connecting the writer to larger social or political groups, as shown in the fotonovela.

Rules Orientation and Parallelism–Uniqueness

The ways cultures develop and apply rules vary around the world. To assess this difference, intercultural researchers have constructed the values of particular and universal orientations. In particularist cultures, the default approach applies rules and decisions depending on relations and context, while universalist cultures emphasize equality of treatment regardless of social position or relation. In other words, instead of the "level playing field" of universalism, the particularist playing field is overtly structured with a specifically tailored set of rules for each social relationship. Research shows that Mexico consistently ranks high on particularism, while the United States tends to favor universalism (Castañeda 1995; Condon 1997; Hampden-Turner and Trompenaars 2000; Hofstede 2010; House et al. 2005; Kras 1991).

The fotonovela shows a more particularist or flexible and unique approach, while the generic pamphlet is more universal. In the fotonovela, each page has a different layout based on visual and verbal information needs, and there is no parallel information or list. Next, and most importantly, the "rules" or subject of cardiovascular health are discussed using the specific relations and context of the Ramírez family. The rules change according to the circumstances—the arrival of the boyfriend raises the blood pressure of the father, a classic particularist approach to rules. The fotonovela does give universal numbers for understanding levels of cholesterol, but these numbers are personalized for the individual filling out the form or box. In addition, the colors used in the fotonovela are much more vibrant and contrastive, emphasizing the dynamic nature of its culture. Finally, this pamphlet downplays the scientific "process" of determining appropriate cholesterol levels, instead focusing on the Ramírez family context and their social relations.

The second pamphlet demonstrates strong universalist tendencies. First, it focuses on generally defining cholesterol levels for everyone, notwithstanding their social or personal situations. Second, this pamphlet presents objective information that emphasizes the scientific and universal nature of health and cholesterol. Third, it presents much of the information in list form, a universalist strategy that underscores the parallelism and readability needed for universalist readers. Also, there is a general page design that persists throughout the whole pamphlet. Fourth, this pamphlet has much more muted—or less dynamic—colors. Finally, the process of determining appropriate cholesterol levels is overt, illustrated by the calculator and the tables used to determine the different levels of cholesterol.

In composition classrooms, these particular–universal differences imply strongly divided preferences for writing styles. As shown by ESL research, two critical patterns of Mexican compositions are (1) uniqueness in paragraph development (non-parallel structures) and (2) more complex, artistic sentence structures (Crawford 2007a; Crawford 2007b; Kail, Sanchez y Lopez 1997; LoCastro 2008; Montaño-Harmon 1991; Simpson 2000; Valero-Garcés 1996). On the other hand, writing pedagogy in the United States usually emphasizes uniformity, parallelism, and a strong reliance on the writer to carefully guide the reader through the text (Hinds 1987).

Public Versus Private and Degree of Involvement

Next, the pamphlets differ in terms of public versus private and specific and whole relations. Figure 7.3 shows public/private relationship circles (developed from Thatcher 2012b and adapted from Trompenaars 1994) that best demonstrate these different approaches.

The specific orientation is characterized by the ease in which a person can enter a private relationship from a public sphere, which is shown by the dashed line. However, once in, that relationship is usually sphere-based and rarely crosses over, and friendship belongs to one or

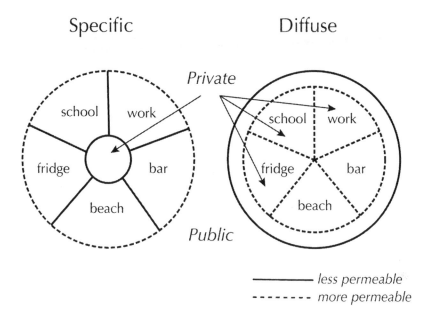

Figure 7.3

two spheres only, with little or no crossover of authority. The diffuse circle shows that it is difficult to pass from a public into a private relationship, signaled by the thick line of the outer circle. And there is a small public/private mixture area between the two circles, but, once inside the larger private sphere (signaled by a dashed smaller circle), the relationship crosses boundaries, and there is no distinguishable private self. Because of its high levels of individualism and universalism, the United States usually ranks high in specific orientation, while Mexico, because of its collective and particular orientations, usually ranks high in diffuse orientation (Castañeda 1995; Hampden-Turner and Trompenaars 2000; Hofstede 2010; House et al. 2005; Kras 1991).

The two NIH pamphlets reflect the differences in specific and diffuse communications. As exemplified in the fotonovela, diffuse communication patterns mean that any topic of discussion must situate the whole person in all his or her aspects and dimensions, including social hierarchies and context. The first thing introduced in the fotonovela is not a definition of good cardiovascular health, but rather the family and their names and roles. Consequently, the health of the family is holistically grounded in their relations, their diet, and their home. Thus, the diffuse patterns about cardiovascular health seem (to specific people) to be hidden in the drama of the family, circling around the point of cholesterol, because diffuse communicators need to understand the whole person before getting to the point.

On the other hand, the US-oriented pamphlet is broken up into specific topics and people, such as doctors, prescription drugs, age, gender, and other concrete components of the person. However, these concrete or specific topics or issues are never brought together into a whole, but are discussed individually. In addition, instead of showing a concrete person or family with names and context, the second pamphlet shows an icon of a person. They are not talking about a specific person, only the part of a person that is related to cardiovascular health, a perhaps extreme example of a specific communication strategy. This pamphlet also promptly gets to the point, with a bulleted introduction as a caption in the left hand corner and an announcement of the topic in the first line. Almost all of the paragraphs have a clear and direct topic sentence, and rarely does a paragraph wander from that topic. Further, the layout of the US-oriented pamphlet is more specific, or—as a diffuse person might say—it is spotty and chaotic, with topics, pictures, and information seemingly scattered all over the place without coherent connection.

In writing classrooms, this difference can show up mainly in directness and how coherence is defined. Specific cultures strongly favor getting to the point quickly and then developing aspects of that point in a related, often linear, fashion. On the other hand, research explains the more diffuse style of Mexican communications (Condon 1997; Kras 1991) as it manifests itself, mostly as planned deviations in argumentative structures that focus on complex combinations of people, issues, and events (Crawford 2007a; Crawford 2007b; Kail, Sanchez y Lopez 1997; LoCastro 2008; Montaño-Harmon 1991; Simpson 2000; Valero-Garcés 1996).

Role of Context in Communication

This value set assesses the role of context in communicative interactions (Hall 1976; 1983). All cultures communicate in contexts, but how they rely on context for meaning differs. Low context means that meaning resides primarily in the explicitly coded part of the communication, not in the surrounding context. Thus, there is great focus on the accuracy of the explicitly coded text, and low context communicators try to program into the communication every verbal sign and cue to carefully guide the reader through the message, meaning that there is an overt emphasis on organizational and transitional strategies that pilot readers through texts. Connor (1996) and Hinds (1987) label this type of writing as "reader friendly," writing that assumes a reduced reliance on the reader to bring their own contextual cues and creates transitions to encourage understanding.

On the other end of the spectrum, high context communication assumes a strong reliance on contextual and social cues for meaning. Here, good writing focuses on how information elucidates the influence of the social context on meaning. High context communicators generally focus on adhering to interpersonal relationships instead of fixed guidelines. There is low attention to detail and high attention to intent. Instead of parallelism, high context communicators prefer novelty so as to match the uniqueness of the evolving relationship in its specific context. To them, parallelism is boring and artificial. Connor (1996) and Hinds (1987) label this type of writing as "reader-responsible" (Connor 1996, 42), or writing in which the reader is expected to fill in the information and create the transitions. Because of its individual, universal, and specific orientations, the United States usually defaults to low context communications, and, for the opposite reasons, Mexico usually defaults to high context communications (Castañeda 1995; Condon 1997; Hall 1976; 1983; Hampden-Turner and Trompenaars 2000; Hofstede 2010; House et al. 2005; Kras 1991).

Both NIH pamphlets exemplify low and high context communications. The generic pamphlet is low context—it concretely codes the message into the language itself, as in the case of determining cholesterol levels. Thus, there is little or no reliance on context to understand what this message means in the lives of the readers. Furthermore, there are many visual and verbal strategies that serve as signposts to guide the reader through the text, including lists, boxes, small graphics and icons, lines across the page, etc. In addition, there is specific text that can be used to accurately quantify levels of cholesterol risk, an approach that is highlighted by the calculator icon. There is also attention to detail, including outlining different types of cholesterol, different risk rates, and other concrete, context-free information. There are also various lists and an overwhelming parallelism.

On the other hand, the fotonovela is classically high context. It communicates the message of improving cardiovascular health by way of the Ramírez family, not from actual codified text. Thus, the reader is supposed to infer the message of improving cardiovascular health through the family's discussion of the topic. Great attention is given to the intentions of the people, specifically the mother in wanting what is best for her family, the father in wanting what is best for him as the father, the grandmother in her role, and the children in their roles. These intentions are highlighted by the perpetual smiles on the characters' faces and the positive language of the captions. In addition, the general outline or organizational pattern of the pamphlet is not topic based, but rather contextual or narrative, using the story to signpost its major sections. Further, much more detail is given to the context of where this happens—the house, the actual food being prepared, the people's names, and the events surrounding the topic. There is much less technical detail in the fotonovela because these details, in the appropriate context, will be worked out within the family's discussion.[4]

Monochronic and Polychronic Time

Cultures view and use time differently, especially in their communications. Polychronic timeframes mean simultaneity, multiple tasks managed at the same time, and apparent disorganization. It focuses on the importance of place and the involvement of people rather than adherence to present schedules. On the other hand, monochronic or sequential timeframes mean linked linear structures of cause and effect, with an organized flow of events (Hall 1976; 1983). Written discourse in monochronic cultures emphasizes linear structures of topics, a direct topic sentence to situate that discourse, and a given/new discourse structure. On the other hand, polychronic communicators favor the orchestration of events, people, places, and issues in discourse. Often, writing in polychronic cultures exemplifies complex syntax and paragraph structures, with many narratives in polychronic or multiple timeframes. Because of its individual, universal, specific, and low context orientations, the United States usually prefers monochronic time orientations, and, for the opposite reasons, Mexico ranks high for polychronic communications (Castañeda 1995; Hampden-Turner and Trompenaars 2000; Hofstede 2010; House et al. 2005; Kras 1991). This different view of time strongly correlates with the universal and particular values associations, especially regarding traffic. Traffic patterns in Ciudad Juárez are generally much more polychronic, with flows that are not nearly as regulated and linear.

The two NIH pamphlets exemplify the differences in monochronic and polychronic timeframes. Because the fotonovela uses narrative to make its point, it manages to (1) tell the story, while at the same time (2) describing high cholesterol, (3) the dietetic connection to high cholesterol, (4) the role of stress and high cholesterol, (5) the connections between age and gender for high cholesterol, and (6) how to reduce high cholesterol to improve health. This is a complex, polychronic orchestration of health, cholesterol, and the Ramírez family. In addition, the layout of the fotonovela reflects the multitasking, or simultaneity, of the Ramírez family.

The second pamphlet is much more linear. It has a listed introduction on the first page, which lays out the exact order of the pamphlet's organization. There are clear distinctions between each section, often highlighted by different colors or a line across the page. There are caption boxes to explain different sections, thus highlighting the different timeframes. Each unit of information is clearly differentiated, either visually or verbally.

TYPIFYING BORDER RHETORICAL AND CULTURAL FUNCTIONINGS

The relations that border university students have with these two rhetorical traditions is complex and far exceeds the usual division between ESL and native speaker approaches to the writing classroom. Thus, in this section, we attempt to flesh out how the two traditions combine at the US–Mexico border to form specific *rhetorical functionings*, and how these functionings might be displayed in US writing classrooms.

Before doing this, we must situate the discussion. First, this mixing does not follow predominant attributions by US border scholars that the US–Mexico border is one of great fluidity, hybridity, and blurring of boundaries. To begin our argument, we quote from Vila (2003), a border sociologist whose experience closely parallels ours:

> The so-called "border studies" approach was so powerful that many of us, graduate students at U.S. universities, went to the U.S.–Mexico border with the "mission" of validating with ethnographic works the ideas of García Canclini, Anzaldúa, and Rosaldo (hybridity, border crossing, third country, etc.), ideas that mostly were developed within a literary criticism framework, not an ethnographic one. However, as soon as I arrived in the region, it became obvious that the border, or at least Ciudad Juárez-El Paso, was different from the way it was habitually portrayed by the most prestigious American border scholars. (608)

As Vila so competently argues from extensive ethnographic research, these border approaches have three significant weaknesses (many of which parallel the theoretical and methodological weaknesses discussed earlier). First, they are based on the assumption that the US side of the border represents the border experience, without considering the Mexican influence, a double ethnocentrism that Thatcher (2012b) similarly criticizes of Anzaldúa's border approaches.

Second, as both Vila (2000; 2003) and Thatcher (2012b) argue, an important corollary to this US ethnocentrism is to paradoxically assume multiple, fluid, and constantly changing identities, but—at the same time—strongly advocate for individual uniqueness and self construction, yielding an Anzaldúa-like avoidance of group affiliation and a consequent fixation on stereotypes. This assumption of the individual as the unit of reference for border studies clearly echoes the earlier discussion of the large gap between global theory and local practices, as well as the very strong penchant for US researchers to have great difficulty moving beyond the individual in intercultural situations (Stewart and Bennett 1991). In fact, we hypothesize that one of the most salient indicators of US acculturation is the movement from group to individual units of identity analysis, with an accompanying fixation on stereotypes.

Third, the final corollary of this US ethnocentrism is that the border is not just one culture with a supposed multiplicity of fluid and ever-changing identity constructions. Rather, as shown by this entire chapter, the border is a complex—and often strategic—sharing and displaying of competing cultural and rhetorical traditions, depending on the rhetorical situation. Vila (2003) explains:

> However, the border is not really one, but multiple, in the sense that not only different people construct distinct borders and disparate identities around those borders, but those different borders acquire a distinct weight in relation to the different subject positions (and the different narratives within those subject positions) people decide to identify with. (616)

From this perspective, Vila (2000; 2003) argues that border identities can serve to either cross or reinforce borders, the title of Vila's 2000 book.

These three weaknesses (US ethnocentrism, ignorance of Mexico/Latin America, and fluid–unique identities) come to fruition in a variety of US-based portrayals of Latin America, such as Baca (2008), who uses the Anzaldúa's Mestizo construct to examine identities in Latin America and the Caribbean. Interestingly, two Mexican scholars, Castro-Gómez and Mendieta (1998), similarly categorize this triple US ethnocentrism as colonialism, or, as

> a new form of metropolitan theorizing *about* Latin America that ignores the traditions of reading and historical memories articulated from Latin America itself. The theoretical agendas of postcolonialism [by US Latin American scholars] are not developed as an instrument in favor of the struggle for Latin American civil society; rather, they follow the impact of the multi-ethnic, -religious and -cultural development that has occurred in countries like the United States. . . . By not distinguishing the two situations, ie, confusing Latin America with U.S.-American Latino, postcolonial theories actually work as a colonialist policy. (13, translated by Barry Thatcher)

In short, using the US-based, individualistic Mestizo trope as a lens for Latin America is a strong case of orientalism and colonizing. Following this same identity theory, Vila (2000; 2003) found it difficult to discuss group identities on the El Paso side of the border without many El Pasoans falling into the Anzaldúa denial of group attributes and strongly advocating for fluid identities. However, on the Ciudad Juárez side, group identity was often the default identity touchstone.

Likewise, Thatcher's experience as a full-time instructor at NMSU, while teaching at two Ciudad Juárez universities and carrying out more than 800 thousand dollars worth of cross-border projects, has led him to precisely the same conclusion as Vila. Almost all of this work involved the Mexican government—*maquiladora*, health, transportation, and personnel collaboration on cross-border projects with their US colleagues—which clearly demonstrated different group orientations. Further, as cofounder of La Revista Latinoamericana de Retórica, co-founder of the US chapter of the Latin American Rhetoric Society, and as a founding member of La Asociación Latinoamericana de Retórica, Thatcher has had ample opportunity to talk with his colleagues from Mexico, Brazil, Chile, Colombia, and Argentina about Anzaldúa (1999) and the Mestizo approach. The customary response: who is Anzaldúa? When they learn she was a Texas Hispanic and US postcolonial scholar, their response is almost word for word like the previous excerpt from Castro-Gómez and Mendieta (1998).

It is from these three perspectives (cross-border view, multiple units of analysis, and strategic identities) that we map out six groups or typologies of rhetorical and cultural functionings along the border that serve as a template or reference point—not as a determiner—for an individual's cultural and linguistic traditions. That simply means that one person can strategically function as Mexican, for example, and reinforce the pejorative views of northern Mexico; or as a Mexican-American, reinforcing the US border; and/or a recent immigrant, reinforcing a crossing of borders. These are strategic rhetorical choices and positionalities that are not entirely fluid. Thus, we have chosen not to turn our analysis of students' relations to the border context and Mexican rhetorical patterns into a discussion of identity, which is fraught with complicated and contentious arguments. Instead, we argue that there are six distinct rhetorical functionings that border residents are capable of using in specific rhetorical situations, based on their value-driven sense of agency.

BORDER IDENTITY: FUNCTIONING, CAPABILITY, AND AGENCY

The model of border rhetorical choices as distinct functions derives from the widely acknowledged work in global human development known as the Human Development and Capability Approach (HDCA 2013). This model helps us understand how one border university student can or cannot be capable of functioning across a wide range of rhetorical contexts, and it has three key terms or variables: *functioning*, *capability*, and *agency*. Functionings are the

> valuable activities and states that make up people's well being—such as a healthy body, being safe, being calm, having a warm friendship, an educated mind, a good job. Functionings are related to goods and income but they describe what a person is able to do or be as a result. When people's basic need for food (a commodity) is met, they enjoy the *functioning* of being well-nourished. (HDCA 2013, 1)

Functionings are much like abstract or acontextual literacy skills, such as an ESL writer being able to compose an English sentence or paragraph. Second, *capabilities* are the "alternative combinations of functionings that are feasible for [a person] to achieve. Put differently, they are 'the substantive freedoms he or she enjoys to lead the kind of life he or she has reason to value'" (HDCA 2013, 2). Although this ESL student might be able to write a paragraph (functioning), this student might not be capable of—or is prohibited from—writing an effective English paragraph for a specific context, which is a capability. Third, *agency* "refers to a person's ability to pursue and realize goals that he or she values and has reason to value. An agent is 'someone who acts and brings about change.' The opposite of a person with agency is someone who is forced, oppressed, or passive" (HDCA 2013, 3). Thus, an ESL writer might be able to compose an effective paragraph (function) for a specific rhetorical situation (capability), but that ESL writer might choose not to write it that way based on her value–drive (agency). Moreover, this approach assumes that all people possess varying degrees of functioning, capability, and agency.

These three concepts directly frame our discussion of writers along the US–Mexico border. We are assuming that different functions exist—such as functioning as a recent immigrant—but people are capable of various functions, depending on their agency and specific capacities and traits. Our goal as researchers, theorists, and teachers is to help our students become more capable of functioning in a great variety of rhetorical contexts, depending on their purpose and audience. Consequently, the following six functions are seen much like strategic cultural/rhetorical scripts that border writers and residents can move between in order to serve their rhetorical purposes and contexts.

SIX KEY CULTURAL AND RHETORICAL
FUNCTIONINGS ON THE US–MEXICO BORDER

Functioning 1: Deeply Rooted Mexican-American

Since US border states (California, Arizona, New Mexico, and Texas) were part of Mexico in the nineteenth century, there are many Mexican-American (or Latino/Hispanic) residents living in the US who can trace their ancestry back five or six generations to the border region. They are often prominent farmers and ranchers, doctors, entrepreneurs, and important business, government, and industry workers. This group adapted itself (often reluctantly) to the change in nationality in the mid-1800s, from Mexican to American. Currently, many more often identify themselves as New Mexicans or Texans, integrating cultural and social patterns from the United States and the US–Mexico border region, but often not from Mexico. People who self identify as such rarely function well in Mexico or find themselves with Mexican nationals. Many in this group speak little Spanish through the generations and are increasingly functioning overtly as Americans, without the Mexican-American descriptor. Many distance themselves from the other border functionings discussed next. In the various cross-border interactions, we have observed several instances when people functioning as Mexican-Americans not only cannot work with Mexican nationals but often portray ambivalent, even hostile views toward Mexico, much as Vila (2000) documents. Many in this group may function best as *Hispanic* or *Latino*, depending on the state. In New Mexico and West Texas, Hispanic is the preferred term, but Latino is the preferred term in California and the rest of Texas, while Arizona seems mixed.

In terms of predominant cultural and rhetorical patterns, this functioning is often indistinguishable from US values, despite many discussions of local differences such as Anzaldúa (1999). Many or most in this group strongly identify with the US rhetorical traditions explained earlier; in fact, some research has documented an *overcompensated* identification with US values, with some from this group hiding their Mexican heritage and exaggerating US values (Vila 2000). The dominant rhetorical functionings in this combination probably include:

- individual patterns that emphasize independent thinking and self-analysis;
- universal orientations of uniformity, parallelism, coherence, and simplifying texts;
- specific approaches that stress direct thesis statements and supporting evidence;

- reliance on the text as the final say in meaning, including great care in detail; and
- linear, polychronic communication strategies.

Not surprisingly, although some in this group might claim Hispanic or Mexican heritages, most will not have faced cultural and rhetorical transfer problems in US writing classrooms, but instead parallel the experiences of mainstream US students.

Nevertheless, it is important to note that the above characteristics are less the product of cultural evolution and more the byproduct of ethnocentric, English-only educational policy and forced assimilation. In addition, we feel the need to point out that there is a large socioeconomic divide that exists within this group, which problematizes their identification. Although we will not delve into class politics, it bears noting that the Mexican-Americans identified above come from essentially privileged backgrounds, whereas our experience has shown that Mexican-Americans from less socioeconomically privileged backgrounds might cling more readily to Mexican linguistic and cultural patterns. Finally, individuals in this functioning are more likely to attempt to reclaim parts of their lost language and traditions, such as with the aims of the Chicano movement and similar associations (Vila 2000).

Functioning 2: Recent Immigrant

The next functioning involves the recent immigrant, most of whom come from Mexico. The key capacity for this function is speaking Spanish like a native, and there is a strong connection to the collective–structured traditions in Mexico, especially self-identification as *Mexican* (as opposed to Hispanic/Latino) and a preference to associate mainly with other recent Mexican immigrants (Vila 2000; 2003). If possible, they frequently travel to Mexico, where many family members still live and where they can function like Mexican nationals. This functioning is populated by multiple classes and income levels, although a higher percentage are working class laborers. People who function as recent immigrants are the most plagued by problems with immigration, since a large number are undocumented and have complicated relationships with US education systems. A key part of functioning as a recent immigrant is the preference for orality and oral-like rhetorical features in their written texts (Thatcher 2006). We have generally observed people functioning as immigrants interact effectively on the Mexican side of the border, but are often challenged with US institutions. This functioning is grounded almost entirely in Mexican rhetorical traditions, and people who function as such often face considerable difficulty performing well in US English writing classrooms.

It's this group for whom the fotonovela was written, and, thus, this group probably brings most—if not all—of these Mexican rhetorical traditions to the US writing classroom, including:

- collective patterns that emphasize social hierarchies, relations, and power through people;
- particular orientations that emphasize originality, uniqueness, novelty, and resistance to uniformity and simplification of texts;
- diffuse approaches that stress developing holistic relations rather than getting straight to the point;
- polychronic prose organization that differs from the usual US linear approach; and
- reliance on context, assuming audiences can read into the communication, and refusing to place all of reality into the writing itself.

Not surprisingly, this group may face considerable difficulty with US rhetorical traditions. Ongoing research needs to determine the challenges of such acculturation.

Functioning 3: Generation 1.5 and Beyond

The most complicated and disparate, this functioning has been labeled as Generation 1.5 and is caught between the two combinations discussed above. People who function as G1.5 are often American-born, US citizens, but their parents or grandparents are from Mexico. Spanish is the default language of this function, but this is Spanish at home with English learned fluently at school and at work (Baca 2000). Often when G1.5 people travel to Mexico to visit family, they cannot function as well and are uncomfortable culturally or rhetorically. A key feature of this functioning is the desire to rapidly acculturate to a specific set of predominant American values—such as individualism and universalism—that are often held in an uneasy tension with the more Mexican values of collectivism and social hierarchy. However, this function assumes many traits from Mexican roots, such as particularism, diffuseness, and polychronicity, but they are grounded locally in US cultural systems (Thatcher 2012b). This function is caught between rhetorical and cultural traditions, with complex and varied attitudes and connections to both systems, a point that Vila (2003) explores more thoroughly. These attitudes include ambivalence about self-identification: some may hide their Spanish or Latino characteristics because of their desire to integrate better into the United States, while others may openly identify themselves as Mexican-American and insist on speaking Spanish (Vila 2000).

In terms of connecting to US and Mexican rhetorical traditions, there are many variations and gradations of this functioning, depending on their historical, social, and/or cultural connections to either Mexico or the United States. Some of these Mexican rhetorical traditions, for example, easily cross into the United States (Thatcher 2012a), such as the family and interpersonal orientations; however, other Mexican traditions—such as time, diffuseness, and high context—might pass less easily into the United States because of strong differences with US economic, educational, and legal systems. Further research needs to address the actual influence of the border on rhetorical traditions (Thatcher 2012a).

Functioning 4: Mexican Nationals

This functioning emphasizes *lo Mexicano* (Mexicanness)—theoretically disconnected from overt US influence. An important sub-function is the *Mexicano fronterizo* (border Mexican), a person who has immigrated to the United States because of better business opportunities, or, more recently, to escape the narco-violence. To function well in this group, people are frequently middle or upper class, have been educated in private Mexican schools, and often speak formal English learned in Mexico. An important feature of this functioning is viewing Latinos, Generation 1.5, or Mexican-American groups with some disdain, accusing them of selling out their Mexican heritage (Vila 2000). This functioning presents complicated relationships with US rhetorical contexts. People who function only in this way often do not identify well with those functioning as recent immigrant or Generation 1.5 because of class–economic differences, as well as the fact that they share more economic, social, and educational values with the predominant US middle class. Furthermore, this combination, because of their deep connections to Mexico, does not connect well with Anglo-Americans either (Condon 1997; Vila 2000). Many people functioning as Mexican nationals are usually educated internationally, not only in the United States, but also Europe and even Asia. Often, these Mexican nationals reside in El Paso but work in Ciudad Juárez.

In terms of relating to the two rhetorical traditions presented in the pamphlet, this combination will also vary considerably. First, one feature of the fotonovela is that it works well with predominantly oral readers, which is common among the Mexican immigrants for whom this fotonovela was designed. Often, the Mexican national is highly literate and would dislike some or most of the more oral- and comic-book-like features of the fotonovela, such as high context and polychronicity. However, many of these Mexican nationals could strongly identify with some of the other values sets, especially collective, particular, and diffuse. Finally, because this group values education and has been formally educated in Mexico, they are less likely to adopt rhetorical traditions from the United States, instead sticking to the rhetorical traditions they learned in Mexican schools. Because they have learned to read and, most importantly, write in a certain style, they are less likely to abandon what they have learned and assimilate to US rhetorical styles, something that recent immigrants and G1.5 have been observed to do.

Functioning 5: Cross-Border, Bilingual, and Bicultural

A fifth functioning is the cross-border, bilingual, and bicultural. People who can function well across the border are comprised mostly of Mexican nationals (mostly *Mexicanos Fronterizos*), such as the growing percentage of students at New Mexico State University and The University of Texas at El Paso who are Mexican nationals from Ciudad Juárez. And a good number of mid-level management and engineers live in El Paso and work in the *maquilas* (a US-run factory) in Ciudad Juárez. To be functional across the border, people must be experienced at traveling frequently across the border and interacting bilingually with people who function in the other five border functions. This group's ability to relate to both rhetorical traditions is complex. The US or generic tradition presented in the pamphlet is often the strategy for business and education, while the fotonovela is often for home and social relations. The mixing of these traditions is common and complicated. They tend to cling firmly to their Mexican culture and traditions, and many would identify as Mexican. They speak Spanish with friends and family, and reserve English for professional situations. Much research is needed to explore the nature of the bicultural, bilingual border residents and their cultural and rhetorical strategies.

Functioning 6: Güeros or Anglos

The final major functioning in southern New Mexico is composed mostly of Anglo Americans—*güeros*, or whites—who are relatively late-comers to the border region. As explained earlier, after the succession of one-third of the Mexican territory to the United States in the mid-1800s,

Anglo-Americans began to arrive in larger numbers. According to the official census (US Census 2011), Anglo-Americans account for about 25 percent of the population in southern New Mexico and 10 percent in west Texas. This is a catch-all group for anyone whose ethnicity is partially white and who is not Hispanic, black, or Asian. This functioning assumes predominant US rhetorical and cultural values as exemplified in the generic pamphlet. This group will often favor the rhetorical strategies presented in the generic pamphlet, but—depending on their literacy levels and assimilation of border culture—may prefer features of the fotonovela.

In conclusion, these typified functionings provide a template to gauge the kinds of rhetorical strategies that students can draw upon in their writing classes. They are not identities themselves, but traditions that border students can draw upon in specific rhetorical situations. For a summary table of these groups, please see Appendix 7.1.

RELATION OF WRITING CURRICULA TO BORDER CONTEXT

As a conclusion, this section hypothesizes about how well the writing curricula at UTEP and NMSU are designed for the border context, or whether it assumes the homogenized, predominant US cultural and rhetorical traditions. And as writing scholars and administrators, one of our major questions concerns how much this design accommodation really matters. As mentioned in the other chapter for this collection, our institutional data show that Mexican nationals and those students whose dominant language is Spanish pass our writing classes as easily or more easily than other students. Consequently, we are not sure what to do about the disconnect between the border context and curriculum. We will, however, hypothesize about the following issues and research questions, based on our experience teaching in the classroom and researching in nonacademic border contexts. Space limitations prohibit a concrete analysis as to why the curriculum is strongly connected to US cultural and rhetorical patterns, but the following lists our own observations.

Writing purpose and exigency

As some research has indicated (Kellog 1995; Leon-Portillo 1996; Thatcher 2006, 2012b), the exigencies that initiate or call for writing generally differ between the United States and Mexico. Because of its collective, particular, diffuse, and high context values, writing in Mexico has strong notary-like purposes (Kellog 1995; Thatcher 2006), often serving to authenticate or formalize existing group relations, much like the fotonovela enacted by the Ramírez family hierarchy. On the other hand, because of its individual, universal, specific, and low context values, writing in the United States is more commonly used as an explicit mechanism to argue or construct an appropriate course of action for more independent, but like-minded, peers or communities. Both curricula at UTEP and NMSU assume more US-like writing purposes, based on relatively independent peers arguing for a course of action in communities, rather than authenticating social relations. Thus, how can students who come from Mexican traditions adapt to more mutually constructive writing purposes?

Reader–Writer relations

As shown by the fotonovela, the Mexican rhetorical tradition historically creates strongly interpersonal (Albert 1996) reader–writer relations, relying on collective, particular, diffuse, and high context values. This method emphasizes roles in the hierarchy and unique approaches to human relations. The US tradition is often more individualistic and universal, assuming equal relations and focusing on persuasion and sound argument. The curricula at UTEP and NMSU do help students address the social and contextual complexities of the writing situation, which is more in line with the interpersonal reality of Mexican rhetoric (Albert 1996). However, the base relation of writer and reader as one of equality (see, for example, Faigley and Selzer 2011) is, therefore, focused on persuasion and argument. Thus, how well can students who come from Mexican traditions adapt their carefully crafted interpersonal/hierarchical approach to the strong, direct, and openly persuasive/argumentative approach?

Information

The fotonovela and generic pamphlet clearly highlight the differences in informational needs. Generally, the US approach emphasizes the low-context depth and detail of a specific topic, while the Mexican approach grounds the topic in more diffuse, interpersonal, and contextual approaches. As explained in the other chapter, it is difficult to assess from course descriptions whether the UTEP and NMSU curricula emphasize the depth and detail of a US approach or the holistically-grounded context of the Mexican approach. Given that the rest of the curriculum is mainly based on predominant US cultural values, it might be interesting to research how students who come from Mexican traditions learn to focus in a more linear, specific, and low context environment, leaving out holistic impulses.

Organization

As demonstrated in both pamphlets, the general organizational tendency of a US approach in the writing classroom should be more linear, parallel, and symmetrical, while the Mexican approach should emphasize uniqueness, deviation, and context and relationship sensitivity. However, like information, it is difficult to assess from course descriptions whether the UTEP and NMSU curricula emphasize the linear, parallel, and symmetrical approach to document and paragraph organization, but—given that the rest of the curriculum is mostly based on predominant US cultural values—they most likely do. Thus, it might be interesting to research how students who come from Mexican traditions learn to develop more linear, parallel, and symmetrical documents and paragraphs, a tendency that we have consistently observed in NMSU students.

Writing as a process

The last key difference for writing programs is the emphasis and nature of the writing process. Since writing in the United States is often the mechanism for constructing courses of action in more low-context, universal ways, the writing process itself is often emphasized over the relations of the social context (Thatcher 2012b). On the other hand, since writing in Mexico is often associated with notary or authenticating purposes, the social relations are emphasized and configured through the writing process itself, which, in turn, takes care of the writing purpose based on formal social and organizational roles. For example, as Thatcher (2012b) explains in a chapter comparing US and Mexican instructional manuals and training, US materials writers

> tend to use parallelism, templating, and repetition in structuring their procedures as a way to emphasize the standardized and rational elements of these processes. These universal approaches focus specifically on achieving a definite outcome, regardless of the ascribed status of the people involved. . . . On the other hand, particularist communication patterns emphasize the dynamic and complex nature of the power relations that are responsible for the specific procedure or transaction. From this

perspective, effective communication means understanding and managing the relations of the people or systems that are responsible for the transaction. Thus, it is very important to understand these ascribed statuses of people involved so that the transaction can be carried out. (291)

Like the fotonovela, the family and interpersonal processes are emphasized, with the assumption that the technical detail of cholesterol levels will be worked out later. The opposite is true for the generic pamphlet: technical processes are strongly highlighted, with the interpersonal or social relevance mostly hidden. As explained in the other chapter, the curricula at UTEP and NMSU are strongly process-based, and the assumptions about process precisely mirror the US cultural values of using writing to construct viable courses of action. To the degree that the curricula at UTEP and NMSU emphasize the writing process as constructing the course of action over authenticating existing social relations, it might be interesting to research how students who come from Mexican traditions adapt to these constructive processes.

CONCLUSION: FIGHTING RE-ENTRENCHMENT

We feel the need to address one of the issues that has plagued the development of the writing programs at UTEP and NMSU: cultural entrenchment and overcompensation. Adler (1991) presents compelling evidence from a range of intercultural studies of organizational behavior, arguing that "organizations worldwide are growing more similar while the behavior of people within the organizations is maintaining its cultural uniqueness." In fact, Adler (1991) believes local cultures tend to resist or even strengthen their cultural customs in the face of international organizational norms (57–58). In other words, when cultures continually face competing cultural norms, they basically re-entrench themselves, often more tenaciously, in their own norms. We see this entrenchment effect (variously distributed) in the border region, which is oddly contradictory. For example, it would appear obvious or normal for NMSU to have a strong ESL program to address the needs of border writers, but just the opposite is true. NMSU's ESL program is housed in the Communication Studies Department, but all ESL courses have the SPCD prefix, meaning *Speech Communication Disorders*; it employs as few non-tenure faculty as possible; and, until recently, it had limited connections to the English department. As a result, foreign ESL students take courses with the words "communication disorders" attached to the course name. In other words, these ESL students are instantly connected to communication disorders. From this perspective, NMSU is re-entrenched in its own Anglo-American world, choosing to ignore that nameless country (Mexico) thirty miles to the south. UTEP seems less entrenched in the Anglo-American culture. It has a much more developed ESL department, and its English department has a unique bilingual, Spanish–English professional writing program. However, these developments are recent—within the last five years. It is only recently that the rhetoric and writing faculty at NMSU and UTEP have begun addressing these larger rhetorical and curriculum issues, which is demonstrated in our companion chapter. This work is heartening, but, not surprisingly, there is still much to do.

Notes

1. For the sake of this chapter, the differences between globalization and transnationalism are not significant enough to merit further distinction. Further, following many researchers, globalization is used because it currently shows how all major global factors influence this interdependence.
2. At this point, for space considerations, we will not engage the traditional Derridian argument that there is nothing outside language. Instead, we view these "non-linguistic" factors as economic, political, and social factors, not directly tied to local issues of moving between two languages such as Spanish and English.
3. Perhaps some readers will feel that using nonacademic writing theory and methodology is unsuitable for academic writing. We believe the opposite is true: because of the great exigencies of globalization, many fields—such as health, manufacturing, and environment—have explored the cultural and rhetorical patterns that occur in global contexts and have developed theories and methodologies that allow us to bridge these differences. Our ESL and multilingual students certainly bring their nonacademic patterns to the university classroom.
4. Very little research has compared the high and low context writings of US and Mexican composition, although quite a bit has documented the high context communications of Mexicans with each other (Castañeda 1995; Condon 1997; Hall 1976, 1983; Kras 1991; Leon-Portillo 1996).

References

Abbott, Don Paul. 1996. *Rhetoric in the New World*. Columbia: University of South Carolina Press.

Adler, Nancy J. 1991. *International Dimensions of Organizational Behavior*. 2nd ed. Boston, Kent: Cengage Learning.

Albert, R. D. 1996. "A Framework and Model for Understanding Latin American and Latino/Hispanic Cultural Patterns." In *Handbook of Intercultural Training*, 2nd ed., ed. D. Landis and R. S. Bhagat, 327–48. Thousand Oaks: Sage Publications.

Anzaldúa, Gloria. 1999. *Borderlands La Frontera*. 3rd ed. San Francisco: Aunt Lute Books.

Baca, Damian. 2008. *Mestiz@ Scripts, Digital Migrations, and the Territories of Writing (New Concepts in Latino American Cultures)*. Hampshire: Palgrave Macmillan. http://dx.doi.org/10.1057/9780230612570.

Baca, I. 2000. *English, Spanish, or Los Dos? Examining Language Behavior among Four English/ Spanish Bilingual Families Residing on the El Paso, Texas/Juárez, México Border.* PhD diss., New Mexico State University.

Balcazar, H., V. Cardenas, H. De Heer, E. Rosenthal, and L. Schulz. 2011. "Ethnic Pride and Cardiovascular Health among Mexican American Adults along the U.S.-Mexico Border." *Hispanic Journal of Behavioral Sciences* 33 (2): 204.

Berry, Patrick W., Gail E. Hawisher, and Cynthia L. Selfe. 2012. *Transnational Literate Lives in Digital Times.* Logan: Computers and Composition Digital Press/Utah State University Press. Accessed from http://ccdigitalpress.org/transnational/.

Bhawuk, D., and H. Triandis. 1996. "The Role of Culture Theory in the Study of Culture and Intercultural Training." In *Handbook of Intercultural Training,* 2nd ed., ed. D. Landis and R. Bhagat, 17–34. Thousand Oaks: Sage.

Bourdieu, P. 1999. *Language and Symbolic Power.* Cambridge: Harvard University Press.

Canagarajah, A. Suresh. 2006. "The Place of World Englishes in Composition: Pluralization Continued." *CCC* 57 (4): 586–619.

Castañeda, J. G. 1995. *The Mexican Shock: Its Meaning for the U.S.* New York: The New Press.

Castro-Gómez, S., and E. Mendieta. 1998. *La Translocalización Discursiva de "Latinoamérica" en Tiempos de la Globalización.* Accessed from http://www.ensayistas.org/critica/teoria /castro/introd.htm.

Condon, J. C. 1997. *Communicating with the Mexicans.* 2nd ed. Yarmouth: Intercultural Press, Inc.

Connor, U. 1996. *Contrastive Rhetoric: Cross-Cultural Aspects of Second-Language Writing.* Cambridge: Cambridge University Press. http://dx.doi.org/10.1017/CBO9781139 524599.

Connor, U., E Nagelhout, and W. Rozycki, eds. 2008. *Contrastive Rhetoric: Reaching to Intercultural Rhetoric.* Amsterdam: John Benjamins. http://dx.doi.org/10.1075/pbns .169.

Crawford, T. 2007a. *ESL Writing in the University of Guanajuato: The Struggle to Enter a Discourse Community.* PhD diss., Canterbury Christ Church University.

Crawford, T. 2007b. "Some Historical and Academic Considerations for the Teaching of Second Language Writing in English in Mexico." *MEXTESOL Journal* 31 (1): 75–90.

Faigley, Lester, and Jack Selzer. 2011. *Good Reasons.* 5th ed. Harlow: Longman.

Grewal, D. S. 2008. *Network Power: The Social Dynamics of Globalization.* New Haven: Yale University Press.

Garza Almanza, Victoriano. 2009. *Publica o Perece* [Publish or Perish]. Ciudad Juárez, Mexico: Colegio de Chihuahua.

Gudykunst, William B. 2005. *Theorizing about Intercultural Communication.* Ann Arbor: University of Michigan Press.

Hall, E. T. 1976. *Beyond Culture.* New York: Doubleday.

Hall, E. T. 1983. *The Dance of Life.* New York: Doubleday.

Hampden-Turner, C., and A. Trompenaars. 2000. *Building Cross-Cultural Competence.* Hoboken: Wiley.

Harklau, L., K. M. Losey, and M. Siegal, eds. 1999. *Generation 1.5 Meets College Composition.* Mahwah: Lawrence Erlbaum Associates.

HDCA. 2013. "Human Development and Capability Association." Accessed from http:// www.hd-ca.org/.

Headland, T. N., K. L. Pike, and M. Harris, eds. 1990. *Emics and Etics: The Insider/Outsider Debate.* Newbury Park: Sage.

Hinds, J. 1987. "Reader Versus Writer Responsibility: A New Typology." In *Writing across Languages: Analysis of L2 Text,* ed. U. Connor, and R. B. Kaplan. 141–152. Reading: Addison-Wesley.

Hofstede, G. 2010. *Cultures and Organizations, Software of the Mind.* 3rd ed. New York: McGraw Hill.

Horner, Bruce, and John Trimbur. 2002. "English Only and U.S. College Composition."
   CCC 53 (4): 594–630.
House, R. J., P. J. Hanges, M. Javidan, P. R. Dorfman, and V. Gupta, eds. 2005. *Culture,*
   Leadership, and Organizations: The GLOBE Study of 62 Societies. Thousand Oaks: Sage
   Publications.
Kail, M., and I. Sanchez y Lopez. 1997. "Referent Introductions in Spanish Narratives as
   a Function of Contextual Constraints: A Cross Linguistic Perspective." *First Language*
   49:17.
Kellog, S. 1995. *Law and the Transformation of Aztec Culture, 1500–1700.* Norman:
   University of Oklahoma Press.
Kras, E. 1991. *Management in Two Cultures.* Yarmouth: Intercultural Press, Inc.
Leon-Portillo, Miguel. 1996. *El Destino de la Palabra. De la Oralidad y los Códices*
   Mesoamericanos a la Escritura Alfabética. México City: El Colegio Nacional Fondo de
   Cultura Económica.
LoCastro, V. 2008. "Long Sentences and Floating Commas: Mexican Students'
   Rhetorical Practices and the Sociocultural Context." In *Contrastive Rhetoric: Reaching to*
   Intercultural Rhetoric, ed. U. Connor, E. Ulla, and W. Nagelhout, 195–217. Amsterdam:
   John Benjamins. http://dx.doi.org/10.1075/pbns.169.13loc.
Lucy, J. 1996. "The Scope of Linguistic Relativity: An Analysis and Review of Empirical
   Research." In *Rethinking Linguistic Relativity,* ed. J. J. Gumperz and S. C. Levison,
   37–69. Cambridge: Cambridge University Press.
Matsuda, Paul, and Aya Matsuda. 2009. "The Erasure of ESL Writers." In *Generation 1.5*
   Meets College Composition, ed. L. Harklau, K. M. Losey, and M. Siegal, 0–64. Mahwah:
   Lawrence Erlbaum Associates.
Matsuda, P. K., and D. A. Atkinson. 2008. "Conversation on Contrastive Rhetoric." In
   Contrastive Rhetoric: Reaching to Intercultural Rhetoric, ed. U. Connor, E. Nagelhout, and
   W. William Rozycki, 277–98. Amsterdam: John Benjamins. http://dx.doi.org/10
   .1075/pbns.169.18mat.
Mejia, Jaime Armin. 2004. "Arts of the US Mexico Contact Zone." In *Crossing Borderlands:*
   Composition and Postcolonial Studies, ed. Andrea Lunsford and Lahoucine Ouzgane,
   171–98. Pittsburgh: University of Pittsburgh Press.
Mesoudi, Alex. 2011. *Cultural Evolution: How Darwinian Theory can Explain Human Culture*
   and Synthesize the Social Sciences. Chicago: University of Chicago Press. http://dx.doi
   .org/10.7208/chicago/9780226520452.001.0001.
Montaño-Harmon, M. 1991. "Discourse Features of Written Mexican Spanish: Current
   Research in Contrastive Rhetoric and its Implications." *Hispania* 74 (2): 417–25.
   http://dx.doi.org/10.2307/344852.
Morris, Michael W., K. Leung, D. Ames, and B. Lickel. 1999. "Views from Inside and
   Outside: Integrating Emic and Etic Insights about Culture and Justice Judgment."
   Academy of Management Review 24.4: 781–796.
National Institute of Health. 2013. *Easy-to-Read English/Spanish Booklets on Heart Health.*
   Accessed from http://www.nhlbi.nih.gov/health/public/heart/other/sp-page.htm.
Pagel, M., Q. Atkinson, A. Calude, and A. Meade. 2013. *Ultraconserved Word Point to Deep*
   Language Ancestry across Eurasia. Cambridge: University of Cambridge Press.
Pennycook, Alistair. 1995. *The Cltural Politics of English as an International Language.*
   London: Addison Wesley Publishing Company.
Hispanic, Pew. 2012. "Hispanic Student Enrollments Reach New Highs in 2011."
   Accessed September 2013. http://www.pewhispanic.org/2012/08/20/hispanic
   -student-enrollments-reach-new-highs-in-2011/
Pike, Kenneth. 1967. *Language in Relation to a Unified Theory of the Structure of Human*
   Behavior. 2nd ed. The Hague: Mouton.
Ruecker, T. 2012. *Writing across Institutions: Studying the Curricular and Extracurricular*
   Journeys of Latino Students Transitioning from High School to College. PhD diss., University

of Texas at El Paso.

Scenters-Zapico. John. 2010. *Generaciones' Narratives.* Logan: Computers and Composition Digital Press/Utah State University Press. Accessed from http://ccdigitalpress.org /generaciones/

Simpson, J. 2000. "Topical Structure Analysis of Academic Paragraphs in English and Spanish." *Journal of Second Language Writing* 9 (3): 293–309. http://dx.doi.org/10 .1016/S1060-3743(00)00029-1.

Stewart, E., and M. Bennett. 1991. *American Cultural Patterns: A Cross-Cultural Perspective.* Rev. ed. Yarmouth, ME: Intercultural Press, Inc.

Swales, John M. 1997. "English as 'Tyronnasauraus Rex.'" *World Englishes* 16 (3): 373–82. http://dx.doi.org/10.1111/1467-971X.00071 http://deepblue.lib.umich.edu /bitstream/.

Thatcher, B. L. 2006. "'Intercultural Rhetoric, Technology, and Writing in Mexican Maquilas.' Special Technology Transfer Edition of *Technical.*" *Communication Quarterly* 15 (3): 383–405.

Thatcher, B. L. 2010. "Editor Introduction to First Edition." *Rhetoric, Professional Communication, and Globalization* 1:1–34. Accessed from www.rpcg.org

Thatcher, B. L. 2012a. "Fotonovelas and Anglo Designs in Health Communications for Spanish-Speaking Residents along the U.S.-Mexico Border." *Rhetoric, Professional Communication, and Globalization* 3: 74–109.

Thatcher, B. L. 2012b. *Intercultural Rhetoric and Professional Communication: Technological Advances and Organizational Behavior.* Hershey: IGI-Global Press.

Trompenaars, Alfons. 1994. *Riding the Waves of Culture: Understanding Diversity in Global Business.* Burr Ridge: Irwin Professional Publishing.

U.S. Census. U. S. 2011. "The Hispanic Population: 2010." Accessed September 2013. http://www.census.gov/prod/cen2010/briefs/c2010br-04.pdf

Ramanathan, Vai, and Dwight Atkinson. 1999. "Individualism, Academic Writing, and ESL Writers." *Journal of Second Language Writing* 8 (1): 45–75. http://dx.doi.org/10 .1016/S1060-3743(99)80112-X.

Valadés, D. 1996. *Retórica Cristiana.* La Ciudad de México: Universidad Nacional Autónoma de México.

Valero-Garcés, C. 1996. "Contrastive ESP Rhetoric: Metatext in Spanish-English Economics Texts." *English for Specific Purposes* 15 (4): 279–94. http://dx.doi.org/10 .1016/S0889-4906(96)00013-0.

Vila, P. 2003. "Processes of Identification on the U.S.-Mexico Border." *Social Science Journal* 40 (4): 607–25. http://dx.doi.org/10.1016/S0362-3319(03)00072-7.

Vila, P. 2000. *Crossing Borders, Reinforcing Borders: Social Categories, Metaphors and Narrative Identities on the U.S.-Mexico Frontier.* Austin, TX: University of Texas Press.

Villanueva, Victor. 1993. *Bootstraps: From an American Academic of Color.* Austin: University of Texas Press.

Appendix 7.1. Six Transient Points of Stabilized Cultural and Rhetorical Identities Along the US–Mexico Border

Transient points of stabilized identities	Relation to dominant Mexican cultural and rhetorical patterns (including Spanish)	Relation to dominant US cultural and rhetorical patterns (including English)
Mexican-American (3rd+ generation American with Mexican ancestry)	• Some remnants of Spanish language and Mexican culture, especially in family and interpersonal contexts. • Ambivalence toward Mexico.	• Significant assimilation of deeply-rooted US cultural values. • Perhaps over-assimilation of US values in some cases.
Recent Immigrant (less than ten years in the US and originally from Mexico or Latin America)	Deeply connected to Mexican cultural and rhetorical patterns, but has mostly oral traditions and limited formal education.	Ambivalent and contextual: learns US patterns sufficiently to function in employment and education, but rejects or ignores other US values.
Generation 1.5 (US-born but from Mexican or Latin American parents)	• Inherits Mexican culture from parents and US culture from education and work. • Family and interpersonal Spanish. • Oral traditions, especially as children; written traditions at school and in English.	• Narratives of academic and economic success are connected to English and US cultural and rhetorical traditions. • Strong affinities for US cultural values of universalism (level playing field) and individualism (relative independence).
Mexican national (born and educated with significant ties to Mexico)	• Strongly and often proudly connects to and identifies with Mexican rhetorical and cultural traditions. • Ambivalence to US dominance, especially historically (hace 160 anos, Nuevo México era México).	• Often in United States to improve economic and academic capacities. • Ambivalence about US cultural and rhetorical traditions. • Academic English with limited practice.
Cross-border and bicultural (live and work on both sides border; bilingual)	• See strengths and weaknesses in both US and Mexican cultural and rhetorical traditions → capacity to leverage strengths and minimize weaknesses according to situation. • Feel both marginalized and empowered at the same time, rooted but rootless. • Most often hide bicultural and bilingual traits, as compared to other groups.	
Anglo-American	• Mexico is the romanticized but dangerous other. • Awareness of bilingual context. • Academic and Walmart Spanish. • Custom of relying on token "Hispanics" to represent the other-than-Anglo identities. • Conflate all border identities into one as "Mexican."	• English monolingual in obvious bilingual context but deeply naturalized US cultural and rhetorical traditions.

Strategic positioning among points of identity in structured contexts	Acculturation issues for NMSU writing and English classes
• Can position him/herself with "Mexican" identities, but more readily identifies with the United States. • Usually cannot function in Mexico. • Often disdains functioning as recent immigrant or G1.5.	• English dominant: very little language or culture issues; most problems are general or concern academic literacy. • Some affinity for select cultural and rhetorical traditions from Mexico, but within a US frame.
• Usually self identifies more with Mexico and has limited experience with US patterns. • Can identify and position as recent immigrant, Mexican national, or Mexican-American.	• Often limited educational, English, and literacy experience. • Strong oral and interpersonal traditions grounded in Mexican rhetorical patterns.
• Can usually move effectively between professional contexts with English, and family contexts with Spanish. • Difficulty functioning as Mexican national, but possibly can as recent immigrant, and usually trying to function as US- or Mexican-American.	The most complex group/set of issues: • Often first-generation college students of supportive parents. • Spanish/Mexican repertoire in certain rhetorical situations and English/US in others. • Great identity complexities and ambivalences.
• Often not reliably informed about nor capable of assuming other points of border identity but can pass as recent immigrant. • Can view other identities as sellouts or culturally suspect.	• Strong academic and learning capacities. • Most issues are linguistic (Spanish → English) and contrastive rhetoric (different genres and functions of communication media in US)
• Adept at positioning themselves as Mexicans, Mexican-Americans, or US-Americans depending on power dynamics. • Ambivalence toward Anglo-Americans.	• Strong general rhetorical skills because of innate systematic nature of their bicultural and bilingual orientation. • Can mix up which rhetorical strategies are appropriate in given contexts.
• Can only position as Anglo-American. • Often completely unaware of other border identities: all are "Mexican." • Unaware of power dynamics and positionality issues among other five border identities.	• NMSU and UTEP generally ground writing and language curriculum in Anglo-American values. • Over-reinforcing US cultural values in light of ever-pressing Mexican and border presence. • Strong predominance of US scholars, such as Anzaldúa, pretending to represent the border or even Mexican experience using only a US-based lens.

8

GLOBALIZATION AND LANGUAGE DIFFERENCE
A Mesodiscursive Approach

Hem Paudel

INTRODUCTION

Writing programs are facing tremendous pressure to address the issue of language difference, not only in the US but also across the whole world (as Bou Ayash's chapter also shows). Our classrooms are becoming more and more multilingual and multidiscoursal (Canagarajah 2006b; Matsuda 1999; 2006) with the constantly expanding trend of globalization—facilitated by the advancement in digital technologies—the rapidly increasing movement of immigration, and the rise in global commerce and trade. In the United States, as Paul K. Matsuda (1999) and Preto-Bay and Hansen (2006) have said, the number of multilingual students has grown exponentially in recent times. Data released by US Department of Education shows that "while the population of five to twenty-four-year-olds grew by 6% between 1979 and 1999, the number who spoke a language other than English at home increased in the same period by 111%" (referenced in Preto-Bay and Hansen 2006, 38). It is predicted that "by 2015, 30% of the school-aged children will be children of immigrants, either first or second generation" (39). This data does not even include international students. In the global context, "non-native" English speakers far outnumber its "native" speakers (Crystal 2003; Leung 2005).[1] As English is used in different discursive contexts, here in the United States and beyond, it's widely diversified by its interactions with various other language practices. Consequently, the central questions that many WPAs are asking today are: How can we address the differences in language use in our classrooms? And what institutional changes and policies can help us overcome the challenges that language diversity may pose in places where monolingual ideology

DOI: 10.7330/9780874219623.c008

has traditionally ruled every aspect of language teaching? Insights from language theories developed in the context of the global spread of English can help us address these questions. Therefore, this chapter tries to briefly assess some of the existing trends in language theories and offer an alternative way of addressing the issues raised above.

In this chapter, I argue that—instead of teaching "standard" English—we need to focus on "difference" itself as the subject of classroom discussions in our writing courses, and that we must pay close attention to the labor-intensive nature of negotiations across languages. Along those lines, I attempt to develop a theory of translingual agency that, first, seeks to go beyond the paradigms of dominant language theories that regard languages as discrete and stable entities, and, second, critiques the romanticized version of multilingual agency, where multilinguals are represented as naturally capable of shuttling across languages. Therefore, I argue that we need to move beyond dwelling on stable language structures or the free-floating agency of individual language users and instead focus more on language use and practice in specific spatio-temporal contexts. In doing so, we must pay attention to the mesodiscursive space, where languages and discourses interact and co-construct each other. When we consider language structurations and agency in this mesodiscursive way, the focus shifts from superficial notions of language diversity to what Pennycook (2008), Kramsch (2006), and others call semiodiversity. After presenting an alternative way to view language difference, I'll discuss some of the major implications of this approach to WPA in terms of principles of curriculum design, placement of ESL students, teacher training, and writing center work.

MAJOR LANGUAGE MODELS

English monolingualism is still dominant in our teaching practices, even if it has been challenged in recent scholarship on language both within writing studies and beyond. Many alternative models—such as world Englishes (WE), English as a lingua franca (ELF), defense of national language (DNL), and multilingualism—have been developed to counter and go beyond monolingual assumptions. However, despite these models' appreciation of the value of diversity in languages and cultures, they still retain some of the fundamental assumptions of monolingual ideology.

As Pennycook (2008) argues, WE, ELF, and DNL give more focus to "form" rather than meaning making by either highlighting how new forms and structures have emerged in localized varieties,[2] by proposing to develop a common core of English language across all varieties,[3] or by defending national language against the hegemonic influence of English.[4] They also assume that languages have a separate and stable core and seem to ignore the fact that languages transform and are transformed by their interactions with other language practices (due to various factors associated with language, including distinct rhetorical and epistemological diversities). Similarly, while focusing on structural differences, they also ignore the role of individual practice in transforming language structures. In other words, these approaches gloss over the role of individual agency, though minimal, in negotiating and transforming both local and global, micro and macro structures. Thus, they retain the traditional tendency of viewing languages as primarily governed by preexisting systems or structures, thereby maintaining assumptions about language fixity even when talking about language diversity.

In place of theorizing the use of English from the perspectives of these three models, the other trend is to advocate multilingualism. The dominant models of multilingualism, unlike monolingualism, do acknowledge the presence of different languages and cultures. However, in many cases, the general and dominant understanding of multilingualism suffers from the same problem as the other approaches. Here, as many European language theorists have said, multilingualism is used to refer to separate competencies in two or more languages. In other words, languages are taken as discrete systems where "the ultimate goal for language learning [is] to become, feel, and speak like an idealized native speaker" (Moore and Gajo 2009, 139). In such cases, bilingualism becomes "double monolingualism" (Heller 2002, 48) and multilingualism is "little more than [the] pluralization of monolingualism" (Pennycook 2010, 10). As in monolingual tradition, language competence is measured in terms of native speaker norms of separate languages. Thus, multilingualism does not serve the broader purposes of enhancing understanding and critical awareness about different discourse practices. Rather, as Pennycook (2008) says, "The struggle over diversity as numerical plurality . . . this focus on glossodiversity at the expense of semiodiversity . . . obscures the potential role of language education in the production of diversity" (34). Therefore, this numerical version of multilingualism/bilingualism retains the dominant tendency to view languages as discrete and formal systems and does not extend beyond native speaker models. Hence, additive multilingualism ignores the inevitability of "traffic" within, among, and between the artificial ideological boundaries separating languages, cultures, and peoples.

In order to avoid monolingual assumptions of the traditional version of multilingualism, many language theorists have offered their own alternative ways of thinking. European linguists, such as Coste and Simon (2009) and Danièle Moore (2006), offered their own alternative ways of theorizing multilingualism, suggesting that "the language competence of bilinguals should not be regarded as the simple sum of two monolingual competences, but should rather be appreciated in conjunction with the user's repertoire of total linguistic resources" (Moore and Gajo 2009, 139). In contrast to the additive model of multilingualism, where multilingualism merely means two or more separate monolingualisms (Canagarajah 2009; Heller 2002; Pennycook 2008), plurilingualism "allows for the interaction and mutual influence of the language in a more dynamic way" (Canagarajah 2009, 22). In short, the plurilingual approach considers linguistic differences that multilinguals bring to language negotiations not as a problem or deficit, but as a resource. I will extend this notion, however, with an equal emphasis that the differences in linguistic traditions and cultural values can work not just as a resource, but also as a constraint in working across cultures and languages.

With its overemphasis on resources, plurilingualism often undermines these constraints, leading them toward romanticization of the agency of multilingual language users. In an attempt to counter monolingual hegemony, this approach "concentrates on the individual rather than the community as its angle of vision" (141) and places more emphasis on the individual as a "social actor, with agency and choice" (Moore and Gajo 2009, 150). The idea of romanticization becomes further substantiated by the fact that plurilingual theorists try to highlight their argument that multilingual individuals, due to their multilingual resources, exercise metalinguistic and metadiscursive awareness (Jessner 2006; Moore 2006). In emphasizing metadiscursive awareness, the plurilingualists tend to underestimate how the social relations and the hegemony of dominant discourse can pose powerful constraints to individuals, consequently pushing multilingualism toward its potential romanticization.

Suresh Canagarajah's (2007) notion of plurilingual competence and his theory of shuttling between languages exemplify such romanticization of multilingualism. His account of shuttling between languages presents multilingual writers as if they can easily *hop on* and *hop off* languages due to their membership in local multilingual communities: "the LFE [lingua franca English] speakers come with the competence in many respects, more advanced than that of the child because of the multilingual practice enjoyed in their local communities—which is then honed through actual interaction" (928). It is perhaps true that multilinguals develop a more open and tolerant attitude toward language difference. However, the habitus built through their multilingual experiences in their local communities may also pose constraints in negotiating language difference in other situations, due to the specific nature of that habitus. For instance, Ramakanta Agnihotri's (2007) study of plurilingual practices in India, especially his description of taxi drivers' communicative practices, outlines his observation that most taxi cab drivers in Banglore are multilingual and can successfully communicate across languages. It is not clear, however, that they would do well outside their locale, though their prior experience might help them negotiate language practices as cab drivers elsewhere. This is because their language habitus is always shaped by the local context of their language use. When applied to students, this illustrates that plurilingual practices in informal and out-of-class situations may not appropriately capture the dynamic of language relations in formal academic situations, where a monolingual ideology remains very strong. That is why, despite their multilingual experiences, many students are governed by monolingual hegemony.

Canagarajah (2006b) uses the example of a Malaysian student from Min-Zhan Lu's (1994) study to illustrate how that student seems to have ignored the powerful presence of English monolingualism, which shapes students in ways to make them avoid "error" as much as possible. This study clearly shows how difficult it is for students to actually shuttle between languages. The expectations within and outside the academy make them want to reproduce the dominant discourse, as in case of the Malayasian student. Even in such a highly encouraging situation, he chose to imitate the conventions of "standard" English. Similarly, the circulation of the same examples over and over again (like that of the Malaysian student in Lu's study and the Arabic student in Canagarajah's (2011) later study) also demonstrates how much students want to reproduce the dominant discourse rather than try to intentionally break it. So, such practice should be complimented by our close attention to implicit traces of difference, especially when using the same language structure/vocabulary for differences in meaning. It seems that plurilingual theorists' concern to debunk monolingualist ideology risks making code-meshing/shuttling between languages a natural competence for all multilingual speakers—something they want to hone all the time.[5] When we focus on such code-meshing practices, we may dismiss how a large number of people are not only forced to but they also desire to imitate the norms of the "standard" language to create difference in meaning, even in their imitation. My major concern is that, by focusing on a few code-meshing practices of expert writers, we are dismissing the struggles of thousands of students in their attempt to "master" standard English.

In summing up the discussion of the romanticization of multilingualism, we can say that plurilingual theorists regard multilinguals as "free-floating" individuals, boosted by their history of language use and unrestrained by the actual contexts in which their negotiating expertise needs to be constantly relocalized through transformative meaning making. These theorists seem to have ignored how changing configurations of both the range of power relations and the power differential ratio in each relation can affect communication. In the context of the still-persisting monolingual tradition in US composition, we must pay attention to how and whether students forge difference in meaning when reproducing standard discourse conventions. The singular focus on code-meshing can risk encouraging teachers to only look for obvious differences and ignore the creative subversion of seemingly-repetitive, imitative acts.

MESODISCURSIVITY AND LANGUAGE USE

As discussed so far, the three major tendencies that I find problematic in terms of theorization of language use are: first, reconstructing a stable linguistic core, thereby ignoring both local heterogeneities and historical changes (WE, ELF and DNL); second, pluralizing monolingualism (additive multilingualism); and third, romanticizing multilingual competence (plurilingualism). Going against the first two tendencies and complicating the third, and based on Pennycook's theory of language as a local practice, this chapter proposes an approach that highlights the always local nature of language use, but with the awareness that it gets somewhat predictable due to the sedimented patterns emerging out of its repetitive nature. And this notion of language, by conceiving language practice as a midway point between little "d" discourse and big "D" Discourse, offers a way to avoid both the stability of language norms and the romanticized theory of multilingual agency implicated in other approaches discussed above. Here, language structure is conceived, unlike in structuralism, as the sedimented patterns emerging from its repetitive use in a particular local space (Pennycook 2010, 9).[6] In this sense, instead of focusing on abstract systems and preexisting standards, we need to highlight how structural patterns emerge and evolve over time through recurring acts of language use in specific locations.

The interplay between individual practice and the shared habitus during a particular instance of exchange makes the assumptions of radical contingency and stability unrealistic. Here, individual language use and social structurations of language are co-dependent and co-constitutive. Therefore, as Pennycook (2010) says, every individual language practice is a "mediating social activity where we do things both because we want to and along lines laid down by habit, propriety, cultural norms or political dictates. It is therefore useful to explore the *meso-political* space of practice that lies between the local and the global" (23, emphasis added).[7]

In other words, we need to pay attention to the meso space instead of overemphasizing the micro at the cost of the macro, as we saw in Canagarajah's (2007) account of plurilingualism, or overemphasizing the macro while undermining the role of the micro, as we saw in all three approaches discussed above. What individuals do does not depend only on what they want; it is also guided by the structuring forces in global/local relations of power. As Bruce Horner (2001) argues, it is important to consider how certain language practices are legitimized while others are delegitimized based on existing power relations in a particular location, and how it is equally vital to create a favorable classroom environment for students to negotiate such politics of language (743).

Hence, I intend to highlight the relationship between language structure and individual practice, especially the idea that they constitute and transform each other. Discarding the theories of language structure as a preexisting system or individual language users as free-floating agents, I propose to view language structure as, in Giddens' (1986) sense, both the "medium and the outcome" of individual language practices (25). So, the focus here is not on "either/or" but on the interplay between the two—how language shapes an individual and how an individual transforms language. Therefore, the meso, the in-between position, means awareness of the tensions between individual agency and the social/historical constraints implicated in language structure on how one exercises that agency. In thinking about the relationships between dominant discourse and individual agency, we must attend to the role of dominant ideology, especially how it can pose constraints to individual agency.

Arjuna Parakrama's (1995) reflections about his own writing gives us a clear sense of how dominant ideology can restrain individuals trying to negotiate across languages:

> I had wanted to write the whole of this book in forms of non-standard English, but it became too difficult because I am very much a product of these standards I wish to problematize. This task to change the way we have looked at language, in concrete as opposed to abstract terms, is

hard—*really* hard because it has much less to do with individual ability
than structural and discursive hegemony (vi)

What Parakrama's example shows is the idea that when one tries to "master" a language/discourse, one is also mastered by that discourse, so
much so that it's difficult for him or her to get out of it and practice delegitimized discourses. Parakrama's case also reveals a few other things. It
clearly shows why being multilingual/multidiscoursal, in Pennycook's
sense of semiodiversity, is so hard. On the one hand, Parakrama was a
graduate student writing his dissertation on the issue of the standardization of English. He was clearly bilingual, perhaps from birth. And he was
also deliberately trying to subvert the dominant discourse. Yet, he still
finds it extremely difficult to shuttle between languages. When considering the writing practices of our students, it is extremely important to
pay attention to the kinds of difficulties Parakrama mentions.[8] However,
on the other hand, it does not mean that his and similar other attempts
to problematize standardized discourse do not have any impact on language ecology. His attempt to problematize the ideology of English
monolingualism, either by using non-standard English or the "standard"
one, does contribute to the changes we've seen over the years in our
understanding of and thinking about language.

While Parakrama's example shows us the difficulty resulting from
one's near-complete entanglements into the dominant language ideology, there lies, in some cases, another kind of difficulty, the difficulty in
switching from the home/local discourse to the dominant.[9] For many
students who do not have strong familiarity with and regular training
in the dominant discourse, the problem arises when they are asked to
write in the dominant discursive tradition and must transition from
their familiar discourse tradition to the dominant one. Think of students entering the US classroom with different experiences of epistemological and discourse practices. They often need to work hard
to fulfill the expectations of the dominant academic discourse. Their
past experiences that shape their habitus often tend to contradict the
dominant discourse practices of the present. To take one example,
many students who come from different academic and cultural traditions may find the combative nature of academic writing in the West
disorienting and challenging.

The case of a recent immigrant from India, Neha Shah—presented
in Fishman and McCarthy's (2001) study—can cast light on the difficulties discussed above. In the writing intensive Intro to Philosophy class,
the instructor, though very sympathetic to the ESL student, thinks Neha
is underprepared for his class. However, Neha thinks she can easily pass

the course. This mismatch between what the instructor and the ESL student think results not only from their conflicting expectations, but also from their different assumptions and experiences about academic writing. The instructor expects Neha to write and read in a way based on Western argument-based writing tradition. He wants her to understand the arguments in philosophical texts, critique their positions, and take a unique position of her own on a particular topic. Neha first thinks she will easily pass this course because she has already completed a bachelor's degree in India. But the kind of writing pattern she used in India is vastly different from her current instructor's expectations. She does not focus on producing argument-based text. Her writing often presents background information in detail and offers her understanding of the assigned texts without including her own argument about the text. Neha's other major problem is that she does not find the texts and the curriculum interesting. When she writes, she focuses on personal or cultural beliefs. The difficulty she goes through, as she herself says in an interview with the researcher, lies in the fact that her knowledge and education have not been recognized in her current university: "She explains that the disruption in her plans caused by this conflict between American and Indian systems made her feel 'sad and sorry' for herself. '[I am like] a traveler [who] does not know which way is correct road to get his or her place'" (Fishman and McCarthy 2001, 198). This is why she goes through a lot of ambivalence regarding the courses she is taking, which is also reflected in her apathy toward her philosophy course. Moreover, it's difficult for her to connect to many of the intellectual and cultural values she is supposed to analyze and appreciate.

By contrast, Neha, as a "traveler" between two cultures, a newcomer to this one, entered Steve's class with different interests and background knowledge—different cultural capital—than her American classmates (Bourdieu, 1982). As a result, she found herself, once again, experiencing bicultural tension, saying that course content was confusing to her, sometimes even upsetting. For example, she was puzzled about her classmates' emotional involvement in discussions of racism after they read Fanon, Carmichael, and hooks (Fishman and McCarthy 2001, 200).

Many of the things discussed in class did not make any sense to her. At the same time, she was not encouraged to use her cultural capital to critique both the ideas in her texts and her own cultural assumptions. This is one major reason why the instructor finds Neha's writing incoherent and disorganized. Perhaps Neha could have done better, had the instructor opened up ways for her and for other students to tap into their own cultural and language resources to enhance their writing and discussion.

Neha's case, while not completely representative of all non-native students, also manifests other challenges that many minority students face. Besides taking two other courses, Neha works as a teaching assistant and also works forty-five hours a week at two off-campus jobs. As many other studies have shown, students like Neha have several commitments while passionately trying to succeed academically in order to have better job prospects in an 'alien' world. The pressure from instructors and their own concerns about linguistic differences make students try to imitate standard discourse. Therefore, it is important for us to not only encourage glossodiversity but also to pay attention to the differences such students create in their attempts to repeat dominant discourse patterns.

What Neha's example shows us is that while we should highlight the importance of in-betweenness, a position in which individuals try to maintain the knowledge and awareness of two or more different discourses, it is equally necessary to caution us to think of such a position as being highly labor-intensive. This is because this meso space allows us to maintain greater agency only when we resist the silencing of delegitimized discourses. Mesodiscursivity is not a "mixture" or "blend" of two discourse practices, as the term hybridity generally means; nor is it a presence of the conventions of two discourse practices, where one of the two is silenced; rather, it is closer to what Bhava (2004) says of "hybridity, a difference 'within', a subject that inhabits a rim of an 'in-between' reality" (19). This mesodiscursive position is important for maintaining a critical distance between the hegemonic discourse practices. The individuals in this meso space are not only informed and shaped by both the micro and the macro, they also inform and transform them in turn. This focus on meso helps us avoid two extreme positions: notions of a metadiscursive awareness[10] for initiating change in discourse practice on the one hand, and discursive imprisonment leading to a complete lack of individual agency on the other (structural/poststructural notions of structure).

Rethinking language practices in terms of mesodiscursivity also causes us to question the tendency to think of everyone as multilingual/ multidiscoursal in the sense of the romanticization of multilingualism posits. We need to make a distinction between actually being multilingual and having a belief in multilingualism, instead of conflating the two and calling everyone multilingual. In the discursive sense that this chapter is using the term multilingualism, or from the perspective of what Pennycook (2010) calls semiodiversity, one does not become multilingual simply by having an open attitude towards speakers of other languages, as many plurilingual theorists and other ELF scholars posit. As Horner, NeCamp, and Donahue (2011) contend, being multilingual does not merely mean being able to speak multiple languages. Therefore, despite people having access to and familiarity with various discourses, and despite them speaking several languages, one discourse always tends to dominate the others in specific situations. In other words, we may all tend to be "multidiscoursal," but, for most of us, one discourse overshadows the rest. Min-Zhan Lu's (1987) description of her bilingual upbringing in China, in an atmosphere where she was sandwiched between the discourse of Western humanism and that of Chinese revolutionary politics, may be illustrative here, even if it does not apply to all situations:

> The homogeneity of home and of school implied that only one discourse could and should be relevant in each place. It led me to believe I should leave behind, turn a deaf ear to, or forget the discourse of the other when I crossed the boundary dividing them. I expected myself to set down one discourse whenever I took up another just as I would take off or put on a particular set of clothes for school or home. (445)

This case is revealing. Even if people may not have parallel situations, they tend to work under pressure—both consciously and unconsciously—from one dominant discourse, depending on which discourses other than the dominant one remain silenced. Even in the above example, the focus is on either one or the other. However, Lu may need to attend to many other discourses and social relations operating simultaneously with the dominant discourse of either Chinese revolutionary politics or Western humanism. Even in case of switching between discourses, she clearly shows her intense struggle. Her experience illustrates that "struggle," the struggle to stop the bleeding over of one discourse into the other, rather than an easy shuttling between them. She says, "writing the book report made me feel that my reading and writing in the 'language' of either home or school could not be free of the interference of the other" (443). Lu's discussion of the metaphoric meaning of "red" and how she used it to transfer the idea of love to revolutionary politics is a clear example of such overlap.[11] This instance clearly demonstrates how difficult it is to shuttle between discourses, because in "shuttling" we often assume a separate existence of each one, instead of seeing how they relate and how individuals are informed by or inform and transform these discourses.

So, to remain consciously mesodiscursive, we must remain well informed about and invested in the positions and discourses that are different from our own, often the ones which are delegitimized by the dominant ideology (the US academic discourse in case of US minority students).[12] Think of one who can speak both English and Nepali languages, but is raised in the Western education system and has been detached from epistemological and discursive practices and material investment in his home country, and is now studying or teaching in the United States. Think of how much pressure she or he feels even in ordinary situations like writing papers for class: often one is forced to adapt to the conventions and requirements of Western academic models. In this context of this meso space, the macro (Western academic) is seen as a force at odds with and, therefore, mediated by the micro (personal commitment to the delegitimized dispositions) emphasis on "localizing" the hegemonic bundling of activities.

Therefore, mesodiscursivity is not a default condition in multilingual places; it requires a conscious and deliberate choice. It requires a commitment to semiodiversity against the grain of hegemonic meanings and ways of meaning making. So, maintaining this mesodiscursive position is not a matter of competence in languages, but a matter of knowing how different discursive practices interact and intersect so that one can be a conscious user of different language practices. Because of this, the attention in US classrooms should be directed more toward diversity in meanings and understandings. Here, attention to mesodiscursivity takes one beyond "language" to think about various social relations and discourses. So, mesodiscursivity relates not only to relations across languages like Spanish, English, or Nepali, but also across discourses of capitalism, gender, and geopolitical relations. Going beyond thinking in terms of glossodiversity in a context where students are required or expected to reproduce the dominant discourse, we must attend to the mesopolitical meaning-making embedded in seeming acts of repetition in a dominant discourse that is socially and historically overvalued at the macro level.

IMPLICATIONS OF A MESODISCURSIVE APPROACH

"It makes me sick—That's how I feel. And that's why a lot of people are not interested. I-am-not [states each word slowly]. What am I saying?—Everybody knows what 'I'm not' means. It's like trying to segregate, you know, you've got like a boundary that sets, you know, you apart from other people. Why?" (Lillis 2001, 85)

"You will need to work on standard edited English, especially if you want to work using this language after you get your degree." (A typical comment on many papers of non-native writers)

Language Difference in Curriculum Design

I begin with these two examples—how linguistic difference is treated and how such treatment affects non-native students—in order to briefly discuss some of the implications of the approach this chapter proposes. While the first quotation above reflects the frustration that many non-mainstream students go through in situations where English is conceived only in monolingual terms, the second quotation represents the dominant approach to correctness in writing, assuming that one major goal of teaching writing is to teach "standard" English. Peruse the major goals or outcomes statements of any US composition program and you will find such a goal highlighted in the very beginning. Even the "WPA Outcomes Statement for First-Year Composition" mentions a similar goal for first year writing courses. It says, "By the end of first-year composition, students should control such surface features as syntax, grammar, punctuation, and spelling," assuming there are fixed conventions that students can and should "master" (Council of Writing Program Administration 2008). This language of *mastery* and the characterization of those features as *surface* features mask how they are, in reality, the result of sedimentations of language practices in specific socio-historical contexts. This dominant tendency toward language conventions promotes the masking of the politics of language "standardization." And this is where the mesodiscursive approach sees the need to change how we approach language conventions, shifting our focus from the masking of politics to formulating outcomes and goals for First Year Writing curriculum.

When the guiding principle in curriculum design assumes difference in language use as deviation/error, it not only upholds the myth of discreteness and stability of a language "system"[13] (Horner, Lu, Royster, and Trimbur 2011; Pennycook 2010), but it also frustrates many students in ways similar to the one we see in the above quotation from Lillis (2001). In many cases, the direct impact of such language beliefs would be students getting a lower grade, the consequences of which can be devastating (loss of scholarship, ineligibility for admission, etc.). Besides the false theoretical assumption, the real practical problem is that most of these non-native students are systematically placed at a disadvantage because the norm often comes from language of the dominant class. Many students who use English differently go through serious frustration and heavy pressure due to the fact that teachers always mark their writing as "incorrect," requiring them to master the dominant variety. For instance, in the quote above, the student feels as if she is "segregat[ed]" simply because she uses "I'm" in place of "I am." Theresa Lillis (2001) rightly points out the political ramifications

of such practice: "Example 1 helps the researcher learn about the significance of a particular textual feature—I'm—to the writer. The writer
doesn't see full versus contracted forms as a question about neutral conventions but rather as having the potential to exclude people, including
herself, from engaging in academia" (360). Such students also often go
through psychological struggle due to the fact that they feel insecure
about their future prospects.

A similar problem persists even when we see language difference
from the perspectives of ELF, WE, DNL, and multilingualism: the focus
will still remain on competence in some variety of English or another
national language.[14] That is, these perspectives still assume that languages are separate and stable. In other words, those who do not use
a particular language or language variety in its purity will suffer. These
perspectives simply shift the problem from one group to another.[15]

Following plurilingual theory in approaching language difference in
curriculum design would also be problematic because it does not take
into account the frustration and the struggle that such students must
endure due to the assumptions that they, as multilinguals, are capable
of shuttling between discourses. Whether it is a code-switching or a
code-meshing pedagogy, both assume that there are separate codes and
that multilinguals can develop a metalinguistic awareness for intentionally switching across languages. Canagarajah (2006a), House (2003a;
2003b), Meierkord (2004), and other linguists cite examples to make
such points. For instance, Canagarajah cites scholars like K. Sivatamby
and Geneva Smitherman to show how multilinguals use strategies of
code-meshing to deliberately resist the norms of standardized discourse
and forge difference in meaning. Though these examples can be
sources of inspiration for many other scholars and students, taking them
as representative of multilingual students would, ironically, perform a
disservice to many other students because such an emphasis ignores
their struggles and difficulties. The problem for most students is that
they cannot have a clear awareness of boundaries, even if such boundaries exist at some abstract level.

So, what is a good option for helping students become more conscious language users, while still respecting the differences in their
writing? First, both as WPAs and as teachers of writing, we should
stop overemphasizing "correctness" in writing and interpreting correctness in terms of the "standard" variety in our curriculum. This
means it is necessary for us to shift our focus from language as a set
of transferrable skills to language as a complex and socially-situated,
meaning-making practice. When we shift our attention to language

use as mesodiscursive, our guiding philosophy in curriculum design becomes engaging students and teachers in developing greater awareness of different ways of meaning making, as well as tolerance toward ambiguities and differences in language use. Instead of making the mastery of surface features of "standard" English the central goal of First Year Writing, we must now try to offer our students an environment where they can rethink historic language conventions, consider their interactions with dominant social ideologies, reflect on the available resources for creatively resisting the hegemony of English monolingualism, and develop a mesodiscursive awareness of language use in specific micro–macro contexts.

Placement and Pedagogy in Writing Classrooms

With the rise in the number of non-native speakers in our composition classes, one central question that has intrigued WPAs is whether to separate non-mainstream (or ESL) students or to mainstream them. When we question abstract categories like "standard English" (often meaning American or British) and ESL,[16] and when we conceive of language as a mesodiscursive practice, the whole logic of both separating and mainstreaming becomes problematic. As dichotomizing between ESL and non-ESL is problematic and as writings of so-called monolingual students demonstrate diverse ways of meaning making, it is better to integrate all ESL and non-ESL students, not because the former can learn from the latter or vice versa, but because they all can learn from every other student in the class as the nature of their language practice varies due to their specific interplay between individual resources and sedimented language patterns.

In this situation, our emphasis should shift from kinds of placement to pedagogy. As discussed above, our focus of teaching should be on promoting an awareness of difference rather than teaching singular and monolithic norms/standards. This is similar to what James Slevin (2001) says in a slightly different context:

> Composition is a discipline, an *educational* practice in the older sense I have sketched, that cannot know itself because we have lost our power to name what we do. Our discipline is about the encounter of different ways of reading and writing; our discipline arises in acts of interpretation and composing, different ways of reading and thinking and persuading brought into our classrooms by students. Our disciplinary work in all its forms, including research, arises from the need and the desirability of promoting and enriching the dialog, already underway. (44)

When we make differences in language use a major emphasis of our teaching, we should reimagine composition as an activity of learning, since it is learning new ways of using language. This mode of teaching writing is similar to what Claire Kramsch (1998) calls the "intercultural speaker model," where the primary aim of language teaching becomes learning various ways of meaning making in micro/macro contexts (17).

However, in most ESL literature, difference is taken in a static sense, assuming that ESL and non-ESL students have certain writing styles. We should instead discard the static notion of difference and use what Kerschbaum (2012) calls "a dynamic, relational, and emergent construct" (616). This means we should be careful in approaching students' writing based on differences in various a priori categories, such as ESL, native speaker, etc. The point of whether to keep ESL students separate or together becomes less important than how we approach difference. It can perhaps be more detrimental to address language difference by separating or integrating students based on who they are or how they look than it actually helps them. Rather, it is better to consider that, as language is always in "translation" and its norms are continually evolving—as Pennycook (2008) and Canagarajah (2006a) say—every student brings a new and different way of meaning making.

Though, theoretically speaking, keeping all students together, ESL or non-ESL, makes more sense than keeping them separate, it's true that—as some ESL scholars have pointed out—ESL students may feel threatened in a classroom with an overwhelming majority of monolingual students due to the influence of monolingual ideology on both ESL and non-ESL students. We therefore need to create "an environment which is less threatening to ESL students" and promote cross-cultural awareness (Matsuda and Silva 2006, 247).

Since one of the major emphases of the mesodiscursive approach to language difference is the difficulty of negotiating across languages and cultures, especially from the minority position, it is important for teachers to create a favorable atmosphere for all students to feel encouraged to tap into their resources and to question the politics of dominant language/discourse conventions. At the same time, monolingual students and teachers can also benefit from learning new ways of reading and writing in such situations. Joseph and Ramani (2012, 29–30), despite advocating additive multilingualism, offer some remarkable examples of how we can engage students in critical enquiry of language politics. They offer a dual language degree, teaching various courses in both English and a local language, knowing that students recognize their own language as a legitimate language of scholarship and intellectual work. Similarly, as a major assignment in their writing class, they ask students to "translate sections of scholarly articles from English into their home languages." They believe that such activities can help students develop a "deeper comprehension of selected Western epistemologies." In the context of US composition, even if a translation assignment may not be appropriate, it is possible to ask students to find scholarly texts translated from other languages—in order to see how rhetorical and organizational patterns relate to and differ from the dominant Western style—and ask them to reflect on the resources they tap into in the process.[17] However, it is extremely important for teachers, as Michael Apple (2011) says, to be ready to learn from differences in meaning-making practices in other languages and to study the historical and cultural contexts contributing to those differences. Therefore, teaching writing in an age of globalization is as demanding as it is rewarding. All students and teachers can enrich their linguistic, epistemological, and cultural repertoire and appreciate the value of diversity.

Teacher Training and Translingual Disposition

I work as a writing consultant in a business school, and I often meet students who say "our teacher takes two points off for every error I have in my paper" or "in my last assignment, I lost twenty points because I had ten article errors." One comment that a student received in his paper drew my attention: "Your paper is very difficult to read because it wanders around." Perhaps due to monolingual training, teachers may still have difficulty with student writing that "wanders around"; they don't have any tolerance toward ambiguities and complexities. This applies, as Matsuda (2006) says, not only to teachers outside the English department, but also to those who teach First Year Writing. This pervasive ideology of English monolingualism still governs how teachers think about language, despite English going through constant transformations in varying sociopolitical contexts. What it says is that writing programs need to work continuously toward changing the dispositions of such teachers because, as Patricia Friedrich (2006) says, they cannot be changed and "implemented overnight" (26). As a mesodiscursive approach underscores the need to pay attention to individual disposition shaped by social structurations, as well as to the possibility of changing such disposition by introducing and investing in alternative discourse practices, it is important to do at least two things regarding teacher training. First, we need to encourage teachers (including graduate teaching assistants (GTAs) and adjuncts, who form the majority of those who teach First

Year Writing) and provide them with the resources, as Patricia Friedrich (2006) says, to learn from recent scholarship on language learning:

> I recommend that both WPAs and faculty read and discuss works in sociolinguistics and particularly in world Englishes. When instructors become aware of the magnitude, the scope, and the many different functions of English around the world, their perceptions of the language tend to change completely, and their sensitivity to issues facing users of the language who are different from themselves seems to grow accordingly. (26)

Second, we can utilize, as Wendy Hesford et al. (2009) advocate, the resources that a diverse group of teachers can bring, especially from their experiences of teaching or learning languages that are different from our mainstream tradition. However, it would be a mistake to assume that non-native or multilingual GTAs/faculty are free from monolingual bias, particularly because the teaching of English is equally (sometimes even more) governed by monolingual ideology, even outside the United States and other English-speaking countries. The sharing of these diverse experiences, by both native and non-native teachers, can help promote greater awareness about language politics and discursive practices.

The Writing Center as an Additional Space

The same approach is necessary to make our work in writing centers more responsible and ethical. As Talinn Phillips, Candace Stewart, and Robert D. Stewart claim, "the writing center provides a third site—a site which, unlike the TESOL or English departments, is already cross-disciplinary—for writing" that addresses the issue of language diversity (Phillips et al. 2006, 89). However, though the writing center can be an appropriate forum for initiating changes in language ideology across the disciplines, the tutoring approach should be radically changed. The following "success" story about the work of an ESL specialist in a writing center offers insight into the problem we may still face if we do not change our approach and instead think of the solution to the presence of ESL students in our classes as hiring more second language specialists:

> Working with the same second language student twice a week for eleven weeks, he reported that the student improved her writing from nearly unreadable prose to high academic English. He surmised that this success emerged from several factors. For example, he insisted that she learn from her own mistakes and from his corrections, thus reducing her mistakes in article usage from twenty or more per page to fewer than five per

> page . . . He also developed a set of templates for her to use when writing article reviews; these templates outlined rhetorical patterns and conventions she might follow, thereby addressing shifts in cultural and rhetorical differences. (Phillips et al. 2006, 42)

The method used here is, in my perception, no different from how mainstream composition teachers with some familiarity with language issues address ESL problems. ESL specialists still focus on language as superficial structure and do not care about how differences in students' use of language can carry different ways of understanding and meaning making.[18] The traditional approach, which does not go beyond surface "errors," fails to account for the link that language conventions have with the micro/macro contexts of its use. The writing center is an appropriate forum to address the issue of language difference, since a majority of visitors to writing centers are non-mainstream students. However, writing center work should not be taken as an alternative space that fully replaces the diversity concerns in our classrooms. Rather, it should complement similar attempts in every regular class. The right approach in the writing center can encourage students to tap into their linguistic and cultural resources and negotiate the hegemony of the dominant discourse. And, in line with what Phillips et al. (2006) argue, writing centers can take the initiative to create awareness in students and faculty across the disciplines about the politics of language and the need to recognize the value of diversity in reading and writing.

CONCLUSION

The three major approaches to language diversity—WE, ELF, and DNL—ignore the emergent nature of language practice by conceiving languages as stable systems. However, other approaches, such as plurilingualism, tend to regard language users as free-floating individuals, thereby downplaying the labor involved in cross-language practices. This chapter, going beyond these two major tendencies, argues that it is necessary to attend to the writer's engagement in mesodiscursive space and respond to various macro and micro relations. In this context, I contend that the act of negotiation that multilinguals engage in is labor-intensive, due to the overwhelming presence of "standard" English in most formal writing situations. Hence, WPAs—whether in the United States or outside—need to be careful when designing writing curricula and training teachers and writing center tutors.

Since language use is a mesodiscursive practice, when designing curricula for teaching writing—in place of emphasizing the mastery of "standard" English—we should focus on engaging students and teachers in developing greater awareness of different ways of meaning making and displaying tolerance toward ambiguities and differences in language use. In the spirit of this language philosophy, we must rethink placement options for ESL students. Instead of separating and/ or mainstreaming ESL students, which rests on the policy of unidirectional monolingualism, we should work toward creating an environment where all diverse students can learn from different ways of constructing meaning, a practice that benefits both mainstream and non-mainstream students. Similarly, teacher training should focus on transforming the disposition of GTAs and composition faculty toward language difference by engaging them in translingual discourse and sharing various experiences working with English and other languages in specific micro/ macro contexts.

This work of transforming the language disposition of composition instructors, though it is labor-intensive, is central to our work because they are the ones who play a significant role in changing the language beliefs of future educators and policy makers. Equally central is the role writing centers can play in this process. Writing centers have a unique role because they are in a position to influence language beliefs of both students and faculty across various disciplines. However, writing center tutors should go beyond a skills-based approach to language difference and instead focus on the various ways students can use the English language and other language resources.

Notes

1. The notion of a native speaker norm has been challenged, as several linguists such as Paikeday (2003) contend that native speaker is "merely an ideal or a convenient linguistic fiction—myth, shibboleth, sacred cow—an etherlike concept with no objective reality to it, albeit embodied in a quasi-privileged class of speakers of each language" (21). Therefore, I am only using the terms "native" and "non-native" for convenience.

2. Braj Kachru's (2005) *Asian Englishes* and Kachru and Nelson's (2006) *World Englishes* are good examples of the world Englishes model.

3. See Jennifer Jenkins (2000), Andy Kirkpatrick (2006), and Barbara Seidlhofer (2006) as examples of the English as lingua franca approach.

4. Phillipson (2001; 2003) and Joseph and Ramani (2006) represent the defense of national language approach to the hegemony of the English language on a global scale.

5. Even if Canagarajah (2011) critiques the Chomskian model of natural competence, he seems to have fallen victim to a similar model by assuming the expertise of multilingual speakers to be "honed by actual interaction." It is quite different to think of language repertoire as a resource for multilingual speakers to tap into

when confronting difficult communicative situations, as well as to think of it as part of natural competence and applicable to all situations.

6. In defining language as a *local* practice, Pennycook (2010) first seeks to go beyond the traditional notion of "context" and takes local to mean the particular space as related to other terms—such as "regional, national, global, universal"—where it is not opposed to what is global, but can also be constitutive of and by such things as global (4). He also avoids interpreting language as a mere instrument of a larger Discourse, always contingent and fluid. Therefore, he calls language a practice that goes midway between the little "d" discourse and the big "D" Discourse (Gee 2008).

7. Pennycook derives his theory of practice from, among others, Bourdieu (1977; 1991) and Giddens (1986), who use the term "practice" or "habitus" to "steer a course between the grand and seemingly deterministic theories of critical social science, where human action is a by-product of larger social structures, and the voluntaristic views of humanism" (Pennycook 2010, 27).

8. For a similar account of the difficult and labor-intensive nature of language negotiation, see Guillaume Gentil's (2005) "Commitments to Academic Biliteracy."

9. I refer to such a division between home/non-dominant and dominant discourse mainly to highlight the fact that there are different practices, but not to say that such a division is water-tight. I do acknowledge that no discourse remains completely unaffected by others.

10. Even Canagarajah's [2006a] notion of shuttling is closer to this position.

11. Lu (1987) presents how language is a site of struggle. In this article, she does not seem to have considered how subversive mimicry could have been an option for resistance. However, her later articles clearly present this idea of reproduction as appropriation and negotiation.

12. Aijaz Ahmad (1994) makes a similar point in a different context. He criticizes postcolonial scholars like Edward Said for their tendency to claim authentic perspective from the periphery. Ahmad believes that US-based international scholars lose their multicultural resources due to both their loss of meaningful contact and material investment in the discourses of their home country as well as their entrapment into the academic culture of the United States.

13. It's not only the dominant monolingual policy/ideology that assumes language fixity. Other language theories that acknowledge diversity also end up holding the same belief, focusing either on ELF or on separate varieties of WE. Therefore, these theories do not help us overcome monolingual ideology in curriculum design.

14. This can be a regional or national variety of "standard" English (American English, Indian English, etc.), a simplified language of communication (ELF), or a national language.

15. Instead of saying something like "If you want to work in the United States, you have to master standard edited English," teachers might say "Use pure Nepali or Nepalese English [if there is such a thing] to be successful in Nepal." So, in the case of the United States, non-native writers may suffer, whereas outside English-speaking countries will include those who do not practice the dominant variety.

16. See Kate Mangelsdorf (2006) and Gail Shuck (2006) for more information on how categories like ESL have become more problematic than useful.

17. As Horner, Lu, Royster, and Trimbur (2011) and Horner, NeCamp, and Donahue (2011) argue, the translation of scholarly texts from other languages can also be used to satisfy second language requirements.

18. For a detailed account of how simple instances of "error" in student writing can mask larger meanings, see Min Zhan Lu's (1994) "Professing Multiculturalism."

References

Agnihotri, Rama K. 2007. "Towards a Pedagogical Paradigm Rooted in Multilinguality." *International Multilingual Research Journal* 1 (2): 79–88. http://dx.d oi.org/10.1080/19313150701489689.

Ahmad, Aijaz. 1994. *Theory: Classes, Nations, and Literatures.* London, New York: Verso.

Apple, Michael W. 2011. "Global Crises, Social Justice, and Teacher Education." *Journal of Teacher Education* 62 (2): 222–34. http://dx.doi.org/10.1177/0022487110385428.

Bhava, Homi K. 2004. *The Location of Culture.* New York: Routledge.

Bourdieu, Pierre. 1977. *Outline of a Theory of Practice.* Trans. Richard Nice. Cambridge: Cambridge University Press. http://dx.doi.org/10.1017/CBO9780511812507.

Bourdieu, Pierre. 1982. "The School as a Conservative Force: Scholastic and Cultural Inequalities." In *Knowledge and Values in Social and Educational Research,* ed. Eric Bredo and Walter Feinberg, 391–407. Philadelphia: Temple University Press.

Bourdieu, Pierre. 1991. *Language and Symbolic Power.* Ed. John Thomson. Trans. Gino Raymond and Matthew Adamson. Cambridge: Harvard University Press.

Canagarajah, Suresh. 2006a. "Toward a Writing Pedagogy of Shuttling between Languages: Learning from Multilingual Writers." *College English* 68 (6): 589–604. http://dx.doi.org /10.2307/25472177.

Canagarajah, Suresh. 2006b. "The Place of World Englishes in Composition: Pluralization Continued." *College Composition and Communication* 57 (4): 586–619.

Canagarajah, Suresh. 2007. "Lingua Franca English, Multilingual Communities, and Language Acquisition." *Modern Language Journal* 91:923–39. http://dx.doi.org/10.1111 /j.1540-4781.2007.00678.x.

Canagarajah, Suresh. 2009. "Multilingual Strategies of Negotiating English: From Conversation to Writing." *JAC* 29 (1–2): 17–48.

Canagarajah, Suresh. 2011. "Codemeshing in Academic Writing: Identifying Teachable Strategies of Translanguaging." *Modern Language Journal* 95 (3): 401–17. http://dx.doi .org/10.1111/j.1540-4781.2011.01207.x.

Coste, Daniel, and Diana-Lee Simon. 2009. "The Plurilingual Social Actor: Language, Citizenship and Education." *International Journal of Multilingualism* 6 (2): 168–85. http://dx.doi.org/10.1080/14790710902846723.

Crystal, David. 2003. *English as a Global Language.* Cambridge: Cambridge University Press. http://dx.doi.org/10.1017/CBO9780511486999.

Fishman, Stephen M., and Lucille McCarthy. 2001. "An ESL Writer and Her Discipline-Based Professor: Making Progress Even When Goals Don't Meet." *Written Communication* 18 (2): 180–228. http://dx.doi.org/10.1177/0741088301018002002.

Friedrich, Patricia. 2006. "Assessing the Needs of Linguistically Diverse First-Year Students: Bringing Together and Telling Apart International ESL, Resident ESL and Monolingual Basic Writers." *WPA: Writing Program Administration* 30 (1–2): 15–36.

Gee, James Paul. 2008. *Social Linguistics and Literacies: Ideology in Discourses.* 3rd ed. London, New York: Rutledge.

Gentil, Guillaume. 2005. "Commitments to Academic Biliteracy: Case Studies of Francophone University Writers." *Written Communication* 22 (4): 421–71. http://dx.doi .org/10.1177/0741088305280350.

Giddens, Anthony. 1986. *The Constitution of Society.* California: University of California Press.

Heller, Monica. 2002. "Globalization and the Commodification of Bilingualism in Canada." In *Globalization and Language Teaching,* ed. David Block and Deborah Cameron, 47–64. London: Rutledge.

Hesford, Wendy, Edgar Singleton, and Ivonne M. García. 2009. "Laboring to Globalize a First-Year Writing Program." In *The Writing Program Interrupted: Making Space for Critical Discourse,* ed. Donna Strickland and Jeanne Gunner, 113–25. Portsmouth, NH: Boynton/Cook Publishers.

Horner, Bruce. 2001. "'Students' Right,' English Only, and Re-imagining the Politics of Language." *College English* 63 (6): 741–58. http://dx.doi.org/10.2307/1350100.

Horner, Bruce, Min-Zhan Lu, Jacqueline Jones Royster, and John Trimbur. 2011. "Language Difference in Writing: Toward a Translingual Approach." *College English* 73 (3): 299–317.

Horner, Bruce, Samantha NeCamp, and Christiana Donahue. 2011. "Toward a Multilingual Composition Scholarship: From English Only to a Translingual Norm." *College Composition and Communication* 63 (2): 269–300.

House, Juliane. 2003a. "English as a Lingua Franca: A Threat to Multilingualism." *Journal of Sociolinguistics* 7 (4): 556–78. http://dx.doi.org/10.1111/j.1467-9841.2003 .00242.x.

House, Juliane. 2003b. "Misunderstanding in Intercultural University Encounter." In *Misunderstanding in Social Life: Discourse Approaches to Problematic Talk*, ed. Juliane House, Gabriele Kasper, and Steven Ross, 22–56. London: Pearson.

Jenkins, Jennifer. 2000. *The Phonology of English as an International Language: New Models, New Forms, New Goals*. Oxford: Oxford University Press.

Jessner, Ulrike. 2006. *Linguistic Awareness in Multilinguals: English as a Third Language*. Edinburgh: Edinburgh University Press. http://dx.doi.org/10.3366/edin burgh/9780748619139.001.0001.

Joseph, Michael, and Esther Ramani. 2006. "English in the World Does Not Mean English Everywhere: The Case for Multilingualism in the ELT/ESL Profession." In Rubdy and Saraceni, 186–200.

Joseph, Michael, and Esther Ramani. 2012. "'Glocalization': Going Beyond the Dichotomy of Global Versus Local through Additive Multilingualism." *International Multilingual Research Journal* 6 (1): 22–34. http://dx.doi.org/10.1080/19313152.2012 .639246.

Kachru, Braj. 2005. *Asian Englishes: Beyond the Canon*. Hong Kong: Hong Kong University Press.

Kachru, Yamuna, and Cecil L. Nelson. 2006. *World Englishes in Asian Contexts*. Hong Kong: Hong Kong University Press.

Kirkpatrick, Andy. 2006. "Which Model of English: Native Speaker, Nativized or Lingua Franca?" In Rubdy and Saraceni, 71–83.

Kerschbaum, Stephanie L. 2012. "Avoiding the Difference Fixation: Identity Categories, Markers of Difference, and the Teaching of Writing." *College Composition and Communication* 63 (4): 616–44.

Kramsch, Claire. 1998. "The Privilege of the Intercultural Speaker." In *Language Learning in Intercultural Perspective: Approaches through Drama and Ethnography*, ed. Michael Byram and Michael Fleming, 16–31. Cambridge: Cambridge University Press.

Kramsch, Claire. 2006. "The Traffic in Meaning." *Asia Pacific Journal of Education* 26 (1): 99–104. http://dx.doi.org/10.1080/02188790600608091.

Leung, Constant. 2005. "Convivial Communication: Recontextualizing Communicative Competence." *International Journal of Applied Linguistics* 15 (2): 119–44. http://dx.doi .org/10.1111/j.1473-4192.2005.00084.x.

Lillis, Theresa. 2001. *Student Writing: Access, Regulation, Desire*. London: Routledge.

Lu, Min-Zhan. 1987. "From Silence to Words: Writing as Struggle." *College English* 49 (4): 437–48. http://dx.doi.org/10.2307/377860.

Lu, Min-Zhan. 1994. "Professing Multiculturalism: The Politics of Style in the Contact Zone." *College Composition and Communication* 45 (4): 442–58. http://dx.doi.org/10 .2307/358759.

Mangelsdorf, Kate. 2006. "Controversies in Second Language Writing: Dilemmas and Decisions in Research and Instruction." *WPA: Writing Program Administration* 30 (1–2): 101–6.

Matsuda, Paul Kei. 1999. "Composition Studies and ESL Writing: A Disciplinary Division of Labor." *College Composition and Communication* 50 (4): 699–721. http://dx.doi.org /10.2307/358488.

Matsuda, Paul Kei. 2006. "The Myth of Linguistic Homogeneity in U.S. College Composition." *College English* 68 (6): 637–51. http://dx.doi.org/10.2307/25472180.

Matsuda, Paul Kei, and Tony Silva. 2006. "Cross-Cultural Composition: Mediated Integration of US and International Students." In *Second Language Writing in the Composition Classroom: A Critical Source Book*, ed. Paul Kei Matsuda, Michelle Cox, Christina Ortmeier-Hooper, and Jay Jordan, 246–59. Boston: Bedford.

Meierkord, Christiane. 2004. "Syntactic Variation in Interactions across International Englishes." *English World-Wide* 25 (1): 109–32. http://dx.doi.org/10.1075/eww.25.1 .06mei.

Moore, Danièle. 2006. "Plurilingualism and Strategic Competence in Context." *International Journal of Multilingualism* 3 (2): 125–38. http://dx.doi.org/10.1080/14790 710608668392.

Moore, Danièle, and Laurent Gajo. 2009. "Introduction – French Voices on Plurilingualism and Pluriculturalism: Theory, Significance, and Perspectives." *International Journal of Multilingualism* 6 (2): 137–53. http://dx.d oi.org/10.1080/14790710902846707.

Paikeday, Thomas M. 2003. *The Native Speaker is Dead!* Toronto, New York: Lexicography.

Parakrama, Arjuna. 1995. *De-hegemonizing Language Standards: Learning from (Post)colonial Englishes about English*. Basingstoke: Macmillan. http://dx.d oi.org/10.1057/9780230371309.

Pennycook, Alastair. 2008. "English as a Language Always in Translation." *European Journal of English Studies* 12 (1): 33–47. http://dx.doi.org/10.1080/13825570801900521.

Pennycook, Alastair. 2010. *Language as a Local Practice*. London, New York: Routledge.

Phillips, Talinn, Candace Stewart, and Robert D. Stewart. 2006. "Geography Lessons, Bridge-building, and Second Language Writers." *WPA: Writing Program Administration* 30 (1–2): 83–100.

Phillipson, Robert. 2001. "English for Globalization or for the World's People?" *International Review of Education* 47 (3/4): 185–200. http://dx.doi.org/10.1023 /A:1017937322957.

Phillipson, Robert. 2003. *English-Only Europe: Challenging Language Policy*. London: Routledge.

Preto-Bay, Ana Maria, and Kristine Hansen. 2006. "Preparing for the Tipping Point: Designing Writing Programs to Meet the Needs of the Changing Population." *WPA: Writing Program Administration* 30 (1/2): 37–57.

Rubdy, Rani, and Mario Saraceni, eds. 2006. *English in the World: Global Rules, Global Roles*. London: Continuum.

Seidlhofer, Barbara. 2006. "English as a Lingua Franca in the Expanding Circle: What It Isn't." In Rudby and Saraceni, 40–50.

Shuck, Gail. 2006. "Combating Monolingualism: A Novice Administrator's Challenge." *WPA: Writing Program Administration* 30 (1–2): 59–82.

Slevin, James. 2001. *Introducing English: Essays in the Intellectual Work of Composition*. Pittsburgh: University of Pittsburgh Press.

Council of Writing Program Administration. 2008. "WPA Outcomes Statement for First-Year Composition." http://wpacouncil.org/positions/outcomes.html.

9

(RE-)SITUATING TRANSLINGUAL WORK FOR WRITING PROGRAM ADMINISTRATION IN CROSS-NATIONAL AND CROSS-LANGUAGE PERSPECTIVES FROM LEBANON AND SINGAPORE

Nancy Bou Ayash

In an increasingly multilingual and multicultural society, where the intermingling and interpenetration of languages, language varieties, and emergent Englishes are expected, the critical question of language difference and its implications for language policy, composition pedagogy, curriculum design, and teacher preparation programs is becoming of utmost concern to US writing program administrators (WPAs). As they come to terms with the linguistic heterogeneity that is growing in number and intensity in writing programs and courses, WPAs are constantly striving to accommodate the academic needs of growing multilingual student populations and better understand and respond to the complexity of their identities, language practices, and written texts. In a recent opinion statement, Bruce Horner et al. (2011) advance a translingual approach to language difference that reconfigures the current work of US writing programs. Enacting a translingual model in US writing programs necessitates ambitious changes in policies and teaching practices that incorporate "*more*, not less" work on and across English(es) and other languages, thereby encouraging "conscious and critical" explorations of the heterogeneity of meanings in scenes of reading and writing (304, emphasis in original). Based upon the confessions of its advocates, an emerging translingual approach in US writing programs is still "at the beginning stages of [its] learning efforts . . ., which by definition will require the ideas and energy of many—including literacy workers using diverse languages, from outside as well as within the Anglo-American sphere" (310). The productivity of translingual work

DOI: 10.7330/9780874219623.c009

in US writing programs and the challenge of meeting its key tenets is, therefore, closely bound to exchanges across national and linguistic borders. In view of such recommendations for increased cross-language and cross-national relations, I focus this chapter on what WPAs can learn about the possible ways to address language difference in their own writing programs. I do so using examples from multilingual countries like Lebanon and Singapore, which have had their own share of struggles and successes with cultural and linguistic diversity.

Perspectives on responses to language diversity in the two postcolonial contexts of Lebanon and Singapore can be useful to WPAs in the United States, especially in planning the proper course for the incorporation of more translingual work in their own writing programs and in striving for official recognition by their own institutions. Lebanon, a former French colony, has shifted from bilingualism followed by cultural–linguistic struggles between Arabic and English/French to the current direction of "full-fledged multilingualism in society as well as in education" (Shaaban and Ghaith 1999, 1). Whereas Singapore, an ex-British colony, still struggles with ethnic tensions as a result of its current bilingual education policy, which is mainly criticized for its failure to capture the complexity of its multilingual realities (see Gopinathan et. al 2004; Rubdy and Tupas 2009). As I show in this chapter, the productivity of advancing translingual directions in US writing programs largely depends on the satisfaction of three interacting conditions, which WPAs still need to more closely examine: (1) attention to the multiplicity of language practices on the ground; (2) fighting for actively multilingual language policies that directly reflect the kind of cultural and linguistic diversity in the classroom; and (3) curriculum design that is in alignment with both language policy and the specific nature of sociolinguistic landscapes.[1] Both multilingual societies have had a long history of grappling with the coexistence of various languages and varieties, as well as the resulting complexities of language contact phenomena. In the remainder of this essay, I offer a description of each context, Lebanese and Singaporean, considering: (1) the active use of a variety of languages; (2) the ongoing histories of language and language-in-education policies; and (3) pedagogical responses to language difference in college writing curricula. In the last section, I explore the dynamic interaction between sociolinguistic realities, language policies, and composition instruction—in light of the globalizing economy and geopolitics in both locations—in relation to the multilingual situation in the United States. Building on and extending Horner et al.'s (2011) recent translingual framework, I conclude by exploring some possible implications for WPAs wishing to institutionalize translingualism in their own writing programs.

LANGUAGE DIVERSITY IN THE CASE OF LEBANON

1. English and Other Languages on the Ground

Lebanon is a multilingual nation with a dynamic linguistic use of major languages—such as Arabic, French, and English—that serve basic communicative, vocational, and educational purposes. The native language, Arabic, is considered diglossic, having two linguistic varieties: an unwritten colloquial Lebanese–Arabic variety, used for various conversational purposes, and another Modern Standard Arabic version, used only in religious, educational, literary, and other formal domains. In addition to the native Arabic language, the majority in Lebanon speaks French as a second foreign language after English, or as the first and English as the second. Other languages, such as Armenian, German, Kurdish, and Farsi, are also actively used by various minority groups in the Lebanese society, mainly as home languages or as languages of instruction in specific regions.

Amid the active use of this specific variety of languages—Arabic alongside English and French—remain the most widely used languages in which daily routines and affairs are conducted in contemporary Lebanese society. With Lebanon characterized by its dynamic flow of languages in various spatiotemporal contexts, it is no surprise, as I will demonstrate in the next two sections, to find special attention allotted to foreign language education.

2. Language and Language-in-Education Policies

French and English in Lebanon were first introduced as foreign languages through the arrival of missionaries in the first half of the nineteenth century, the most prominent of which were the French Jesuits and the American Evangelical Protestants. These missionaries introduced western influences into the Lebanese educational system by establishing bilingual schools and institutions of higher education across the country. However, the status of the English language in Lebanon altered drastically amid French rule in the middle of the twentieth century, which strategically foregrounded the political, military, and economic presence of the French. In addition, cultural and linguistic pollination through imposing French educational systems and a strict language policy chiefly promoted the far-reaching dominance of French.

After reclaiming its independence from French colonization in 1943, the first Lebanese government issued various declarations for strengthening the native Arabic language and reviving its high status through establishing independent educational institutions and designing new national curricula. Up until the late twentieth century, discussions about language policy in Lebanese society spurred a series of heated debates among various groups. With the country arising from an extended civil war period, the choice of language for communication and education was immediately associated with ideological orientations and political affiliations, either with France or the United States. During that period, foreign languages also "spread along sectarian lines"—Catholics and Maronite Christians who held strong affinities for France as their "savior" in a Muslim-dominated region learned only French, most Muslims studied Arabic, and the Druzes, the Greek Orthodox, and some Muslims who had ties with American Protestants preferred English (Diab 2000, 178). Such controversy around issues of national identity and belongingness being connected to language choice was gradually resolved through declaring Arabic as the only official language in the country besides placing equal emphasis on the teaching and learning of French and English at all education levels.

Under such pre-university educational reform, along with an emphasis on the native Arabic language, instruction in either English or French is mandatory at the primary and secondary levels. Moreover, under the new curriculum developed by the National Center for Education Research and Development (NCERD),[2] equal weight is given to the native language and either one of the two foreign languages, and instruction in the second foreign language is introduced in the seventh grade.[3] These measures were deemed necessary, given the failure of an Arabic-only educational policy experiment in 1975, a policy which overlooked the dissemination of French and English in Lebanese culture and its educational system (Diab 2006, 82). Such official directions toward preserving and promoting multilingualism were a realistic reflection of the proliferation of foreign languages in daily functions, in addition to the various privileges that such multilingual competence ensured the Lebanese people, both locally and globally (Shaaban and Ghaith 1999, 6). The history of language and educational policy in Lebanon reflects an official movement in primary and secondary education toward resisting monolingual directions, signaled through early attempts to either implement an Arabic-only policy or prioritize one language over the other. As the case of Lebanon illustrates, there is evidence of an increased attention toward the multiplicity of languages that are needed in daily life, as well as evidence of official efforts toward strengthening the balance among the vibrant languages in the country.

3. Language Ideologies and Curriculum Design

Alongside the official recognition of the central role of foreign language education at the primary and secondary level, in this section I consider the place of translingualism in relation to tensions with deeply infiltrated monolingual ideologies.[4]

The importance of reflecting not only workplace dynamics but also the linguistic realities and real challenges of cross-border exchanges in the business and technical world is increasingly acknowledged in professional writing courses through the growing process of composing business and technical documents in multiple languages. Unlike traditional writing assignments, which reflect dominant expectations for high quality writing as being exclusively in Standard Written English (SWE), or the more accommodative assignments that make room for alternative compositions (only in exploratory and early drafts, leaving SWE to more polished final versions), these writing assignments cross the traditional linguistic boundaries that separate SWE from other linguistic repertoires in the writing classroom. They include explicit invitations for writing students to compose business and technical documents in French and/or Arabic alongside English according to changing purposes, audiences, and contexts. Follow-up writing assignments ask students to critically reflect on the various stylistic and rhetorical choices they made when working with a plurality of languages and patchworks of meanings. Making such pedagogical spaces for linguistic diversity and resourcefulness grew out of the need to address the requirements of the job market in which the majority of university graduates find jobs, either in Lebanon, neighboring Arabic-speaking countries, France, other European, or even African countries, where written communication in Arabic and/or French in addition to English is a must.

The dispersion of similar subversive pedagogies into composition has been extremely slow, thereby leading to a discrepancy between the academic writing and the professional writing courses. Though the diverse language situation in Lebanon has managed to find its way into professional writing classrooms, academic writing teachers are still hesitant to encourage cross-language relations. The use of Arabic and other languages in the English writing classroom is limited to oral interactions and clarifications for complexity in content. Even teachers who explicitly make textual spaces for nonstandard varieties of English and other languages, and who encourage critical engagements with such texts, end up adhering to universal standards of written English in their formal assessments.

In terms of the level of commitment to translingualism in Lebanese writing classrooms, what is of particular interest is that—while translingual work has gradually started seeping into professional writing—residual forces of monolingual ideologies are still prevalent in composition. This is a clear indication that "[s]trong justifications from the push of the job market have only empowered some professional writing teachers to take initial steps towards translingual work while the dominance of monolingualist ideologies in the academic knowledge market in Lebanon as well as internationally has kept those in the academic realm clinging to conformity" to standardized rules and prescribed writing conventions (Bou Ayash 2014, 190).

LANGUAGE DIVERSITY IN THE CASE OF SINGAPORE

1. English and Other Languages on the Ground

The second multilingual context also characterized by the complexity of its linguistic situation is Singapore. The present language make-up in Singapore is a direct result of British colonialism and immense immigration movements. The Singaporean society is mainly comprised of three major ethnic groups—Chinese, Malay, and Indians—that speak a diversity of home languages and language varieties. Here, English is used to facilitate communication and cultural transmission within these diverse ethnic communities. As a result of this interaction and intermingling, Singlish, a local hybrid variety of English, is widely used by growing numbers of Singaporeans (Chua 2007, 86).

2. Language and Language-in-Education Policies

Each ethnic group in Singaporean society, as Quentin Dixon describes, used a wide variety of home languages before the adoption of the 1966 bilingual policy (Dixon 2005, 26). After unsuccessful attempts to offer education in any of the four official languages (English, Mandarin for the Chinese, Malay for the Malays, and Tamil for the Indians) along with compulsory proficiency in another official language, the Singaporean government developed a modified bilingual education policy. Following the lead of the colonial government, the government of independent Singapore retained the language of its colonizers and appointed to it the role of a lingua franca that mainly facilitates *inter*ethnic and *intra*ethnic communication between major groups across the country (Rubdy et al. 2008, 40). Under Singapore's bilingual education policy, English is the language of interethnic communication, while the other three official mother tongues—given second language status—are prominent markers of Singaporean speakers' ethnicity and are considered the "languages of cultural transmission" due to their symbolic power (Rubdy and Tupas 2009, 330).

Singapore has molded an educational system that caters to the demands of economic globalization, with English being the sole language of all content-area instruction. In order to ensure that western influences on Singaporeans are counterbalanced amid the sweeping influences of globalization, Singapore's policymakers have also granted special attention to the teaching and learning of the mother tongues as second languages. The government's politically motivated efforts are exactly what Rubdy and Tupas (2009) describe as a "two-pronged response to globalization"—remaining open to yet critical of swamping global forces (318). In addition to the English medium of instruction, the study of one of the mother tongues as a second language through primary, secondary, and junior college levels is compulsory.

The notion of "mother tongue" in the case of Singapore is officially defined as communal property based on one's ethnicity, which is primarily determined by that of the father instead of the individual's experiences and linguistic exposure or affinity (Wee 2002, 285). In a multiracial society like Singapore, given such a problematic conception of mother tongue, it is no surprise that many Singaporeans struggle to study and use a mother language, even claiming it to be so tough that they might not perceive it as such or even perceive themselves as native speakers of that language. The Malays are the only ethnic group that is more likely to be assigned a mother tongue that actually corresponds to their home language. Most individuals in the Chinese community have grown up with dialects other than Mandarin as the state-legislated mother tongue, such as Hokkien, Cantonese, and Teochew, and many Indians speak other Indo-European languages at home, such as Hindi, Punjabi, and other Indian dialects (Dixon 2005, 26). As a result of the sensitivity of language issues in an ethnically divided state like Singapore, there are constant political, cultural, and ideological tensions that are not fully captured by the official language and educational policies. Amid government attempts to silence valid issues of identity, policies in Singapore continue to serve as fertile ground for further ethnic and social tensions under a complex linguistic situation.

3. Language Ideologies and Curriculum Design

In response to growing language difference in the Singaporean society, as well as perceived threats from the local Singapore variety of English (i.e., Singlish), Prime Minister GohChok Tong launched a nationwide "Speak Good English Movement" (SGEM) in 2000 to enshrine Singapore's economic development and modernization. With the slogan of "Speak Well, Be Understood," this official movement highlights the importance of maintaining national and international intelligibility through preserving and promoting specific aspects of Standard English (SE) (McKay and Bokhorst-Heng 2008, 93; Speak Good English Movement 2000). This pro-SE campaign has forced its way into the teaching and learning of spoken and written English. In Catherine Chua's (2007) terms, "literacy is equated with proficiency in the standard variety," and the local variety of English is stigmatized and constructed as "a source of literacy and communication problems" under this campaign. Persistant use of Singlish in written, oral, and visual compositions is viewed by the Singaporean government as "hurt[ing] the Republic's aim to be a First World Economy" and contaminating the mastery of SE (81–82). The English language and writing instructors are viewed as "standard bearers" and are "morally obligated to compensate for" what is perceived as "a lack, a deficit" and a broken, "bastardized" form of English propagating among young language users in Singapore (McKay and Bokhorst-Heng 2008, 106–107). While many linguists and educators argue that "Singlish and [Standard] English can co-exist" (see Chua 2007; Gopinathan et al. 2004), the main aim of Singapore's government is to eradicate such cultural and linguistic anomalies in students' writing and language usage.

Despite such political efforts to champion SE, with the accelerating spread of digital media technologies, Singlish is still an integral, practical part of the literacy and language practices of overwhelmingly large numbers of Singaporeans, who regard it as a marker of national identity (see Chua 2007). The dynamic use of Singlish is clearly portrayed in the Speak Good Singlish Movement's (SGSM) Facebook webpage, founded in 2010, with its revolutionary slogan: "Let the Singlish Renaissance Begin!" This movement's primary mission is establishing that:

> [A group of Singaporeans] are tired of people confusing Singlish with broken English. [They] are tired of people pretending to speak Singlish by speaking bad English. [They] are tired of people caricaturizing Singlish speakers as uncouth and unintelligent. If [other Singaporeans] don't bother to learn the subtle rules of a natural evolving language, then [they cannot] conclude that it is simple, shallow, and useless! Singlish is full of cultural nuances and wordplay, and it pulls together the best in

the grammar, syntax, and vocabulary of many languages. (Speak Good Singlish Movement 2010)

As Christopher Stroud argues in his research on the practices and ideologies of multilingualism in social and politically transforming economies like Singapore, these vibrant virtual spaces for multilayered processes of linguistic innovation are moving the setting of linguistic norms and standards away from the hands of governments, official bodies, and policy makers and into the public sphere (Stroud 2007, 530).

As can be seen, what seems to be lacking in the Singaporean context are pedagogical invitations for cross-linguistic border crossings, the subsequent reinvigoration of the teaching and learning of English, and living Singaporean languages in a way that is not fixated merely on the mastery of language and writing skills but, instead, oriented toward meaningful linguistic and cultural exchanges (see Gopinathan et al. 2004; Rubdy and Tupas 2009). A pedagogical model that accounts for the distinctive patterns of Singaporean Englishes as legitimate variants in their own right, rather than deviations from SE, is far more realistic in maintaining the waves of Singapore's cultural plurality and diverse language practices in an ever-changing globalized society, as well as in mirroring Singaporean learners' own experiences of actual Singaporean life and the world.

PROMISES AND CHALLENGES OF TRANSLINGUAL ACTIVISM IN US WRITING PROGRAMS: LEARNING FROM LEBANON AND SINGAPORE

The current comparative analysis highlights powerful linguistic and ideological tensions that are being resolved and negotiated in completely diverse ways in these different multilingual societies. In small countries like Lebanon and Singapore, who have no natural resources other than strategic locations and strong dependence on trade and commerce, negotiations of conflicting tensions between a dominant monolingual ideology[5] and emerging ideologies of translingualism are mainly driven by geopolitical relations and economic considerations. These two economically-dependent countries can tell us a great deal about how the new, globalized economy values language(s) and language practice(s) in two radically different ways through investments in: (1) the dominance of SE, where the needs of the changing economy and the global market in Singapore have motivated the official persistence of the indoctrination of SE as a commodified lingua franca as well as an ostensible, cross-ethnic link language; and (2) cross-language relations, where economic and vocational considerations in Lebanon have been the basic motivation for pursuing more translingual work, particularly in the professional writing realm. As English has no governmental role in Lebanon, the country's historical relations with France and other Arabic-speaking countries in the Middle East have rendered emerging cross-language initiatives a necessity for cultural openness and ongoing political, economic, trade, and intercultural relations. However, the discourse and logic of economic domination in Singapore, which explicitly links the achievement of greater economic capital to the possession of SE (i.e., the sole variety deemed globally recognizable by those in power), accounts for the instigation of the government-sponsored SGEM. While Singapore represents the mastery of SE as an investment in economic and cultural capital, Lebanon seems to be heading toward "commodified translingualism," which treats translingual practice as a highly marketable commodity in the business domain (Bou Ayash 2014, 193).

In comparison with multilingual countries like Lebanon and Singapore that more readily adopt and adapt their language policies and practices under economic driving forces, the economic and geopolitical domination of the United States might explain the dissemination of longstanding monolingual ideologies in its tacit language policies and, subsequently, in current composition pedagogies and assessment practices. The tacit English-only policy, as Horner and Trimbur (2002) argue, is built upon the modernist ideology of "one nation, one language" and continues to pervasively inform US writing instruction, research, and program administration. This implicit policy is based on troubling "reified notions of language and socio-cultural identity," under which a language users' identity is not only identified with a single language but is also projected as bounded and unchangeable (608). In one of the world's most culturally and linguistically diverse nations, US multilingualism remains the statistical but not the cultural norm. There have been recent initiatives by the US government and the Modern Language Association (MLA), as Scott Wible argues, to promote multilingualism among US citizens and improve the nations' foreign language education, yet such attempts remain predominantly influenced by national security concerns and geopolitical and cultural self-interests (Wible 2009, 463).

In light of the accelerating spread of linguistic and cultural diversity emerging, from both human migration and twenty-first-century digital media technologies, growing numbers of US composition scholars and WPAs are detecting a pressing need for more equitable and aggressive boundary transgression. These scholars are calling for a variety of reforms, including: rethinking language myths and traditional dispositions toward language and language difference (Canagarajah 2006; Horner and Lu 2007, 2013; Horner and Trimbur 2002; Horner et al. 2011; Lu 2006; Matsuda 2006, and many others); reorienting the internationalization of disciplinary trade (Donahue 2008; 2009; Hall 2009); and reconfiguring labor within WPA, composition pedagogy, and language policy (Canagarajah 2006; Hesford et al. 2009; Horner et al. 2010; 2011; Lu 1999; 2004; Schaub 2003; Shuck 2006; Tardy 2011). Knowing that these compositionists, along with many others, have ventured into laboring against the order of global economy and geopolitical hegemony, transitioning (along with writing students) into newly emerging translingual zones where not many cannot claim expertise, renders such an endeavor challenging, yet more promising.

The work of other literacy laborers in both Lebanon and Singapore provides various insights that should be viewed as exigent moments for institutionalizing translingualism in US writing programs. The ongoing histories of language education policy and practice in Lebanon and Singapore can provide a representative model of some of the difficulties and opportunities of pursuing a translingual approach in the US. The current cross-national and cross-linguistic perspectives shed light on shared concerns regarding struggles with monolingual ideologies, which are mainly prevalent through the alarming singularity of relations between individual's ethnic and linguistic identities, evident in Singapore, and through the surviving desire to preserve language standards in writing instruction and assessment in Lebanon and, to a larger extent, Singapore.

When considering the level of commitment to translingualism, it is productive to think of the three multilingual locations of Lebanon, Singapore, and the US as representing three different scenarios in relation to their responses to language diversity, especially regarding: (1) the local specificity of sociolinguistic landscapes, where language users and learners construct meaning through the use of multiple languages and language practices for specific purposes, needs, and contexts in their daily functions; (2) the official language, language-in-education policies, and their degree of attention to sociolinguistic landscapes; and (3) writing curriculum design and the corresponding educational responses to sociolinguistic landscapes. I would further argue that sufficiently accounting for the interactional and sociolinguistic dimensions of languages and language practices on the ground in *both* language policies and teaching practices constitutes an ideal condition for the institutionalization of translingualism in US writing programs. We can therefore consider these multilingual contexts as representing three different linguistic models from their responses to each of the above three dimensions (see Table 9.1 below).

With its official recognition of the multiplicity of language resources on the ground, coupled with efforts to incorporate these into the writing curriculum, Lebanon comes the closest to satisfying these three favorable conditions for translingualism, despite traces of conservatism in teaching and assessment practices. What is noteworthy about Lebanon's language policy and educational legislations is that they are, to some extent, more realistic in mirroring and maintaining the waves of cultural plurality and diverse language practices in an ever-changing globalized society and, thus, are more relevant to local language users' and learners' actual lived experiences. Though Lebanon has adopted official policies that capture the dynamism of local linguistic resources, the encroachment of other languages into the traditionally English sphere of the academic writing classroom remains heavily determined by the nature of language ideologies governing curriculum design. Such observations from Lebanon, therefore, demonstrate the insufficiency of having adequate multilingual language policies if they are not coupled with aggressive changes in curriculum design to more forcefully invite translingual work.

As for the case of Singapore, in spite of the vibrant nature of its sociolinguistic landscape, curriculum design is still predominantly guided by the same conventional language ideologies as those promoting its official SGEM. The language situation in Singapore, therefore, illustrates the case of "additive" multilingualism, which some might argue is equivalent to the "pluralization of monolingualism" (Makoni and Pennycook 2007, 22). Singaporean language policies and language-in-education policies promote the primacy of SE—as the vocational opportunities are inevitably linked to desired language competences and skills. In light of this lack of fit between political/economical concerns of the state and actual Singaporean multilingual realities, and in order to move beyond pedagogical focus on the mastery of standard forms and instead establish translingual language relations, what is missing in the Singaporean scenario is official recognition in their policies and practices of the distinctive patterns of Singaporean languages and Englishes "as legitimate variants in their own right" (Rubdy and Tupas 2009, 320), and no longer as errors or deviations from SE.

How are these cross-national and cross-linguistic perspectives from postcolonial contexts of direct relevance to US WPAs? The above conditions for more favorable language ideologies in writing program

Table 9.1 The Nature of Translingualism on the Ground, in Policies, and in Practices

	Sociolinguistic Landscapes	Policies	Curriculum Design	Language Relations Model
LEBANON	Statistical and cultural norm	Capturing the complexity of sociolinguistic realities	Emerging translingualism with residual monolingual ideologies	Commodified Translingualism
SINGAPORE	Statistical and cultural norm	Promoting pluralization of monolingualism (fluency in an enumeration of discrete, stable languages) Problematic compartmentalization of language and ethnic identity	Deeply-infiltrated monolingual ideologies (SEGM)	Traditional Additive Multilingualism
UNITED STATES	Statistical not cultural norm	Predominantly monolingual (tacit English-only)	Predominantly informed by longstanding monolingual ideologies (tacit English-only)	Monolingualism

policies, curriculum design, and pedagogical and assessment practices are still not fully available, and thereby require the continued attention of WPAs who aspire to take up a translingual approach. With regards to sociolinguistic realities, multilingualism in the United States—unlike in Lebanon and Singapore—is still the statistical but not the cultural norm. Despite the richness of the US language situation, insufficient attention in state and national educational policies and practices to the actual multiplicity of cultural and linguistic repertoires on the ground still persists.

Differences in the navigation of linguistic resources in all three multilingual locations illustrate the exigency for closer attention by US WPAs and compositionists, especially those embracing a translingual approach to language difference. Perspectives from Lebanon and Singapore, who have had their own share of dealing with the complexities of language difference, lead us to the following conclusions about how we can start contesting monolingualist assumptions about identity and language and enact translingual directions in our own writing programs and courses. First, a full appreciation of the wealth of US sociolinguistic landscapes requires careful handling of the problems that result from associating language with ethnic and racial identities, and increased attention to the actual value of translingualism in sociolinguistic landscapes. Second, the kind of actively multilingual language policy seen in Lebanon is exactly what US compositionists must continue to fight for, a language policy where all writing students can engage in translingual language practices in their public, personal, academic, and professional lives. WPAs can take the initial step toward enacting translingual language relations by being aware of and recognizing the complexity and diversity of language relations among changing student populations in their own program policies. This entails crafting and recrafting program statements and policies[6] that not only show tolerance and appreciation of students' linguistic and discursive resources, but also acknowledge and promote their agency in constantly working and reworking these resources in their writing[7]. Third, we must fight for curriculum change by bridging the gap between language learning and actual language use in ways that attend to the dynamic sociolinguistic dimensions of language use, where no language remains fixed or operates in isolation. One of the first steps toward taking a translingual approach is to view language standards and conventions as negotiable and changeable according to culture, genre, academic discipline, media, and modality, rather than predetermined and fixed entities.[8] WPAs must also create space in writing curricula for the full multiplicity of languages and discourses in their students' repertoire, as well as increase opportunities for more deliberative inquiries about how students are strategically using and navigating these resources and toward what specific ends.[9]

Essential for implementing a translingual approach, this comparative study of the nature and operation of language relations in various locations can be insightful for US WPAs who are aspiring to institutionalize translingualism, especially since it illustrates what seems to be missing in all three multilingual sites under consideration: more aggressive integration of translingual language practices into language policies, writing pedagogies, and curriculum design. Indulging in this new line of work—in which no one can "yet claim expertise" (Horner et al. 2011, 309)—obviously requires the collaborative efforts of all, both in the United States and in other multilingual countries: WPAs, instructors of writing in English and other languages, and most of all our writing students, who inevitably possess ample experience and expertise working across differences in both physical and virtual communicative contexts.

Notes

1. Throughout this chapter, I adopt Alastair Pennycook's (2010) notion of "language landscapes," which transport us into the temporality and spatiality of language, thereby allowing us to closely "see how different linguistic resources are used, different worlds evoked, different possibilities engaged in as people use the linguistic wherewithal around them" (69).

2. NCERD is a specialized center within the Ministry of Education that is entrusted with curricular design and reform.

3. Most private schools usually start introducing the second language as early as first or fourth grade, some even earlier depending on the availability of staff members and educational resources.

4. I base the perspectives in this section on the specific case of one American-style university, the American University of Beirut (AUB), where I draw my examples from my past teaching experiences and personal communications with local practitioners. In various higher education institutions in Lebanon (e.g. AUB, Notre Dame University-Louaize, etc.), there are no composition programs—in the North American sense—but rather communication skills programs with a long tradition of being designed and directed by applied linguists and staffed by faculty trained in TESOL and Applied Linguistics. Alongside the nationwide acknowledgement of the primacy of writing in Lebanese higher education, through the establishment of writing centers and the introduction of WAC/WID courses, attention to oral communication skills in the teaching and learning of language and writing still persists.

5. It is worth pointing out that monolingual ideologies in these postcolonial nations are not limited to English as the surviving cultural influence of American missionaries in Lebanon, or the political marker of British culture in Singapore, but also extend to other languages, such as the French language of the former colonials, the native Arabic language in the case of Lebanon, and the mother tongues in the case of Singapore.

6. See Tardy (2011) for an example of a local survey.

7. For more on manifestations of writerly agency in student work, see Horner and Lu (2013).

8. See Lu (1999) for an early pedagogy that encourages critical deliberation about the standards and conventions of written English and the inevitable (re)working of these in light of asymmetrical power relations along the lines of ethnicity, race, gender, national origin, language background, social class, etc.

9. Refer to Bou Ayash (2013) for examples of sequenced writing assignments that promote cross-language relations.

References

Bou Ayash. Nancy. 2013. "Hi-ein, Hi نيي or يينHi? Translingual Practices from Lebanon and Mainstream Literacy Education." In *Literacy as Translingual Practice: Between Communities and Classrooms*, ed. Suresh Canagarajah, 96–103. New York: Routledge.

Bou Ayash, Nancy. 2014. "U.S. Translingualism through a Cross-National and Cross-Linguistic Lens." In *Reworking English in Rhetoric and Composition: Global Interrogations, Local Interventions*, ed. Bruce Horner and Karen Kopelson, 181–98. Carbondale: Southern Illinois University Press.

Canagarajah, Suresh. 2006. "The Place of World Englishes in Composition: Pluralization Continued." *College Composition and Communication* 57 (4): 586–619.

Chua, Catherine. 2007. "Singapore's Literacy Policy and its Conflicting Ideologies." In *Language Planning and Policy: Issues in Language Planning and Literacy*, ed. Anthony Liddicoat, 76–88. Clevedon: Multilingual Matters.

Diab, Rula. 2000. "Political and Socio-Cultural Factors in Foreign Language Education: The Case of Lebanon." *Texas Papers in Foreign Language Education* 5 (1): 177–87.

Diab, Rula. 2006. "University Students' Beliefs about Learning English and French in Lebanon." *System* 34 (1): 80–96. http://dx.doi.org/10.1016/j.system.2005.06.014.

Dixon, L. Quentin. 2005. "Bilingual Education Policy in Singapore: An Analysis of its Socio-historical Roots and Current Academic Outcomes." *International Journal of Bilingual Education and Bilingualism* 8 (1): 25–47. http://dx.doi.org/10.1080/jBEB.v8.i1.pg25.

Donahue, Christiane. 2008. "Cautionary Tales: Ideals and Realities in Twenty-First Century Higher Education." *Pedagogy* 8 (3): 537–53. http://dx.doi.org/10.1215/15314200-2008-011.

Donahue, Christiane. 2009. "Internationalization and Composition Studies: Reorienting the Discourse." *College Composition and Communication* 61 (2): 212–43.

Gopinathan, Saravanan, Ho Wah Kam, and Vanithamani Saravanan. 2004. "Ethnicity Management and Language Education Policy: Towards a Modified Model of Language Education in Singapore." In *Beyond Rituals and Riots – Ethnic Pluralism and Social Cohesion in Singapore*, ed. Ah Eng Lai, 228–57. Singapore: Eastern University Press.

Hall, Jonathan. 2009. "WAC/WID in the Next America: Re-thinking Professional Identity in the Age of the Multilingual Majority." *WAC Journal* 20:33–47.

Hesford, Wendy, Edgar Singleton, and Ivonne García. 2009. "Laboring to Globalize a First-year Writing Program." In *The Writing Program Interrupted: Making Space for Critical Discourse*, ed. Donna Strickland and Jeanne Gunner, 113–25. Portsmouth, NH: Boynton/Cook Heinemann.

Horner, Bruce, and John Trimbur. 2002. "English Only and U.S. College Composition." *College Composition and Communication* 53 (4): 594–630. http://dx.doi.org/10.2307/1512118.

Horner, Bruce, Min-Zhan Lu, and Paul Kei Matsuda, eds. 2010. *Cross-Language Relations in Composition*. Carbondale: Southern Illinois University Press.

Horner, Bruce, Min-Zhan Lu, John Trimbur, and Jacqueline Jones Royster. 2011. "Language Difference: Toward a Translingual Approach." *College English* 73 (3): 299–317.

Horner, Bruce, and Min-Zhan Lu. 2007. "Resisting Monolingualism in 'English': Reading and Writing the Politics of Language." In *Rethinking English in Schools: A New and Constructive Stage*, ed. Viv Ellis, Carol Fox, and Brian Street, 141–57. London: Continuum.

Horner, Bruce, and Min-Zhan Lu. 2013. "Translingual Literacy, Language Difference, and Matters of Agency." *College English* 75 (6): 582–607.

Lu, Min-Zhan. 2004. "An Essay on the Work of Composition: Composing English against the Order of Fast Capitalism." *College Composition and Communication* 56 (1): 16–50. http://dx.doi.org/10.2307/4140679.

Lu, Min-Zhan. 2006. "Living-English Work." *College English* 68 (6): 605–18. http://dx.doi.org/10.2307/25472178.

Lu, Min-Zhan. 1999. "Professing Multiculturalism: Teaching the Politics of Style." In *Representing the 'Other': Basic Writers and the Teaching of Basic Writing* 166, ed. Bruce Horner and Min-Zhan Lu, 166–90. Urbana, IL: National Council of Teachers of English.

Makoni, Sinfree, and Alastair Pennycook. 2007. *Disinventing and Reconstituting Languages*. Clevedon: Buffalo.

Matsuda, Paul Kei. 2006. "The Myth of Linguistic Homogeneity in U.S. College Composition." *College English* 68 (6): 637–51. http://dx.doi.org/10.2307/25472180.

McKay, Sandra Lee, and Wendy Bokhorst-Heng. 2008. *International English in its Sociolinguistic Contexts: Towards a Socially Sensitive EIL Pedagogy.* New York: Routledge.

Pennycook, Alastair. 2010. *Language as a Local Practice.* Milton Park. Abingdon: Routledge.

Rubdy, Rani, and T. Ruanni F. Tupas. 2009. "A Country in Focus: Research in Applied Linguistics and Language Teaching and Learning in Singapore (2000–2007)." *Language Teaching* 42 (3): 317–40. http://dx.doi.org/10.1017/S026144480900576X.

Rubdy, Rani, Sandra Lee Mckay, Lubna Alsagoff, and Wendy Bokhorst-Heng. 2008. "Enacting English Language Ownership in the Outer Circle: A Study of Singaporean Indians' Orientations to English Norms." *World Englishes* 27 (1): 40–67. http://dx.doi .org/10.1111/j.1467-971X.2008.00535.x.

Schaub, Mark. 2003. "Beyond These Shores: An Argument for Internationalizing Composition." *Pedagogy* 3 (1): 85–98. http://dx.doi.org/10.1215/15314200-3-1-85.

Shaaban, Kassim, and Ghazi Ghaith. 1999. "Lebanon's Language-in-Education Policies: From Bilingualism to Trilingualism." *Language Problems and Language Planning* 23 (1): 1–16. http://dx.doi.org/10.1075/lplp.23.1.01leb.

Shuck, Gail. 2006. "Combating Monolingualism: A Novice Administrator's Challenge." *WPA* 30 (1–2): 59–82.

"Speak Good English Movement." 2000. Accessed November 25, 2010. http://www .goodenglish.org.sg.

"Speak Good Singlish Movement." 2010. Accessed June 11, 2012. https://www.facebook .com/MySGSM.

Stroud, Christopher. 2007. "Multilingualism in Ex-Colonial States." In *Handbook of Multilingualism and Multilingual Communication,* ed. Peter Auer and Li Wei, 509–38. Berlin: Mouton de Gruyter.

Tardy, Christine M. 2011. "Enacting and Transforming Local Language Policies." *College Composition and Communication* 62 (4): 634–61.

Wee, Loinel. 2002. "When English is Not a Mother Tongue: Linguistic Ownership and the Eurasian Community in Singapore." *Journal of Multilingual and Multicultural Development* 23 (4): 282–95. http://dx.doi.org/10.1080/01434630208666470.

Wible, Scott. 2009. "Composing Alternatives to a National Security Language Policy." *College English* 71 (5): 460–85.

10

DISCOURSES OF INTERNATIONALIZATION AND DIVERSITY IN US UNIVERSITIES AND WRITING PROGRAMS

Christine M. Tardy

Internationalization in higher education generally refers to the process of incorporating international or intercultural dimensions through, for instance, study abroad programs, international students and scholars, "off-shore" programs or international branch campuses, and/or programs and institutes that take an explicitly global focus. Data on the internationalization of higher education in the United States consistently point to growth in these areas. With regard to student mobility, David Graddol estimates that two to three million students worldwide study outside the borders of their home countries each year. The greatest number study in the United States and the United Kingdom, but Germany, France, Australia, and China all host more than 100,000 students annually (Graddol 2006). According to the Institute of International Education (IIE), the majority of international students in the United States currently come from East Asia, especially China, India, and South Korea (Institute of International Education 2010b). US-based students who study abroad are also a part of this educational global mobility, and the past thirteen years have seen a rise in their participation in such programs. In the 2008–2009 academic year, about 50 percent of the 260,327 US students studying abroad traveled to Europe, though China was the fifth most common destination overall (Institute of International Education 2010a). And it is not just students who travel abroad for academic purposes—in 2009–2010, over 115,000 scholars also worked outside of their home countries (Institute of International Education 2010b). Finally, in addition to a global movement tied to education, there are a growing number of students at US universities who might be considered "transnational," or who hold close ties to two

DOI: 10.7330/9780874219623.c010

or more countries. These students may include immigrants or children of immigrants, refugees, and expatriates, and their numbers are largely unaccounted for because they are domestic students.

Internationalization has indeed become not just a fact of educational life but also a popular buzzword among university administrators. Derek Bok (2006, citing Lambert 1989) notes that a strong majority of university presidents identify the internationalization of undergraduate education as "very important." Given the expansion of international mobility and universities' interest in developing students' global awareness, we might expect to also find a growing emphasis on foreign language (FL) education in US higher education—after all, language is one important element of internationalism. At first glance, this appears to be the case; research carried out by the Modern Language Association found enrollment in non-English language courses to have steadily increased since 1995. The study estimates about 1.6 million enrollments in language courses (excluding Latin and Ancient Greek) in 2009, with about half of those attributed to Spanish-language classes (Furman et al. 2010). However, when FL course enrollments are considered in relation to overall university enrollments, a slightly different picture emerges. In 1960, there were 16.1 modern language course enrollments per 100 total student enrollments; by 2009, that number had dropped to 8.6. Perhaps even more discouraging is the fact that the vast majority of language course enrollments are at the introductory (78 percent) rather than the advanced (22 percent) level (Furman et al. 2010). And in the current economic climate of deep university budget cuts, the fate of many language programs is now in question, especially those in less commonly-taught languages or languages not deemed to be of critical importance (Foderaro 2010).

This relative lack of institutional emphasis on language study in the face of a purported heightened interest in global awareness presents a somewhat surprising paradox and suggests that language is not necessarily considered an intricate or essential part of internationalization—at least not in the United States (see Kubota 2009 for a discussion of additional pervasive paradoxes). Yet, the role of language in and its relationship to internationalization, most specifically in higher education, should be of particular interest to WPAs, who are responsible for administering the only required language-related instruction at many institutions. International and transnational students take requisite courses in first-year writing, business writing, or technical writing; domestic students in these courses go on to study abroad and participate in jobs that require them to communicate—often in writing—with people from all over the world. In other words, writing courses (to which language is integral) must respond to local patterns of internationalization, and, in some cases, they may even shape such patterns.

While many of the other chapters in this collection examine specific contexts and practices of writing/writing programs from an international perspective, I will explore the ways in which US universities and their writing programs *talk about* internationalization, creating and reinforcing dominant institutional discourses. At most colleges and universities, it would be difficult for institutional messages about the value of international perspectives to go unnoticed, by either students or faculty. These messages have become part of our missions, strategic plans, curricular changes, and even bottom lines, consciously or unconsciously constructing enduring discourses. These discourses, I contend, are significant because they shape the ways in which students, faculty, and administrators understand and respond to internationalization and all of its components, including language. In this chapter, I focus specifically on the dominant discourses found in university and writing program web pages, sharing a critical analysis of these texts. My goal in this research is to make visible the discourses that structure our institutional spaces, and argue that such visibility is necessary in order to enact change.

DOMINANT DISCOURSES AND CRITICAL DISCOURSE ANALYSIS

Norman Fairclough (2003) defines discourses as "ways of representing aspects of the world." In his view,

> Different discourses are different perspectives on the world, and they are associated with the different relations people have to the world, which in turn depends on their positions in the world, their social and personal identities, and the social relationships in which they stand to other people. Discourses not only represent the world as it is (or rather is seen to be), they are also projective, imaginaries, representing possible worlds which are different from the actual world, and tied in to projects to change the world in particular directions. (124)

Fairclough's definition is productive for my analysis because of its emphasis on projected representations. When students, faculty, and administrators, for example, repeatedly encounter particular representations of social relationships, those representations may eventually become normative and assumed; such assumptions guide or shape our future actions and interactions.

Critical discourse analysis (CDA) aims to expose underlying discourses and their assumptions and offers a tool for doing so by examining how such representations are constructed specifically through language. Fairclough's framework of CDA calls for identifying the main parts of the represented world (or the main "themes") and the perspectives or points of view from which they are represented. CDA specifically examines how linguistic features are used to realize discourses; such features may include vocabulary choices, semantic relations (e.g., synonymy, antonymy), patterns of co-occurrence of words, metaphor, presuppositions, and systems for classifying parts of the world. As Fairclough points out, multiple discourses often co-exist though certain discourses may become dominant, thereby reflecting an assumed or naturalized order of things.

CDA usually focuses on public texts because of their broad reach and critical role in shaping perceptions. In the case of universities, such public genres might include institutional websites, mission statements, viewbooks, or brochures, all of which carry a primarily promotional aim. While the expressions of identity and ideology found in these kinds of texts may or may not reflect actual institutional practices, they are worthy of study because they play a significant role in establishing perceptions of both the institution and the ideologies privileged by the institution.

STUDYING PUBLIC DISCOURSES IN HIGHER EDUCATION

The study I share here was prompted by the discursive tensions I observed in my own institutional context and in the academy more generally. These are the tensions which coalesce around the discourses of internationalization in higher education, in which global engagement and diversity are put forth as important values while issues of linguistic diversity, support for international students, or multilingualism are often largely ignored (see, for example, Horner and Trimbur 2002; Matsuda 2006; Tardy 2011). My interest in the power of texts as discursive manifestations led me to ask how such issues are represented through an institution's public genres, where most universities' or writing programs' "official" positions and ideologies are presented. My analysis was therefore guided by two primary questions:

1. What are the dominant discourses of internationalization and diversity as presented on US university and writing program websites?

2. Where does language fit within these discursive matrices?

My choice for considering both internationalization and diversity in my analysis is rooted in my perception that these two values are often discursively, if not practically, linked in higher education and composition studies. For instance, my former university's web page rather prominently displays the following description of the values embraced by a "global campus":

A global society on campus

We are the largest Catholic university in the country; we're also widely known for welcoming students and employees **from all ethnicities, religions and backgrounds**. Some might see those two facts as conflicting, but we see them as complementary. By **nurturing diversity** and being intentional about incorporating **multiple viewpoints** into academic and student life, we are providing learning experiences that **better reflect—and prepare students for—the world**. (DePaul University 2011, emphasis added)

Scholarly explorations of US higher education, such as those of Derek Bok (2006) and Martha Nussbaum (1997), similarly conjoin these constructs; for example, Nussbaum describes a globalized society as "a context of diversity" (51). Within composition studies scholarship, internationalization and diversity have also been coupled, as international and transnational students have been discussed primarily in terms of the diverse backgrounds and resources they bring to our classrooms. By analyzing both of these constructs, I hope to gain insight into any discursive intersections and locate language within these larger constellations.

My analysis focused on a corpus of websites from twenty-eight US universities, drawn from IIE's lists of institutions with the highest numbers of international and study abroad students as of 2007–2008, the most recent data available at the time of my research.[1] The corpus included fifteen institutions with the highest international student enrollment and fifteen institutions with the highest study abroad participation, compiled by taking the top five institutions from each of three institution types: doctorate, master's, and baccalaureate (see Table 10.1). Two schools appeared on both lists, resulting in a total of twenty-eight institutions included in the study. These schools were intentionally selected because I expected them to value internationalization and its related dimensions.

The final corpus was fairly representative in terms of institution type (public/private), geographic region, and size, with a slight bias toward larger institutions and those located in the western United States (see Table 10.2). This collection also includes institutions with varying missions, such as prominent research-focused institutions, professionally-oriented schools, small liberal arts colleges, and state universities accessible to a broad student population.

For each institution, I first examined a series of university web pages: the university homepage; the university mission statement; and any

Table 10.1 Research Corpus Institutions

Institution Type	Top International Student Enrollments, 2007–2008	Top Study Abroad Student Participation, 2007–2008
Doctorate	University of Southern California New York University Columbia University University of Illinois (Urbana-Champaign) Purdue University	New York University Michigan State University University of Minnesota (Twin Cities) The University of Texas at Austin University of California Los Angeles
Master's	San José State University San Francisco State University California State University (CSU)–Northridge CSU–Fullerton CSU–Long Beach	Elon University James Madison University California Polytechnic State University CSU–Long Beach Villanova University
Baccalaureate	SUNY Fashion Institute of Technology Brigham Young University–Hawaii Utah Valley University Brigham Young University–Idaho Mount Holyoke College	Saint Olaf College Oberlin College Calvin College DePauw University University of Richmond

Table 10.2 Demographic Profile of Institutions Studied

Institution Type	Public	15
	Private	13
Institution Size	30,000 <	13
	15,000–29,999	4
	5,000–14,999	4
	< 4,999	7
Geographic Region	Pacific	1
	West	10
	Midwest	8
	South	4
	East	5

prominent pages focused on diversity, globalization, and/or international initiatives geared toward a broad audience. My intention was to look at the most *immediately available* web content, rather than to carry out an extensive search, in order to gain a sense of the pages that typical users of the site would likely encounter. Next, I turned my attention to these same universities' writing program pages, including: the homepage (or, when multiple programs existed, the first-year writing program), the program mission or goal statement, individual course descriptions, and any information related to working with diverse students in the program.[2] By first examining dominant institutional discourses on internationalization, I hoped to gain insight into how the discourses of writing programs might reflect, challenge, or even resist those dominant university discourses.

For each page examined, I noted linguistic features that represented aspects of internationalization or diversity. For instance, I noted common words (and their variant forms) used to represent those concepts (e.g., "global," "international," "worldly"), common collocations used in relation to those concepts (e.g., "global community," "global marketplace," "global reach"), and common themes or components of the concept (e.g., leadership, engagement). Because I was working with multimodal texts, I also took note of any visual features that corresponded to internationalization and diversity. Such features, in the case of websites, may be even more powerful in representing meaning than verbal features. After collecting all of these features for comparison, I also noted absences—such as themes that were not present or collocations that were rare or absent, drawing on the notion of what Huckin (2002) calls "textual silences." Finally, I identified the ways in which language was present or absent as a component of the discourses identified in these public texts.

DOMINANT DISCOURSES OF UNIVERSITY WEB PAGES

To gain a sense of how prominent international references were on the university websites, I first looked at the homepage of each institution. These pages are accessed by the largest number of viewers, including current students, faculty, and administrators; prospective students and their parents; prospective employees; and a wide range of other people who have some interest in the university. As such, the homepage is important in creating an institutional identity and reflecting a certain set of assets and values. International references were apparent on many of the twenty-eight homepages I analyzed:

Nine sites (32%) included images with international references

Eight sites (29%) included a major link for global programs or initiatives (common link titles were "Global," "International," or "International Presence")

Three sites (11%) included a major link for study abroad

One site (3%) included a major link for international students

A small number of homepages contained a prominent menu of links related to international initiatives, including sub-categories such

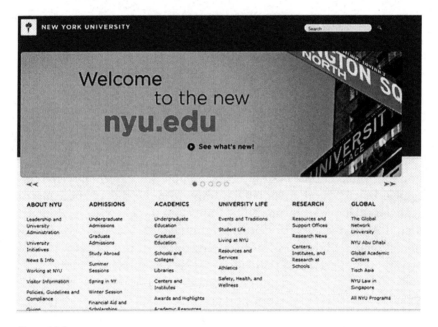

Figure 10.1

as institutes, off-shore branch campuses, and study abroad (see Figure 10.1), ensuring that even the most casual viewer was aware of the institution's global reach. After analyzing a university homepage, I examined its mission statement to identify the extent to which international issues played a role in the university's official purpose and self-image; I then looked at any high-level pages[3] that addressed diversity in order to identify the extent to which discourses of diversity overlapped with discourses of internationalization.

Analyzing the texts and images of all of these pages, I identified two main discourses of internationalization. The first reflects themes of economic globalization and US dominance in the global "marketplace." This representation of the university (or its students) as *global leaders in a global market* is found in more than one-third of the sites, consisting primarily of large research universities. For instance, Columbia describes itself as "one of the world's most important centers of research," NYU claims to develop students' "potential for leadership in a global world," and the University of Illinois describes their alumni as "leaders of international corporations." Many schools, such as the University of Minnesota, describe their emphasis on "conducting high-quality research [and] scholarship . . . that benefit students, scholars, and communities across

Figure 10.2

the state, the nation, and the world." The University of Texas at Austin frames its work as "vital in the increasingly multicultural state of Texas and global market place."

These arguments of economic leadership are reinforced through images that situate the university as a global "capitol" or an institution with global impact (Figure 10.1), and which represent students as future (or current) world leaders (Figure 10.2). Such discourses reflect an export model, in which the US university develops a commodity that is valued and exported worldwide for the benefit of others. Interestingly, Ravinder Sidhu (2006) identifies similar discourses among academic commentary on international education in his study of universities and globalization.

A second major discourse of internationalization on these institutional web pages is that of the university and its students as *participants in a global community*. In contrast to these hierarchical (even hegemonic) representations of global leadership, in which some countries appear to leverage greater educational capital than others, themes of global participation represent these relations more laterally or communally—though still often from a US-centric perspective. More than one-third of the university websites express this ideology, often employing the common phrases of "global citizen" or "citizen of the world." For example, Mount Holyoke College aims to foster "the alliance of liberal arts education with purposeful engagement in the world," while San José State

Figure 10.3

University cites as one of its goals, "Multi-cultural and global perspectives gained through intellectual and social exchange with people of diverse economic and ethnic backgrounds." Others emphasize their desire to prepare students to become "global citizens . . . in and of the world" (NYU), "responsible and knowledgeable citizens of the world," (St. Olaf), and "global citizens and informed leaders motivated by concern for the common good" (Elon). This discourse of global citizenship is often reinforced through images of flags from various countries or photographs of students in contexts outside of the United States (see Figure 10.3). Notably, it also emphasizes affiliation and communal engagement rather than competition and dominance.

Universities that express internationalization in terms of global citizenship tend to be small, often elite, liberal arts colleges rather than large research universities, and many have religious affiliations. Rather than developing knowledge as capital to be exported, global competence and experience are assigned value in this discourse.

It should also be noted that, as Fairclough states, competing discourses can often be found sitting side-by-side. In this case, the values of global economic dominance and global participation are often found on the same institutional sites, or even in the same sentence, as evident in the above quote from Elon University. Such tensions remind us that discourses are almost never uniform and "pure," and that they must also be read with a critical eye—a statement about the importance of global participation from an institution with an explicit missionary focus may, after all, be disguising a rather different agenda.

I now turn to analyzing diversity discourses in their own right. By shifting our vantage point, we can identify the ways in which these two broader discourses might intersect with institutions' public texts. Diversity, much like internationalization, is a value that is frequently touted in US education in an almost obligatory way. In the websites I examined, it was most often represented visually (and racially) in photographs of students and/or faculty of color. Although nearly all of these institutional sites included separate pages specifically focused on the issue of diversity, only two contained a prominent and direct link from the homepage. That said, mentions of diversity permeated nearly all of the websites I examined. Most often, the term was used in reference to underrepresented student groups, and most particularly students of color. However, the term has been broadened institutionally to address gender, disabilities, underrepresented ideas, international students, and, in some cases, language. In the web texts in my corpus, *diverse* (and its counterparts) collocated with words like *community*, *campus*, *students*, *people*, *ideas*, and *perspectives*. Diversity was described as something to be *embraced*, *appreciated*, *celebrated*, *respected*, *sustained*, *acknowledged*, and *valued*.

These discourses of diversity represent the world as a complicated place of difference, though one that can be (somewhat idyllically) transformed into a cohesive and synergistic community. Some universities stressed the importance of helping students contend with such difference, developing "global competencies" (California Polytechnic State University) that would prepare them "to succeed in a multi-cultural world" (Elon). Nearly all institutions drew semantic connections between "diversity" and the "campus community," emphasizing inclusivity. Finally, diversity was associated with potentially marginalized students; many universities made note of the support and resources they offered to historically underrepresented students. San José State University, for example, claimed to "use diversity as an educational resource and knowledge domain for students, and as a central ingredient for their academic success." In all of these cases, however, it should be noted that the university assumed the position of the dominant center, essentially inviting difference into the academic community and, thus, monitoring and controlling the ways in which diversity would impact the university itself.

The converging values placed on internationalization *and* diversity would suggest that perhaps multilingualism—an important element of both—might be assigned some symbolic capital in this discursive marketplace, though this was generally not the case. Language was referenced in only two universities' diversity statements, and a just handful of institutions referred to the diversity of languages spoken on campus, as in these examples:

> "Many [students] **speak two or more languages**, including a number who
>   have completed missions for The Church of Jesus Christ of Latter-day
>   Saints" (BYU-Hawaii)
> "Mount Holyoke's faculty and staff speak more than 50 languages."
>   (Mount Holyoke)
> "six academic **language houses** and one diversity house" (St. Olaf)

In other cases, language was referred to among the aspects of global competencies that students could develop, such as NYU's assertion that "Graduates of Global Liberal Studies will be world citizens, **proficient in a foreign language**, engaged in international cultures." Just one institution (CSU–Fullerton) included a menu tab on the homepage that linked students to a Spanish-language site. Overall, however, language was not a prominent theme of either diversity or internationalization.

These dominant university discourses set up a particular worldview and set of values, and they make up the discursive environment in which decisions about writing programs are made, ranging from funding to staffing to curriculum. The dominant discourses identified in my analysis represent a world in which students should be prepared to participate in an international economy, perhaps as a global leader or as a global citizen. They portray a world of diversity, though not necessarily one that values multilingualism. In what ways might these representations of the world be taken up, adapted, or challenged by writing programs within these institutional spaces?

DOMINANT DISCOURSES OF WRITING PROGRAM WEB PAGES

Examining the web-based discourses of university writing programs is somewhat more problematic, as some programs in my corpus did not have a web presence, while others included only minimal content on their online spaces. In addition, writing programs' web content tends to be written for current students, so these sites do not share the promotional agenda of university sites, nor do they appear to be professionally designed or tested, as the university homepages have most certainly been. In other words, these writing program websites are directed primarily to an internal audience —students, faculty, possibly administrators—who are in search of information about the program, the curriculum, and specific courses. I didn't necessarily expect these more pragmatically focused sites to include the same messages as the university sites regarding internationalization, diversity, and language; instead, I hoped to identify the prominence and nature of these discourses in the program's self-presentation, as well as to understand the extent to which they draw upon, echo, or even counter the discourses found in the university pages.

Only a small number of writing programs in my sample linked their identities to the institutional discourse of *global leadership*, with about one-fifth emphasizing writing as a tool for global transformation in their program goals or objectives. These sites described writing as something that students can use "to transform culture" (Calvin College) or to "change oneself and the world" (Elon). Just one program, SUNY's Fashion Institute of Technology, linked its program goals explicitly to the *global marketplace*, stating that "in today's complex global economy, excellent communication skills are essential." It may be the case that more specialized writing programs—such as those focused on professional communication—tap into these discourses of globalization more commonly than programs that focus primarily (or exclusively) on first year writing.

A discourse of students as *participants in a global community* was never presented in program goals, but it was evident in the goals and descriptions for specific courses in a small number of programs. Three programs offered descriptions of themed sections, including sections which emphasized international issues. The writing program at St. Olaf College, for example, offered first year courses with titles like "Considering Global Poverty" and "Our World through the Artistic Lens," with the latter description stating that students will "focus on a range of issues relating to the global community." And San José State University described its business writing course as teaching students to "communicate appropriately and effectively in cross-cultural situations." These are course options, rather than requirements, but they do suggest an attempt to integrate global issues into the curriculum, adopting the discourse of the *global community*.

It is possible—even likely—that other programs in my sample offer courses with themes relevant to globalization or diversity, but do not include descriptions of these courses on their websites. My interest here, however, is not in what the programs *do* but rather *how they present what they do* to a wider audience, including what they choose to articulate and how. This analysis suggests that, at least in early 2010, even writing programs at institutions with a strong international focus drew upon discourses of internationalization only minimally in their external self-presentations. It could be the case that, for most writing programs, global topics are configured as a means for practicing writing rather than as relevant competencies of writing. Such an understanding would assume that writing classrooms are relatively homogenous, or at least that any existing international diversity (cultural, ethnic, linguistic) does not play a critical role in university writing.

This is not to suggest that diversity, like internationalization, was largely invisible in these programs' web spaces. While references to diversity were not present in every program page, they were found at ten of the twenty-eight institutions. Unlike the university websites, these sites rarely made direct use of the word *diversity*; references were more likely to be implied, as in the following examples:

- "We are dedicated to serving the writing needs of all USC students" (USC, writing program homepage).
- "[the program] assists traditional and non-traditional students who want to improve their writing skills" (Utah Valley University, writing program homepage).

Similarly, while the university webpages paired *diversity* with words like *campus, community, people,* and *ideas,* the three writing programs that used the word *diversity* linked it to *communities, cultural groups, skills, backgrounds,* and *experiences.* Diversity, it seems, takes on a slightly different discursive undertone here, emphasizing difference over shared spaces or inclusivity. On the university websites, diversity is something to be embraced, sustained, and valued, but on the writing program sites, it is something to be served and responded to. This is a discourse of *diversity as distinct needs* that programs can accommodate, adopting the type of deficit model that practitioners in second language writing have long critiqued.

Another relatively common discursive message on these writing program pages is that of *diversity as a topic or object of study.* Four programs describe program goals, course goals, or course descriptions related to studying diversity in this way. On their program homepages, CSU–Northridge states that students will "Analyze and compare perspective, meaning, and style in different texts, including those that reflect multicultural images and voices," and Michigan State University offers a description of a first year writing course section that "involves drafting, revising, and editing compositions derived from readings on the experience of American ethnic and racial groups to develop skills in narration, persuasion, analysis, and documentation."

Perhaps surprisingly, only three writing programs in my corpus linked diversity to the development of skills for communicating with diverse groups. In two of these cases, this connection is made in more specialized, often advanced writing courses; in the third case, the description is included in a student guide:

- ". . . communicate appropriately and effectively in cross-cultural situations" (San José State, business communications course description).
- "topics of inquiry . . . may include . . . the challenges of representing or appropriating other cultures, and the difficulties of writing and communicating within diverse communities" (Oberlin, advanced composition course description).
- "[writing] empowers us to understand different conventions, genres, groups, societies, and cultures" (Purdue, student guide).

It is certainly possible that communication within and across diverse groups is simply not a goal of most writing programs. The WPA Outcomes Statement for First-Year Composition, for example, makes no mention of writing in cross-cultural or diverse communities, and most writing teachers already find it challenging to address rhetorical skills, standard language skills, and now digital and multimodal competencies in the short timeframe of their courses (Council of Writing Program Administrators 2008).

This rationale may also explain why a discourse that is so prominent in university webpages—*diversity as a resource*—appears to be so rare, almost absent, in writing program websites. Only two programs that I analyzed represented diversity as a resource. University of Minnesota explains on their program homepage that instructors draw "on students' diverse skills, backgrounds, and experiences . . . [to] lead students to discern and participate in important public and university-level conversations." The only other similar reference was found in a course description for St. Olaf College: "There will be specific opportunities to explore cultural perceptions with international students on campus." While this latter example situates diversity as a resource, it simultaneously represents diversity as difference (note that international students are specifically marked here) and as an object of study. This approach risks framing non-US students as the exotic "other," only there to benefit the domestic student. Here we see echoes of larger institutional discourses on diversity in which the university seems to sanction and create particular forms of diversity for the purposes of benefitting dominant student groups and the university itself.

Within the specific context of writing programs, which deal fundamentally with language, it may strike readers as somewhat surprising that linguistic diversity was never explicitly described on these websites. However, language was not entirely invisible. Nine of the twenty-eight programs—about one-third—identify courses that are designed for linguistically diverse students, such as "ESL sections" or "international sections" of first year writing. While such courses offer, on the one hand, an important structure for meeting the needs of many multilingual students, on the other, they present a *discourse of containment*—as Matsuda (2006) has argued—excluding this population from the "mainstream" program and marking them as "other," while monolingual students retain the status of the unmarked norm.

Each of the labels that writing programs adopt in referring to multilingual, international, or transnational populations emphasize different aspects of these writers' identities. Among the websites in this sample, eight adopted labels that may be interpreted as representing multilingual writers as linguistically deficient: "non-native speakers of English" (4), "English Language Learners" (2), "students who would benefit from supplemental English Language assistance" (1), and "students with English as their second language" (1). In contrast, two programs used the term *multilingual students* or *speakers*, and one referred to them simply as *international students*. In both cases, these labels tend to emphasize the resources that such students bring to the university and their writing courses. Clearly, however, the issue of labeling is complex—perhaps even one of the greatest challenges programs face in attracting the target student population to their courses. In the end, the discursive message that such labels may send are often less important administratively than the logistical goal of attracting students.

I believe it is fair to say that, when language is acknowledged on these programs' websites, it is often represented somewhat statically, as a commodity that students need to gain access to. Four programs identify the development of "standard edited English" as a goal, and four programs note that students will develop skills in diverse styles and genres (often in addition to standard edited English). Programs that support multilingual students through special sections of writing demonstrate a commitment to this population and an acknowledgment of the international and linguistic diversity of their local context, but, at the same time, these students become marked as deficient. On the other hand, programs that make no mention of multilingual writers or diverse populations on their websites (even if they do offer sections or other support systems specifically for them) may unintentionally represent the program as serving an unmarked homogenous population.

CONCLUSION

The analysis I've shared reveals, in many cases, a disconnect between university and writing program discourses of internationalization and diversity. A cynical reading of this distinction might be that the universities' messages here are merely cosmetic, a result of marketing research and intentional branding rather than a reflection of institutional values or actions. In fact, writing programs on the ground may be doing much more to support global citizenship and promote inclusion for diverse students than universities as a whole. Nevertheless, institutional messages on public spaces like websites are important because they set up particular relationships and representations of the world, or at least of one local space.

Composition journals and conferences have increasingly embraced international issues[4]—including supporting multilingual writers in our classrooms and integrating international scholarship into our research conversations. Yet, there have been far fewer discussions of how these issues relate to broader institutional missions or strategies. This chapter has turned to critical discourse analysis as one way to explore these relationships. Such an approach can help composition scholars in general and WPAs in particular understand the discourses of our institutions, the ways those discourses might shape writing program decisions and practices, and how we might construct our own program spaces to reflect (and create) the values we want to embrace and embody.

My analysis of a small subset of US university websites suggests that these institutions tend to draw on discourses of global leadership in a global marketplace, global citizenship, diversity as inclusion, and diversity as a resource—but language is rarely an integral part of these discourses. Such a finding has implications for writing programs, which deal directly with language skills. When linguistic diversity or multilingual competence is not promoted as an institutional value, English (or, more specifically, standard American English) more easily assumes symbolic capital. Program decisions regarding placement measures, forms of summative assessment, and program goals and objectives, for example, may all be influenced by dominant university discourses, which tend to paint a picture of linguistic homogeneity even within an international and diverse institution. My argument here is not that these dominant discourses *control* writing program decisions, but rather that such decisions are made *within* these discourses, and that WPAs can therefore benefit from understanding their larger discursive environments.

Such an understanding can also inform the rhetorical strategies that WPAs adopt in affecting change. By identifying institutional values and messages, WPAs might be better able to situate their program's needs within larger institutional priorities. If internationalization and diversity are values that are visibly reflected in a university's public discourses, identifying links to related initiatives may be of great benefit to a writing program. Neither internationalization nor diversity were prominent themes in the writing program web pages I examined, suggesting that we may not be articulating (for ourselves or our institutions) the ways in which these values may contribute to university initiatives in these areas. Indeed, there may be financial and curricular benefits to demonstrating more clearly to upper administration the values that our writing programs place on internationalization, as well as how writing instruction can play a role in developing students' global competencies. In other words, WPAs working at institutions that grant symbolic (and often material) capital to global initiatives may find they can tap into such values—riding the current global bandwagon, so to speak—and appropriate them in order to reorient their own missions, program and course goals, and even program structures. Those at universities with strategic plans or university-wide learning outcomes that include an international focus may seek to incorporate such goals and language into their own program and course goals. Cross-cultural sections of first-year writing, such as the model described by Matsuda and Silva (1999), offer one example of an alternative structure.

All of this is not to suggest that writing programs simply adopt university discourses—as the critical analysis in this chapter shows, not all of these discourses may reflect our disciplinary values, nor may they benefit all of our students. Instead, I am suggesting that WPAs examine the discourses they construct—in their online spaces, their program goals and objectives, their mission statements, and their faculty handbooks—as well as the extent to which those discourses reflect their program values. If a program recognizes linguistic diversity and global perspectives to be important aspects of writing and writing instruction, it should consider how those values are not just embedded in the curriculum but are also represented publicly to students, faculty, and university administrators.

It is perhaps an important reminder that I examined the public discourses of institutions specifically recognized for their numbers of students who study beyond their home borders. It would seem to be a safe assumption that these schools do value internationalization on some level, perhaps even more so than peer institutions that place less emphasis on transnational education. Yet, within even these institutions, discourses of global citizenship or linguistic pluralism appear very rarely in their writing programs' public texts. From that perspective, this small-scale analysis reinforces arguments made by writing scholars—such as Suresh Canagarajah (2006), Paul Kei Matsuda (2006), and Christiane Donahue (2009)—who say that dominant discourses within composition studies in general and US writing programs in particular continue to reflect and reinforce a myth of linguistic homogeneity. The unmarked student is still, by and large, assumed to be a US-educated monolingual English speaker; meanwhile, international students and bilingual transnational students may serve as sources of diversity, whose perspectives can at times enrich "mainstream" students' experiences, but who are "special" populations that may require language support outside of the conventional structure.

The danger here is that such representations become naturalized, making it a challenge to reimagine alternative discourses, such as those that privilege multilingual students, that value linguistic resources, or even that mark monolingual students as linguistically deficient. Yet, dominant discourses—such as those identified here—can be disrupted once they have been made visible. Doing so can help move us toward the creation of new public discourses that challenge our assumptions of language difference as deficit and shift the marketplace of linguistic and cultural capital within higher education.

Notes

1. More recently available data show an almost identical list of top institutions.
2. As websites are frequently updated, it should be noted that this research was collected during the spring of 2010; therefore, some of the content and design may have changed since that time.
3. I use the expression "high-level pages" to refer to pages that are just one or two links away from the homepage. These pages tend to include public relations material (e.g., mission statements, letters from the president, etc.) or pages for divisions or offices within the university (e.g., Office of Diversity).
4. In this light, it is interesting to note that the 2008 WPA task force report (Anson 2008) on internationalization focuses on enhancing the international perspectives of WPAs—as well as the organization and the journal—rather than on shifting the programs they administer or the ways in which they represent those programs.

References

Anson, Chris. 2008. "WPA Task Force on Internationalization: Final Report." *Council of Writing Program Administrators.* http://wpacouncil.org/files/finalreport_0.pdf.

Bok, Derek. 2006. *Our Underachieving Colleges.* Princeton, NJ: Princeton University Press.

Canagarajah, A. Suresh. 2006. "The Place of World Englishes in Composition: Pluralization Continued." *College Composition and Communication* 57:586–619.

DePaul University. 2011. "About DePaul." http://www.depaul.edu/about/Pages/default.aspx. Accessed February 1, 2011.

Council of Writing Program Administrators. 2008. "WPA Outcomes Statement for First-Year Composition." Council of Writing Program Administrators. http://www.wpacouncil.org.

Donahue, Christiane. 2009. "'Internationalization' and Composition Studies: Reorienting the Discourse." *College Composition and Communication* 61:212–43.

Fairclough, Norman. 2003. *Analyzing Discourse: Textual Analysis for Social Research.* London: Routledge.

Foderaro, Lisa W. "Budget-Cutting Colleges Bid Some Languages Adieu." *New York Times,* December 3, 2010. Accessed June 5, 2011. http://www.nytimes.com/2010/12/05/education/05languages.html?pagewanted=all.

Furman, Nelly, David Goldberg, and Natalia Lusin. 2010. "Enrollments in Language Other Than English in United States Institution of Higher Education, Fall 2009." Modern Language Association of America. http://www.mla.org/2009_enrollmentsurvey.

Graddol, David. 2006. *English Next.* London: British Council; http://www.britishcouncil.org/english.

Horner, Bruce, and John Trimbur. 2002. "English Only and U.S. College Composition." *College Composition and Communication* 53 (4): 594–630. http://dx.doi.org/10.2307/1512118.

Huckin, Thomas N. 2002. "Textual Silence and the Discourse of Homelessness." *Discourse & Society* 13 (3): 347–72. http://dx.doi.org/10.1177/0957926502013003054.

Institute of International Education. 2010a. "Top 25 Destinations of U.S. Study Abroad Students, 2007/08–2008/09." *Open Doors Report on International Educational Exchange.* http://www.iie.org/en/Research-and-Publications/Open-Doors/Data/US-Study-Abroad/Leading-Destinations/2007-09.

Institute of International Education. 2010b. "Top 25 Places of Origin of International Students, 2008/09–2009/10." *Open Doors Report on International Educational Exchange.* http://www.iie.org/en/Research-and-Publications/Open-Doors/Data/International-Students/Leading-Places-of-Origin/2008-10.

Kubota, Ryuko. 2009. "Internationalization of Universities: Paradoxes and Responsibilities." *Modern Language Journal* 93 (4): 612–6. http://dx.doi.org/10.1111/j.1540-4781.2009.00934.x.

Lambert, Richard D. 1989. *International Studies and the Undergraduate.* Washington, DC: American Council on Education.

Matsuda, Paul Kei. 2006. "The Myth of Linguistic Homogeneity in U.S. College Composition." *College English* 68 (6): 637–51. http://dx.doi.org/10.2307/25472180.

Matsuda, Paul Kei, and Tony Silva. 1999. "Cross-Cultural Composition: Mediated Integration of U.S. and International Students." *Composition Studies* 27:15–30.

Nussbaum, Martha C. 1997. *Cultivating Humanity: A Classical Defense of Reform in Liberal Education.* Cambridge, MA: Harvard University Press.

Sidhu, Ravinder K. 2006. *Universities and Globalization: To Market, To Market.* Mahwah, NJ: Lawrence Erlbaum Associates.

Tardy, Christine M. 2011. "Enacting and Transforming Local Language Policies." *College Composition and Communication* 62:634–61.

PART III

Transnational Engagement

11

DISPOSABLE DRUDGERY
Outsourcing Goes to College

Rebecca Dingo, Rachel Riedner, and Jennifer Wingard

INTRODUCTION

In the fall semester of 2009, Lori Whisenant, director of business law and ethics at the University of Houston's Bauer School of Business, made news (at least academic news) by outsourcing the grading for her writing in the disciplines (WID) course. She contracted with EduMetry Inc., a company whose US base is in the suburbs of Washington DC, but whose labor pool is drawn heavily from Bangladesh, Malaysia, and India (June 2010). EduMetry promises those who use its services that their employees possess at least a master's-level degree, and that they will provide "robust feedback" (RichFeedback LLC 2012b) on student assignments, allowing faculty to focus on more "mission-critical activities"[1] (EduMetry Inc. 2010a). For Whisenant, the economic benefits provided by EduMetry far outweighed the costs, which averaged $12 per individual assignment graded as opposed to $5,584.50 for each TA per semester.[2]

Upon first read, Whisenant's decision is shocking. Much like the current discussions of Massive Open Online Courses (MOOCs) and the implementation of automated essay grading programs, humanities scholars and those who hold fast to the notion that universities must provide a full-spectrum liberal education are beginning to recognize the targeted strategies of the corporate university. In many ways, the ability for one professor to outsource her grading to an offshore company is indeed of deep concern. However, this move did not begin when Whisenant signed on with EduMetry; rather, it began when she partnered with the University of Houston's writing center to train the undergraduate graders who staffed her course. Those graders generated inconsistent results, so Whisenant then joined with the UH English department to employ

DOI: 10.7330/9780874219623.c011

graduate-level TAs. Each student worker employed under Whisenant, however, was taught to facilitate writing instruction. These facilitators did not look at writing merely as a means of knowledge transmission. Therefore, the training the undergraduates received through the writing center, as well as the training the TAs brought to her course, was already unintelligible to Whisenant because it did not replicate what *she* thought writing or grading should be.

In its best incarnation, the partnerships between the writing center and its disciplinary partners allow for an intellectual exchange of ideas, methods, and ultimately the construction of a course curriculum that places writing at the center of nontraditional writing intensive courses. However, that model does not always work. As with many WAC/WID partnerships, the centrality and inclusion of writing pedagogy in discipline-specific courses is often only as strong as the buy-in of the professor. In other words, as we will discuss in more depth throughout this chapter, Whisenant did not see writing as central to the work of her course. Instead, she saw it as the neutral medium through which her students would deliver answers about the course's core curriculum. And that disconnect between the mission of the UH writing center and Whisenant's view of writing as purely functional (with the TAs assigned to work for her caught in between) allowed her to quite readily outsource the grading for the writing assignments in her course.

In this chapter, we use this incident *not* to report the consequences of Whisenant's choices as a piece of academic lore, but rather as a case study that offers a way for rhetoric and composition scholars to foreground the many contexts—globalized and institutional, material and ideological—under which twenty-first-century WAC/WID labor practices may take place. Like writing itself, these contexts are not neutral; they entail substantive risks. We seek to highlight the unevenness with which labor and knowledge are valued in first and third world contexts, and especially in first world universities. Our response to this critique is to offer a transnational feminist analytic, one that offers a way to understand and confront university labor practices, particularly labor practices in writing programs within our present global milieu.

Drawing from the praxis of transnational feminist theory, we map how decisions made at UH are linked with other, broader practices and have repercussions both locally and globally. Instead of using the TAs assigned by the English department for the course (suddenly leaving those TAs without employment), the professor hired graders whose came from "two-thirds" world nations. Our transnational feminist analysis, which considers the UH incident both broadly and specifically, lays bare competing structures of globalized power often hidden from our everyday experiences as workers—i.e., scholars, teachers, and administrators. As a result, we take into account local institutional and state structures, as well as the commonplace neoliberal ideologies that made it possible (and even seem ethical) for this professor to outsource her grading.

We recognize that this incident is specific to UH. Yet, it occurred not just due to local politics but also because of significant global economic, social, and political changes over the last twenty-five years, especially in the rise of neoliberal economics and governmentality, as well as an ideological belief that writing is not central to learning, but merely a means of reporting knowledge. We argue that, in order to really understand how deeply universities and writing programs have felt this shift toward global neoliberalism, rhetoric and composition scholars must keep in mind how local institutions are closely tied to the global, as well as to institutional beliefs that often produce an uneven allocation of funding. Our analysis therefore connects labor and monetary exchange (i.e., shifting funds from UH to EduMetry and then to Bangalore) to uneven economic circumstances, unequal relations of power, and supranational effects. Crucially, these financial practices and labor shifts create and maintain different iterations of institutional power that reinforce inequality across disciplines, departments, and, in this instance, global work sites.

For this reason, the UH case of outsourcing exemplifies why WAC/WID practitioners should be attentive to the labor risks of global neoliberalism and, as we will emphasize, how they can be informed by a transnational feminist rhetorical analysis that links specific local and global labor practices and globalized ideologies of neoliberalism.[3] A transnational feminist analysis enables us to analyze the globalized labor contexts in which our seemingly local WAC/WID practices are situated and to which WAC/WID ultimately might contribute. As we argue, a transnational feminist analytic draws attention to how local labor conditions are globally situated, and how these linkages are unseen, under-theorized, and (for the most part) not part of current WAC/WID scholarship and debate.[4]

Our approach extends our discipline's active attention to labor issues in a US context[5] by framing US-based university labor practices within a global context—decisions made at UH (i.e., in the US) have a real impact on workers locally *and* elsewhere (i.e., those who reside in the two-thirds world). Our aim, in other words, is to shift WAC/WID frameworks and conversations to explicitly connect local practices (within specific locales) to the global relationships in which they are embedded, and to offer transnational feminism as way of making this move. We have picked a particular location (Houston) and case study (a uniquely egregious one) that highlights global labor inequalities and the structural contradictions in which they are situated. While this case study is certainly not exemplary of all WAC/WID practices at UH and elsewhere, it does point to the global reach of university decisions, including curricular decisions that are part of common WAC/WID practices.

This example demonstrates how WAC/WID practices are implicated in globalization. The case study points to a risk that WAC/WID programs face when participating in uneven and unequal labor structures, especially as universities are becoming increasingly strapped for resources. The decisions regarding how those resources are allocated are frames within ideological structures that do not permit or encourage a full understanding of the methods, research, or theoretical underpinnings of writing instruction. Instead, we find views like Whisenant's, wherein writing is seen as a neutral medium of transmission through which assessment can happen. That fundamental assumption exacerbates the uneven institutional economic situations in which WAC/WID writing centers—like the one at UH or programs across the US and abroad—find themselves. This case study also points to the potential that faculty, contingent laborers, and administrators will take on more and more duties with less and less resources because of the uneven distribution of funding and prestige that certain departments carry. Furthermore, as a method of cost cutting within universities, outsourcing labor that is not as highly valued, such as writing instruction, may begin to look more appealing to universities as a means of addressing growing budget constraints.

The UH context, then, compels us to raise the following questions:

- What are the economic, labor, political, and ideological linkages between each group involved—the professor, the graduate student TAs, the undergraduate students, and the outsourced workers in India?
- What are the uneven local and global structural relationships and discursive conditions that can allow for academic outsourcing?
- Where can political interventions be made? How can labor practices be changed?

We use these questions to uncover relationships among the material effects of labor, economic structures, institutional arrangements, ideological assumptions, and the unforeseen impact of policies and decisions made by seemingly disconnected actors (Dingo 2012). As a result, this chapter argues that—if practitioners of rhetoric and composition are moving our disciplinary knowledge, practices, and commitments across borders—we must carefully think through and take into account transnational structures that make this movement possible: geopolitical history, economics, and cultural norms and assumptions, to name a few.

OUTSOURCED!: THE DRUDGERY OF GRADING GOES GLOBAL

The EduMetry Virtual TA website, in describing the company's contribution to UH, writes: "RichFeedback helped the University of Houston by handling the more labor-intensive aspects of providing rich feedback and rubric-based scoring. We helped students know their weaknesses through specific feedback and suggested ways to improve their work" (RichFeedback LLC 2012c). The assumption throughout the website is that giving feedback on student writing and/or assessing student assignments is "drudgery," a wearisome and distasteful toil that (in the nineteenth-century industrial capitalist meaning of the word) is only suitable for servants and factory workers. Grading is not worthy of faculty engagement, nor is it cost-effective to have instructors spend their valuable time assessing their students' writing. Therefore, grading is passed onto TAs. However, in the current context, due to economic decisions in the state of Texas, even TAs may be considered too expensive, since they receive a (low) first world wage. The solution to this "drudgery," time suck, and economic hardship is to use a service—such as EduMetry—whose sole focus is to assess and give feedback on student writing. In other words, the global workers do the drudgery (i.e., work that is servile and, to use Donna Strickland's (2011) term, mechanistic) so the first world faculty do not have to do it.

In her book, *The Managerial Unconsciousness in the History of Composition Studies*, Strickland describes how, for university-based scholars, the labor of grading writing is often assumed to be "mechanistic" and "separate from . . . intellectual work," which is the supposed mission of the university (Strickland 2011, 19). She discusses at length the social and political history of the university (and, indeed, of composition programs), which splits the mechanical aspects of writing instruction and the intellectual work done throughout the rest of the university as a means of keeping composition teachers (and scholars) under-classed. She outlines the belief that writing instruction and the work it entails (i.e., grading) is less than intellectual, because it is about the production of correct prose rather than writing as a means of engagement with ideas. Furthermore, Strickland points out that this ideology is gendered because it presumes that writing instruction, and the grading associated with it, is less intellectual and "softer" than research.

To return to our example, in the use of the term "expert," one might assume that EduMetry is providing decently paid jobs for "professional" and "educated" workers who speak English well and who happen to come from low-income nations. This presumed expertise goes against the dominant US image of outsourcing as involving the transfer of low-skill and low-pay jobs, such as factory work, to developing nations and the exploitation of workers in those locations. However, EduMetry claims that its workers are not low-skill, low-waged factory workers at all. Rather, in EduMetry discourse, they are trained experts who take on outsourced "professional" work[6]—(EduMetry Inc. 2010c)—completely different from the exploitative process documented throughout third world sweatshops in the latter part of the twentieth century and even more recently. Indeed, as Whisenant told *The Chronicle of Higher Education*: "This is what [EduMetry workers] *do* for a living. We're working with *professionals*" (June 2010, emphasis added). However, Whisenant claims the outsourced work is *now* performed by professionals. The implication here is that, prior to the move to EduMetry, the work done by Whisenant's TAs employed through UH's English department was done by novices. Therefore, it made more sense to partner with professionals, no matter how removed from the classroom, because—she assumed—they would give the students in her course a better educational experience.

What Whisenant did not account for, however, was that the work being done by her TAs included more than just scoring and/or grading. From their perspective, they were partnered with her course to help facilitate writing instruction within a business course. They were instructed to follow the model provided by the UH writing center, which trains and assigns both graduate and undergraduate facilitators to writing intensive courses across the university. The UH writing center seeks to partner with courses across the disciplines in order to assist and support professors in specialized fields with writing instruction (University of Houston 2012b). The graduate TAs and undergraduate facilitators the writing center employs are given specialized training to provide in-person or online specialized support in all aspects of the writing process, not just grading.

Whisenant's choice to outsource the grading to Edumetry TAs was not just a dodgy proposition regarding labor practice; it also revealed her lack of knowledge about and respect for the trained writing instruction provided in her course. She saw writing as merely a method of assessment of student learning, not a means of engaging course material. Therefore, when novice TAs did not give feedback speedily enough, she saw their tardy response as a lack of professionalism. In other words, Whisenant believed a professional grader could turn a written assignment around quickly, with comments, because they would merely be commenting on how well the student answered the content questions, or perhaps how well they adhered to standard grammar and usage rules. The professional graders were not expected to provide comments on style, development, or any of the other complexities that are a part of teaching academic writing.

In the UH example, grading, often seen as a menial aspect of the teaching of writing, is contracted out of US-based classrooms and institutions. The purpose of grading writing is to assess student mastery of the material and check grammatical and mechanical errors (i.e., "fixing" papers). Grading quantifies student performance of a writing task and, as such, is usually considered by US faculty as a (boring, menial) managerial task. In this conceptualization, writing is seen as a quantifiable format, one which can be assessed outside the classroom/university context in which it was produced. Writing is not an intellectual process through which students engage material, much less contribute to social discourse and knowledge production. Therefore, outsourcing grading fits in with Strickland's discussion of the teaching of writing as mechanistic, gendered labor, and grading as unsubstantial, surface-level work (Strickland 2011).

In this use of outsourced "menial" instruction in a former colony (or what is often referred to as a "developing nation"), we see traces of the neocolonialism that has become central to the twenty-first-century global economy. This relationship between disciplinary specialists in the first world and grading "experts" in the periphery echoes a former colonial relationship between India and Great Britain. India now has a fast growing professional middle class (and the fastest growing lower class), in large part due to the Structural Adjustment Policies (SAPs) of the 1990s. These SAPs mandated that India partner with first world nations and provide labor, especially in the areas of telecommunications, technology, industry, and now education. As a result, India has vast reserves of professionalized, though exploitable, labor, since Indian workers are tied to wealthy foreign companies who profit off of their hard work. This labor can be cheaply hired to perform tasks in US universities that are seen as less than intellectual, such as grading papers. EduMetry asserts that all of their experts are not only post-baccalaureate, but they are also proficient in standard written English (Rich Feedback LLC 2012a).

They are therefore sufficiently trained in the English language to do the un-intellectual work of grading. Because they were educated in an English-speaking, (post)colonial system, EduMetry experts have gained adequate language expertise, which allows them to provide inexpensive services to Western educational institutions. At this moment, we see a clear division of labor that is structured along first world–third world divisions. While intellectual work is performed by privileged, discipline-based specialists in first world locations, less valued and less interesting work such as grading—what we've called drudgery—can be done by (presumed) grading "experts" in former colonial locations that have now entered a postcolonial era but, to a large extent, remain underdeveloped nations. This relationship between knowledge producers in first world locations and skilled workers in third world countries sustains an unequal positioning of expertise and division of labor, thus maintaining (neo)colonial political relationships.

OUTSOURCED!: THE LOCAL IMPACT OF OUTSOURCING

In the above discussion, we pointed out traces of the uneven, colonial relationship in outsourcing. There's also an uneven division of labor between the teaching of writing, grading, and teaching a subject. Taken together, these raise additional risks for WAC/WID. As a result, in addition to its resonance with colonial labor relationships, Whisenant's choice to outsource grading has professional, institutional, and curricular implications for UH. Her choice raises questions as to whether Whisenant was a good and ethical teacher/employer, and whether TAs are effective educators for undergraduates.[7] Indeed, the *Chronicle of Higher Education* used the Whisenant incident to address the merits of writing instruction using grading practices, the place of TAs, and university and administrative responsibilities to TAs, as well as individual professors' responsibilities in a writing intensive business course (June 2010). Reader comments about the article were both supportive of Whisenant's choice to outsource the grading—"Since the course is 'business law and ethics' and is taught by a lawyer (see her website), the decision to outsource the feedback for the "writing in the discipline" component of the course seems not only prudent but also quite effective in meeting the varied goals of the course." (Comment 72)—as well as critical of her lack of interaction with her students' writing, the non-use of US labor, and her inattention to the education and training of the university TAs. All ninety-five comments in the *Chronicle* reveal complex perspectives on teaching in higher education during this historical moment when jobs, resources, and (especially, state education) money are at a premium (June 2010).

Yet what is not immediately clear in the *Chronicle* article (nor reflected in the comments) is the built-in, firmly-situated, and uneven local–global political and economic structures we begin to trace above, and which this case exemplifies in other ways. Although UH is a US-based public university, the Bauer Business School's practices mirror global corporate practices that either (1) obfuscate the relationship between product–worker, monetary exchange, and the state's interests in corporate/educative initiatives or (2) celebrate the relationship between product–worker and corporation as a boon for the worker, without closely examining pay and working conditions. Moreover, Bauer draws much of its monetary support from global corporate sponsors, such as Exxon and Halliburton, and allows those sponsors to provide stipulations within Bauer's curriculum. In other words, Bauer is implicated—through its curriculum, administrative relationships, and economic structures—in a powerful corporate culture that has a global reach. Local decisions and practices at Bauer have both a local (i.e., TA labor) and a global (Bengali graders) impact.

Ultimately, this UH case illustrates how complex "transglocal" (Scott 2012) networks (within a local WID program) and economic ideologies can exacerbate uneven structural power relationships at home and abroad. This particular instance privileges outsourcing and demonstrates neoliberal governmentality, the art of governing that manages people, goods, wealth, and social coherence as a justification for state power (Brown 2003).[8] Neoliberal government and supranational policies support "unfettered market forces" (Giddens 1998, 12) and "fiscal austerity, privatization, market liberalization, and governmental stabilization" (Duggan 2003, xii), which are all pro-capitalist. Historically, neoliberalism arose alongside the expansion of contemporary globalization. Neoliberal policies and ideologies have impelled globalization and the transnational exchange of goods, services, people, political practices, knowledge, and culture, while also driving the movement of people, texts, labor, and jobs across borders. As a result, contemporary globalization has had uneven material consequences throughout different regions of the world, due to the rise of neoliberalism's market-driven approach to economic and social policy. Neoliberal policy supports private enterprise and open markets, advocating that trade liberalization is more "efficient" than state action. Thus, to some extent, Whisenant's curricular decisions and actions can be explained by neoliberal policy and ideology that is widely accepted by corporations, supranational organizations, governments, and other powerful institutions.

At the same time that neoliberalism shapes policy and ideology in powerful global institutions, neoliberal economics has also occasioned a drop in funding for state-supported activities (such as education) because free trade agreements have reduced (or erased) the tariffs and taxes typically required when exchanging goods across borders—the very taxes that help support the work of the state. Likewise, because industrial work has moved from high-income nations to mid/low-income nations, citizens from high-income nations have faced unemployment while others face labor exploitation. By reading neoliberal ideologies present in the UH case (and unfolding the complex layers of the situation through a transnational feminist analysis), we can see how seemingly disconnected global policies and local decisions are connected to each other and are both shaped by neoliberalism. Perhaps part of Whisenant's decision to outsource her grading had to do with saving her department money, or resulted from an increase in the student-to-faculty ratio made necessary by decreased state funding, etc. Whatever her specific reasons, we argue that her decision took place within the context of neoliberal economic policies and labor practices.

Much like Strickland's (2011) recognition of the gendered structures of US composition, the outsourcing of grading is premised upon neoliberalism's raced and classed economic and geopolitical aims. In other words, ideologies of neoliberalism trickle into our everyday lived experiences,[9] manifesting themselves within particular values and actions around employment and education: entrepreneurship, competition, individual choice, self-interest, and self-empowerment. Ultimately, these ideologies result in a perceived disconnection from wider structures of power, despite our being embedded within those very structures. Thus, neoliberalism functions across and connects several scales—policy, economy, culture, personal—and it extends into educational employment structures and disciplinary divisions and knowledge.

In such a situation, neoliberal policies and ideologies have material ramifications for faculty, graduate student workers, and professional workers within the United States and in labor sites that are linked to the United States. For example, although the writing intensive courses at UH are loosely joined under the WID moniker, individual faculty set both the curricular and ideological uses for writing within each individual course. More to the point, there is no centralized curriculum, little oversight, and minimal agreed-upon concept of writing; what the curriculum requires is merely a word-count designation for "writing intensive" courses. This loose curricular structure, coupled with Houston's culture of privatization,[10] runs the risk of interpolating professors (and students) into a neoliberal curriculum whereby outsourced classroom practices can be deployed easily and without much consequence.

Through this critique of the UH case, we aim to consider the neoliberal contexts in which local and global labor is situated and put forth a transnational feminist analytic that draws attention to how local labor conditions are globally positioned. The *location* of education and the *labor* of education are discursively disengaged in a neoliberal context (i.e., we do not see how location and labor are imbricated with one another); therefore, the constitutive relationship between labor and education is obfuscated. While we know that the lead professor is employed by UH, the course itself is being partially orchestrated elsewhere—far away in Bangalore. In other words, the virtual TAs are not present, or unseen, in the physical classroom. As this case makes clear, outsourcing labor creates uneven, cross-national connectives.

As scholars engaged in transnational studies, we find it necessary to—in the words of Khagram and Levitt (2007)—"uncover, analyze, and conceptualize similarities, differences, and interactions among trans-societal and trans-organizational realities, including the ways in which they shape bordered and bounded phenomena and dynamics across time and space" (10–11). As transnational feminists, we add an analytic and political edge (as we demonstrate further below) by tracing how escalating global capitalism can create conditions of economic exploitation and inequality for workers while maintaining a high standard of cost/benefit return for larger, more powerful institutions (such as UH).

In order to understand the UH situation through a transnational feminist lens, we must juxtapose each actor's situation and consider how the US-based TAs have a relationship with the virtual TAs, how their material conditions rely upon each other, and how the ideology of "cost-cutting equals value" has penetrated the university. While the virtual TAs in Bangalore may now have employment, it is at the cost of the employment of UH graduate teaching assistants. Consequently, to better understand this situation through a transnational lens, we might think in terms of scales of power. Transnational feminists trace power at a variety of scales—the economic, social, and political conditions of contemporary neoliberalism, neocolonialism, and neoimperialism across nations—analyzing how various scales of power link diverse nations and people and shape them in similar, different, and sometimes unequal ways. In addition, transnational feminists examine the roles that state and supranational power, history, and class relations—as well as sexual, gendered, raced, and ethnic expectations—play in the making and unmaking of nations and nation-states, and, in the UH example, knowledge production.

THE MATERIAL EFFECTS OF THE NEOLIBERAL UNIVERSITY

The C.T. Bauer College of Business at the University of Houston is a multimillion-dollar college within the university. As we've noted, it is supported by outside donations from large corporations like Halliburton and ExxonMobil. These corporations are not silent donors. In fact, it is well known that they attach their donations to explicit curricular expectations for UH's students. For example, they support corporate citizenship requirements (such as community service, unpaid internships, and the demonstration of ethical behavior). They also influence the curriculum by standardizing the content of particular courses so that graduates have the mark of a decidedly "Bauer" education. These expectations are seemingly benign. However, by tying the curricular and ethical expectations for students to corporate dollars, Bauer has created a college that is saturated with neoliberal ideologies and imbued with an explicit neoliberal pedagogy.

That neoliberal pedagogy can be readily seen in Whisenant's writing intensive business law and ethics courses. Even though these courses were designed to fit within the university's WID requirement (which, as we discussed previously, is a weakly conceived institutional requirement), it also serves as a site where Bauer students satisfy the writing requirements set forth by the Bauer corporate partners. These requirements have little to do with practices developed by disciplinary-based scholars, such as process-based writing or writing-to-learn strategies. Instead, they mostly focus on "clarity" and "grammar," which are often grouped under "good written communication skills."

According to both the *Chronicle of Higher Education* and EduMetry, Whisenant incorporated five case-based writing assignments into her course (June 2010 and RichFeedback LLC 2012c). Neither source explained exactly what these assignments were, but the *Chronicle* did cite a 5,000-word-count standard for the course as a whole (June 2010). Also, EduMetry boasts that it "assessed [these] assignments for the C. T. Bauer College of Business against UH-approved rubrics that address critical thinking, written communication and knowledge application" (RichFeedback LLC 2012c). Because the language of the rubric used by EduMetry includes the term "knowledge application" rather than "knowledge production" or "knowledge synthesis," we assume that the case studies in Whisenant's course are reproductions of provable sets of information. These assignments do not reflect an individual student's process of knowledge production or show how students themselves exchange new knowledge.

One reason for our assumption about "knowledge application" comes from critiques of corporate knowledge production by Stanley Aronowitz (2000). In *The Knowledge Factory*, Aronowitz warns that when neoliberal educational practices enter the university, they change how the university and knowledge production functions at its core, transforming into a model of pure information dissemination and non-creative scholarship and learning. For Aronowitz, the move toward a "corporatizing" of curriculum in university classrooms affects students by rewarding them for regurgitating knowledge rather than creating sustained inquiries based on intellectual curiosity. As a result, assignments created within the context of neoliberal education are cogs in the machine of a course that can be assessed and refined outside of the exchange of ideas.[11] Thus, in this educational framework, writing assignments do not need to be graded by the professor because they are not part of the intellectual exchange of the course. Instead, writing assignments are merely quantifiable measurements of discrete student learning. Either the student knows the information and can reproduce it or she cannot. Any grader, even one in Bangalore, can easily make that judgment. Again, Strickland's variation between knowledge and drudgery is reproduced both within the US classroom and abroad.

A symptom of the downfall of the Keynesian economic system—wherein national and state governments invested in services (such as welfare, education, and health care, to name a few) that supported their citizens—is that we have removed (or outsourced) so much funding from state education that schools can only produce measurements and quotas, not liberal democratic citizens. Moreover, this sort of citizenship is not measurable. This post-Keynesian, neoliberal form of education does not prepare students to analyze information; rather, it teaches them how to consume information quickly, without connection—to file facts, images, and blurbs—and without integrating bits of information with historical, political, and economic processes and forces.

The UH case clearly illustrates the ideological infiltration of neoliberalism into the curriculum. In addition, it is easily outsourced because writing can be measured through an "unbiased and detailed and objective evaluation of [student] work," which is communicated through a predetermined but decontextualized rubric (RichFeedback LLC 2012c). Writing is not judged on its ability to produce knowledge or synthesize and combine multiple sites of knowledge; instead, the EduMetry virtual TAs assess how well students *apply* the knowledge given them. When writing is integrated into the learning of a course, and not just seen as a product or tool for assessment, it can become an instrument of knowledge production, contributing to a pedagogical model that Paulo Freire ultimately describes as emancipatory (Freire 2000). Clearly, this is not the model to which the Bauer College of Business subscribes.

It is the ideology that grading is mechanistic and that writing itself is merely a means of displaying a student's knowledge that allows for the outsourcing of grading so readily. Yes, of course there is an economic component, which we have explained earlier in this chapter, but there also exists an ideology about the function of writing, grading, and its place within the university classroom. Whisenant had already "outsourced" the teaching of writing in her course to TAs from the UH writing center. She was not connected to the teaching of writing, nor did she see it as a central part of her curriculum. Instead, writing was the mechanism, the medium through which the knowledge she was responsible for could be tested, and, as such, any contact with the grading, responding, or feedback was not as important as her course's curriculum. Thus, responding to writing was drudgery.

However, when students are not given the opportunity to engage with their writing or their writing instructor in any meaningful way, it becomes a mere process of regurgitation that is easily disposed of or commodified. Likewise, since that writing has little meaning, it also becomes disposable, much like the UH TAs who were downsized to make room for the cheaper, more expert, outsourced labor of the virtual TAs in Bangalore. Because both the professor and the students do not have a relationship with these virtual TAs, it becomes even easier to dispose of them as well, since they—to some extent—are unseen in the classroom. These TAs are machine-like and dehumanized, simply outputting the results of each writing assignment. As a result, this situation redefines relationships of power between students, graders, and the professor, perhaps making students feel like more justified consumers.

FROM TA LABOR TO GLOBALLY OUTSOURCED LABOR

Whisenant's course was important on a local, institutional level because it provided direct funding to two English department TAs. Because of its "corporate partners," Bauer has the money to employ graduate students from departments across campus to assist professors within their WID courses. Occasionally, Bauer partners with the writing center, which staffs both undergraduate and graduate tutors who act as facilitators in the writing studios connected to the larger business courses. In our example, Bauer sought English department TAs whose labor was given over to Bauer because of their assumed expertise in writing instruction. The partnership stipulated that the business school would provide the funding for those two TAs, and these TAs would provide writing instruction via grading and commenting on student texts. Therefore, in hopes of gaining "expertise" in writing feedback for their large section (seventy-five students per section) WID course, Bauer provided funding to a unit that is traditionally underfunded within the university—the English department.[12]

This partnership *should* have been beneficial to both Bauer and the English department: Bauer got "expert" labor, and English got monetary support in the form of funding for much needed TAs. However, when viewed through a transnational lens, we can see that the power relationship between English and Bauer is uneven. Bauer controls the resources in this situation—i.e., the funding stream—and, therefore, they can do the hiring, the firing, or the outsourcing. The English department merely provided two very vulnerable, and ultimately disposable, graduate TAs who have minimal protections for job security. In the end, the "expertise" offered by the TAs had little or no value because their understanding of the job—to facilitate the teaching of writing as an intellectual process—was far different than Whisenant's understanding of what TAs should do—grade student papers while quickly looking for errors based on the understanding of course material and/or standard usage. And, because these TAs were providing feedback on each student's "writing," they were taking far longer to grade each paper and were providing feedback that Whisenant viewed as unnecessary for the students in her course. Whisenant did not see the value in these TAs, so they quickly became disposable, or at least not worth their stipends. Therefore, within the neoliberal university, if one's intellectual project is not valued, one's labor will not be valued either.

Whisenant is quoted in the *Chronicle of Higher Education* as saying: "Our graders were great, but they were not experts in providing feedback" (June 2010). And, because they were not "experts," she did not feel the need to keep them on the payroll. Whisenant did not work with her TAs to develop their skills, nor did she seek assistance from the English department when she began to notice the TAs were not providing the feedback she wanted. Part of the promise of being a teaching assistant is the opportunity to learn *how* to become a better instructor. Assessment, feedback, teaching, and planning courses/syllabi are all parts of the education that TAs should receive when they work with faculty. Even one of the commenters on the *Chronicle* article questions: "How will the TAs learn and grow as educators if they aren't given a chance to actually fulfill the job of TAs?" (June 2010).

But Whisenant did not see it as her place to mentor her TAs. In fact, she did not view them as *her* TAs at all. From the very beginning, it was assumed that the TAs were there because they were already trained, either by their home department or by the UH writing center. So, instead of the TAs working *with* Whisenant, they worked—much like the graders in Bangalore—*for* her at a remove. In this instance, the English department partnered with Whisenant, following the same model established by the UH writing center. However, instead of replicating a successful partnership wherein the writing center provides both upper division undergraduate facilitators and graduate student TAs to bridge the gap between core curriculum and writing instruction, the lack of support and desire from Whisenant to fully engage as a faculty partner demonstrates how the partnership can break down. If the instructor is not involved, does not help TAs plan, or just sees the work of the writing center as a service, the teaching of writing across the curriculum can become further separated from a course.

As easy as it is to vilify Whisenant, if we consider the work of the writing center as a service provided by the university to its many constituents, and if TAs are provided either through the writing center or directly from the English department, Whisenant has already, in a sense, outsourced the writing/grading component of her course. She just did it locally. Therefore, if Whisenant is not truly collaborating with the writing center or the English department to incorporate writing pedagogy into her course, she could very well understand her relationship with the writing center or the English department as one of outsourcing. Consequently, the move to outsource her grading to already trained "experts" in Bangalore is not really that surprising.

If we examine her choice within the neoliberal framework of cost/benefit, the EduMetry experts seem like a much more solid choice than the UH TAs because: (1) they come already fully trained, (2) they are cheaper, and (3) they follow a grading rubric based on Whisenant's own outcomes. According to EduMetry, their "virtual TAs" are "your expert teaching assistants" (RichFeedback LLC 2012b), who are degreed and well versed in standard written English, but are never identified because "it is about the process and not the individual" (RichFeedback LLC 2012a). The UH TAs are assigned to the class to be a bridge between the core curriculum and writing instruction. Therefore, each paper should receive individual comments because each student, as per writing theory, has their own issues to improve upon. However, because Whisenant did not see writing instruction as integral to her curriculum, those individual comments were viewed as incompetence and could be shed in the name of money and expertise. The expertise EduMetry is selling, then, is quite different from the traditional TA expertise developed at the university. Instead of students interacting with a TA who (1) works with the instructor, (2) sits in the class, (3) understands the material, and (4) develops somewhat of a rapport with both the students and the professor, the EduMetry TAs merely read decontextualized (at worst) or limitedly-contextualized (at best) texts and then comment on and grade them.

Although EduMetry tells us it is important that "experts" grade our students' papers, the underlying message here is that grading writing (like the grading of a Scantron or multiple choice test) can be done by anyone anywhere, and for relatively little money. Although we don't know the specific compensation provided to EduMetry workers, we do know that Whisenant was able to save money by reassigning the funds from her unused TAs.[13] If each course enrolls seventy-five students, two courses run each semester, and each course contains five case study assignments per course, Whisenant and the Bauer business college were paying about $9,000 per semester. That is well under the amount that one TA would make. Furthermore, the fee for outsourced grading went first through a US company, then a Bengali company, and ultimately to the actual "experts." There is an assumption that because they are "experts," we are not exploiting inexperienced labor, that this is fundamentally different from the way sweatshops in low-income nations without labor laws, for example, might exploit labor. However, when one actually breaks down the economics of the EduMetry system, the amount of money provided to these "experts" must be grim indeed.

In other words, this case demonstrates how WID courses can contribute to the globalized exploitation of labor. As we mention above, there have been sustained discussions and scholarship in the field of rhetoric and composition (and elsewhere) about labor and fair wages for academic workers. This case, however, is something else, much like the labor issues we have seen throughout the greater US job market—it is an outsourcing of "expendable waged labor." Both the outsourced workers and the US TAs' economic situation may be linked by international trade, in addition to the fact that both are not thriving in this transnational economy. We have seen how economic trade agreements—such as the North American Free Trade Agreement of 1995 (NAFTA), which expanded labor exploitation and remapped communities along the US–Mexico border—have ramifications at home and abroad. NAFTA has significantly downsized industrial labor in the US, and has also contributed to the extreme rise of the service sector economy, which, due to other neoliberal policies of the 1990s, does not provide benefits (health, retirement, etc.) or consistent salaried labor. On the Mexican side of the US border, shantytowns have sprung up alongside factories, where people live in extreme poverty, unable to afford the very items they assemble. There is also a direct correlation between the rise of factories and crime; in Ciudad Juarez, a town along the border, the rates of rape, kidnapping, and the disappearance of female factory workers has increased since NAFTA went into effect. Ultimately, policy and outsourcing can have unforeseen or unpredictable effects.

This sort of initial outsourcing of US labor had, until recently, been limited to factories and what was described as "low-skilled" work. In the UII example, however, the outsourced workers in Bangalore do the same work that US middle-class workers do, but for significantly reduced wages. Workers, such as TAs, may face unemployment and growing debts[14] due to a lack of job security that their jobs may have formerly provided, which compounds the already grim job prospects for so many graduates in the humanities. By the same token, these US-based TAs might be able to sustain some portion of their first world lifestyle, since the exploitation of other workers across the globe enables US companies to keep the cost of consumer products down. Yet, the TAs may share a common material condition with their Bangalore counterparts, who also may not receive a living wage, benefits, childcare, or vacation. Both are vulnerable and disposable, though the degree of this varies by location.

Working against common representations of the disenfranchised, poor factory worker, EduMetry emphasizes that its workers are "experts" with "at least a masters level degree" (RichFeedback LLC 2012d). The target audience for EduMetry's publicity might assume these workers have fair labor conditions, since they are clearly labeled as educated; we might assume that they, much like we promise college-educated students in the United States, will be compensated, given health benefits, treated fairly. However, because the work is not done within the United States, even the scant labor protections given to US workers are not afforded to the workers of EduMetry. And, like the sweatshop workers in free trade zones, these workers are hired because they will work for far less than a US-based TA. Furthermore, since the work is characterized as "drudgery," we can perhaps extrapolate that there is a factory-like quality to the employment structure. And, because of the separate nature (through the writing center) of writing instruction at UH, Whisenant was able to see the writing in her course as tangential, mechanistic, and already outsourced. (The ideology of the place of WID as tangential and the responsibility of an external entity helped facilitate Whisenant's move to outsource her grading to Bangalore.)

A transnational analysis enables us to point to global power relationships that the UH case reveals. The graders Whisenant hired through EduMetry are outside the institutional culture and structures of UH—they work in a different time and place, and they are divorced from the students and the content of the course. Furthermore, the outsourced workers have no institutional support or recourse (that we know of) regarding their employment. Therefore, the effect of neoliberal capitalism is that the labor of grading, and the graders themselves, are *outside* the system and its networks of communication between the professor and the students.

Outsourced labor differentiates and outlines a political space between those who are directly and deeply involved in academic life and those who are not. Riedner and Mahoney (2008) have argued that outsourced workers support the university community insofar as their labor makes possible the conditions of its education. Simultaneously, outsourced workers are structurally and ideologically *outside* insofar as they are not imagined as part of the university community itself. These labor decisions expose how both groups of TAs are undervalued for different ideological reasons that serve the same neoliberal cost-cutting aims. Perhaps UH TAs have better benefits, but, as graders, they have no power within the university structure because their work was not seen as valuable. By contrast, EduMetry graders, who performed their task to Whisenant's satisfaction, were simply absent from the scene altogether.

CONCLUSION

As the UH example demonstrates, there are global ramifications of local neoliberal practices, ideologies, and pedagogies for WAC/WID work. Ryan Claycomb and Randi Gray Kristensen note that, because of its strong relationship with disciplinary practices, the WID movement has a high vulnerability in "potential complicity with the corporatization of the university and its use of writing as an instrumentalist component of the production of labor capital for the workforce" (Claycomb and Kristensen 2009, 11). They argue that it becomes easy for WAC/WID programs to simply "serve" the desires of the discipline or the university, particularly if the program is dependent upon funding from external disciplinary units that do not take into account the impact of global ideologies, practices, and structures of the university. This kind of "service" to disciplines can obfuscate relationships between product–worker, monetary exchange, and the state's interests in corporate/educative initiatives, as we previously illustrated. Furthermore, these material inequalities are supported by neoliberal ideological assumptions that allow certain programmatic wants and structures to override others.[15]

From the UH example, we demonstrate how the addition of a transnational feminist analytic enables a more thorough understanding of the networked power linkages across the university and the globe. The ideas of distance/proximity, migration, flows, and exchanges are at the heart of a transnational feminist framework, and these ideas deal directly with connections among space, place, and location. Transnational feminists attempt to place discrete events (like the UH case study) into these complex systems, focusing on how these individual events interact with larger systemic flows of power. Therefore, instead of merely learning the specifics of a disciplinary writing (at best) or creative writing pedagogy that "serves" a discipline, a transnational feminist analytic allows WAC/WID practitioners to connect institutional decisions, individual situations, and local cases within global systemic contexts. Transnational feminist analyses, then, can help to create sites of activism that challenge both local and global oppression.

Decisions made at the University of Houston have a real impact on workers elsewhere. UH is a powerful institution, one that has both the resources of the state of Texas and influential private interests. As such, it is not just a local place—to students, faculty, and staff—but it is a global institution constituted by transnational relations. Because of its global status, decisions made at UH (by individual faculty and administrators) carry and perpetuate the practices of transnational neoliberalisms. Whisenant's decision to outsource her grading to Bangalore extended the neoliberal ideology and labor relations of the university to local places around the world (Massey 2004).

The political aim of this analytic is to challenge and change the relations that a global institution such as UH creates, as well as expose the underlying assumptions about knowledge production and the place of writing that allow for the ease of outsourcing grading. This intervention requires a pedagogical approach, where teaching is not just situated in but linked to networks of power that disseminate to and from powerful global places. The political exigency of the UH case creates a responsibility for people and places elsewhere, while maintaining a focus on local material relations and contexts. The goal, Doreen Massey (2004) argues, is "opening up a politics of place which does not deprive of meaning those lines of connections, relations and practices, that construct place, but that also go beyond it" (9).

To summarize our argument, a transnational feminist analytic applied to WID/WAC practices allows us to:

1. Become more aware of the complex, networked ideological and material power relationships at work, both locally and globally.

2. Avoid becoming complicit with neoliberal economic structures that organize our world and reaffirm uneven power relationships throughout the university and the globe.

3. Analyze and intervene in uncritical labor and pedagogical practices of the global university, recognize the impact and reach of global universities, and view this global reach as a site of political intervention.

If we can begin to recognize and educate ourselves, then we can advocate for WAC/WID programs that prioritize their expertise, and give them the much-needed material resources to support their efforts. In other words, by learning to map institutional/global power structures and ideological assumptions, WAC/WID directors can understand how both ideological and material power interacts and corresponds with our current political moment.

Notes

1. "About Us," on the EduMetry Inc. website, *EduMetry: Learning Outcomes Management*, http://edumetry.com/about-us.php (site discontinued). According to EduMetry, "mission-critical" activities for faculty include "teaching, improving their courses, and research" from "Benefits" on the EduMetry Inc. website, http://edumetry .com/benefits.php (site discontinued). Of course, this begs the question: is feedback necessarily divorced from teaching, course improvement, or even research?

2. These numbers were based on the amount of money provided in salary to English TAs at UH divided by two. TAs are nine-month, two-semester employees, so Whisenant removed the cost the business school provided to the writing center for the TA's labor and funneled it to EduMetry. The crux was that these TAs were under contract and still received their stipend; it just had to be covered by the English department's budget, not Bauer's.

3. See Dingo (2012) and Wingard (2012) for further discussion of transnational feminist rhetorical analysis.

4. Some scholars have examined the internationalization and cross-national ramifications of WAC/WID work. Christine Donahue (2009), for example, has critiqued the field of writing studies at large for blindly celebrating the international turn in our field, which often actually look like colonialist or pluralistic projects that seek to export a form of American (composition) exceptionalism, while uncritically embracing "other" ways of writing and arguing. She ultimately requests that

scholars think about the blind spots in our scholarship, where power between and among nations structures our pedagogies and practices.

5. For examples of this attention to labor issues, see Bousquet (2008), Giroux (2007), Schell (1998), and Strickland (2011).

6. "Careers," on the EduMetry Inc. website, *EduMetry: Learning Outcomes Management*, http://edumetry.com/careers.php (site discontinued).

7. This situation also reveals the politics of labor for graduate students, who may not have the time, resources, or training to adequately respond to student papers.

8. Wendy Brown (2003), in her discussion of what she calls neoliberal governmentality, notes the shift in political thought from liberal democracy to neoliberal logics: "In making the individual fully responsible for her- or himself, neoliberalism equates moral responsibility with rational action; it erases the discrepancy between economic and moral behavior by configuring morality entirely as a matter of rational deliberation about costs, benefits, and consequences" (6). According to Brown, neoliberalism removes the buffer between economics and morals, creating a world wherein moral decisions are made from a cost-benefit analysis of what will affect the self.

9. See Brown (2003) and Riedner and Mahoney (2008) for more.

10. Like the rest of Texas, the city of Houston is staunchly pro-business. From the lack of citywide zoning (meaning that property can be developed for business or residential anywhere in the city) to the lack of personal, business, or state income tax, Houston is invested in business and private property rather than social services or municipalities. These material conditions go hand in hand with an ideology that privileges the individual over the communal. Texans, and Houstonians in particular, strongly embody the American ideal of the "cowboy" or "self-made man." It is each individual's right and responsibility to take care of themselves, their property, and their own livelihood, and they must do this without government intervention.

11. We recognize that this mode of assignment design and assessment is not unique to neoliberal universities. There are other, older educational models where students are rewarded for reproducing knowledge rather than for sustained inquiry. However, our argument is that the neoliberal model, with its emphasis on information dissemination as the core value of the university and as central to its self-defined mission, is part of a new phase of global capital.

12. These numbers come from the University of Houston and C.T. Bauer College of Business administration websites. They are significantly different from the numbers reported in the *Chronicle of Higher Education* article, which cites two sections per semester (250 students), each staffed by seven TAs. We do not know which numbers are truly accurate for the 2009–2010 academic year; however, for the 2011–2012 academic year, our numbers are correct.

13. The UH TAs make about $11,360 a year.

14. According to several recent articles in publications such as the *New York Times*, the *Wall Street Journal*, and the *Atlantic*, college graduates are exiting the university with far more debt than ever before. Graduate students are not immune to this trend. Due to salary compression, lack of unionization, and longer degree-completion averages, graduate students are entering the job market with record student debt. And often those debts are unsecured private debts, not the federal loans (either subsidized or unsubsidized) of the past.

15. The argument that the humanities bolsters the work of the sciences, engineering, and business schools, but does not have the monetary or institutional power to sway any curricular or institutional changes, has been well documented in the *New York Times*, the *Chronicle of Higher Education*, and *Inside Higher Ed*.

References

Aronowitz, Stanley. 2000. *The Knowledge Factory: Dismantling the Corporate University and Creating True Higher Learning.* Boston. Beacon Press.

Brown, Wendy. 2003. "Neoliberalism and the End of Liberal Democracy." *Theory and Event* 7 (1). http://muse.jhu.edu/login?auth=0&type=summary&url=/journals/theory_and_event/v007/7.1brown.html

Bousquet, Marc. 2008. *How the University Works: Higher Education and the Low-Wage Nation.* New York: New York University Press.

Claycomb, Randi, and Ryan Kristensen. 2009. *Writing against the Curriculum: Anti-disciplinarily in the Writing and Cultural Studies Classroom.* Lantham, MD: Lexington Books.

Dingo, Rebecca. 2012. *Networking Arguments: Rhetoric, Transnational Feminism, and Public Policy Writing.* Pittsburgh, PA: U of Pittsburgh P.

Donahue, Christine. 2009. "'Internationalization' and Composition Studies: Reorienting the Discourse." *CCC* 61 (2): 212–43.

Duggan, Lisa. 2003. *Twilight of Equality: Neoliberalism, Cultural Politics, and the Attack on Democracy.* Boston: Beacon Press.

EduMetry Inc. 2010a. "About Us." *EduMetry: Learning Outcomes Management.* http://edumetry.com/about-us.php. Accessed July 2010 (site discontinued).

EduMetry Inc. 2010b. "Benefits." *EduMetry: Learning Outcomes Management.* http://edumetry.com/benefits.php. Accessed July 2010 (site discontinued).

EduMetry Inc. 2010c. "Careers." *EduMetry: Learning Outcomes Management.* http://edumetry.com/careers.php. Accessed July 2010 (site discontinued).

Freire, Paulo. 2000. *Pedagogy of the Oppressed.* New York: Continuum.

Giddens, Anthony. 1998. *The Third Way: The Renewal of Social Democracy.* Cambridge: Polity.

Giroux, Henry A. 2007. *The University in Chains: Confronting the Military-Industrial-Academic Complex.* Boulder: Paradigm Publishers.

June, Audry Williams. 2010. "Some Papers are Uploaded to Bangalore to be Graded." *Chronicle of Higher Education* 4 (April). http://chronicle.com/article/Outsourced-Grading-With/64954/.

Khagram, Sanjeev, and Peggy Levitt. 2007. "Constructing Transnational Studies." In *The Transnational Studies Reader: Intersections and Innovations,* ed. Peggy Levitt and Sanjeev Khagram, 10–11. New York: Routledge.

Massey, Doreen. 2004. "Geographies of Responsibility." *Human Geography* 86 (1): 5–18.

Rich Feedback LLC. 2012a. "Benefits." *Virtual-TA: Your Expert Teaching Assistant.* http://www.virtual-ta.com/benefits.php.

RichFeedback LLC. 2012b. "Home." *Virtual-TA: Your Expert Teaching Assistant.* http://www.virtual-ta.com/.

RichFeedback LLC. 2012c. "Success Stories." *Virtual-TA: Your Expert Teaching Assistant.* http://www.virtual-ta.com/success-stories.php#1.

RichFeedback LLC. 2012d. "Careers" *Virtual-TA: Your Expert Teaching Assistant.* http://www.virtual-ta.com/careers.php.

Riedner, Rachel, and Kevin Mahoney. 2008. *Democracies to Come: Rhetorical Action, Neoliberalism, and Communities of Resistance.* Lantham, MD: Lexington Books.

Schell, Eileen E. 1998. *Gypsy Academics and Mother-Teachers: Gender, Contingent Labor, and Writing Instruction.* Portsmouth, NH: Boynton/Cook Publishers.

Scott, J. Blake. 2012. "Tracking 'Transglocal' Risks in Pharmaceutical Development: Novartis's Challenge of Indian Patent Law." In *The Megarhetorics of Global Development,* ed. Rebecca Dingo and J. Blake Scott, 29–43. Pittsburgh. PA: U of Pittsburgh P.

Strickland, Donna. 2011. *The Managerial Unconscious in the History of Composition Studies.* Carbondale, IL: SIUP.

University of Houston. 2012a. "C.T. Bauer College of Business." *University of Houston* http://www.bauer.uh.edu/.

University of Houston. 2012b. "Mission." *Writing Center.* http://www.uh.edu/writecen /mission.php

Wingard, Jennifer. 2012. *Branded Bodies, Rhetoric, and the Neoliberal Nation-State.* Lanham, MD: Lexington Books.

12

ECONOMIES OF COMPOSITION
Mapping Transnational Writing Programs in US Community Colleges

Wendy Olson

Community colleges are expanding their work in the teaching of English literacy skills, and they do so for a growing culturally and linguistically varied English language learning student population. As JoAnne Crandall and Ken Sheppard note in a report they developed for the Council for Advancement of Adult Literacy, "ESL is now the largest department at Miami-Dada Community College, and the largest ESL program in the world is located at Santa Monica Community College" (Crandall and Sheppard 2004, 6). Not coincidently, approximately one-fourth of the students enrolled in community colleges are immigrants. Furthermore, given the institutional emphasis on access, resident multilingual writers and Generation 1.5 students are among the diverse population of students who enroll regularly in basic writing and composition classes in community colleges. At the same time, a trend that accompanies the growth of international students in community colleges—and one that reflects the rise of standard English as a global commodity—includes offering intensive English language programs specifically designed for international students.

As part of global economic restructuring, US community colleges are reaching out to—and, in some cases, aggressively marketing to—international students. They market their English product as an inexpensive commodity that international students can obtain on their two-year campuses before entering US universities. In doing so, they participate in what Min-Zhan Lu (2004) identifies as "a discourse of flexible accumulation" around English language instruction—English skills are advertised as commodities to be consumed and used in the service of a global free market (43–44). Approaching English as a commodity, this discourse

DOI: 10.7330/9780874219623.c012

of flexible accumulation illustrates a post-fordist restructuring, wherein communication and the emergence of a global language are intricately tied to the rise and globalization of capitalism (Fairclough 2002, 164).

In furthering the notion of English as a commodity, these community college programs reveal a monolingual approach to literacy acquisition, an approach that assumes the acquisition of only one language as the norm. Horner and Trimbur (2002) elaborate on the significance of this ideological disposition for the teaching of writing in the United States: it "purifies the social identity of U.S. Americans as English speakers, privileges the use of language as written English, and then charts the pedagogical and curricular development of language that points inexorably toward mastery of written English" (607). In other words, this monolingual approach to literacy perpetuates the myth of a homogenous English language; reinscribes the overvaluing of standard, edited English; and, subsequently, influences how we go about teaching writing. One unfortunate outcome of this process is that it can reinforce a writing curriculum that supports a reductive notion of literacy and literacy acquisition. As contemporary approaches to composition theory suggest, such reductive pedagogical approaches—which are often associated with a current–traditional pedadogy—do not work because they do not provide for a rhetorically situated understanding of language use and the production of academic writing. Consequently, students moving from such programs into college-level courses that demand students attend to and negotiate the expectations and writing conventions of different academic disciplines could very well be at a disadvantage.

In order to better understand this trend, and the curricular and pedagogical implications of these courses, I conducted a study of English language learning programs[1] at two-year colleges in the state of Washington. There are thirty-two two-year colleges within the state of Washington, twenty-eight community colleges and four technical colleges. Of the twenty-eight community colleges, four colleges provide ESL courses, but have no program designed specifically for international students. Though these four colleges do enroll international students, their ESL programs generally provide instruction for local immigrants. One college provides an intensive language program designed for international students, which it outsources to Kaplan. Of the remaining twenty-four colleges, each offers either an "English language learning program" (ELLP) or an "intensive English program" (IEP), in addition to ESL programs. These programs are offered as a curricular sequence embedded within broader international programs designed to accommodate international students specifically. For the purposes of this study, I focused on these latter twenty-four community colleges in order to examine how this monolingual ideology persists even within a transnational context.

Often, ESL and ELLP/IEP are housed in the same academic department, though this is not always the case. Beyond the fact that the programs cater to two distinct student populations, a few other distinguishing markers exist between the ESL and ELLP/IEP courses. In some cases, the ESL courses are offered at a significantly reduced rate as non-credit-bearing courses. In contrast, international students pay full tuition at the non-resident—sometimes even the non-resident/out-of-country—rate. For example, at one college, international students are charged approximately $9,000 per quarter for the equivalent of 12 credit hours, while students enrolled in ESL classes are charged $25 per quarter. Furthermore, while the ESL courses focus primarily on speaking, reading, grammar, and minimal writing—what I categorize as primarily a linguistic proficiency curriculum—the ELLP/IEP courses also include college writing preparation within their curricular sequence. While the curricula for the ELLP/IEP courses range from English linguistic proficiency (speaking/reading/grammar) to pre-college composition, I focus primarily on the pre-college writing courses in my extended analysis, since these are the courses wherein students are likely to be introduced to academic writing expectations and conventions.

While my focus was primarily on the rise of English language programs, my research methods included data gathering of programmatic materials from across the spectrum of literacy and writing instruction programs at each of the twenty-four colleges: ESL, ELL/IE, developmental/basic writing (in some cases including adult basic skills programs), and composition. The data I gathered included program descriptions and brochures, taken primarily from program websites; course descriptions, as provided in college catalogs; and course syllabi, when available. I cross-referenced data to examine patterns with respect to similarities and differences across course curricula, course goals and objectives, sequencing among courses, curricular transfer across programs, programmatic goals and objectives, and institutional positioning and location (i.e., where programs are housed) within the broader community college mission. In doing so, I approached the research with the following questions in mind: How do these programs fit within the community college mission and philosophy? How are the courses designed, and in what ways do they or do they not align with best practices in composition theory? What are the pedagogical implications of these distinct curricular and programmatic formations?

In what follows, I provide a description of the community college context and situate the emergence of ELLPs within the two-year college enterprise. Next, I examine how a discourse of flexible accumulation circulates in the brochures and webpage descriptions of IEPs at community colleges in Washington. This discourse of flexible accumulation treats English as a commodity, wherein "the acquisition of a language, whether a standardized or peripheralized English, is associated with the image of someone first buying or inheriting a ready-made, self-evident, discrete object—a tool (of communication) or a key (to success)—and then learning to use that object like an expert" (Lu 2004, 25). In particular, I look to map the ways in which this discourse professes English as a thing that might be acquired and (efficiently) used, primarily in the service of a global marketplace: a commodity. Subsequently, I move to articulate the ways in which this commodification shapes and influences the curricular and programmatic structures of English language instruction at these two-year institutions, and, as such, is complicit in furthering an autonomous literacy model founded upon a monolingual ideology. Given this context, I conclude with some recommendations for how WPAs at two-year colleges might approach their work in ways that resist this monolingual tendency and advocate for a more nuanced sense of literacy acquisition within their institutions.

THE TWO-YEAR COLLEGE

Community colleges are a rich resource for examining this complex process of literacy instruction because of the particular role they play in US higher education. Perhaps most notably, community colleges are open admissions institutions. Consequently, community colleges are often idealized as central to providing a point of access into higher education for nontraditional students. In a variation on what Harvey Graff (1979) has termed "the literacy myth," this idealized access to education is also assumed to confer social and economic mobility. However, the material realization of this promise of access is greatly compromised in a tiered and stratified educational system, a system wherein community colleges are located at the bottom of the hierarchy. How well community colleges are able to deliver on their promise of educational access—if they even succeed at all—is severely constrained by a number of circumstances that are realized in particular ways, including: how resources and funding are distributed, the legislative policies and politics unique to the two-year college, and the institutional mission, structures, and practices. In particular, community colleges are vulnerable to the creep of corporate practices into administrative and budget decision making. Thus, as Keven Doughtery (2001) notes, critics of the community college system have argued that, "although it may let in otherwise excluded students, the community college fails to deliver the educational and occupational opportunity it promises" (6).

In his 1960 study, educational sociologist Burton R. Clark described this phenomenon as the "cooling out" function of community colleges, which he portrayed as structural—on the one hand, students are admitted into the institution; on the other hand, a significant number of admitted students fail to obtain two-year degrees and/or transfer to four-year institutions. If students are not dismissed outright from the institution, they are discouraged from the transfer track and encouraged toward a vocational track (Clark 1960, 571–72). Clark argues that the community college system itself necessarily functions to sort and delay students along educational tracks. Following Clark, Doughtery (2001) complicates this structuralist perspective and identifies this consequence as the "contradictory nature" of the community college, tracing its emanation from the historical debate over the community college's originating mission and subsequent impact (44). As Anderson, Alfonso, and Sun (2006) note of Doughtery's analysis, "the contradictory nature of community colleges is attributed to the multiple goals and the different influences and forces, both ideological and economic, that constrain and shape the evolution of these institutions" (426). Thus, the community college's contradictory nature is not an outcome of design but rather effect. Literacy instruction within two-year colleges is deeply implicated in this debate because of the ways in which literacy standards can function as gatekeepers within educational institutions.

Perhaps the most notable and critiqued instance of this "cooling off" effect is represented in basic writing courses, often referred to as "remedial" or "developmental" writing instruction, within two-year college settings. Identified years ago by Albert Kitzhaber (1963, 7) as "sub- (and sometimes sub-sub) remedial English"—since multiple pre-college courses exist—these courses have historically carried no institutional credit and must be completed sequentially as prerequisites for FYC. For those students required to enroll in such courses, moving through this pre-college writing curriculum can significantly slow down their progress toward a degree. As Ira Shor (1997) has more recently remarked, these courses have "added an extra sorting-out gate in front of the comp gate, a curricular mechanism to secure unequal power relations" within higher education (92). Because multiple basic writing classes exist at community colleges, this gate-keeping function can significantly impact students.[2]

The rise of ELLPs/IEPs within two-year colleges might be seen as yet another manifestation of this remediation dilemma. On the one hand, in keeping with their mission to provide access to higher education, these open-admission institutions enroll international students, promising to provide them with the academic skills necessary to successfully perform within US institutions of higher education. On the other hand, they do so under a curricular structure of pre-college courses that segregate students from native English users, and within programs that often delay progress toward the degree. Certainly, similar to critiques of basic writing courses that follow this kind of mechanical, non-contextualized approach to literacy instruction,[3] such courses are founded upon an autonomous literacy model—a point I take up in more detail later in this chapter. For now, the point I want to make is that the rise of ELLPs within US community colleges must be situated in their history of remediation, which in turn must be understood with respect to the multiple and sometimes contradictory missions of such institutions as they exist within the broader political economy of US higher education.

At the same time, these programs must be understood within the context of the increasing competition for students across institutions of higher education. Whereas, historically, two-year colleges and four-year institutions tended to draw and admit distinctly different populations of students, the rise of for-profit postsecondary institutions, along with decreased state support for public four-year institutions, has meant that community colleges are now competing with four-year colleges and universities for student enrollment. These factors, according to educational theorist John S. Levin (2005)—alongside the community colleges' "have not" status in higher education and coupled with the cultural effects of neoliberalism—have resulted in an entrepreneurial culture among community colleges (11–12). Because of this competition for both students and resources, community colleges have shifted their goals and internal resources in favor of economic development, a shift that includes the expansion of ELLPs for international students (15).

Consequently, more and more international students are enrolling in US community colleges. As Crandall and Sheppard (2004) observe in their report, "international students seeking English instruction increasingly prefer community college programs because they are less expensive than those offered by either commercial English language schools or universities" (6). Indeed, the comparable 2010–2011 out-of-state tuition rates for public institutions of higher education in Washington confirm as much. Out-of-state tuition at four-year public schools ranged from $15,323 to $26,324, while out-of-state tuition at two-year public schools ranged from \$3,615 to \$9,588 (O'Leary 2010). Thus, the out-of-state savings for international students enrolling in Washington's community colleges is substantial. Subsequently, "from 2008 to 2009, community colleges experienced a 10.5 percent international student enrollment growth—the highest of any type of U.S. higher education institution" (Tellefeson, para. 6). Though enrollment has slowed some since 2008–2009, international student enrollment in US community colleges remains steady, with students from Vietnam, Mexico, Hong Kong, Nepal, and Indonesia disproportionately represented in particular (Clark, para. 6).

Because of their unique position—a position that highlights the ways in which the contradictory logic of capitalism functions in US higher education—community colleges evidence a particular kind of commodification within the broader political economy of higher education. While the rhetoric of democracy and access is often employed in describing this role of community colleges, the reality is that the mission and goals of community colleges are also constrained by outside forces (such as fast capitalism) and restructured from within in order to survive. In particular, as John S. Levin (2007) observes, the community college's historical emphasis on student access and community have recently altered due to globalization and neoliberalism, both of which contribute to the corporatization of higher education and the competition for students and resources among all post-secondary institutions. The growing emphasis on English language instruction is just one example of how community colleges have shifted their curricular focus toward the demands of a global economy. As discussed later, this shift necessarily impacts not only the curriculum, but also pedagogical approaches. In the following section, I examine descriptions of English language programs as portrayed through the brochures and websites of programs across Washington community colleges. In doing so, I trace the ways in which the discourse of flexible accumulation permeates the programs.

THE DISCOURSE OF FLEXIBLE ACCUMULATION AND MONOLINGUALISM

In their competition for students, community colleges often advertise as providing affordable education options in the increasingly expensive realm of higher education. This particular pitch is employed consistently to attract international students to Washington's community colleges. In most cases, affordability is bundled together with a number of other attributes to suggest that students will receive the best educational value at the two-year college. This list of attributes varies somewhat, but consistently includes such benefits as the opportunity to learn in small classes, and on campuses that are located in "safe" and "friendly" communities. Further items often highlighted include preparation for transfer to four-year schools, and often even conditional admittance to various local universities. Indeed, the international student brochure for one community college advises prospective students that "many students start at a community college in the United States because they offer smaller classes, more personal contact, and cost less than four-year universities." The pamphlet goes on to proclaim that "with careful planning, students can transfer to *any* university in the USA" (emphasis added). Thus, it is suggested that students are paying not just for an education; they are also investing in and procuring a certain quality of life—and lifestyle—when they decide to enroll in a US community college. They are accumulating both economic and cultural capital.

Embedded within this narrative of social and cultural mobility is the trope of American exceptionalism. In a number of these program descriptions, the community college experience is made to stand in synecdochically for the whole of the American education system, providing students with a superior educational experience. One institution observes that its "international students have transferred to many different universities, such as the University of Washington, Washington State University, Seattle University, University of Utah, Arizona State University, and the University of Oregon," while another institution lists "easy transfer to prestigious universities" among its promises to prospective international students. Stressing the portability of this English commodity, another campus advises that "students with a degree from an American University also have a better chance of getting a good job in their home country." Among this list of accruements, flexible access to English language instruction is emphasized. This flexible accumulation resembles post-fordist tendencies of production, whereby education is specialized and individualized to scale.

As noted above, in the state of Washington, twenty-four out of the thirty-four public two-year schools currently provide English language intensive programs. Eighteen of these programs are listed as featured programs at Community College U.S.A. (Study in the USA 2011). Echoing the discourse of flexible accumulation, these programs offer international students a variety of English language instructional options. All of them provide a sequence of classes and levels, and many offer three to five levels of instruction related to pre-college writing.

These levels range from beginning to introductory to advanced, with beginning most often being described as appropriate for students with very little or even no English skills.

Furthermore, most programs emphasize that TOEFL is not a prerequisite for enrollment, an additional benefit. As described in the informational materials for one intercity community college, "No official test score? No problem! Students can take a placement exam upon arrival." The description explaining why a minimum TOEFL score is accepted, but not required, at another urban community college further suggests that this option is to the student's advantage: "we prefer to assess your English once you arrive, and place you in the appropriate class. With the right class placement, your academic performance is likely to be better, therefore improving your chances of being admitted to a top university." In the discourse of flexible accumulation, even placement options are circulated as consumer goods, commodities that are carefully chosen and consumed in the interest of improving one's educational capital. One effect of this discourse is that it reinforces language use as a commodity, too.

This discourse of accumulation reflects one of the ways in which English now functions as a curricular economy within two-year institutions. With the inclusion of higher education in the General Agreement on Trade in Services (GATS), community colleges are particularly vulnerable to the reconfigurations of fast capitalism (United Nations Educational, Scientific, and Cultural Organization 2012). In the wake of community colleges' entrepreneurial restructuring, and the global response to English's rise in value, US community colleges are tailoring their educational programs in order to provide new consumers (international students) with a global product (standard English). What is at stake in this process is a cultural logic that reinscribes the standardization of English through what Horner and Trimbur (2002) identify as a monolingual ideology. Among other concerns, this monolingual ideology contributes to a reductive notion of how language is both acquired and used.

"A tacit language policy of unidirectional monolingualism," according to Horner and Trimbur (2002), "continues to exert a powerful influence on our teaching, our writing programs, and our impact on U.S. culture" (595). This influence is further fueled by the global economy and transnational politics that inform English's role as a global lingua franca. Undergirding monolingualism in the teaching of English is a privileging of "English" not only as a singular, static concept, but also as a standard for editing. As Matsuda (2006) explains, such a policy "makes moving students toward the dominant variety of English the only conceivable way of dealing with language issues in composition instruction" (637). In other words, a monolingualist approach affects both what is taught (standard, edited English) and how it is taught. Implicit within the monolingualist rhetoric of flexible accumulation is the assumption that literacy is a discrete skill and literacy acquisition can occur in a vacuum.

This particular positioning of literacy and literacy acquisition exposes what Brian Street (2003) has identified as an "autonomous" literacy model, a model that defines literacy simply as a static skill set to be cognitively mastered (78). Furthermore, the notion that literacy and literacy acquisition are "neutral," "universal," and "benign" is reinforced (77), which fails to recognize what Deborah Brandt (2001) describes as literacy sponsorship—the ways in which literacy is harnessed and managed for particular uses by particular forces (19–20). We see this model represented not only within the discourse of accumulation that pervades our ELLPs, but also within programs' course descriptions and course syllabi. As noted above, and similar to the ongoing practice of multiple, discrete levels of basic writing courses within two-year colleges, all of the programs in this study offer a number of English language learning courses that students must move through sequentially, based on their placement scores. Depending on placement, one program requires students to progress through up to four courses dealing explicitly with composition, what I would describe as remedial writing courses designated exclusively for international students: "Intermediate Writing and Applied Grammar," "Advanced Writing and Applied Grammar," "Upper Advanced Grammar," and "College Grammar Support."[4]

The curricular distinctions among these courses reproduce an autonomous literacy model in that they focus on elements of writing as discrete skills to be mastered before moving onto the next, presumed-to-be more complex task. The first two courses are distinguished in their curriculum by focusing on sentence and paragraph construction ("Intermediate Writing and Applied Grammar") and paragraph and essay construction ("Advanced Writing and Applied Grammar"). The third and fourth courses require concurrent enrollment in English composition. "Upper Advanced Grammar," which focuses on "grammar review and application to expository essays and informative summaries," requires concurrent enrollment in "Writing Fundamentals" (the pre-college writing course that directly precedes the FYC sequence), which focuses on expository writing, summarizing, and mechanics. "College Grammar Support," which focuses on "grammar review and application to writing persuasive essays, information summaries, and critiques of college-level articles," requires concurrent enrollment in "English Composition I" (the first in a sequence of three required FYC courses). In addressing sentence, paragraph, and essay construction as separate, sequentially-mastered skills, the curriculum reveals what Mike Rose (2011) and Joseph Harris (1995), among others, critique as a building-blocks, developmental approach to writing instruction (Harris 1995, 29; Rose 2011, para. 3). This approach is problematic and pedagogically ill-informed because it does not reflect an understanding of writing as a contextualized practice. And, as noted above, it risks unwittingly reinforcing a monolingual approach to language acquisition in higher education.

A syllabus for "Advanced Writing and Applied Grammar" further illustrates the characteristics of this autonomous literacy model. The objectives for the course are listed as follows:

1. Write introductions, conclusions, and transitions to create a clear line of thought in paragraphs and essays; ethically use academic documentation style to indicate quotation, paraphrase, and summary.

2. Write simple, compound, and complex sentences using complete, accurate word order, and appropriate verb tenses and punctuation.

3. Demonstrate clear improvement in identifying and editing individual problems of grammar and syntax in your writing.

While the curriculum does include revision as a means for accomplishing the above goals, it also approaches grammar instruction through isolated exercises, including a "particular emphasis on correction and practice of sentence-level grammar." In addition, the trajectory of the course moves from sentence types (topic sentences and conclusion sentences) to paragraph types to essay types, with an overarching emphasis on modes (narrative, compare/contrast, cause/effect, and argument). Not only is this literacy model implicated in the reproduction of a monolingual policy of English instruction by overemphasizing "correct," "accurate," and "standard" English, but is also reinforces a deficit model of literacy instruction. This deficit model ignores the other, sometimes multiple languages—and thus literacies—that international students bring to the classroom, consequently missing out on the opportunity to use them as "resources for producing meaning in writing, speaking, reading, and listening" (Horner et al. 2011, 303).

TRANSLINGUALISM AND WPA WORK

In a recent opinion piece published in *College English*, Horner, Lu, Royster, and Trimbur (2011) argue for a translingual approach to writing instruction. According to the authors, a translingual approach recognizes language difference and variation as a resource rather than a problem within the composition classroom. In contrast to a monolingual approach, this approach "acknowledges that deviations from dominant expectations need not be errors; that conformity need not be automatically advisable; and that writers' purposes and readers' conventional expectations are neither fixed nor unified" (304). In particular, they suggest that monolingual pedagogical and curricular structures that focus on mastery of language proficiency and use as discrete, static skills need to be revised in light of our field's understanding of language and literacy practices as varied, multiple, and fluid. Such an approach might serve as a useful framework for negotiating—and potentially reimaging—the programmatic and curricular structures that affect the teaching of writing at two-year colleges, particularly as it impacts international students. Jody Milward (2010), a two-year college professor and former chair of the Two-Year College English Association, agrees. In "Resistance to the 'English Only' Movement: Implications for Two-Year College Composition," she emphasizes the linguistically diverse student body of community colleges in general, as well as the pedagogical challenges associated with serving such a diverse student body. Milward notes that "problems with placement" and "a lack of integration between ELL levels and programs" make it difficult to address composition from a multilingual pedagogical approach (223). She further explains that the combination of a highly contingent faculty and a curriculum driven by textbooks compounds the problem (225).

In line with my own observations in this chapter, Milward (2010) argues that "composition scholars must pay more attention to ELL programs—from ESL noncredit to community college transfer to bachelor's degree—through cross-institutional collaborations" (223). In addition to advocating for multilingual-friendly pedagogies and assignments, Milward identifies a number of programmatic and institutional changes, including: requiring ELL preparation for composition instructors, ongoing professional development for faculty, support for interdepartmental collaboration, and reframing the public rhetoric that undergirds monolingualism. Along with Milward's valuable suggestions, I believe we need to revise the curricular structures that support monolingual pedagogies, such as revamping outdated program models and assessment practices that support (and are supported by) a monolingual approach to the teaching of writing.

It is important to note that in recent years the field of composition has impacted the teaching of English/writing in two-year colleges.

According to Nist and Raines (1995, 62), approximately half of all permanent faculty in community colleges are "newcomers" (recent hires through national searches), and—as is the case in universities—these new faculty members have studied in a climate in which training in composition pedagogies is often required, at least through one graduate seminar. I suggest that this phenomenon, at least in part, has impacted the ways in which composition and basic writing are taught at community colleges. For example, Washington community colleges have basic writing programs that are shaped after stretch models and linked learning communities. In keeping with an understanding of literacy instruction as social/material practice, I'd like to see more two-year programs develop these kinds of alternative models/structures, particularly in ESL and intensive language instruction programs. Doing so affords more possibility for supporting a rhetorical pedagogy that emphasizes English/Englishes as contextually situated and not universal.

Revision to programmatic structures necessarily means rethinking programmatic assessment practices as well. Rather than high-stakes assessment, such as end-of-term computer testing, I suggest instituting portfolio assessment, which has already been adopted in a number of FYC and basic writing classrooms across community colleges. While some critiques of portfolio assessment are understandably valid (including the ways in which "process" is easily commodified, thus rendering its intended pedagogical aims ineffective), these portfolios include, at the very least, multiple writing artifacts by which students' writing is assessed. Furthermore, with multiple writing artifacts being considered in portfolio assessment, English language learners in particular are better positioned to negotiate how they both use and make use of English/Englishes. Portfolio assessment is also useful in that it can easily function as an assessment "bridge" between programs, thereby providing a curricular foundation for sequencing and integration across programs, such as ELL and composition.

In elaborating a list of possibilities for supporting a translingual pedagogy, it becomes clear that such programmatic and institutional change does not manifest on its own. Even as individual faculty members attempt to implement a translingual pedagogy within their own classrooms, their efforts are often limited or even thwarted by curricular or programmatic policies that maintain a monolingual view of language instruction. Such pedagogical transformation, I argue, requires institutional agency, particularly in a climate where 67 percent of faculty are part-time (Bartholomae 2011, 13). This kind of agency might be afforded by a writing program administrator, since—as David Martins demonstrates in his introduction to this collection—WPAs are institutionally situated to reflect and act on the broader, more nuanced understandings of how transnational contexts inform and influence contemporary writing programs.

Identifying and supporting WPAs in two-year colleges, however, can be a complicated task. Given that two-year colleges often lack the institutional support and needed release time for WPA, Tim Taylor (2009) describes WPA at two-year colleges as necessarily collaborative and decentered, with writing program structures varied and often ad hoc in nature (128). As such, Jeffrey Klausman's (2008) observation that most community colleges lack WPAs and thus lack writing programs is significant (239). He suggests that, without a WPA, writing instruction at two-year colleges resembles a collection of classes rather than a coherent program. And, when we understand that writing instruction at two-year colleges is parceled across various programs, we can see how the problem of coherence might be magnified in this institutional context. Consequently, in order to provide better support for programmatic coherence and development, both Taylor and Klausman call for more institutional attention to writing program administration at two-year colleges. Such support might serve to facilitate interdepartmental dialogues about pedagogical best practices, as well as cross-institutional conversations and collaborations, all of which would surely contribute to improving institutional awareness and understanding of transnational contexts and pedagogies.

Interestingly, the above list of suggestions for supporting a translingual approach are echoed in Susan K. Miller-Cochran's (2010) identification of administrative practices that WPAs should follow as part of their professional obligation to students:

- Incorporate attention to second language writing issues into preparation of teaching assistants;

- Consider training and experience with second language writers as part of the standards for hiring faculty in writing programs;

- Incorporate these issues into the curriculum itself through pedagogical strategies. . . .

- Make second language writing part of the graduate curriculum for students specializing in rhetoric and composition. (217)

As Miller-Cochran observes, implementing such strategies to develop a curriculum that supports language diversity often requires significant structural and substantive change. And, as others have noted, WPAs are uniquely situated to enact such institutional change. Sue McLeod

(1995), for example, argues that WPAs can function as "change agents," bringing about curricular transformation through institutional and committee structures (113). Geoffrey Chase (2002), too, suggests that programmatic change requires a WPA in order to provide a "comprehensive, holistic approach that acknowledges how the various levels of any composition program are interconnected" and tied to the larger institution (244). In short, I argue that, because the important work of pedagogical and curricular reform cannot occur without attention to the institutional context, WPAs can function to mitigate the effects of English's globalization on writing programs and students; in doing so, they can serve to guide and facilitate a transnational approach to composition that takes language diversity seriously.

CONCLUSION

In "An Essay on the Work of Composition," Lu (2004) draws our attention to the ways in which English functions as a global commodity: "The pressure to acquire and use English," she writes, "is increasingly becoming a lived reality for peoples stratified by labels such as Native-Speaking, Educated, Developed Countries, or Democracy and their Others" (20). By pointing out the ways in which various uses of English are embedded in global capital, she reminds us that literacy functions as an economy, and that how literacies are valued—and devalued—constitutes a system of power. She goes on to argue that what we do in ESL instruction is implicated in this process, and that—more often than not—we adopt this commodity approach in our teaching (25). An understanding of how English language instruction functions in two-year colleges is an essential part of this discussion. Because a growing number of international students are enrolling in US community colleges, and because community colleges play a particularly significant role within US higher education as open-access institutions, they are an important site for investigating this process of literacy instruction and commodification within the US education system.

In providing the above analysis, I posit that college composition is necessarily a transnational enterprise within US higher education. As such, I depict two distinct configurations of transnational composition. First, drawing on the work of Bruce Horner, Min-Zhan Lu, John Trimbur, Paul Kei Matsuda, and others, I read the enterprise of transnational composition as an articulation of English as tied to global politics, and—at the very least—the acknowledgment of the ways in which standard English functions as a myth and as cultural–global capital. This acknowledgment is rooted in an understanding of how writing instruction in US higher education has evolved as a monolingual enterprise that functions to control language use through English-only assumptions and policies (Horner and Trimbur 2002, 594–95). And it is this manifestation of transnational composition in US community colleges that I move to critique.

Second, and perhaps more importantly, I articulate a critical approach to transnational composition as a strategic politic, a politic of "talking back" to the myth of standardized English and the accompanying mechanisms of language control. In this case, I move to contextualize transnational composition as a social/material practice, as a process shaped by materiality, history, and possibility. This politic affords opportunities for a more progressive pedagogy, one that attends to English/Englishes and embraces our field's understanding of language as epistemic, and a pedagogy more in line with what Horner, Lu, Royster, and Trimbur (2011) describe as a translingual approach (303). Therefore, I also speculate on how such a pedagogy might be realized within the specific sociomaterial conditions of the twenty-first century, US community colleges, and their various writing program structures. Crucial to the implementation and maintenance of a successful translingual pedagogy is an understanding of the ways in which distinct institutional and programmatic structures, policies, and practices might both limit and support pedagogical reform. In closing, I suggest that transnational composition can function as a kind of generative politicizing and potential reshaping of the various material structures and sites of literacy instruction that occur on two-year campuses. An integral part of realizing such work is a critical engagement with writing program administration as both an apparatus and an agent for change.

Notes

1. Some colleges identify their programs as "English language learning programs," whiles others use the term "intensive language programs" instead. I use both interchangeably throughout this chapter.
2. See, for example, Adams, Gearhart, Miller, and Roberts' (2009) study of student attrition in basic writing classes at their two-year institution.
3. For example, see Adler-Kassner and Harrington (2002), Carter (2008), and Rose (2011).
4. Additional course requirements for speaking, reading, and grammar exist. However, since my focus is on composition, I have limited my analysis to courses that directly address pre-college-level and college-level writing instruction.

References

Adams, Peter, Sarah Gearhart, Robert Miller, and Anne Roberts. 2009. "The Accelerated Learning Program: Throwing Open the Gates." *Journal of Basic Writing* 28 (2): 50–69.

Adler-Kassner, Linda, and Susanmarie Harrington. 2002. *Basic Writing as a Political Act: Public Conversations About Writing and Literacy.* Creskill. Hampton Press.

Anderson, Gregory M., Mariana Alfonso, and Jeffrey C. Sun. 2006. "Rethinking Cooling Out at Public Community Colleges: An Examination of Fiscal and Demographic Trends in Higher Education." *Teachers College Record* 108 (3): 422–51. http://dx.doi.org/10.1111/j.1467-9620.2006.00657.x.

Bartholomae, David. 2011. "Teaching on and off the Tenure Track: Highlights from the ADE Survey of Staffing Patterns in English." *Pedagogy* 11 (1): 7–32. http://dx.doi.org/10.1215/15314200-2010-012.

Brandt, Deborah. 2001. *Literacy in American Lives.* Cambridge: Cambridge University Press. http://dx.doi.org/10.1017/CBO9780511810237.

Carter, Shannon. 2008. *The Way Literacy Lives: Rhetorical Dexterity and Basic Writing Instruction.* Albany: State University of New York Press.

Chase, Geoffery. 2002. "Redefining Composition, Managing Change, and the Role of the WPA." In *The Allyn & Bacon Sourcebook for Writing Program Administrators*, ed. Irene Ward and William J. Carpenter, 243–51. New York: Longman.

Clark, Burton C. 1960. "The Cooling-Out Function in Higher Education." *American Journal of Sociology* 65 (6): 569–76. http://dx.doi.org/10.1086/222787.

Clark, Nick. "Internationalizing the Community College Campus." World Education News & Reviews 25 (9). *http://www.wes.org/ewenr/12oct/practical.htm.* Accessed May 4, 2012.

Crandall, JoAnn, and Ken Sheppard. 2004. *Adult ESL and the Community College.* New York: Council for Advancement of Adult Literacy.

Doughtery, Kevin J. 2001. *The Contradictory College: The Conflicts, Origins, Impacts, and Futures of the Community College.* Albany: State University of New York Press.

Fairclough, Norman. 2002. "Language in New Capitalism." *Discourse & Society* 13 (2): 163–66. http://dx.doi.org/10.1177/0957926502013002404.

Graff, Harvey J. 1979. *The Literacy Myth: Literacy and Social Structure in the Nineteenth Century City.* New York: Academic Press.

Harris, Joseph. 1995. "Negotiating the Contact Zone." *Journal of Basic Writing* 14 (1): 27–42.

Horner, Bruce, Min-Zhan Lu, Jacqueline Jones Royster, and John Trimbur. 2011. "Language Difference in Writing: Toward a Translingual Approach." *College English* 73 (3): 303–21.

Horner, Bruce, and John Trimbur. 2002. "English Only and U.S. College Composition." *College Composition and Communication* 53 (4): 594–630. http://dx.doi.org/10.2307/1512118.

Kitzhaber, Albert R. 1963. *The Two-Year College & the Teaching of English: A Report of the Incoming President of the National Council of Teachers of English to the Executive Committee, November 1963. Champagne.* NCTE.

Klausman, Jeffrey. 2008. "Mapping the Terrain: The Two-Year College Writing Program." *Teaching English in the Two-Year College* 35 (March): 238–51.

Levin, John S. 2005. "The Business Culture of the Community College: Students as Consumers; Students as Commodities." *New Directions for Higher Education* 129 (Spring): 11–26. http://dx.doi.org/10.1002/he.169.

Levin, John S. 2007. *Nontraditional Students and Community Colleges: The Conflict of Justice and Neoliberalism.* New York: Palgrave Macmillan. http://dx.doi.org/10.1057/9780230607286.

Lu, Min-Zhan. 2004. "An Essay on the Work of Composition: Composing English against the Order of Fast Capitalism." *College Composition and Communication* 56 (1): 16–50. http://dx.doi.org/10.2307/4140679.

Matsuda, Paul Kei. 2006. "The Myth of Linguistic Homogeneity in U.S. College Composition." *College English* 69 (6): 637–51. http://dx.doi.org/10.2307/25472180.

McLeod, Susan. 1995. "The Foreigner: WAC Directors as Agents of Change." In *Resituating Writing: Constructing and Administrating Writing Programs*, ed. Joseph Janangelo and Kristine Hansen, 108–16. Portsmouth: Boynton/Cook.

Milward, Jody. 2010. "Resistance to the 'English Only' Movement: Implications for Two-Year College Composition." In *Cross-Language Relations in Composition*, ed. Bruce Horner, Min-Zhan Lu, and Paul Kei Matsuda, 221–29. Carbondale: Southern Illinois UP.

Miller-Cochran, Susan K. 2010. "Language Diversity and the Responsibility of the WPA." In *Cross Language Relations in Composition*, ed. Bruce Horner, Min-Zhan Lu, and Paul Kei Matsuda, 221–29. Carbondale: Southern Illinois UP.

Nist, Elizabeth A., and Helon H. Raines. 1995. "Two-Year Colleges: Expanding and Claiming Our Majority." In *Resituating Writing: Constructing and Administrating Writing Programs*, ed. Joseph Janangelo and Kristine Hansen, 59–70. Portsmouth: Boynton/Cook.

O'Leary, Brian. 2010. "Tuition over Time, 1999, 2010." *Chronicle of Higher Education.* October 28. http://chronicle.com/article/Interactive-Tool-Tuition-Over/125043/.

Rose, Mike. 2011. "Remediation at the Crossroads." Editorial. *Inside Higher Education* 21 (April). https://www.insidehighered.com/views/2011/04/21/rose_remedial_education_at_a_crossroads

Shor, Ira. 1997. "Our Apartheid: Writing Instruction and Inequity." *Journal of Basic Writing* 16 (1): 91–104.

Street, Brian. 2003. "What's 'New' in Literacy Studies? Critical Approaches to Literacy in Theory and Practice." *Current Issues in Comparative Education* 5 (2): 77–91.

Study in the USA. 2011. "Featured Programs." Community Colleges USA, http://communitycollegesusa.com/en/schools/featured-programs/. Accessed July 1, 2011.

Taylor, Tim. 2009. "Writing Program Administration at the Two-Year College: Ghosts in the Machine." *WPA: Writing Program Administration* 32 (3): 120–39.

Tellefesen, Robyn. 2011. "Interest in Vocational Training is Up Among International Students." *My Global Education.* http://www.myglobaleducation.com/article/v/16132/interest-vocational-education-is-up-among-international/. Accessed July 10, 2011.

United Nations Educational, Scientific, and Cultural Organization. 2012. "Basic Information on GATS," Studying Abroad, http://www.unesco.org/education/studyingabroad/highlights/global_forum/gats_he/basics_he_trade_main.shtml. Accessed May 4, 2012.

13

FROM "EDUCATING THE OTHER" TO CROSS-BOUNDARY KNOWLEDGE-MAKING
Globally Networked Learning Environments as Critical Sites of Writing Program Administration

Doreen Starke-Meyerring

We never educate directly, but indirectly by means of the environment. Whether we permit chance environments to do the work, or whether we design environments for the purpose makes a great difference.
—John Dewey (1961, 19)

Writing program administration, like teaching, is a political act with consequences.
—Strickland and Gunner (2009, xiii)

From its beginnings as scholarly work, writing program administration has been understood—in Bruffee's (1978) prescient words—as "not managerial, but directly educational," as deeply concerned with, in a Deweyan (1961) sense, designing environments and conditions that allow for and facilitate student learning. From the beginning, writing program administrators have understood that this educational mission is highly political—that it involves daily struggle and activism to bring about the institutional change that allows for new learning environments to emerge and take hold. Indeed, early on in his editorial explaining the need for a Council for Writing Program Administrators, Bruffee urged us to pay attention to "the limitations built in structurally" in institutions that greatly influence the teaching and learning of writing (7). As a result, WPAs have a long history of activism dedicated to this daily struggle in their roles as change agents, politicians, and leaders (Adler-Kassner 2008; Hesse 2002; McLeod 1995; 2007). Strickland and Gunner (2009) capture this political nature of WPA

DOI: 10.7330/9780874219623.c013

work by describing it—like teaching and writing—as "a political act with consequences" (xiii).

As I show in this chapter, it is these traditions of WPA work—the long standing commitment to student learning environments, and the concomitant deep sense of the political nature and institutional struggle involved in that commitment—that position WPAs particularly well for re-envisioning learning environments in globalizing higher education, both within rhetoric and writing studies programs and, importantly, across the university. As I argue, globalization in higher education is, in many ways, about the daily struggle at the heart of WPA work—it is about how, in Dewey's (1961) and Bruffee's (1978) sense, learning environments will be designed, what kind of learning they will facilitate, who gets to participate, who is learning with/from whom, and whose knowledge counts. In globalizing higher education, I suggest, the daily struggle of WPA work evolves around these questions: To what extent will normalized and habitual "common-sense" local ways of knowing and learning be reproduced in traditional courses packaged for one-way sales in online or offshore global markets? Or, to what extent will they be opened up for mutual inquiry and collaboration in globally networked learning environments (GNLEs), that is, learning environments that rest on robust partnerships extending across institutional, linguistic, national, or other boundaries in order to facilitate faculty and student participation in the shaping of an emerging global social and economic order (Starke-Meyerring 2005; 2010; Starke-Meyerring, Duin, and Palvetzian 2007; Starke-Meyerring and Wilson 2008)?

Teachers and scholars of writing have been at the forefront of the struggle over the shape of learning environments in globalizing higher education, and consequently they have begun to develop partnered courses and programs, often from the grassroots and in the face of considerable local, institutional inertia and constraints (e.g., Anderson et al. 2010; Boehm, Kurthen, and Aniola-Jedrzejek 2010; Crabtree et al. 2008; Du-Babcock and Varner 2008; Dubinsky 2008; Herrington 2004; 2005; 2008; 2010; Herrington and Tretyakov 2005; Kennon 2008; Maylath, Vandepitte, and Mousten 2008; McNair and Paretti 2010; McNair, Paretti, and Kakar 2008; Mousten, Vandepitte, and Maylath 2008; Paretti and McNair 2008; Paretti, McNair, and Holloway-Attaway 2007; Rainey, Smith, and Barnes 2008; Sapp 2004; Starke-Meyerring and Andrews 2006; 2010; Zhu et al., 2005). These emerging, partnered learning environments provide the inspiration for this chapter because they constitute critical sites for WPA as they offer important opportunities for re-seeing writing programs and WPA work in globalizing higher education.

Like much WPA work, these learning environments are intensely political; in Scott's (2009) words, they are "deeply interwoven with the broad organizational, economic, and political aspects of the business of higher education" (54). And, particularly important for GNLEs as intercultural encounters extend beyond institutional boundaries, that business is "deeply embedded in and framed by the symbolic and material conditions of neo/colonization, imperialism and globalization" (Sorrells 2011, 180). For WPA work, attention to these broader geopolitical conditions is vital because neoliberal global policies, such as those of the World Trade Organization, have rendered higher education a privatized commodity to be traded in global markets. At the same time, the neoliberal redirection of public funds away from public institutions, such as higher education, has pushed institutions and programs to position themselves in global markets with expansionist initiatives for the purpose of revenue generation from international tuition dollars. Writing programs often hold the key to success for such expansionist projects, specifically for the participation of international students enrolled in them. After all, those students are largely evaluated on their writing, of course—the extent to which they comply with the discursive disciplinary norms of Western academic traditions. Given the role writing programs play in these contexts, WPAs may increasingly be called upon to ensure and facilitate these processes of assimilation within global expansionist projects.

It is in light of these pressures that, I think, emerging GNLEs offer an important and timely critical space for pause and reflection. These GNLEs raise important questions for the study and teaching of writing in higher education and, thus, for WPA work: How might we understand the situatedness of writing programs in the struggle over the neoliberal globalization project? What opportunities do emerging GNLEs offer to help us explore and rethink the roles writing programs can play in globalizing higher education? What new questions do they raise for the study and teaching of writing, as well as for WPA work?

In addressing these questions, the purpose of this chapter is rather modest: it is not to provide interventions or prescriptive recommendations for WPA work in the context of globalization, or even specifically for the design of GNLEs; rather, in the spirit of this book, my purpose here is to pause and reflect on emerging learning environments for the possibilities they offer in the study and teaching of writing in globalizing higher education. In exploring these questions, I hope to contribute to existing dialogue about what the study and teaching of writing can do in this context, as well as what implications these possibilities have for WPA work. Specifically, I argue that GNLEs can offer alternative spaces to traditional expansionist transmission models of "educating the Other" (Luke 2010) as they are reproduced in the current neoliberal globalization of higher education. To tease out the ways in which GNLEs allow us to imagine these alternatives, I first briefly sketch some of the geopolitical conditions of the neoliberal globalization project and the ways in which it has pushed for expansionist models in the global marketization of higher education. I then highlight some of the dimensions of GNLEs that allow us to explore their potential as alternatives to expansionist projects and to position and re-see writing programs as critical sites of WPA work in globalizing higher education.

GNLES AND WPA WORK AS SITUATED IN THE GEO-POLITICS OF NEOLIBERAL GLOBALIZATION

In order to explore ways in which GNLEs offer alternatives to dominant practices of globalization in higher education, it is first important to situate GNLEs as critical sites for WPA work in the geopolitics of neoliberal globalization. As Scott (2009) observes, neoliberal policies are familiar to WPAs as they have placed higher education and writing programs in situations "in which legislative mandates and budgetary restraints increasingly discipline every decision-making at all levels of public institutions" (54). Scott goes on to list some of the consequences for higher education and writing programs, which are worth quoting at length as they highlight important characteristics of the institutional environments in which WPAs reside and GNLEs have been emerging. Specifically, Scott points to "a gradual rise in academic administration, paralleled by a decline in tenure-track faculty as a proportion of total faculty; movement toward cheaper instruction that involves raising the number of students in each class; increasing efficiencies through distance education programs; expanding the numbers of courses taught by non-tenured faculty; and increased pressure on faculty from all disciplines to seek external funding for research" (54). These shifting conditions are also part of the larger neoliberal globalization project, which has shaped higher education in profound ways and has important implications for the roles of writing programs in this process, therefore requiring our close attention.

Much has been written about neoliberal globalization as a corporate and state-driven sociopolitical and economic project, which goes far beyond what can be discussed in this chapter. For the purpose of historicizing and situating GNLES as alternate, critical sites of WPA, it is important to note that, perhaps not accidentally, the emergence of

WPA scholarship coincides temporally with the emergence of the neo-liberal globalization project. Trimbur (2009), for example, traces the emergence of WPA as "a recognizable form of academic work" (vii) to the 1970s and 1980s, a time period that has also been identified as the recognizable beginnings of the neoliberal globalization project (Giroux 2004; Harvey 2007; Scholte 2005). Trimbur describes that period as a time of tension between democratizing projects, such as the open admissions movement pushed for by civil rights and the Reagan-era return to unconstrained and anti-democratic capitalism. Ever since, in one way or another, the neoliberal globalization project—with its many dimensions—has deeply impacted WPA work, as Adler-Kassner (2008) indicates, for example, in tracing the "accountability" shift in higher education institutions to that same time period.

The 1980s also marked the end of the Cold War, and thus the failure of twentieth-century attempts (in some parts of the world) to construct alternative forms of social organization in capitalism. Throughout much of the second half of the twentieth century, those attempts spurred the socialization and placing of public constraints on capital, for example, in the form of labor or environmental protection laws, social security, public welfare, public access to higher education, etc. Surfacing toward the end of the Cold War, then, the project of neoliberal globalization has largely been about the reversal of this socialization and the removal of public constraints on capital. Accordingly, the project has been characterized by the reduction or even removal of public influence and policies that might impede profits—including policies regulating investment, policies securing environmental and labor rights protection, or programs facilitating social justice—as well as the redirection of public funds away from public institutions serving the public good (Giroux 2004; Harvey 2007; Marginson 2007; Scholte 2005). This link between the desocialization of capital and the end of the Cold War is important because it suggests that the neoliberal project is not a short-lived phase, but rather a return to desocialized capitalism. Accordingly, the tensions and struggles Trimbur (2009) identifies between democratizing projects and anti-democratic, desocialized capitalism will likely intensify, with GNLEs an important site in this struggle.

Much of this struggle has been shaped by two trends. First, the battle for public participation in democratic deliberation, since much deliberation and decision making about public policy has been moved to global economic institutions—such as the WTO—and taken behind closed doors (Stiglitz 2006; della Porta et al. 2006), including decisions about turning higher education into a globally-traded, privatized service industry

(Bassett 2006; Verger 2009). For rhetoric and writing studies, a field that has traditionally understood its subject matter as involving the facilitation of citizen participation in democratic deliberation and decision making, this exclusion of the public from global decision making, especially concerning higher education, has been particularly problematic.

Second, the inclusion of higher education in global trade agreements was driven by a push for global market expansion. Accordingly, hundreds of millions of public and private dollars were invested in establishing mostly Western or Western-dominated higher education marketing consortia and e-learning initiatives, such as Fathom or UK eUniversity, which largely reproduced existing courses and programs for online delivery and sales in global markets (Marginson 2004). These initiatives generally used an expansionist model of globalizing higher education, a model that, as Luke (2010) notes, continues the colonial tradition of "educating the Other." According to Luke, this tradition has its roots in the eighteenth–twentieth-century efforts of colonial powers to train colonial subjects "with the requisite bodily disposition, cultural traits, linguistic facility and technical expertise to represent empire and, where needed, to build colonial infrastructure and operate its institutions" (46).

The purpose of these global marketing consortia was mainly to sell Western higher education courses and programs, usually in one direction—from the anglophone West to what were perceived to be profitable emerging markets, most notably in Asia. As Marginson (2004) notes, most of these initial global marketing consortia have since failed and closed down, but the expansionist vision of selling higher education in global markets continues to dominate decision making, and can be expected to remain prominent as public funds continue to be redirected away from public institutions (Marginson 2007; Rhoads and Torres 2007; Torres 2008).

As Selfe (1999) argues, traditional expansionist models of global learning in higher education are certainly worth our close attention. Most important, these models approximate educational colonization as they repackage local courses and programs online for global sales, despite their situatedness in the geopolitical and institutional contexts in which they were designed, thus reproducing, legitimizing, and advancing assumptions, values, and knowledge-making practices that largely serve the needs and interests of these contexts. This is not to say that there are no multidirectional relationships or diverse ways in which the expansionist model is taken up in geopolitical locations, such as through selective adoption, adaptation, or resistance. Rather, this model remains rooted in an expansionist global market.

Continued during the Cold War, particularly by Cold-War superpowers, the expansionist transmission model of "educating the Other" was largely motivated by the then prominent imperative to form international subject positions in line with dominant Cold War ideologies. As Luke (2010) points out, with the end of the Cold War, the main motivation for expansionist models of "educating the Other" shifted to outperform an ideological competitor focused on revenue generation. In the context of neoliberal globalization, with its redirection of funds away from public institutions, that motivation will likely continue to provide the larger geopolitical context for both GNLEs and WPA work in globalizing higher education, which raises an important question: How can writing programs position themselves in relation to the neoliberal globalization of higher education, and, specifically, what opportunities might GNLEs offer for this purpose?

BEYOND "EDUCATING THE OTHER": GNLES AS ALTERNATIVES IN RHETORIC AND WRITING STUDIES

GNLEs offer alternative approaches to the one-way, expansionist sale of higher education in global markets by creating collaborative, partnered learning environments for mutual inquiry. Rhetoric and writing studies faculty have taken richly diverse approaches to the design of such partnered learning environments, ranging from civic engagement projects with local community organizations to partnered online course environments to entire international joint degree programs across universities and across national boundaries. These learning environments exhibit a number of dimensions that offer new opportunities for repositioning and rethinking writing programs in globalizing higher education. I focus here on five dimensions that are particularly useful for this purpose, and that also constitute key areas of WPA work: (1) the geopolitical dimension, (2) the pedagogical/collaborative dimension, (3) the language dimension, (4) the technological dimension, and (5) the structural–institutional dimension. All of these dimensions reflect continua rather than either/or dichotomies.

Geopolitical Dimension: Toward a Multifaceted Geopolitic of Rhetoric and Writing

One dimension that has come to characterize partnered learning environments designed to address questions of globalization is the geopolitical situatedness of partners, including their geopolitical location.

While many faculty have developed partnerships across national bound-aries (e.g., Anderson et al. 2010; Boehm, Kurthen, and Aniola-Jedrzejek 2010; Du-Babcock and Varner 2008; Herrington and Tretyakov 2005; Maylath, Vandepitte, and Mousten 2008; McNair and Paretti 2010; Rainey, Smith, and Barnes 2008; Sapp 2004; Starke-Meyerring and Andrews 2006; Zhu et al. 2005), others have worked with partners in local communities (Dubinsky 2008), and a few have begun to integrate local community partners and partners in other national locations (Crabtree et al. 2008). Working with the local community, Dubinsky (2008), for example, has extended his proposal and report writing course to include community activists and immigrants through a part-nership with the local YMCA in an effort to overcome the isolation of immigrant women and facilitate their integration into the community. This partnered learning environment allows students in his course to experience the rhetorical work of proposals and reports in creating a shared understanding among local community activists, immigrants, and funding associations, and ultimately mobilize the resources needed to act on this understanding and implement programs that facilitate immigrant integration into the community.

Others have built partnered learning environments to connect with students and colleagues across national borders. Working within the context of developmental and introductory composition and English for Specific Purposes (ESP) courses, the Sharing Cultures Project, for example, brings together students from a developmental writing course in the United States, an academic writing course in South Africa, and an English course for law students in Russia to collaborate on vari-ous course projects in ways that allow students to probe and engage dominant narratives of national identities (Blum Malley, Ruiters, and Gulyaeva 2011). Similarly, the Cross-Cultural Rhetoric Project (2014) provides a partnered learning environment for students from univer-sities in the United States, Sweden, and other countries (Alfano 2009; O'Brien and Eriksson 2010).

Working in the context of a professional communication and trans-lation program, the Transatlantic Project likewise brings together tech-nical communication students and faculty from the United States and translation students and faculty from several European countries in online partnered learning environments. These students and faculty collaborate on a writing and translation project in order to examine locally-situated cultural assumptions and the work their texts do in local environments (Maylath, Vandepitte, and Mousten 2008; Mousten, Vandepitte, and Maylath 2008). Along similar lines, linking students in a technical communication course at a US university with students in an "English for engineers" course in Sweden, Anderson, Bergman, Bradley, Gustafsson, and Matzke (2010) devote their GNLE work to facilitating the participation of students in practices of online peer review as a way of developing new and alternative perspectives on their work.

Similarly, the Global Classroom Project brings together technical communication students in the United States with students from across disciplines in Russian universities to collaborate on joint research projects in a digital communication course (Herrington 2004; 2005; 2008; 2010; Herrington and Tretyakov, 2005; Kennon 2008). Engineering communication faculty have also designed transnational collaborative online learning environments across disciplines to help students learn how to critically assess language practices and technology designs in order to build productive relational spaces and shared practices for online collaborative work (McNair and Paretti 2010; McNair, Paretti, and Kakar 2008; Paretti and McNair 2008; Paretti, McNair, and Holloway-Attaway 2007). Business communication faculty have also taken advantage of digital technologies to build partnered learning environments that facilitate collaborative projects among students across national borders (Du-Babcock and Varner 2008; Starke-Meyerring and Andrews, 2006; 2010; Zhu et al. 2005).

While a large number of partnered learning environments operate across national boundaries, some partnerships involve activities that both extend across national boundaries and connect with local communities. Crabtree, Sapp, Malespín, and Norori (2008), for example, describe a comprehensive partnership initiative between a US university and a Nicaraguan university, in which the professional writing program and the communication program play an important role. Centered on their institutions' shared missions of promoting social justice and civic engagement, this partnership includes multiple components—ranging from faculty development to faculty and student exchange to course and program development for civic engagement—with US and Nicaraguan students collaborating on civic engagement projects with local poor communities in Nicaragua and in the United States. Crabtree and her colleagues situate their geopolitical decisions explicitly in the struggle for global social justice in an effort to counteract the consequences of "the colonial history, market bias, and corporate monopolistic character of contemporary . . . globalization" (Crabtree et al. 2008, 88).

As Crabtree and her colleagues indicate, the geopolitical dimension of GNLEs—situated in the struggle over the neoliberal globalization project—allows us to imagine ways in which writing courses and programs can move beyond traditional thinking in "national/international," "us/them," "global/local" and other binaries that undergird expansionist initiatives and international programs. Rather than internationalization, GNLEs allow us to address the struggle over competing visions of an emerging global and social/economic order and to explore how those visions are articulated, shaped, quelled, or contested within or across different geopolitical locations. In other words, they offer new ways for writing programs to explore and collaboratively address the questions raised by the neoliberal globalization project about public interest, social justice, and public participation in democratic decision making. In shifting beyond traditional internationalist thinking, as Dubinsky (2008) illustrates, those questions may well need to be addressed in local communities.

Whether conceived within and/or across geopolitical locations, GNLEs offer new opportunities for students to question dominant narratives underpinning global neoliberal agendas within their communities and beyond. Herrington's ten years of work with the Global Classroom Project (Herrington, 2004; 2005; 2008; 2010; Herrington and Tretyakov 2005; Kennon 2008), for example, illustrates the ways in which students work with peers in diverse geopolitical locations to question and reframe dominant narratives of global events, wars, economic crises, or the environmental exploitation presented in national media outlets. Working with faculty and students in Russian and US universities, the Global Classroom Project, for example, engaged in a deliberate effort to overcome dominant Cold-War enemy narratives, helping students probe such dominant narratives and build relationships that transcend them. Moreover, whether the students work together to study the debate surrounding genetically modified foods pushed by transnational corporations in Europe and the United States, or whether they examine the representations (or the absence thereof) in Russian and US media of the contested exploitation of natural resources and environmental destruction on Russia's Sakhalin Island by Western oil companies, they learn vital lessons in rhetoric and writing and, thus, in participation in global environments, such as how competing local and global interests are advanced rhetorically and with what consequences for local communities and beyond.

As these examples suggest, GNLEs may allow us to not only move beyond "internationalization" with its nationalist "us versus them" binaries, but may also provide opportunities for probing normalized nationalist narratives that often go unquestioned in traditional "international" thinking, programming, and curriculum design. Yet, as Stuart Hall

(1996) argues, "ideas of 'national identity' and 'national greatness' are intimately bound up with imperial supremacy, tinged with racist connotations, and underpinned by a four-century-long history of colonization, world market supremacy, imperial expansion and global destiny over native peoples" (43). GNLEs, then, can open up new spaces for mutual inquiry into such narratives and the interests they serve.

Although sketched only in broad strokes here, the geopolitical dimension of GNLEs provides rich and exciting opportunities for imagining and positioning writing courses and programs in relation to the neoliberal globalization project, as well as for facilitating the participation of students and faculty in the democratic deliberation of an emerging global social and economic order. At the same time, it seems that current events—from "Occupy" movements around the world to worldwide student protests against the increasing neoliberal privatization of higher education—provide both ample urgency and opportunity for imagining such partnered curricula and the pedagogies and collaborations that make them possible.

Pedagogical/Collaborative Dimension: From "Educating the Other" to Cross-Boundary Knowledge-Making

As the previous examples illustrate, GNLEs involve collaboration among both faculty and students within and/or across geopolitical locations to explore and engage in the geopolitics of globalization. This partnership may evolve around shared and/or separate pedagogical goals, but, regardless, it is this grounding in partnership and collaborative pedagogy that bestows the greatest potential on GNLEs as critical sites for reimagining the study and teaching of writing in globalizing higher education, and for realizing—or even extending—the potential offered by their geopolitical dimension. In other words, it is their pedagogical dimension that offers the greatest potential to challenge the dominant expansionist transmission model of "educating the Other" and of envisioning collaborative alternatives.

Important for WPA work, this potential is deeply rooted in our disciplinary understanding of rhetoric and writing as regularized rhetorical practices through which subject positions, power relations, hierarchies, and social worlds are produced, maintained, reproduced, and normalized. That normalization, as we have learned, is the work of regularized discourse or genres, which human collectives (e.g., institutions, organizations, communities) develop and organize over time in order to produce the desired or privileged outcomes, along with the social hierarchies, power relations, and subject positions needed to produce those outcomes (Bawarshi and Reiff 2010; Bazerman, Bonini, and Figueiredo 2009; Coe, Lingard, and Teslenko 2002).

As many writing studies researchers have pointed out, it is the habitual and repeated nature of these practices—their rootedness in habit, routine, and tradition; their deep implication in the reproduction of locally-situated sociocultural and material conditions as well as subject positions—that make them appear normal, commonsensical, and beyond questioning (e.g., Coe et al. 2002; Paré 2002). As such, they normalize the activities, the power relationships, and the ways in which knowledge is produced, or, whose knowledge or what kinds of evidence are acceptable. As Paré (2002) notes, however, the normalcy of the genres in which we participate occasionally becomes "cracked," visible, and available for inquiry. According to Paré, such disruptions of the status quo occur, for example, "when an event occurs that does not match the anticipated, socially construed exigence to which the genre responds; or, . . . when the genre is stretched too wide, and its forms and actions are inappropriate or ill-suited to the occasion . . .; [or] when newcomers first begin to participate in a genre and find it 'unnatural'" (61). In GNLEs, such opportunities for critical inquiry into the status quo emerge when we encounter and explore alternative genres that organize, reproduce, and normalize the ways of thinking, writing, and doing in diverse geopolitical locations.

This critical work of inquiring into normalized ways of knowing, doing, and being is at the heart of GNLEs. Indeed, GNLEs can offer purposefully designed spaces for this work—spaces that make the normalcy of local genres available for inquiry and negotiation when participants bring to their encounters their normalized, locally-situated ways of writing and knowing and at the same time experience alternative genres that organize, reproduce, and normalize the ways of thinking, writing, knowing, and doing in different geopolitical locations. In other words, through partnership and collaboration, GNLEs can open up local institutional frameworks for what I call cross-boundary knowledge-making—that is, for mutual inquiry into the understanding, questioning, re-seeing, and negotiation of normalized, locally-bounded ways of knowing, doing, and being that (re)produce, organize, and normalize the activities of the communities, institutions, and disciplines in which we participate. That mutual inquiry into and negotiation of normalized practices in turn allow us to draw upon diverse ways of knowing and develop shared practices for knowledge-making across boundaries of habitual, locally-situated contexts.

In GNLEs, then, it is the convergence of partnership, collaboration, and our rhetorical understanding of how "common sense" is produced, maintained, and questioned that bestows GNLEs with their potential as alternative critical sites for re-envisioning both writing programs specifically and higher education more generally. Unlike the one-directional transmission model of "educating the Other," GNLEs open up the boundaries between courses, institutions, and communities for collaboration and new ways of teaching, learning, and knowing.

Understood as participating in the geopolitics of globalization and as a vehicle for new ways of questioning and negotiating knowledge, GNLEs can take us beyond traditional notions of increasing diversity, fostering intercultural awareness, or learning about the Other/Other cultures. Indeed, any classroom will be populated with students committed or subjected to a diverse range of identity narratives across lines of gender, sexuality, race, nation, religion, language, class, and more. However, while traditional classrooms expect students to work within the dominant pedagogical and institutional framework of a local course, GNLEs can open up that framework for cross-boundary knowledge-making—that is, for inquiry, negotiation, and reconstruction through partnership across boundaries. As a part of this engagement, the locally-situated, habitual, and normalized knowledge-making practices in each geopolitical location become available for inquiry, with negotiation, reflection, and reconstruction equally brought to bear on the teaching and learning experiences of the teachers and students in the shared learning environment.

Of course, GNLEs offer these opportunities, not just for students, but also for faculty, as they inquire into each other's pedagogies and negotiate the design of their partnered learning environment. To provide a brief example, we might briefly consider the syllabus or course outline as one of the most common genres that organizes how a course is to unfold: what students and instructors are to read, write, and say, when, and with what expectations. Like any genre, the syllabus inscribes expectations, such as who gets to write it, when, when it will be handed out, what role it will play in a course, and what it will contain (e.g., a course description, learning objectives, course readings and materials, an academic integrity or plagiarism statement, class policies, a statement facilitating disability access, a weekly schedule, course requirements, evaluation criteria and procedures, and so on, all of which reflect local institutional practices and requirements). For partnered learning environments, the syllabus—as a genre—not only organizes local institutional pedagogy, but it also inscribes and normalizes pedagogical values and assumptions historically produced in institutional and national academic traditions. For example, as Singham (2007) points out, the syllabus assumes that each student will be at the same level of preparedness for the course and will achieve the required learning objectives in the same way and the same amount of time, regardless of students' prior learning and life experiences.

Moreover, a syllabus inscribes such values as what kind of knowledge counts, whose knowledge counts, who determines the learning outcomes, how much flexibility there is for learners, how intellectual property is to be valued (e.g., plagiarism statements), and so on. As Wilson (2013) argues, what is a rather sedimented and often highly constrained genre—subject to local institutional policies—becomes a site of negotiation in GNLEs, rendering normalized assumptions open for questioning. For example, how is the work of the syllabus organized in the institutional environments of partnering faculty? Is that work perhaps absent (e.g., the task of threatening students with consequences for non-normative attribution practices)? Or does the genre perhaps orchestrate learning and knowledge-making in rather different ways? With different assumptions? If so, or if the genre does not exist, what might that mean about which learning and knowledge-making practices are valued? Would a syllabus perhaps seem needlessly constraining, legalistic, prescriptive, or controlling in a different institutional setting? Or is the genre so saturated with local institutional demands, assumptions, norms, and requirements that it becomes untenable? A hindrance? How might culturally-situated statements be negotiated? Or not? And what do competing policies regulating writing and language mean for student collaboration across boundaries?

These examples illustrate that, in order to realize their potential, GNLEs depend on equal partnerships that use the knowledge, perspectives, and contributions from all partners in order to develop peer-produced curricula and pedagogies (Starke-Meyerring et al. 2008). A GNLE in which one partner dominates the curriculum, readings, and technological design will therefore likely defy its purpose. Rather than imposing the pedagogical practices of one partner, GNLEs are characterized by the sensitive inquiry into, mutual learning from, and negotiation of the pedagogical practices that reflect the local curricula, institutional goals, and needs of all partners and participants involved.

Therefore, as Herrington (2008) notes, sustainable partnerships for globally networked learning require thoughtful and intricate processes of relationship development at multiple levels, which take into account the specific institutional practices, constraints, policies, and infrastructures that characterize the working conditions of partners and shape the ways in which writing is thought of and taught in a given institutional setting. WPAs involved in the development of GNLEs need to attend to power imbalances in such partnerships, as partners often work under unequal conditions or constraints in terms of work-load, resources, pressures emerging from tight publication schedules or evaluation/testing procedures, and other institutional or local pol-icy conditions. And, of particular relevance for WPA work, questions of power imbalance might be reflected in the questions GNLEs raise about language.

Language Dimension: From Privileged Varieties of English to a Robust Politic of Language

The language dimension of GNLEs also offers unique opportunities for re-seeing writing programs in globalizing higher education, as this dimension also involves complex decisions, such as decisions about the language of interaction or the roles of the diverse languages of par-ticipants in a partnered learning environment. Indeed, GNLEs gener-ate and challenge us to address new and pressing questions that can facilitate a more robust engagement with the politics of language. For example, how do we rethink our understanding of language in these environments? Whose language is taught? How? How do speakers of dif-ferent languages interact or write collaboratively? How do we, as writing studies researchers have increasingly argued, move beyond a traditional focus on monolingual policies or privileged varieties of a language, such as standard American English, to engage in the politics of language (Canagarajah 2002; Cox et al. 2010; Horner, Lu, and Matsuda 2010; Melton 2008)? How do we collaborate with research fields, such as trans-lation studies or second language studies, that help us address these questions? How do we build partnerships between these fields in order to achieve the interdisciplinary collaboration that has emerged as a vital component for the teaching of writing in globalizing environments?

Indeed, GNLEs have taken up questions of language in complex ways. Craig, Poe, and González-Rojas (2010), for example, focus their GNLE work on addressing questions of language through a WAC/ English as a Foreign Language (EFL) partnership that addresses the diverse needs of both partners—a WAC program at a US university and EFL programs at two Mexican universities. One of the goals, for exam-ple, involves facilitating the participation of graduate students and pro-fessors at Mexican universities whose first language is not English in the

English-dominant academic writing and publishing system, whose exclusion of non-Western based scholars and involvement in the reproduction of Western dominance in global knowledge production has been well documented (Canagarajah 2002; Flowerdew and Li 2009). Another goal involves learning more about EFL pedagogies that might address the needs of the large numbers of international graduate students at the US university.

Along similar lines, the Transatlantic Partnership Project (Mousten, Vandepitte, and Maylath 2008) is deeply concerned with facilitating students' critical participation as professionals in global, multilingual workplaces that are characterized by unequal power relations. Students learn not only how texts are situated in and reproduce local practices, values, and assumptions—which become available for questioning in the process of translation—but also how power relations between professionals working in English as a first language and those attempting to translate their work into other languages might constrain the ways in which these texts travel between the two.

Technological Dimension: Negotiating the Politics of Technology

Questions about the politics of language in GNLEs intersect in important ways with questions about the politics of technology, since many of the partnerships that extend across national boundaries depend heavily on digital technologies, and, in many cases, exist solely in online environments. Some, such as the partnership described by Crabtree and her colleagues (Crabtree et al. 2008), include activities both online (e.g., teaching a joint course online) and "on the ground" (e.g., faculty and student exchanges), as well as civic engagement initiatives in local communities. Others emerge largely through activities "on the ground" when the partnerships operate at the program level.

Regardless of what specific technology is used, GNLEs raise new questions about the politics of technology in the study and teaching of writing. For example, since many of these learning environments are digitally mediated or have digital components, how do the politics of language interact with the politics of technology in facilitating, enabling, or constraining cross-boundary knowledge-making? As McCool (2008) illustrates in his study of the collaborative design of a module on the Sonoran biosphere by a US and a Mexican environmental NGO (non-governmental organization), digital technologies reflect and reproduce the assumptions, metaphors, and ways of thinking, as well as the sociocultural, political, and material conditions of their design. In this way, as much research on writing and technologies confirms, decisions about the design, use, and regulation of technologies are always highly political (e.g., Bazerman 2011; Grabill 2007; Selfe 1999; Starke-Meyerring 2009).

How, then, are diverse, competing, or even incommensurable assumptions, practices, and expectations for social interaction negotiated in such designs? Whose locally-situated practices might be privileged or marginalized by a given technological design? Given this consequential political dimension of language and technology, how are institutional infrastructures ensured that allow for collaborative and equal decision making about the digital environments that will facilitate the work and interactions in GNLEs (Starke-Meyerring and Wilson 2008)? And, specifically, how do faculty and students in GNLEs negotiate competing values, norms, and laws that regulate questions of copyright, fair use, privacy, attribution, access, etc., across institutional, national, and other policy frameworks (Rife 2010)?

Structural–Institutional Dimension: Engaging Local Unifying Logics

In many ways, decisions about geopolitical, pedagogical, language, and technology questions in GNLEs are deeply situated within the institutional infrastructure and policy environments in which both partners work, and these are, of course, environments that are designed to reproduce the established practices of locally-bounded courses and programs. Everything—from budget lines, institutional support infrastructure, course evaluation policies, and course design or syllabus policies to various learning technologies—makes the sharing or even collaborative design of learning environments beyond institutional walls difficult (Starke-Meyerring et al. 2008). Budget lines, for example, reproduce a deep traditional split between disciplinary programs and other institutional units, with resources relevant to the design of GNLEs (such as study abroad programs, instructional design programs, faculty development programs, community partnership programs, etc.), making funding for GNLE initiatives difficult and providing few incentives for the kinds of cross-campus partnership networks that are vital for developing and sustaining GNLEs. Nor do budgets account for the much increased workloads involved in not only thinking through one's own pedagogical design, but also in inquiring into and learning the pedagogical practices, institutional constraints, and affordances of partners, let alone co-constructing and realizing a collaborative pedagogy and learning environment.

Along similar lines, institutional support infrastructure, such as web-based learning environments, are often locked and limited to students officially enrolled in local institutions, making a partnered learning environment—perhaps with faculty and students from different institutions—difficult. Moreover, traditional learning environments are often built with proprietary software, which impedes the adaptation of technology for building a shared learning environment that reflects the goals and image of the partnership, let alone the values and practices of all partners. Likewise, course evaluation procedures as a genre system reproduce, normalize, and require compliance with assumptions about learning in traditional, institutionally-bounded courses, leaving little room for the intensity, complexity, ambiguity, and unpredictability that characterizes a learning experience that extends across institutional boundaries.

This unifying cultural logic of institutional environments can be rather entrenched in its longstanding historical roots. Drawing on Herzberg's anthropological study of institutions, Fox (2009) explains that, historically, higher education institutions have played important roles in the formation of nation states, and that their original logic therefore involved the "unifying ideological work of creating and maintaining a common identity" (16). That logic, of course, directly supports expansionist transmission models of globalizing higher education, which advance that "unifying ideological work" and identity, but render the open, collaborative, questioning cross-boundary work of GNLEs difficult. Therefore it is not surprising that faculty pursuing (or wishing to pursue) partnerships for GNLEs identified local institutional policy and infrastructure environments as the most frequent challenge they faced (Starke-Meyerring, Duin, and Palvetzian 2007). Interestingly, it was not external factors, such as working with different semester schedules or time zones, but local institutional culture that proved challenging.

The institutional dimension affects partnering faculty in many ways, perhaps most notably in the extent to which they are able to engage in GNLE work—for example, whether the partnership will focus on the course level or perhaps extend to the program level. Given the rootedness of higher education institutions in logics of unified identity work and nation building, given the strong emphasis on reproducing established practices, and given current economic pressures toward developing expansionist programs for global markets, many GNLEs operate in the face of considerable institutional inertia and therefore come from grassroots, often focusing on the course level (Starke-Meyerring et al. 2008). Program-level GNLEs in rhetoric and writing studies that are committed to the creation of alternatives to expansionist transmission models may be more difficult to achieve, unless the institutional mission allows for sufficient space for such a commitment. The partnership initiative described by Crabtree and her colleagues, for example, pursues a mission that is closely aligned with their own institutional missions of social justice in the face of global inequities (Crabtree et al. 2008).

Given the complex institutional dimension of GNLEs, WPA work is essential to their success. As WPA scholarship has emphasized for a long time, advancing new learning environments is a highly political act that involves engaging in institutional change. As Strickland and Gunner (2009) put it, WPAs are deeply aware that "it isn't just teaching but institutions that need to change if the good practices that composition scholars develop and teach are to have real effect" (xii). To be sure, that process—as Strickland and Gunner's collection demonstrates—is wrought with difficulties, especially since writing programs have often inherited disconcerting labor practices (Grabill et al. 2003) that are exacerbated by the neoliberal globalization project (Scott 2009). However, if the GNLEs that are emerging in our field are any indication, the alternative ways of envisioning writing programs and higher education—which offer a vital new reason for the long-term struggle of WPAs—are now more important than ever.

CONCLUSION

As teachers, scholars, and WPAs, we are inextricably situated in the larger neoliberal project of globalization, with all of its consequences for writing, knowing, teaching, and learning. Indeed, in the context of privatized, expansionist, and global market-driven program structures designed for the purpose of revenue generation in the face of decreasing public funding for higher education, the significance of writing programs—such as WID/WAC programs, for example—cannot be overstated, given the unique role these programs play in these expansionist settings.

However, even in situations where our institutional contexts position us in global expansionist projects, GNLEs allow us to carve out alternative learning spaces that can help question, redirect, and reshape dominant transmission models of "educating the Other." They do so by encouraging faculty and students to inquire into, re-see, and negotiate the locally-situated, normalized ways of writing, thinking, knowing, learning, and teaching, as well as the ways in which these intersect with complex geopolitical dynamics.

There is, of course, no guarantee that such spaces cannot be co-opted, or that they escape the reproduction of dominant narratives and power relations. Surely, such spaces may be co-opted by institutions as "internationalization on the cheap," or as revenue sources by foregrounding the economics of recruiting international students into joint programs for their tuition dollars. Moreover, unequal power relations between partners may well be inadvertently reproduced in a myriad of ways—for example, by means of language choices and practices; by means of the technological design that may reflect and reproduce the practices, values, and assumptions of one partner over those of another; as a result of institutional demands on their faculty for compliance with local institutional norms; or as a result of unequal workloads, access to resources, and so on. There is also no guarantee that dominant narratives—such as national narratives of supremacy—are not being reproduced, but are made available for probing and questioning.

Nevertheless, within the project of neoliberal globalization, GNLEs offer learning environments that actively undermine the one-way expansionist sale of higher education by creating a collaborative space for mutual inquiry that opens up the normalized common sense of established discursive regimes. As such, GNLEs offer a critical space for pedagogical activism, facilitated, albeit not secured, by their design. In doing so, they exemplify the complexity of creating alternative spaces that is so familiar to WPAs—a complexity that recognizes the dynamics between compliance with established practices, while at the same time managing to create and introduce spaces for alternative ways of doing, thinking, knowing, teaching, and learning.

In short, globally networked learning environments are important sites of struggle, where the battle over the globalization of higher education is played out and where writing programs play important roles. And, as WPAs are deeply aware, these learning environments are highly consequential. The questions at stake in GNLEs are significant indeed: Whose knowledge counts? Who is invited to participate in the production of knowledge? Who learns whose knowledge? Will the knowledge of a privileged region (whose interest that knowledge serves) be "transmitted" to those in less privileged regions? Or, will learners come together and inquire into the local habits and traditions of knowing, what values those reproduce, in whose interests they work, and whose knowledge is privileged? How do power relations shaped by the current geopolitics of globalization affect faculty and students as learners and citizens, as well as the various communities in which they participate? And, as Luke (2010) asks, "Whose material and ideological interests are at play?" (16).

In raising these questions, GNLEs both depend on and challenge WPAs to extend and rethink our understanding of what writing, knowing, learning, and teaching can be and do in globalizing higher education.

References

Adler-Kassner, L. 2008. *The Activist WPA: Changing Stories about Writing and Writers.* Logan, UT: Utah State UP.

Alfano, C. 2009. "Hardwiring Connections Between Students: Group Work, Social Networks, and Connecting Students Across Cultures." Paper presented at CCCC, San Francisco, 12 March.

Anderson, P., B. Bergman, L. Bradley, M. Gustafsson, and A. Matzke. 2010. "Peer Reviewing Across the Atlantic: Patterns and Trends in L1 and L2 Comments made in an Asynchronous Online Collaborative Learning Exchange between Technical Communication Students in Sweden and in the United States." *Journal of Business and Technical Communication* 24 (3): 296–322. http://dx.doi.org/10.1177/1050651910363270.

Bassett, R. M. 2006. *The WTO and the University: Globalization, GATS, and American Higher Education.* New York: Routledge.

Bawarshi, A., and M. J. Reiff. 2010. *Genre: An Introduction to History, Theory, Research, and Pedagogy.* West Lafayette, IN: Parlor Press and WAC Clearinghouse.

Bazerman, C. 2011. "Electrons are Cheap, Society is Dear." In *Writing (in) Knowledge Societies*, ed. D. Starke-Meyerring, A. Paré, N. Artemeva, M. Horne, and L. Yousoubova. West Lafayette, IN: Parlor Press and WAC Clearinghouse. Accessed at http://wac.colostate.edu/books/winks/.

Bazerman, C., A. Bonini, and D. Figueiredo, eds. 2009. *Genre in a Changing World.* Parlor Press and WAC Clearinghouse. Accessed at http://wac.colostate.edu/books/genre/.

Boehm, D., H. Kurthen, and L. Aniola-Jedrzejek. 2010. "Do International Online Collaborative Learning Projects Impact Ethnocentrism?" *E-Learning and Digital Media* 7 (2): 133–46. http://dx.doi.org/10.2304/elea.2010.7.2.133.

Blum Malley, S., J. Ruiters, and E. Gulyaeva. 2011. "Navigating Epistemologies, Methodologies, and Pedagogies in Collaborative, International Writing Research." Presentation at Writing Research across Borders II, Fairfax, VA, Feb 2011.

Bruffee, K. 1978. "Editorial." *WPA: Writing Program Administration* 1:6–12.

Canagarajah, A. S. 2002. *A Geopolitics of Academic Writing. Pittsburgh Series in Composition, Literacy, and Culture.* Pittsburgh: University of Pittsburgh Press.

Coe, R., L. Lingard, and T. Teslenko, eds. 2002. *The Rhetoric and Ideology of Genre.* Cresskill, NJ: Hampton.

Cox, M., J. Jordan, C. Ortmeier-Hooper, and G. Schwartz, eds. 2010. *Reinventing Identities in Second-Language Writing.* Urbana, IL: NCTE.

Crabtree, R. D. D. A., Sapp, J. A. Malespín, and G. Norori. 2008. "Realizing the University Mission in Partnership with Nicaragua: Internationalization, Diversity, and Social Justice." In *Designing Global Learning Environments: Visionary Partnerships, Policies, and Pedagogies*, ed. D. Starke-Meyerring and M. Wilson, 87-107. Rotterdam, Netherlands: Sense Publishers.

Craig, J., M. Poe, and M. F. González-Rojas. 2010. "Professional Communication Education in a Global Context: A collaboration between the Massachusetts Institute of Technology, Instituto Tecnológico y de Estudios Superiores de Monterrey, Mexico, and Universidad de Quintana Roo, Mexico." *Journal of Business and Technical Communication* 24 (3): 267–95. http://dx.doi.org/10.1177/1050651910363269.

della Porta, D., M. Andretta, L. Mosca, and H. Reiter, eds. 2006. *Globalization from Below: Transnational Activists and Protest Networks.* Minneapolis, MN: U of Minnesota Press.

Dewey, J. 1961. *Democracy and Education: An Introduction to the Philosophy of Education.* New York: MacMillan.

Du-Babcock, B., and I. Varner. I. 2008. "Intercultural Business Communication in Action: Analysis of an International Videoconference." In *Designing Global Learning Environments: Visionary Partnerships, Policies, and Pedagogies,* ed. D. Starke-Meyerring and M. Wilson, 156–69. Rotterdam, Netherlands: Sense Publishers.

Dubinsky, J. 2008. "When the Global is Local: Building a Local, Global Community." In *Designing Global Learning Environments: Visionary Partnerships, Policies, and Pedagogies,* ed. D. Starke-Meyerring and M. Wilson, 170–84. Rotterdam, Netherlands: Sense Publishers.

Flowerdew, J., and Y. Li. 2009. "English or Chinese? The Trade-off between Local and International Publication among Chinese Academics in the Humanities and Social Sciences." *Journal of Second Language Writing* 18 (1): 1–16. http://dx.doi.org/10 .1016/j.jslw.2008.09.005.

Fox, T. 2009. "Standards and Purity: Understanding Institutional Strategies to Insure Homogeneity." In *The Writing Program Interrupted: Making Spaces for Critical Discourse,* ed. D. Strickland and J. Gunner, 14–27. Portsmouth, NH: Boynton/Cook.

Giroux, H. 2004. *The Terror of Neoliberalism: Authoritarianism and the Eclipse of Democracy.* Boulder, CO: Paradigm Publishers.

Grabill, J. T. 2007. *Writing Community Change: Designing Technologies for Citizen Action.* Cresskill, NJ: Hampton Press.

Grabill, J. T., J. E. Porter, S. Blythe, and L. Miles. 2003. "Institutional Critique Revisited." *Work and Days* 21:219–37.

Hall, S. 1996. "The Problem of Ideology: Marxism without Guarantees." In *Stuart Hall: Critical Dialogues in Cultural Studies,* ed. D. Morley and K.-H. Chen, 25–48. London, New York: Routledge.

Harvey, D. 2007. *A Brief History of Neoliberalism.* Oxford, UK: Oxford UP.

Herrington, T., and Y. Tretyakov. 2005. "The Global Classroom Project: Troublemaking and Troubleshooting." In *Online Education: Global Questions, Local Answers,* ed. K. Cargile Cook and K. Grant-Davie, 267–83. Amityville, NY: Baywood.

Herrington, T. 2004. "Where in the World is the Global Classroom Project?" In *If Classrooms Matter: Progressive Visions of Educational Environments,* ed. J. Di Leo and W. Jacobs, 197–210. New York: Routledge.

Herrington, T. 2005. "Linking Russia and America in Web Forums: The Global Classroom Project." In *Technical Communication and the World Wide Web,* ed. M. Day and C. Lipson, 167–92. Mahwah, NJ: Erlbaum Publishers.

Herrington, T. 2008. "The Global Classroom Project: Multiple Relationships in Global Partnering." In *Designing Global Learning Environments: Visionary Partnerships, Policies, and Pedagogies,* ed. D. Starke-Meyerring and M. Wilson, 37–51. Rotterdam, Netherlands: Sense Publishers.

Herrington, T. 2010. "Crossing Global Boundaries: Beyond Intercultural Communication." *Journal of Business and Technical Communication* 24:516–39.

Hesse, D. 2002. "Politics and the WPA: Traveling Through and Past Realms of Expertise." In *The Writing Program Administrator's Resource: A Guide to Reflective Institutional Practice,* ed. S. C. Brown and T. Enos, 41–58. Mahwah, NJ: Erlbaum.

Horner, B., M. Z. Lu, and P. K. Matsuda, eds. 2010. *Cross-language Relations in Composition.* Carbondale, IL: Southern Illinois UP.

Kennon, J. 2008. "International Collaboration and Cross-cultural Communication: The Global Classroom Project." In *Designing Global Learning Environments: Visionary Partnerships, Policies, and Pedagogies,* ed. D. Starke-Meyerring and M. Wilson, 114–28. Rotterdam, Netherlands: Sense Publishers.

Luke, A. 2010. "Educating the Other: Standpoint and the 'Internationalisation' of Higher Education." In *Global Inequalities in Higher Education: Whose Interests are we Serving?* ed. V. Carpentier and E. Unterhalter, 43–65. London: Palgrave/MacMillan.

Marginson, S. 2004. "Don't Leave me Hanging on the Anglophone: The Potential for Online Distance Higher Education in the Asia-Pacific Region." *Higher Education Quarterly* 58 (2–3): 74–113. http://dx.doi.org/10.1111/j.1468-2273.2004.00263.x.

Marginson, S., ed. 2007. *Prospects of Higher Education: Globalization, Market Competition, Public Goods and the Future of the University.* Rotterdam: Sense.

Maylath, B., S. Vandepitte, and B. Mousten. 2008. "Growing Grassroots Partnerships: Trans-Atlantic Collaboration between American Instructors and Students of Technical Writing and European Instructors and Students of Translation." In *Designing Global Learning Environments: Visionary Partnerships, Policies, and Pedagogies*, ed. D. Starke-Meyerring and M. Wilson, 52–66. Rotterdam, Netherlands: Sense Publishers.

McCool, M. 2008. "Negotiating the Design of Globally Networked Learning Environments." In *Designing Global Learning Environments: Visionary Partnerships, Policies, and Pedagogies*, ed. D. Starke-Meyerring and M. Wilson, 200–217. Rotterdam, Netherlands: Sense Publishers.

McLeod, S. H. 1995. "The Foreigner: WAC Directors as Agents of Change." In *Resituating Writing: Constructing and Administering Writing Programs*, ed. J. Janangelo and K. Hansen, 108–16. Portsmouth, NH: Boynton-Cook/Heinemann.

McLeod, S. H. 2007. *Writing Program Administration.* West Lafayette, IN: Parlor Press and WAC Clearinghouse; http://wac.colostate.edu.

McNair, L. D., M. C. Paretti, and A. Kakar. 2008. "Case Study of Prior Knowledge: Expectations and Identity Constructions in Interdisciplinary, Cross-cultural, Virtual Collaboration." *International Journal of Engineering Education* 24:386–99.

McNair, L., and M. Paretti. 2010. "Activity Theory, Speech Acts, and the 'Doctrine of Infelicity': Connecting Language and Technology in Globally Networked Learning Environments." *Journal of Business and Technical Communication* 24 (3): 323–57. http://dx.doi.org/10.1177/1050651910363275.

Melton, J. 2008. "Beyond Standard English: Rethinking in Globally Networked Learning Environments." In *Designing Global Learning Environments: Visionary Partnerships, Policies, and Pedagogies*, ed. D. Starke-Meyerring and M. Wilson, 185–99. Rotterdam, Netherlands: Sense Publishers.

Mousten, B., S. Vandepitte, and B. Maylath. B. 2008. "Intercultural Collaboration in the Trans-Atlantic Project: Pedagogical Theories and Practices in Teaching Procedural Instructions across Cultural Contexts." In *Designing Global Learning Environments: Visionary Partnerships, Policies, and Pedagogies*, ed. D. Starke-Meyerring, and M. Wilson, 129–44. Rotterdam, Netherlands: Sense Publishers.

O'Brien, A. J., and A. Eriksson. 2010. "Cross-cultural Connections: Intercultural Learning for Global Citizenship." In *Intercultural Communication Competence: Educating the Global Citizen*, ed. M. Alagic, M., G. M. Rimmington, F. C. Liu, and K. L. Gibson, 1–19. Learn International Series, New Delhi: MacMillan Publishers.

Paré, A. 2002. "Genre and Identity: Individuals, Institutions, and Ideology." In *The Rhetoric and Ideology of Genre*, ed. R. Coe, L. Lingard, and T. Teslenko, 57–71. Cresskill, NJ: Hampton.

Paretti, M. C., and L. D. McNair. 2008. "Communicating in Global Virtual Teams: Managing Complex Activity Systems." In *Handbook of Research on Virtual Workplaces and the New Nature of Business Practices*, ed. P. Zemliansky and K. St. Amant, 24–38. Hershey: Idea Group. http://dx.doi.org/10.4018/978-1-59904-893-2.ch003.

Paretti, M. C., L. D. McNair, and L. Holloway-Attaway. 2007. "Teaching Technical Communication in an Era of Distributed Work: A Case Study of Collaboration between U.S. and Swedish Students." *Technical Communication Quarterly* 16 (3): 327–52. http://dx.doi.org/10.1080/10572250701291087.

Rainey, K., H. Smith, and C. Barnes. 2008. "Steps and Missteps in Negotiating a Joint Degree Program with a Chinese University." In *Designing Global Learning Environments: Visionary Partnerships, Policies, and Pedagogies*, ed. D. Starke-Meyerring and M. Wilson, 67–86. Rotterdam, Netherlands: Sense Publishers.

Rhoads, R. A., and C. A. Torres, eds. 2007. *The University, State and the Market: The Political Economy of Globalization in the Americas*. Stanford, CA: Stanford UP.

Rife, M. C. 2010. "Cross-Cultural Collisions in Cyberspace: Case Studies of International Legal Issues for Educators Working in Globally Networked Learning Environments." *E-Learning and Digital Media* 7 (2):147–59. http://dx.doi.org/10.2304/elea.2010.7.2.147.

Sapp, D. A. 2004. "Global Partnerships in Business Communication: An Institutional Collaboration between the United States and Cuba." *Business Communication Quarterly* 67 (3): 267–80. http://dx.doi.org/10.1177/1080569904268051.

Scholte, J. 2005. *Globalization: A critical introduction*. London: Palgrave Macmillan.

Scott, T. 2009. "How We Do What We Do: Facing the Contradictory Political Economics of Writing Programs." In *The Writing Program Interrupted: Making Spaces for Critical Discourse*, ed. D. Strickland and J. Gunner, 41–55. Portsmouth, NH: Boynton/Cook.

Selfe, C. 1999. *Technology and Literacy in the Twenty-First Century: The Perils of Not Paying Attention*. Carbondale, IL: Southern Illinois University Press.

Singham, M. 2007. "Death to the Syllabus!" *Liberal Education* 93:52–56.

Sorrells, K. 2011. "Re-imagining Intercultural Communication in the Context of Globalization." In *Handbook of Critical Intercultural Communication*, ed. T. K. Nakayama and R. T. Halualani, 171–89. Oxford, UK: Wiley-Blackwell. http://dx.doi.org/10.1002/9781444390681.ch11.

Starke-Meyerring, D. 2005. "Meeting the Challenges of Globalization: A Framework for Global Literacies in Professional Communication Programs." *Journal of Business and Technical Communication* 19 (4): 468–99. http://dx.doi.org/10.1177/1050651905278033.

Starke-Meyerring, D., and M. Wilson, eds. 2008. *In Designing Global Learning Environments: Visionary Partnerships, Policies, and Pedagogies*. Rotterdam, Netherlands: Sense Publishers.

Starke-Meyerring, D. 2009. "The Contested Materialities of Writing in Digital Environments: Implications for Writing Development." In *Handbook of Writing Development*, ed. R. Beard, D. Myhill, M. Nystrand, and J. Riley, 506–26. Thousand Oaks, CA: Sage. http://dx.doi.org/10.4135/9780857021069.n35.

Starke-Meyerring, D. 2010. "Globally Networked Learning Environments in Professional Communication: Challenging Normalized Ways of Learning, Teaching, and Knowing." *Journal of Business and Technical Communication* 24 (3): 259–66. http://dx.doi.org/10.1177/1050651910363266.

Starke-Meyerring, D., and D. Andrews. 2006. "Building a Shared Virtual Learning Culture: An International Classroom Partnership." *Business Communication Quarterly* 69 (1): 25–49. http://dx.doi.org/10.1177/1080569905285543.

Starke-Meyerring, D., and D. Andrews. 2010. "Building a Culture of Intercultural Learning: Assessment in a Virtual Team Project." In *Assessment in Technical and Professional Communication*, ed. M. Hundleby and J. Allen. Amityville, NY: Baywood. http://dx.doi.org/10.2190/AITC13.

Starke-Meyerring, D., A. H. Duin, and T. Palvetzian. 2007. "Global Partnerships: Positioning Technical Communication Programs in the Context of Globalization." *Technical Communication Quarterly* 16 (2): 139–74. http://dx.doi.org/10.1080/10572250709336558.

Starke-Meyerring, D., A. H. Duin, T. Palvetzian, and M. Wilson. 2008. "Enabling and Sustaining Globally Networked Learning Environments: Visionary Partnerships and Policies." In *Designing Global Learning Environments: Visionary Partnerships, Policies, and*

Pedagogies, ed. D. Starke-Meyerring and M. Wilson, 139–74. Rotterdam, Netherlands: Sense Publishers.

Stiglitz, J. 2006. *Making Globalization Work*. New York: Norton.

Strickland, D., and J. Gunner. 2009. "Opening Up: Toward a Critical Discourse for Writing Program Administration." In *The Writing Program Interrupted: Making Space for Critical Discourse*, ed. D. Strickland and J. Gunner, xi–xv. Portsmouth, NH: Boynton/Cook.

Torres, A. C. 2008. *Education and Neoliberal Globalization*. NY: Routledge.

Trimbur, J. 2009. *"Foreword"* to The Writing Program Interrupted: Making Space for Critical *Discourse*, ed. D. Strickland and J. Gunner. Portsmouth, NH: Boynton/Cook.

Verger, A. 2009. *WTO/GATS and the Global Politics of Higher Education*. Abingdon: Routledge.

Wilson, M. 2013. "An Inquiry into Faculty Partners' Work and Negotiation of Globally Networked Learning Environments within Higher Education Institutions." Doctoral dissertation, McGill University, Canada.

Zhu, Y., E. Gareis, J. O'Keefe Bazzoni, and D. Rolland. 2005. "A Collaborative Online Project between New Zealand and New York." *Business Communication Quarterly* 68 (1): 81–96. http://dx.doi.org/10.1177/1080569904273715.

Afterword

TRANSNATIONAL WRITING PROGRAM ADMINISTRATION[1]

Bruce Horner

While local conditions remain at the forefront of WPA, transnational activities are thoroughly shifting the questions we ask about writing curricula, the space and place in which writing happens, and the cultural and linguistic issues at the heart of the relationships forged in literacy work. In the global expansion of higher education, the tension between economic and pedagogical interests strongly influences decisions made about what kinds of programs to offer and how to offer them. Writing teachers and administrators involved in the creation or development of international programs must negotiate these tensions based upon what they know and value about learning, teaching, and writing. This collection of essays demonstrates how "transnational writing program administration" challenges taken-for-granted assumptions regarding program identity, curriculum and pedagogical effectiveness, logistics and quality assurance, faculty and student demographics, innovative partnerships and research, and the infrastructure needed to support writing instruction in higher education.

—David S. Martins, Introduction

Transnational writing program administration by definition engages encounters with difference. Transnational writing programs offer different sets of coordinates by which to (re)locate writing and its teaching— in space, culture, geopolitical relations, language—thereby posing alternative notions of writing and its teaching and enabling us to rethink our practices and beliefs that all too often have been understood as simply "the norm." In presenting such programs, this collection contributes to ongoing challenges to longstanding ideological blinders that render as universals what are in fact local (US) cultural presuppositions and practices with postsecondary writing and writing instruction.[1]

In bringing to light significant differences in practices and beliefs about (postsecondary) writing and writing instruction, these essays

DOI: 10.7330/9780874219623.c014

individually and the collection as a whole participate in a larger global movement in literacy studies to rethink literacy and its learning and teaching. In that movement, literacy has been shown to be not a universal, singular, autonomous, and neutral entity in form and effect, but rather plural ("literac-ies"), diverse, and ideological; located and manifested differently in different material social contexts; and subject to manifesting and effecting specific and diverse power relations—in short, literacy as multiple, diverse sets of practices existing in hierarchical relations of power to one another.[2] Within the boundaries set by the collection's focus on postsecondary writing instruction, the chapters describe a comparable diversity of practices and beliefs. At least on the surface, some of these differences might appear trivial, if no less difficult to traverse: different time zones, semester schedules, student residential patterns, and technology. Some of these differences are seemingly more consequential: different traditions of teaching and researching writing; different languages and language ecologies, including official language policies and actual linguistic practices; different attitudes toward and uses for writing in college; and different student populations. From these chapters, WPAs can see that the familiar answers to the familiar question "What is college writing?" are grossly inadequate when a global—rather than a purely US—scope for "college" is assumed. In short, these chapters provide strong challenges to foundationalist beliefs in the singularity, uniformity, and universality of dominant US treatments of college writing and its teaching, and thus to the "missionary" approach to transnational writing program administration that converts the unenlightened residing elsewhere to the blessings of "our" ways. As Anson and Donahue put it in their chapter, there is, after all, more than one way to farm.

As the authors of several of the chapters in this collection confess, there is a tension in the transnational work of WPAs. Specifically, the positioning of WPAs as "experts" on writing who are ostensibly qualified to direct writing programs anywhere, which is based on a monolithic conception of postsecondary writing and writing instruction that is contradicted by the realities of difference they encounter and engage in their experience working transnationally. Of course, one response to that encounter, at least in theory, would be to retreat to a foundationalist approach—i.e., to assume that, in fact, there is/was a single, universal, "normal" postsecondary writing curriculum, and that the job of WPAs is to implement such a curriculum in the programs they direct (and to eliminate, or "correct," any practices and beliefs at odds with that curriculum). Understandably and rightly, none of these chapters advocates or aligns itself with such an approach.

However, this leaves open the question of how (else) to understand and engage with difference—what it might mean, in the words of contributor Nancy Bou Ayash, to work *with* others engaged in the study and teaching of postsecondary writing. I argue that particular ways by which we understand difference frequently limit our response to it, leading— if not to attempts at its eradication—then to reifications of difference that preclude the kind of working "with" difference for which Bou Ayash, and indeed the authors as a whole, argue. I call attention here to three related, limiting tendencies that accompany and contribute to such reifications: (1) the tendency to conceive of difference in purely spatialized terms; (2) often as a consequence, the tendency to mistake official representations of beliefs and practices at a given locale for the full range of these; and (3) in tending to differences between practices and beliefs at specific locations, overlooking the relation of these to shared global forces, thereby allowing those forces to go unchecked and unchallenged.

It is perhaps not surprising that differences in programs defined in terms of spatial location would be understood spatially: spatial distance equates in many ways, not all trivial, to difference. Anson and Donahue observe that assuming writing programs outside the United States will look like those in the United States can obscure the diverse forms (and names, not always identified as "programs") that these take. Bou Ayash notes significant differences in language ecologies—policies and practices—between the United States, Singapore, and Lebanon. Alfano and O'Brien discover a litany of differences in not only time zones but also course schedules, technological resources, and class sizes. However, if these differences are conceptualized in purely spatial terms—what the beliefs and practices are "there" versus "here"—there is a danger of trading in a monolithic conception of writing and writing programs for an "essentialism of the fragments," a mosaic or cloisonné understanding of these differences (see Gibson-Graham 1996, 74). Differences are thereby reified rather than understood, in material/social terms, as active representations that are historical and ideological. Such reifications achieve definitional sharpness through erasure of the contingent, relational, partial (selective, incomplete, temporal, and interested) character of their representations of difference (see Gal and Irvine 1995, 974–75). In such reifications, official accounts of the identities, practices, beliefs, needs, and desires of the inhabitants of a particular location are mistaken for the full range and historically changeable nature of these. Importantly, this reification obtains—in representations (and understandings) of both the different/"other" ("there") and the seemingly familiar ("here")—obscuring overlaps between and differences within specific localities, the interrelations among these localities, the changing character of all of them, and their shared susceptibility to global forces of, for example, neoliberalism.

The travel across space can thus become an exercise in what Michael Byram has identified as "tourism" rather than the work of "the sojourner." Byram explains that, whereas "the tourist hopes . . . that what they have traveled to see will not change . . . and . . . that their own way of living will be enriched but not fundamentally changed" by the travel from here to there, the sojourner "produces effects on a society which challenges its unquestioned and unconscious beliefs, behaviours, and meanings, and whose own beliefs, behaviours and meanings are in turn challenged and expected to change" (Byram 1997, 1). Despite the dominance of tourism as a model for travel, "The experience of the sojourner is potentially more valuable . . . both for societies and for individuals, since the state of the world is such that societies and individuals have no alternative but proximity, interaction and relationship as the conditions of existence" (2). In other words, as tempting as it might be to be simple (good) tourists, conditions not of our choosing inevitably lead those of us engaged in transnational work to be, instead, sojourners.

Engagement in the work of the sojourner means accepting interaction—rather than preserving ostensibly fixed, discrete, and uniform differences—as the norm. Without discounting the need for sensitivity to difference to avoid the sins of the missionary foundationalist in developing writing programs across spatial distances, the very fact of transnational writing program administration requires such interaction and poses challenges to the beliefs and practices of both the sojourner and the "host" institution or location, as well as of the students, faculty, and administrators involved at both sites. Given the labor required to simply establish and maintain transnational writing programs, to which many of the chapters in this collection attest, this can be a daunting task, and it's entirely understandable that some may be tempted instead to adopt a touristic stance that accommodates, rather than engages with, difference: the liberal stance of tolerance. So, for example, when faced with anxieties at Saudi Arabia's Dar Al-Hekma College (DAH) about use of textbooks that investigate homosexuality and represent women engaging in activities that are taboo in Saudi Arabia, Anson and Donahue report that the program accommodated this cultural difference by choosing a textbook with more culturally "appropriate" content: difference was thus tolerated rather than engaged. Interestingly, however, the cultural blandness of the preferred textbook content led to student complaints about feeling a lack of purpose for their writing: a lack of actual engagement with difference has led, Anson and Donahue report, to students being "*disengaged* from their writing" (chapter 1, emphasis added). Additionally, the ostensible (official) need for the students to be protected from culturally objectionable content—content that made the original textbook selections "unusable"—were contradicted by students' expressed needs (perhaps desires) for the opportunity to engage with such objectionable content. Thus, we see the problem of a reification of differences leading to an obscuring of the full range of practices, beliefs, needs, and desires of those "there," as well as the changeable and changing nature of all of these.

Anson and Donahue identify the source of that reification in an "import" model based on the assumption that "'learning to write' is independent of complex cultural practices, ideologies, and activity systems" (chapter 1). The hope, they explain—at least among officials at DAH—was to have an "ideologically neutral structure into which [the officials could] fill culturally relevant (or entirely neutral) content": in Byram's (1997) terms, touristic enrichment without engagement or change. This is the neoliberal fantasy of a friction-free transmission of knowledge, services, and goods, a fantasy that the liberal stance of tolerance for and accommodation of difference aims to accomplish. But, like Byram's wannabe tourist, the experience of travel in fact requires more substantive engagement with difference and change, both from the locals and from the would-be tourists themselves.

This friction gives a different significance to the insistence—made explicit in many of the chapters here—that "context is all." While this slogan rightly argues against a decontextualized approach to the work of writing program administration, which all the authors in this collection oppose, "context" must be understood not as fixed but as an emerging, ongoing, contested, and contestable product of a variety of agents. That is, context must be located not only in (empty) space but in time and the social, as material social practice and the ongoing product of that practice, including that of the researcher/administrator. What passes for the local "context" is neither the whole story, nor the end of the story, but a fragment of ongoing, unfinished, and contested narratives. Understanding the local "context" of DAH in this way, for example, would allow for greater consideration of the full range of competing needs, desires, beliefs, and practices about writing among DAH students, which are obscured by reified representations of these narratives. To Thatcher, Montoya, and Medina-López's predominantly synchronic analysis of differences between the bordering locales of El Paso and

Ciudad Juárez, and between the different rhetorical traditions of Mexico and the United States, such an understanding of contexts would likewise add both a greater sense of changes over time and a greater acknowledgment of the contribution their analyses make toward maintaining a sense of the defining characteristics of each context. Likewise, the sense of "here" from which US transnational WPAs may start would, from this perspective, itself need to be similarly contextualized. For example, while some accounts of "rhetoric" might appear to have a privileged, longstanding, and dominant position in the US field of rhetoric and composition that distinguishes it from traditions of studying and teaching writing elsewhere, other accounts may bring out the strong, if currently unacknowledged, role of linguistics and education in the history of composition, thereby enabling us to recognize and make use of significant overlaps between the US study of composition and traditions of studying and teaching writing elsewhere.

The need to rethink "context" is especially pertinent to efforts at defining "context" primarily in terms of local (students') needs. Aside from the problematic designation of the (distant) locals as, well, needy (with the corresponding designation of the WPA as parental provider figure), a focus on "needs" can often take the form of a putatively "practical" acceptance of dominant definitions of our limits of the possible—resignation to and accommodation of what the dominant has identified as the "*hard facts*, often of power or money in their existing and established forms" (Williams 1983, 259, emphasis in original). This reification of context in terms of fixed needs occludes the very real, if unacknowledged, practical needs and desires of students and faculty to change existing and established forms, demands, beliefs, and practices—what Williams identifies as the "'*whole* truth of this situation' (which can allow that an existing reality is changeable or is changing)" (259, emphasis added). For example, the focus in US writing programs on the *need* for ELL's to learn English omits from consideration the needs, and even desires, of English monolingual students to broaden their linguistic repertoires, of ELL students to develop their own linguistic repertoires beyond "English only," of faculty to help students engage in writing that contests dominant institutional demands for and practices with writing, and so on.

A further limitation of reifications of difference in space is that the focus on the specific, fixed location or context can lead us to treat these in isolation and thereby overlook the relational character of what we find there, as well as the global forces to which individual, local practices necessarily represent responses. Deborah Brandt and Katie Clinton, in a critique of work in literacy studies emphasizing the situated character of specific literacy practices, have pointed out that—while these studies have been salutary in dismantling monolithic notions of literacy as a single, uniform, stable, and autonomous entity—the focus on the "local" may "exaggerat[e] the power of local contexts to set or reveal the forms and meanings that literacy takes" (Brandt and Clinton 2002, 338). As they explain,

> Literacy in use more often than not serves multiple interests, incorporating individual agents and their locales into larger enterprises that play out away from the immediate scene. Further, literate practices depend on powerful and consolidating technologies—technologies that are themselves susceptible to sometimes abrupt transformations that can destabilize the functions, uses, values, and meanings of literacy anywhere. In truth, if reading and writing are means by which people reach—and are reached by—other contexts, then more is going on locally than just local practice. The field has learned much from the recent turn to "local literacies." But might something be lost when we ascribe to local contexts' responses to pressures that originate in distant decisions, especially when seemingly local appropriations of literacy may in fact be culminations of literate designs originating elsewhere? (338)

Several of the chapters in this collection testify to the power of such "distant decisions." David Martins recounts discovering—to his surprise—that his position was "shaped by international contexts," that none of his colleagues or superiors could describe with any clarity, and that he was working in conditions "not of [his] own making" that were apparently "influenced more by economic interests . . . than educational ones" (introduction). As Rebecca Dingo, Rachel Riedner, and Jennifer Wingard warn, "seemingly local WAC/WID practices" need to be understood by considering the "globalized labor contexts" in which these are situated (chapter 11). Certainly, the gendered character of much writing instruction as "women's work" (and therefore not real work deserving real compensation and status) appears to be anything but a "local" phenomenon (see not only the vast literature on US reliance on contingent labor in composition, but also chapters here by Anson and Donahue, Dingo et al., Brunk-Chavez et al., Olson, and Bruce describing similar conditions), and therefore which must be treated as something other than merely "local"—say, a peculiar cultural habit of the natives. The alternative to recognizing the global pressures shaping local practice is to treat these as the "hard facts" of isolated localities, which should be accommodated as technical problems susceptible to technical solutions. At least some of the solutions that Alfano and O'Brien propose, for example, appear to be aimed at just such accommodations. On the one hand, these solutions seem eminently reasonable: making adjustments to conditions not of the participants' choosing or production in order to enable all parties to reach their goals. On the other hand, at least some of the differences in these accommodations are of the kind that would merit challenging if the project is to achieve its aim of helping students "know how to communicate and collaborate with others across the globe" (chapter 2). Likewise, some of the aims of the project itself might be worth questioning. For example, while it may seem laudable to help students learn "how best to collaborate on writing-based assignments, taking the steps of the writing process as a series of tasks to be negotiated with others from diverse cultural contexts and institutional settings with varying expectations about what it means to read and to write well" in order to prepare students "both for their futures in a mediated global world and for their careers working with teams consisting of people from diverse cultural and social backgrounds," the alignment of these "intercultural competencies" with the demands of the "new work order" of fast capitalism might well give the project's directors and, more importantly, the projects' teachers and students pause, especially to the extent that the particular uses to which such competencies might be put go unnamed (chapter 2; see Gee et al. 1998). Likewise, the insistence on working not just transnationally but transcontinentally to achieve such competencies might be questioned to the extent that the habits of mind the project is to develop—curiosity, openness, engagement, creativity, persistence "(the ability to sustain interest in and attention to short- and long-term projects)," responsibility, and flexibility "(the ability to adapt to situations, expectations, or demands)"—would seem not in themselves to require cross-continental communication, once we recognize differences within as well as across continents (and national borders). Christine Tardy's revealing analysis in chapter 10 of the contradictory and questionable ideologies in university website representations of their international character is helpful here in providing a useful model for identifying the "distant decisions" made by powerful actors—with which WPAs must contend—and the questionable uses for which transnational writing programs may be intended by those actors, notwithstanding the actual, quite different, uses to which WPAs, teachers, and students may put these.

In other words, I argue that, in their encounters with difference, transnational WPAs can not only learn from others' beliefs about writing and teaching practices and rethink their own, but they can also work with their partners to change them. If these practices are diverse, subject to change, and ideological, then we should not shy away from our engagement with the ideological work of transnational writing program administration, now understood precisely as (inevitably) ideological rather than local/universal or quaint or autonomous. As many of the chapters in this collection make clear, engaging in transnational writing program administration can force recognition of the ideological forces at work in the development of those programs (see chapters 1, 4, 6, 8, 9, 10, 11, and 12, as well as the introduction). The alternative, however, is not to escape from ideology but to engage ourselves more directly in the ideological struggle over writing. That struggle occurs most powerfully in the day-to-day decisions, teaching practices, and representations of these struggles by WPAs, writing teachers, and their students. As the contributions to this collection make clear, transnational writing programs are a powerful site for engagement in just such work.

Notes

1. On the tendency in scholarship to treat Anglo-American sites as the universal norm, see Lillis and Curry (2010).
2. For a sampling of the more prominent studies in this voluminous discussion, see Barton and Hamilton (1998), Barton, Hamilton, and Ivanič (2000), Brandt (2001), Cope and Kalantzis (2000), Heath (1983), and Street (1984).

References

Barton, David, and Mary Hamilton. 1998. *Local Literacies: Reading and Writing in One Community*. London: Routledge. http://dx.doi.org/10.4324/9780203448885.

Barton, David, Mary Hamilton, and Roz Ivani , eds. 2000. *Situated Literacies: Reading and Writing in Context*. New York: Routledge.

Brandt, Deborah. 2001. *Literacy in American Lives*. Cambridge University Press. http://dx.doi.org/10.1017/CBO9780511810237.

Brandt, Deborah, and Katie Clinton. 2002. "Limits of the Local: Expanding Perspectives on Literacy as a Social Practice." *Journal of Literacy Research* 34 (3): 337–56. http://dx.doi.org/10.1207/s15548430jlr3403_4.

Byram, Michael. 1997. *Teaching and Assessing Intercultural Communicative Competence*. Clevedon, England: Multilingual Matters.

Cope, Bill, and Mary Kalantzis, eds. 2000. *Multiliteracies: Literacy Learning and the Design of Social Futures*. London: Routledge.

Gal, Susan, and Judith T. Irvine. 1995. "The Boundaries of Languages and Disciplines: How Ideologies Construct Difference." *Social Research* 62 (4): 967–1001.

Gee, James Paul, Glynda Hull, and Colin Lankshear. 1998. *The New Work Order: Behind the Language of the New Capitalism*. Boulder, CO: Westview Press.

Gibson-Graham, J. K. 1996. *The End of Capitalism (As We Knew It)*. Minneapolis: University of Minnesota Press.

Heath, Shirley Brice. 1983. *Ways with Words: Language, Life, and Work in Communities and Classrooms*. Cambridge: Cambridge University Press.

Lillis, Theresa, and Mary Jane Curry. 2010. *Academic Writing in a Global Context: The Politics and Practices of Publishing in English*. London: Routledge.

Street, Brian. 1984. *Literacy in Theory and Practice.* Cambridge: Cambridge University Press.

Williams, Raymond. 1983. *Keywords: A Vocabulary of Culture and Society.* New York: Oxford University Press.

CONTRIBUTORS

CHRISTINE ALFANO is a Lecturer in the Program in Writing and Rhetoric at Stanford University.

CHRIS M. ANSON is University Distinguished Professor and Director of the Campus Writing and Speaking Program at North Carolina State University.

NANCY BOU AYASH is an Assistant Professor in the Department of English at the University of Washington.

SHANTI BRUCE is Associate Professor, Chair of the Master of Arts in Writing Program, and coordinator of the undergraduate writing program at Nova Southeastern University in Fort Lauderdale, Florida.

BETH BRUNK-CHAVEZ is the Director of the First-Year Composition program at University of Texas at El Paso.

REBECCA DINGO is an assistant professor in English and Women's Studies at the University of Missouri.

CHRISTIANE DONAHUE is the Director of the Institute for Writing and Rhetoric at Dartmouth College.

KRYSTYNA GOLKOWSKA is a Senior Lecturer in the Pre-medical Program at Weill Cornell Medical College in Qatar.

BRUCE HORNER is Endowed Chair in Rhetoric and Composition at the University of Louisville.

KATE MANGELSDORF is a Professor of Rhetoric and Writing Studies and Director of University Writing Programs at University of Texas, El Paso.

DAVID S. MARTINS is Associate Professor and founding director of the University Writing Program at Rochester Institute of Technology.

KELLY MEDINA-LÓPEZ is a Ph.D. student in the department of Rhetoric and Professional Communication at New Mexico State University.

IAN MILLER teaches writing at the Weill Cornell Medical College in Qatar.

OMAR MONTOYA is a graduate student in the Rhetoric and Professional Communication Program at New Mexico State University.

ALYSSA O'BRIEN is a Lecturer in the Program in Writing and Rhetoric at Stanford University.

WENDY OLSON is Assistant Professor of English in the College of Liberal Arts at Washington State University, Vancouver.

HEM PAUDEL is a doctoral candidate in Rhetoric and Composition, University of Louisville.

RACHEL RIEDNER is Associate Professor of Writing and Women's Studies at the George Washington University.

DUDLEY W. REYNOLDS is a Teaching Professor of English at Carnegie Mellon University Qatar where he is the lead instructor for the first-year writing program.

MARY ANN RISHEL is a Professor in the Humanities who teaches the First-Year Writing Seminar in the Pre-medical program at Weill Cornell Medical College in Qatar.

RODNEY SHARKEY teaches writing through literature in the Pre-medical Program at Weill Cornell Medical College in Qatar.

DOREEN STARKE-MEYERRING is an Associate Professor of Rhetoric and Writing studies in the Department of Integrated Studies in Education at McGill University in Montreal, Canada.

CHRISTINE M. TARDY is an Associate Professor in the Department of English and Associate Director of the Writing Program at the University of Arizona.

BARRY THATCHER is an Associate Professor of Rhetoric and Professional Communication at New Mexico State University.

ALFREDO URZUA-BELTRAN is an Assistant Professor in the Department of Languages and Linguistics at the University of Texas, El Paso.

KATHRYN VALENTINE is an Associate Professor of Rhetoric and Professional Communication at New Mexico State University.

AUTUMN WATTS serves as the Writing Center Coordinator at Weill Cornell Medical College in Qatar.

ALAN S. WEBER is an Assistant Professor of English who teaches the first-year Writing Seminar in humanities in the Pre-medical Program at Weill Cornell Medical College in Qatar.

JENNIFER WINGARD is an Associate Professor of Rhetoric, Composition, and Pedagogy and a faculty affiliate to the Women's Studies Program at the University of Houston.

PATRICIA WOJAHN is the Associate Department Head and Director of Writing Programs at New Mexico State University.

DANIELLE ZAWODNY WETZEL is Teaching Professor & Director of First-Year Writing at Carnegie Mellon University.

INDEX